ABRAHAM LINCOLN

Readers can review an online supplemental appendix to *Abraham Lincoln: Great American Historians on Our Sixteenth President* A C-SPAN Book on the Internet at http://www.c-span.org/lincolnbook

Available on this C-SPAN Web page are:

- Complete transcript of each featured author's interview
- Video of each author's interview
- A slideshow of photos from the book
- Podcasts about the book and about Lincoln
- Links to C-SPAN's other Lincoln sites

A C-SPAN BOOK

BRIAN LAMB AND
SUSAN SWAIN
EDITORS

ABRAHAM LINCOLN

GREAT AMERICAN
HISTORIANS ON OUR
SIXTEENTH PRESIDENT

PublicAffairs
New York

Published in the United States by PublicAffairs™,
a member of the Perseus Books Group.

Library of Congress Cataloging-in-Publication Data

Abraham Lincoln : great American historians on our sixteenth
    president / Brian Lamb and Susan Swain, editors.—1st ed.
        p. cm.
    Includes index.
    ISBN 978-1-58648-676-1
    1. Lincoln, Abraham, 1809–1865—Miscellanea.   2. Lincoln,
Abraham, 1809–1865—Anniversaries, etc.   3. Presidents—
United States—Biography.   I. Lamb, Brian, 1941–
II. Swain, Susan.
E457.2.A1445   2009
973.7092—dc22

                                                    2008034572

First Edition

10 9 8 7 6 5 4 3 2 1

CONTENTS

PART 2
WARTIME PRESIDENT

PART 3
CHARACTER

PART 4
IN MEMORY

PART 5
LINCOLN'S WORDS

INTRODUCTION

In the summer of 1993, I was indulging in a regular habit—scouting out new nonfiction releases at my local bookstore, the now-defunct Brentano's in Arlington, Virginia—when I spotted an interesting title on top of a stack: Harold Holzer's *Lincoln-Douglas Debates*. It was a history book with a contemporary connection: The 1992 campaign, and especially the quadrennial ritual of presidential debates, seemed to generate more than the usual amount of disparagement. Time and again, critics would invoke the 1858 matchup between Abraham Lincoln and incumbent Senator Stephen A. Douglas, the alternative to increasingly shallow and sound-bite-driven campaigns.

That chance encounter with Holzer's book became the genesis of a sixteen-year relationship between our television network, C-SPAN, and the sixteenth president of the United States. It will come as no surprise, then, that C-SPAN has committed itself to being the "television network of the Lincoln bicentennial," agreeing to cover many of the major events planned by a federally appointed bicentennial commission. Visitors to C-SPAN's Web site (www.C-SPAN.org/Lincoln200years) can find hundreds of hours of our original Lincoln-related video, with more to come. Meanwhile, our friends at PublicAffairs, with whom we have published four previous books, joined forces with us to produce this edited collection of Lincoln essays, featuring the views and scholarship of more than fifty writers and historians drawn from C-SPAN's programming archive.

Now, back to that Brentano's. Our sixteen-year interest in Lincoln began with Harold Holzer, co-chair of the Lincoln Bicentennial Commission and one of the nation's best-regarded Lincoln scholars. When not dissecting Lincoln's prose, Holzer serves as senior vice president for external affairs at New York's Metropolitan Museum of Art. Harold gave us an hour-long interview about his debate book for C-SPAN's long-running author series, *Booknotes*. This was our introduction to the large, passionate, and sometimes tempestuous community of Lincoln scholars, amateur historians, archivists, writers, researchers, impersonators, museum curators, teachers, collectors, and critics, all of whom contribute to a national conversation about Lincoln that has been taking place for more than one hundred and fifty years.

It's a dialogue that constantly surprises. For example, from that initial Holzer interview, we learned that the Lincoln-Douglas debates, while historically significant, supply a poor model for candidates in the digital age, when bloggers and social networkers often set the pace for daily political coverage. Lincoln and Douglas met on seven stages across the state of Illinois. Each debate was three hours in length, much longer than nearly all of today's feature films. The 1858 version of one-on-one rhetorical combat consisted of an hour-long speech by one candidate, followed by a ninety-minute rebuttal, and then a half-hour closer by the initial debater.

This somewhat leisurely format became familiar to C-SPAN viewers in 1994 when we set out upon one of our most ambitious and rewarding productions ever—working with all seven of those Illinois debate towns to re-stage each of the Lincoln-Douglas debates in its entirety. Then-colleague Maura Pierce spent hours on the phone, making connections in the relevant communities and piecing together a vast amount of research. C-SPAN's education consultant for the project—master educator and longtime friend Dr. John Splaine—helped spearhead the publication of a companion guide to the televised debates. Finally, in the late summer of 1994, C-SPAN producers and technicians descended upon the Illinois prairie, trailing in their wake production trucks, cameras, generators, and portable satellite uplinks.

On April 13, 1996, as a byproduct of the Lincoln-Douglas debates, I found myself in the basement ballroom of a Best Western hotel in Springfield, just blocks from the Illinois state capitol. I had agreed to be keynote speaker for the annual convention of the Abraham Lincoln Presenters. Looking out from the podium, I saw before me fifty-seven Abrahams—tall, short, fat, and lean. There were bearded Abes and a few clean-shaven ones. Some sat side-by-side with their modern-day Marys; others worked the Lincoln circuit solo. My remarks to the group were window-dressing for in-depth sessions on the fine art of Lincoln presenting. One speaker offered advice that resonated when he told the assembled Abrahams, "If you expect to be treated seriously, never work for free; charge at least $300 an event." Readers of this book, which has several descriptions of Lincoln's relationship with money, might find themselves thinking that Lincoln himself would have agreed heartily with this counsel.

In the wake of our debates project, C-SPAN's Lincoln coverage seemed to take root and flower in many directions. Reflecting the impressive number of new Lincoln book titles each year, their authors became a reliable part of *Booknotes*'s weekly interviews; *Book TV*, C-SPAN2's weekend nonfiction book channel, sent videojournalist Richard Hall to Gettysburg to tape hours of the Lincoln Forum's annual discussion to air on our network; Mark Farkas, our network's executive producer for history, produced with his team several specials on the life and times of our sixteenth president; while the 2005 opening of the Abraham Lincoln Presidential Library and Museum led to several live telecasts from Springfield. Working with presidential historian Richard Norton Smith, the museum's founding executive director, C-SPAN's education department sponsored a national essay contest for high school seniors. The winner, then-eighteen-year-old Mihan Lee of Virginia, read her essay on Lincoln's "New Birth of Freedom," as part of the museum's opening ceremony before President George W. Bush, a crowd of national and Illinois dignitaries, and other assembled Lincoln fans.

To this day, Abraham Lincoln remains elusive. His law partner William Herndon once referred to his friend as "the most shut-mouthed man he ever knew." The many sides of Lincoln, first revealed to C-SPAN viewers through these interviews and special productions, are contained here in a single volume. *Abraham Lincoln* draws from C-SPAN interviews with some of the people best versed in United States history and in the history of Lincoln and the Civil War. It includes, as well, perspectives from a variety of other American writers who have sat before C-SPAN cameras.

Many aspects of the Lincoln story offer thought-provoking parallels to issues as fresh as this morning's headlines. The Abraham Lincoln that lives in these brief essays is much more compelling than the simple rail-splitter we know from schoolbook days.

Here are just a few observations taken from the highly personal portrait of Lincoln that unfolds through the writers featured in this book:

- Abraham Lincoln was striving, ambitious, and eager to get ahead.
  —*David Herbert Donald*

- Ever since he was young, he wanted to accomplish something so worthy that his story would be told after he died.
  —*Doris Kearns Goodwin*

- Lincoln was shrewd. . . . Lincoln could be ruthless where his political interests were concerned. —*Richard Norton Smith*

- Apparently Lincoln wanted to look like Lincoln. He stood out in a crowd, and he used his appearance like a badge. —*John Y. Simon*

- Lincoln had within him a terrible bent toward what he called the "hypo"—what we might today call manic depression.
  —*Alan Guelzo*

Lincoln also demonstrates that he could quickly adapt technology for political and policy gain:

- He was really the godfather of the Pacific railroad.
  —*David Haward Bain*

- Lincoln spent more time in the Telegraph Office than in any other place, save the White House itself. The Telegraph Office was the first Situation Room. —*Tom Wheeler*

- What Lincoln realized was this new democratic art was the art of the people. It was inexpensive, not elite. Just as Lincoln represented the democratic impulses of America, photography represented those impulses, as well. —*David Ward*

Among the clashing opinions on Lincoln and race are these:

- Obviously, Lincoln was not for equality in 1858. —*Harold Holzer*

- He was a gradual emancipationist. —*James McPherson*

- He understood and Frederick Douglass understood . . . the condition for emancipation was the Union. —*Walter Berns*

- Contrary to what most people think, Abraham Lincoln's deepest desire was to deport all black people and create an all-white nation . . . he worked feverishly to create deportation plans.
  —*Lerone Bennett, Jr.*

- What the Emancipation Proclamation did was give African Americans hope. When they heard about it, they understood that the most powerful man in the nation had sided with them.
  —*Edna Medford*

When Abraham Lincoln was assassinated in 1865, one-third of Northerners turned out to either see his corpse or view his funeral train on its twelve-day journey home to Springfield. Since that day, no fewer than sixteen thousand books have been written about Lincoln. Each in its own way attempts to unravel the mystery of this one-term congressman from Illinois, a man who had complex relationships with his family, whose election in 1860 caused seven states to secede before he was inaugurated, whose decision to wage war to preserve the Union caused the deaths of 625,000 soldiers, and whose views on race are ambiguous enough to inspire passionate debate 143 years after his death. Our hope is that readers will find explanations of their own in the words of the fifty-six writers who appear in this book and in the richly textured Lincoln it depicts.

We greatly value the willingness of the featured historians and authors to share their scholarship with C-SPAN audiences. We believe that the snapshots of their work we have provided will encourage you to read more of what they've done. And to facilitate that, we've included short biographies of every author and created a Web site with full transcripts and the original video of their C-SPAN interviews. It's also important to note that any royalties C-SPAN derives from this book will be directed to the nonprofit C-SPAN Education Foundation, which creates classroom materials for middle and secondary teachers.

In 2009, as the nation marks the two hundredth anniversary of Abraham Lincoln's birth, we hope *Abraham Lincoln* and the related television programming that C-SPAN produces will contribute to the ongoing dialogue about Lincoln, presidential power, leadership, racial reconciliation, and American values.

Brian Lamb
with assistance from Susan Swain
Washington, DC
July 2008

ABOUT THE COVER ILLUSTRATION

Based on the U.S. Five Dollar Bill

Abraham Lincoln posed for the photograph on which this engraving was later based just three days before his fifty-fifth birthday, on Tuesday, February 9, 1864. The original was taken at Mathew Brady's gallery on Pennsylvania Avenue in Washington. Historians regard the sitting that day as the most productive of Lincoln's many visits to photographers over the years. It yielded the famous penny profile, the well-known picture of Lincoln looking at a book with his son, Tad, and two magisterial portraits later adapted for the five-dollar bill. This is the second, most recent five-dollar bill engraving. What set this Brady encounter apart was that a formally trained artist, not a photographer, posed the president—New York painter Francis B. Carpenter, who was then currently engaged in a project to paint Lincoln and his cabinet at the first reading of the Emancipation Proclamation in July 1862. (This gigantic finished painting now hangs in the U.S. Capitol.) Carpenter, seeking formal new photographs he could adapt for his oil on canvas, likely arranged all the poses at Brady's that day (Brady himself was probably on the battlefield, taking pictures outdoors, and was by then too blind to make plates himself). Lincoln's son Robert later called one of the photographs made that day the best he had ever seen of his father. If they looked different to Robert, and to modern viewers, there is yet another explanation: On this day, for no particular reason anyone has ever learned, Lincoln parted his hair on the right, not the left. The result was a modest but noticeable image transformation—one reason, perhaps, why the images have been so widely used for coins and currency over the years.

Harold Holzer
Co-chair, U.S. Abraham Lincoln Bicentennial Commission

A NOTE TO READERS ON STYLE

The essays in this book, from historians and authors, have all been crafted from televised C-SPAN interviews. Most were conducted for our long-running *Booknotes* series. Others came from *Q&A*, our Sunday evening interview program, and several were drawn from *Book TV's* interview programs, *In Depth* and *After Words*. A few were conducted for special history programs about Abraham Lincoln.

The transcripts of longer interviews have been excerpted, and the C-SPAN interviewers' questions were omitted to achieve an essay style. Essays are minimally edited so that readers can read authors in their own words. We took care to remain faithful to each author's original meaning; brackets and ellipses, respectively, were used to indicate where words were added or deleted within paragraphs. Capitalization of the first few words in the body of an essay signals where we have pieced together non-sequential portions of the interviews for clarity of thought.

Whether the authors are featured in longer chapters, or in a short take on a specific topic, the purpose of this book is to give you a taste of our featured historians' voices, insights, and scholarship on Abraham Lincoln—at least, in part with the hope that readers will seek out the authors' original works. To that end, the index contains brief biographies of featured authors. In keeping with C-SPAN's public affairs mission and commitment to providing the whole picture, complete transcripts of our interviews with authors—along with video and other features—are available at our Web site, www.c-span.org/lincolnbook.

As with the four previous books based on C-SPAN's author interviews, any of its royalties from the sale of this book will go to the C-SPAN Education Foundation.

THE LIFE OF
ABRAHAM LINCOLN

1809   Lincoln is born to Thomas and Nancy Hanks Lincoln in a one-room log cabin, near what is now Hodgenville, Kentucky.

1811   The Lincolns move to a farm on Knob Creek.

1816   The Lincolns move to Indiana, settling near present-day Gentryville.

1818   Nancy Hanks Lincoln dies of "milk sickness."

1819   Thomas Lincoln remarries in Elizabethtown, Kentucky, to Sarah Bush Johnston, a widow with three children.

1830   The Lincolns move to Illinois, settling in Macon County near what is now Decatur.

1831   Abraham Lincoln, twenty-two, moves to New Salem. He works as a laborer, a clerk in one grocery store, and becomes part owner of another. Later, he serves as town postmaster and as a surveyor. He reportedly was romantically involved with two women—Mary Owens and Ann Rutledge.

1832   Lincoln enlists in a local militia, the Thirty-First Regiment of Illinois, following the governor's call for troops at the breakout of the Black Hawk War. He serves for fifty-one days but sees no action. His fellow militiamen elect him as their captain.

        Lincoln is defeated in his first run for the Illinois General Assembly as a Whig Party candidate.

1834   Lincoln is elected to the Illinois General Assembly, representing Sangamon County. He begins to study law.

1836   Lincoln is re-elected to the state legislature.

        Abraham Lincoln receives a license to practice law from the Illinois Supreme Court.

1837   Lincoln, twenty-eight, moves to Springfield, sharing a room with Joshua Speed. He becomes a junior law partner of John Todd Stuart, Mary Todd's cousin.

He and eight other Whigs push successfully to have the state capital moved from Vandalia to Springfield.

1838   Lincoln wins a third term in the Illinois General Assembly.

1839   Lincoln travels the Eighth Judicial Circuit, practicing law.

He meets Mary Todd at a Springfield ball.

1840   Lincoln wins a fourth term to the Illinois General Assembly. Abraham and Mary begin courting.

1841   Lincoln and Mary break off their engagement. Ending the law partnership with Stuart, Lincoln becomes a law partner of Stephen T. Logan.

1842   Lincoln, thirty-three, and Mary, twenty-three, begin courting again in secret and are later married.

1843   Robert Todd Lincoln, their first son, is born at the Globe Tavern rooming house.

Lincoln loses nomination for Congress.

1844   Lincoln buys his first and only home, at Eighth and Jackson Streets in Springfield, for $1,500. He sets up a new law practice with William H. Herndon as his junior partner.

1846   Edward Baker Lincoln is born at the Lincoln home.

Lincoln is elected to the U.S. House of Representatives as a Whig.

1848   Lincoln delivers speech in Congress opposing the Mexican War.

He is not re-nominated for a second term.

1849   Lincoln proposes legislation to begin abolishing slavery in the District of Columbia.

Lincoln fails to win a federal post from new president Zachary Taylor.

1850   Edward Baker Lincoln, three years and ten months old, dies at the Lincoln home, probably of tuberculosis.

William Wallace Lincoln is born at the Lincoln home.

1853   Thomas (Tad) Lincoln is born at the Lincoln home.

1854   The Kansas-Nebraska Act, giving individual territories the right to determine whether or not they would legalize slavery, becomes law.

Lincoln is re-elected to the Illinois Legislature. He withdraws to pursue a run for the U.S. Senate, a race he eventually quits after throwing his support to Lyman Trumbull to ensure a Republican victory.

1857   The Supreme Court, led by Chief Justice Roger Taney, issues its Dred Scott opinion with seven of nine justices agreeing that no slave or their descendents could be U.S. citizens. Lincoln speaks out against the ruling.

1858   Lincoln delivers his "House Divided" speech after securing the Republican nomination for U.S. Senate. He faces incumbent Democrat Stephen A. Douglas, and the two meet in seven debates across the state.

1859   Illinois Legislature re-elects Douglas to the U.S. Senate over Lincoln by a vote of fifty-four to forty-six.

1860   Lincoln is chosen by the Republican National Convention in Chicago as its candidate for president of the United States.

Lincoln is elected the sixteenth president of the United States, defeating Stephen Douglas (Northern Democratic Party); John C. Breckinridge (Southern Democratic Party); and John Bell (Constitutional Union Party). His vice president is Hannibal Hamlin of Maine.

Lincoln grows a beard at the urging of an eleven-year-old letter-writing girl from Westfield, New York.

South Carolina becomes the first state to secede from the Union.

1861   The Confederate States of America are established. Jefferson Davis is selected as president; Alexander H. Stephens is vice president.

Lincoln gives his Farewell Address to Springfield a day before his fifty-second birthday. It takes him twelve days to reach Washington, DC, where he is inaugurated president.

1861   The Civil War begins with the April 12 attack on Fort Sumter,
(cont.)   Charleston (SC) by the Confederacy. Union forces at Fort Sumter
surrender. Lincoln issues a call for seventy-five thousand
volunteers.

Confederate forces win the battle of Bull Run in Manassas, Virginia.

1862   William Wallace Lincoln, eleven, dies at the White House, probably
of typhoid fever.

Confederate forces win the second battle of Bull Run; Union wins
Battle of Antietam, in Maryland.

1863   Lincoln issues the Emancipation Proclamation.

The battle of Gettysburg (PA) is a Union victory.

The battle of Vicksburg (MS) is a Union victory.

Lincoln delivers the Gettysburg Address at the dedication of
National Soldiers' Cemetery.

1864   The National Union Party (a temporary name for the Republican
Party used to advance the notion of a reunited nation) nominates
Lincoln for re-election at its convention in Baltimore. Hamlin
replaced on ticket by Andrew Johnson, a Tennessee Democrat.

Union forces take control of Atlanta.

Lincoln is re-elected, defeating General George B. McClellan, the
Democratic candidate.

General William T. Sherman presents captured Savannah (GA)
to Abraham Lincoln as an "early Christmas gift."

1865   Lincoln delivers his Second Inaugural Address.

General Robert E. Lee and his Army of Northern Virginia
surrender at Appomattox Court House, Virginia, to Union General
Ulysses S. Grant.

Lincoln is shot at Ford's Theatre by John Wilkes Booth while
watching *Our American Cousin*. The next morning, he dies at the
Petersen Boarding House at age fifty-six.

A funeral train, with Lincoln's remains and those of his son Willie,
departs Washington, DC, beginning a twelve-day trip back to

Springfield, Illinois. His remains are interred at Oak Ridge Cemetery in Springfield.

The Thirteenth Amendment, abolishing slavery, is ratified.

1882   Mary Todd Lincoln dies in Springfield at age sixty-four.

1922   The Lincoln Memorial is dedicated in Washington, DC.

Sources include The National Park Service Web site,
http://www.nps.gov/liho/historyculture/lincolnchronology.htm.

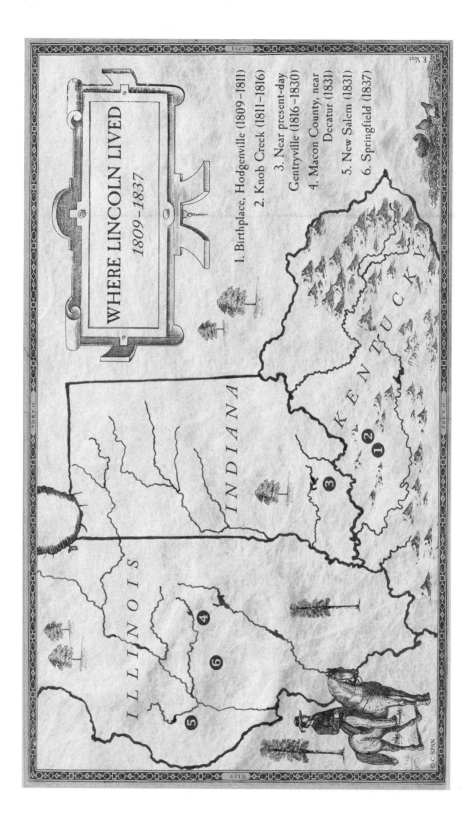

WHERE LINCOLN LIVED
1809–1837

1. Birthplace, Hodgenville (1809–1811)
2. Knob Creek (1811–1816)
3. Near present-day Gentryville (1816–1830)
4. Macon County, near Decatur (1831)
5. New Salem (1831)
6. Springfield (1837)

INDIANA

KENTUCKY

ILLINOIS

E. Vest

© C-SPAN

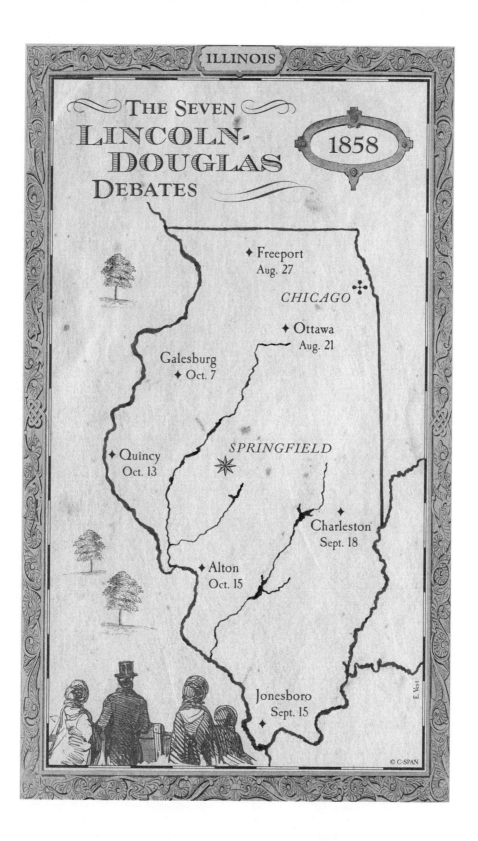

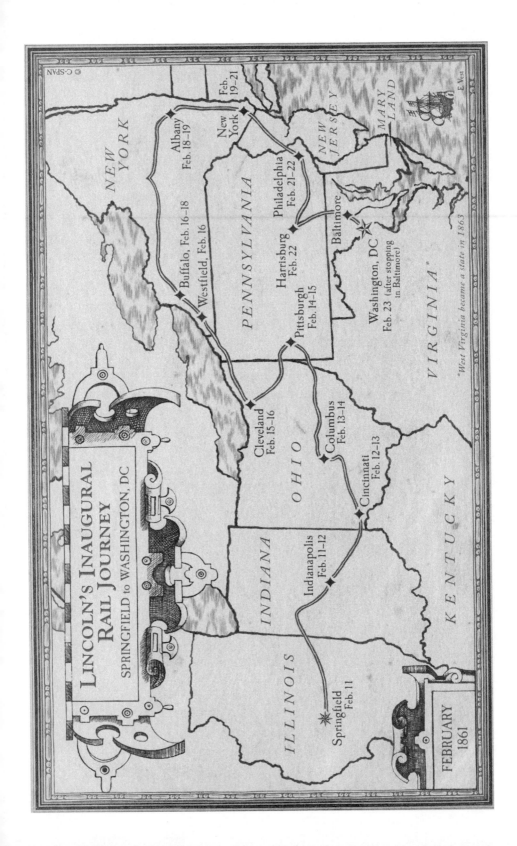

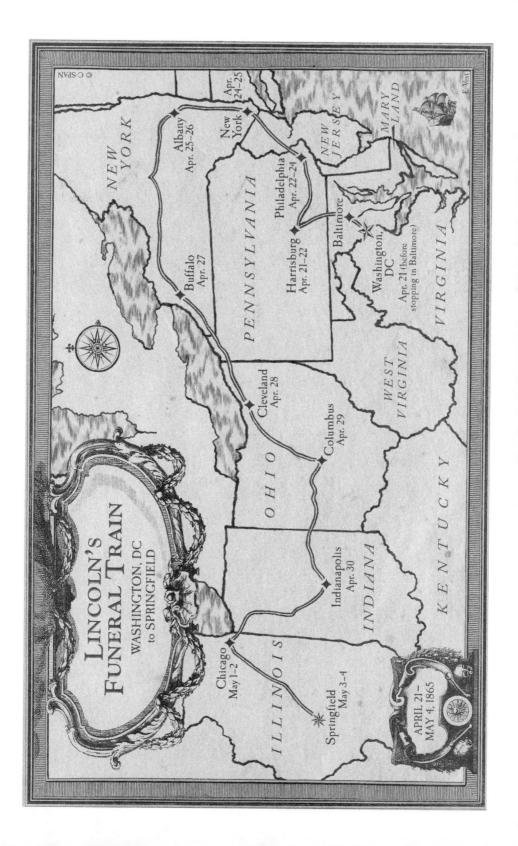

LINCOLN'S
FUNERAL TRAIN
WASHINGTON, DC
to SPRINGFIELD

APRIL 21–
MAY 4, 1865

Chicago
May 1–2

Springfield
May 3–4

Indianapolis
Apr. 30

Columbus
Apr. 29

Cleveland
Apr. 28

Buffalo
Apr. 27

Albany
Apr. 25–26

New York
Apr. 24–25

Philadelphia
Apr. 22–24

Harrisburg
Apr. 21–22

Baltimore

Washington,
DC
Apr. 21 (before
stopping in Baltimore)

ILLINOIS

INDIANA

OHIO

NEW YORK

PENNSYLVANIA

NEW JERSEY

MARYLAND

WEST VIRGINIA

VIRGINIA

KENTUCKY

© C-SPAN

F. Vest

PART 1

LOG CABIN
TO WHITE HOUSE

Early Years

MARK NEELY, JR.

Pulitzer Prize–winning author Mark Neely is a professor of history at Pennsylvania State University. He appeared on C-SPAN's Booknotes *on April 26, 1994, to discuss his book,* The Last Best Hope of Earth: Abraham Lincoln and the Promise of America, *published by Harvard University Press.*

Abraham Lincoln loved his family, but historians have not found his family particularly lovable. His wife, Mary Todd Lincoln, eventually became rather grasping and materialistic and complaining. And his children—because both Mary Todd and Abraham themselves had not very happy youths, they wanted their children to have happy childhoods, and so they spoiled their children. Their children, to the degree that we can approach them from the few meager documents available, are not especially attractive. More important, it seemed to me that if we focus on these things, we are not focusing on what made Lincoln great, and that is essentially the last five years of his life, the presidency.

Abraham Lincoln was born in 1809 in Kentucky near Hodgenville. His father was named Thomas, and his mother was named Nancy Hanks Lincoln. His mother was illiterate. His father could, as Abraham said later in his life, "bunglingly sign his own name but was otherwise illiterate." Thomas hadn't had many opportunities in life. Abraham Lincoln's grandfather, after whom he was named—Thomas Lincoln's father, Abraham—had been killed by Indians while settling a farm in Kentucky. Even so, [Thomas Lincoln] managed to buy with cash three different farms in Kentucky and was attempting to better himself. But he became the victim of a very bad land-title system. Title insurance didn't exist in those days, so when you bought a piece of land in Kentucky, as Abraham Lincoln's father did, essentially you didn't know what you were getting.

Kentucky was a crazy quilt of overlapping land claims. You were responsible for the survey yourself. The survey was conducted by the system of metes and bounds so that the boundaries of these farms would be described in the documentary record as "trees and rocks and streams," all features of the landscape that moved, and so most of the pieces of land in Kentucky had disputed title. Thomas fell victim to this and, in disgust, left Kentucky with his seven-year-old son, Abraham, for Indiana, where the land was surveyed by the federal government and came under the land ordinance of 1785, laid off in neat mile-wide squares, and where title was much more secure. So from the Kentucky origins, Thomas Lincoln then moved with his family to Indiana, far southern Indiana, just across the Ohio River from Kentucky.

Abraham was a modest man. He didn't write an autobiography. He didn't keep a diary. He was a genuinely modest man—a little secretive, in fact, about his past. We do know something about those early years because once he became famous—actually, after his assassination—his former law partner, William Herndon, conducted an oral history. He interviewed, either in person or by letter, old settlers in Indiana and Illinois who had known Abraham when he was a youth. Those reminiscences tell us what we know about the early years of Lincoln's life. They are fraught with great difficulties in use. As you can imagine, if someone came to interview you, and you'd grown up with Abraham Lincoln, and someone asked you, "Did you know Abraham Lincoln?" you'd say, "Sure, I taught him everything he knew." They tended to exaggerate the person's role in Lincoln's life, and they're not altogether trustworthy, but they tell us something.

[LINCOLN LIVED IN Indiana for] fourteen years. He left the state when he was twenty-one. His mother died when he was nine years old, and within a year his father remarried a widow named Sarah Bush Johnston Lincoln. She proved to be a wonderful mother. In the many books written on Lincoln, no one ever says an unkind word about Sarah Bush Johnston.

Abraham had a younger brother, who died at a very early age, and an older sister, who died in childbirth. Abraham, who grew up in what we could consider pretty rough circumstances in rural Indiana, [became acquainted with] death at an early age. It left him with a tragic view of life and mixed feelings about his hardscrabble past. In 1830, the Lincolns moved first to Coles County, and Lincoln helped his father build a cabin there, but he left his father's house at that point. Lincoln did not get along very well with his father. We don't know why. My own speculation is that Abraham Lincoln was very ambitious. By the time his son knew him well, Thomas Lincoln was beginning to lose his ambition. Those farms he'd bought in Kentucky and the sour experience there of having the title spoiled and then moving to Indiana—and he didn't prosper there—I think these experiences, as well as to some degree the people he associated with, sapped Thomas's ambition. By the time Abraham had a conscious view of his father, he may have seen him as somewhat ambitionless. I don't know. That's purely speculation. But he did not get along very well with his father and left his home for good to live in New Salem, Illinois. New Salem is a small log-cabin community, a ghost town now, maintained as a national park site. In Lincoln's day, it was a small log-cabin community near Springfield, Illinois.

ANN RUTLEDGE WAS THE YOUNG woman in whom Lincoln was first interested—a young woman who lived in New Salem. Lincoln apparently courted her. She died tragically at a very early age, which saddened him greatly. End of story. That's all we know about it. Not long afterward, he was courting another woman, so I think that the idea that Rutledge's death somehow altered his life forever after has got to be exaggerated. I think that he had considerable familiarity with death in his own family—a younger brother, an older sister in childbirth, his mother. People on the frontier knew about death. Whatever his relationship with Ann Rutledge, I don't think it had as profound an effect as some sentimentalists in the past have thought.

IN 1842 HE MARRIED Mary Todd, a Kentuckian who came from a much more privileged background, well-educated. Women did not have many educational opportunities, especially west of the Appalachians. She had been to finishing school. She spoke French fluently. She had an extraordinary interest in politics for a woman of the era, and she was for Abraham Lincoln quite a catch.

She moved in the most exalted social circles in Springfield. She had gone to live with her sister who was married and living there, and [she and Lincoln] met in the political society of Springfield, probably at a social occasion.

They had four children. . . . They were all boys, and only one, Robert Todd Lincoln, lived to a ripe old age. He died in 1926 at age eighty-three. But the other three boys died at early ages—four, eleven, and eighteen.

THE ONLY HOME LINCOLN ever owned was in Springfield, and when you see the Victorian taste in which this home is decorated you'll be reminded that this is a nineteenth-century, bourgeois, Victorian man, who left the log cabin behind. When you go to the restored state legislature you'll say, "Ah, this is Lincoln's real arena here."

LINCOLN WAS A TEETOTALER, but he was not self-righteous about it. He did briefly sell alcohol in a little store in New Salem. He did not use tobacco, which was very unusual in those days—and, again, here is a little bit of an unappreciated advantage that Abraham Lincoln had—he avoided what we now call diseases of choice. He didn't probably know he was doing it, but by avoiding alcohol and by avoiding smoking he helped his physical constitution. He had fabulous health, and that's a real advantage to a president because of the grueling schedule. He worked essentially from seven in the morning until eleven at night, and there was no Kennebunkport, no Rancho Mirage, no Camp David, no vacations. He worked almost every day he was president. He had a major cabinet meeting in December 1861 on a diplomatic crisis, on Christmas Day. He worked on New Year's Day, a traditional day for a White House open house, and would shake the hands of thousands of people. He worked every day of the year—no vacations, a grueling schedule—and having good health gave him a big advantage.

He was not conventionally and outwardly religious; that is to say, he was not a formal member of any church. He went to church, he rented a pew, he of course invoked the divinity in his speeches, but what his private religious views were, we don't know. This is typical of what I would call Abraham Lincoln's biographical inaccessibility. On these personal and private things, we will never know because he didn't tell.

IT'S INTERESTING THAT Lincoln became a politician before he became anything else. He ran for public office when he was twenty-three years old in a new state. He lost the first time, but the second time he won. He ran for the lower house of the state legislature. When he went to the state legislature, he met people with bigger horizons than New Salem. Among them was John Todd Stuart, a prominent Whig, who encouraged Lincoln to study law. Lincoln's prospects were not very great, and at one point he thought maybe he'd become a blacksmith. He needed some outside encouragement. He just had such a meager education—only a year of formal school. He didn't learn polished grammar until after he was twenty-one years old. He didn't learn basic geometry until he was forty. He thought his educational background was too limited to become a lawyer, and it took some encouragement from somebody else. But Stuart encouraged him, and Lincoln started reading on his own, and by 1836 he could become a lawyer.

He served four terms in the Illinois Legislature, followed by a brief period in which he didn't hold public office, but he was basically angling to be congressman from his district. Then in 1846 he was elected to the United States Congress. He served one term in that congress from 1847 to 1849, the only national office he held before becoming president.

One of the major differences between the United States and, say, the governments of Western Europe—the parliamentary systems that are popular there—is that we have our elections by the clock. The elections come every four years—even the presidential election, whether we want one or not. Then there are the off-year congressional elections. But in parliamentary systems, if the government becomes unpopular and loses a vote of confidence, they hold the election then. So, in a sense, they hold elections when they need them. We don't. We hold elections when they're constitutionally stipulated.

For Lincoln's era, elections were not nearly so standardized. Only the presidential election came every four years. The states held their elections whenever they wanted to. The result was that somewhere in the United States at almost any time there was an election going on. When Abraham Lincoln was president, the Civil War lasted forty-eight months, and in twenty-four of those months there was a major election somewhere in the United States. The result? Not only the politicians but the people, too, were constantly preoccupied, excited, agitated, and interested in politics.

A perfect proof of this excitement was voter turnout. We are not content, certainly, but we are used, in these days, to seeing a voter turnout that barely exceeds 50 percent of the eligible electorate during presidential elections. When Lincoln was elected in 1860, the voter turnout in the North was more than 80 percent of eligible voters, and this in an era when the electoral districts were very large. It might take a day's buggy ride into the polling place—a day in and out. It took some sacrifice to vote, but people did, and in large numbers.

[Between 1849 and his 1858 Senate race] Lincoln maintained an interest in politics, though he did not have a particularly active political career. He mostly devoted himself to his law practice. Immediately after leaving Congress in 1849, he sought an appointed office from the Taylor administration—the presidency of Zachary Taylor. Lincoln thought he deserved it because he'd worked very hard for Taylor's election, but he didn't get it. It disappointed him. He went home to Springfield and devoted himself more diligently than ever to his law practice, and it's conceivable that he might have left politics had there not been a very big development in 1854, which was the Kansas-Nebraska Act.

When he first entered politics, Abraham Lincoln chose to become a member of the Whig Party for deeply principled reasons, but as it turned out in Illinois this was betting on the wrong horse. Illinois was a Democratic state. The Whig party never could muster enough popularity to elect a

senator or a governor, and so Lincoln had a quietly successful political career in a party that wasn't particularly successful in Illinois. Lincoln wasn't a
failure. He went as far as you could go as a Whig in a Democratic state.

A Whig was, first off, a person who opposed the Democrats of Andrew
Jackson. But second, and probably what really drew Lincoln to the Whig
Party, was that the Whigs had a program for economic development of the
West. It emphasized [a transportation network of] government-built or
-supported canals, roads, and railroads that would crisscross the West. It emphasized some substantial banks that would provide a currency—a sound
circulating medium—for the country, and, sort of surprising for a man born
in a log cabin, the Whigs were also a party of high protective tariffs to develop manufacturing. If you take the program of the party—transportation,
commerce, banks, roads, railroads—it's essentially a developer's dream.
That's what the West needed, and that's what Abraham Lincoln needed. It
solved the problems of his youth. He grew up on a hardscrabble farm, first
in Kentucky and then in southern Indiana, where if there were no banks
you couldn't get a bank loan. How are you going to improve yourself if
there is not enough money around, if there's not transportation to market?
[The Whig Party offered] political solutions to the problems [that his family
experienced].

IN NINETEENTH-CENTURY America, people got so excited about politics
that by the time elections rolled around there were often scuffles in the
streets, canings of newspaper editors who had printed some calumny about
a politician, and a little violence at the polls. When the political campaigns
got very heated . . . a politician would challenge another politician to a
duel. Lincoln was challenged to a duel by a Democratic politician named
James Shields, and it was a very interesting event in Lincoln's life. Lincoln
avoided fighting the duel. That detail tells you something important: he was
to some degree a little exempt from the rougher standards of masculine behavior in nineteenth-century America. He didn't like to hunt. He was not a
violent man. Although he was a good wrestler, he didn't have a vengeful nature, and he wasn't about to fight a duel.

Being the challenged party, it was Lincoln's privilege to stipulate the [du-
eling] weapons. Lincoln stipulated that they would fight with large cavalry
broadswords, and with these heavy swords a plank was to be placed on the
ground over which neither party could cross, and they were to duel with
these swords on either side of this plank. Well, the trick here is that Abraham Lincoln was six feet four inches tall and had a very long reach, and
Shields was rather shorter. So it was a completely unfair contest and ridiculous. By setting these terms, Lincoln was making fun of the institution of

dueling, and yet he went along far enough to set the terms. Later, he was ashamed of his behavior and didn't want to talk about it.

[ONE LINCOLN STORY I LIKE is that] Abraham Lincoln wrote to Gen. William T. Sherman during the Civil War. Sherman was busy. He had just captured Atlanta and was getting ready to march to the sea. But it was a presidential election year, 1864, and in those days they didn't have absentee voting. Many soldiers who were eligible to vote would be campaigning in the South and couldn't get home to vote.

Lincoln wrote a letter to General Sherman asking him, since there was a very tight state election in Indiana, to furlough as many soldiers as he could to vote in that state's election. He said, "This isn't an order." Lincoln was commander in chief, but he didn't order [Sherman to do his bidding]. But Lincoln said, "It's important to the army that the Republicans win this election."

Sherman hated politicians and politics, and he wasn't very cooperative. But it's wonderfully illuminating about Abraham Lincoln's abilities and character. He always took the high road, and he never neglected the low road. He knew all the tricks of the trade, and when he needed them he would use them. This is an advantage, of course, that the president has over the opposition party—that is, he could suggest to the generals that they furlough soldiers to vote.

★ ★
★

Origins and Influences

ALLEN C. GUELZO

Allen C. Guelzo is the Henry R. Luce Professor of the Civil War Era and Professor of History at Gettysburg College. He is a two-time winner of the Lincoln Prize for his books Abraham Lincoln: Redeemer President *and* Lincoln's Emancipation Proclamation: The End of Slavery in America. *Mr. Guelzo appeared on C-SPAN's* Booknotes *on April 16, 2000, to discuss* Redeemer President, *which was published by William B. Eerdmans.*

Abraham Lincoln was born February 12, 1809. He was the only surviving son of Thomas and Nancy Hanks Lincoln. There was at least one brother who we know was born, Thomas, but he died in infancy. There might, in fact, have been another Lincoln sibling, but we're still waiting for some documents on that. He had one older sister, Sarah, who was born several years before he was. She died shortly after she married, during childbirth.

Lincoln grew up, first, in Kentucky. Then, his family moved to Indiana, where they could find cheaper land and more secure land titles. Indiana was in the old Northwest Territory, so the federal government guaranteed land titles. Thomas Lincoln, Abraham's father, moved there to get a secure title for a farm. Lincoln grew up there in southwestern Indiana, until his family moved for the last time to Illinois. After they moved to Illinois, he turned twenty-one and moved out on his own to New Salem, Illinois, which was then an up-and-coming town. People thought it was going to be the most important commercial center in central Illinois.

He had lived approximately eight years in Kentucky. He was in Indiana another thirteen years and then lived in Illinois up until the time of his election [as president] in 1860. He had probably not more than a year, all told, [of formal schooling]. He said that he went perhaps four winters to what was at least a passing resemblance to an elementary school. People often say that this shows that Lincoln was not a man of great education. Well, yes, it does show that, and, no, it doesn't. Lincoln liked, sometimes, to poke fun at his own lack of education. When he had to fill out an entry for the *Biographical Dictionary of Congress*, and it came to the space for education, he wrote only "defective." Mind you, all these other people in the House were writing in "Yale," "Harvard," or "Princeton." In truth, Lincoln probably got as good an elementary education as one was likely to get on the Western frontier and, in fact, any place in America in the 1820s outside the major cities. The thing he actually regretted the most was not having a college education. He felt very keenly the lack of a college education all throughout his life. He felt it made him sit a couple of steps below these younger lawyers—who were coming out West—and especially the people that he had to work with [later] in Washington.

Lincoln's mother died in 1818, and it's hard to know exactly what the impact of her death was. Certainly, one of the difficulties it presented was that Thomas Lincoln became a single parent, but he quickly remarried. He returned to Kentucky. There was a lady there with whom he had had an acquaintance over the years. She was a widow. He went directly to her and said, "I'm a widower, you're a widow. I have needs, you have needs. Let's marry and do it straight off." And they did.

So Sarah Bush Johnston became Sarah Lincoln. She came up to Indiana with her own three children, and she really became a mother to Abraham Lincoln. The story about stepmothers—from the Brothers Grimm—is always of the wicked stepmother and the father who gets taken advantage of. For Abraham Lincoln, it was almost the exact opposite. He loved Sarah Bush Johnston Lincoln, and she loved him. It was his father who he had real distance from, real trouble getting along with. His father died in 1851. The difficulties he had with his father were longstanding. Lincoln declined a request to come to the dying man's bedside. He stayed in Springfield and did not attend the funeral.

[IN ILLINOIS], HE WAS A CLERK in a store and established a store of his own, which failed. Then he took up law and moved to Springfield, which became the capital of Illinois. Its becoming the capital had a lot to do with Abraham Lincoln: Lincoln was elected to the state legislature and one of his earliest achievements as a state legislator was to get the capital moved to Springfield from Vandalia.

He [joined] the United States House of Representatives after he was elected in the 1840s. He ran unsuccessfully for the United States Senate in 1855; he ran again, in 1858, and then was elected the sixteenth president in 1860, just in time for the American Civil War to break out.

He married in 1842 . . . [but] when you talk about Abraham Lincoln's love life, you have to begin with Ann Rutledge. Ann Rutledge was the daughter of what was the principal family of New Salem. James Rutledge was one of the co-founders of the New Salem town. Ann Rutledge, his daughter, was originally betrothed to another settler in New Salem, who went back East. She lost contact with him. And all the evidence that we have, most of which was gathered by William Herndon within a few years after Lincoln's death, suggests that Abraham Lincoln and Ann Rutledge really did have an understanding, if not an outright engagement, to be married. But she died before anything further could take place.

We don't know [her age] exactly, but she was doubtless in her twenties, about the same age as Lincoln. Lincoln said years afterward that he often thought of her, was convinced she would have made a wonderful wife, and thought much about the Rutledge family and what had become of them. A number of the Rutledges served in the Union Army during the war. In a sense, the Rutledges were connected to Abraham Lincoln as Union supporters.

[After the death of Ann Rutledge, Lincoln] went on the rebound. The sister of a friend came to town and put Abraham Lincoln and her sister together. Her name was Mary Owens. She was from Kentucky. She was well-read, she was articulate, and it was rumored she had some means. Lincoln, for a while, was seriously interested in her, evidently proposed to her, but one thing led to another, and she turned him down. One reason she turned him down was because, by that point, he had moved to Springfield, had entered into law, and it was clear that his interests were much wider afield than she was content with. So she declined the final offer of marriage that he made.

There are, in fact, two letters that have survived concerning Mary Owens, and they make very torturous reading because it was evident that in Lincoln's case, here was a young man who, on the rebound, had made a proposal or something that sounded like a proposal. Afterward, he had second thoughts and wrote a very curious letter to Mary Owens in which he said, "If you'd like to back out of this, well, I wouldn't object. I'm not going to force you, but if you've decided that I'm really not the man for you, then it's OK with me." What do you do with a letter like that? She read it for what it was, and she basically said, "No, I don't think we're going to get married. I will let you go because I see that that's what you really want to do."

Mary Todd came onto the scene of Lincoln's life fairly soon after he came to Springfield. She had a sister, Elizabeth, who was married and living in Springfield, and she came from a home environment where a lot of encouragement was given to her to leave. Her mother had died fairly early on. Her father, Robert Todd, had remarried, and Mary and her stepmother did not get along. By the time Mary was seventeen, there were fairly strong hints being put out that she should be looking to get married and move on. She went to live in Springfield with her sister, who was married to Ninian Edwards, [a member of] one of the most influential political families in all of central Illinois. It was there, probably in 1839, that she and Abraham Lincoln were first introduced.

Here's where the story gets complicated. At that point, Lincoln seems to have been entranced with her because she was talented, she was witty, she was good looking, and she was also related to a very important political family. Lincoln had political ambitions. He apparently made some kind of proposal to her. They had some kind of understanding and then, once again, [he had] second thoughts—the second thoughts being caused by Matilda Edwards, who was a relative of Mary Todd's. From the evidence that we have, it seems that Lincoln fell head over heels in love with Matilda Edwards, but she had no interest whatsoever in him.

So there he was, apparently having this crush on this other girl, having made this promise to Mary Todd. Something happened—we don't know exactly what—but the arrangement he had with Mary Todd fell through. It was a catastrophe because if he had second thoughts about marrying Mary Todd, he now had third thoughts about the wisdom of having broken off any kind of engagement. At that point, two things came into play: one was he saw that he'd cooked his goose politically with the Edwards family. The other thing was that here was a young man, with no great financial prospects of his own—he'd come up the hard way. He had only one thing that he could advertise for himself and that was his honesty, his sense of honor. Here, this man who thought that honor was the only card he had to play had done the most dishonorable thing he could do by breaking that engagement. As a result, within two years, mutual friends got them back together, and Mary Todd and Abraham Lincoln were married in November of 1842.

LINCOLN HAD WITHIN HIM A terrible bent toward what he called the "hypo," what we might today call manic depression. When Lincoln went down psychologically, so to speak, he went far down. Whenever the understanding of Mary Todd [about their betrothal] unraveled, that was the same moment at which his best friend [Joshua] Speed, whom he'd roomed with for years, was leaving Illinois to move back to Kentucky. It was also the moment when his political career in the Illinois state legislature had hit the skids. All the great bills, all the great initiatives, all the great public works projects Lincoln had sponsored as a state legislator had been smashed by 1840. All of those events came together right at the end of the year 1840 and the beginning of 1841, and it spun Lincoln into a deep depression, so deep that people said that Lincoln's depressions scared them, that they were afraid if they left sharp objects around, Lincoln might harm himself.

[LINCOLN] CLEARLY IS A central figure in the central event of our history, which is the Civil War. The Civil War—and Lincoln articulated this better than anyone else—was the testing event of the idea of a democratic republic. We take too much for granted today . . . that the idea of democracy is the ideal to which everyone should aspire. A hundred and thirty-five years ago, that wasn't the case. There were very few republics, very few things that could be described as a democracy. They were looked upon as chancy.

If you wanted stability, what you were supposed to have was a monarchy—an aristocracy and a king who could guarantee stability day in and day out. To be part of a democracy was to take a tremendous risk and especially in the United States, with a republic that was dedicated to a proposition that all men are created equal. That was really to put yourself at a big political risk. The Civil War was the litmus test as to whether democracies could hold together or whether they were doomed just to fly apart into various kinds of special interests.

GEORGE BRINTON MCCLELLAN, major general during the Civil War, had been recruited at the very beginning of the war after the terrible Union defeat at First Bull Run to take command of the Union armies. He was put in overall command of Union forces, but he was also given specific responsibility for creating the Army of the Potomac, the Union army that would . . . carry the war into the Confederacy and hopefully defeat the Confederate army and capture the Confederate capital at Richmond.

McClellan took up his task in the summer of 1861. He built a wonderful army. He was a great organizer, a tremendously talented engineer. If management consultants had existed in 1860, his was the résumé that every management consultant in the country would take as an example. There was only one problem: he didn't like to fight, which is a strange thing for a general.

He was a comparatively young man, thirty-four years old, but he had talent coming out of every pore. What's more, the army that he organized loved him. When he would ride down the ranks of men on review parade, they would cheer. One of his staff officers said that McClellan had this peculiar little way of taking off his cap and spinning it on his finger, and the men would just be cheering. On the campaign, he would carry around a small printing press so that he could regularly print up and distribute bulletins and exhortations to the men in the ranks. When he took them on the great campaign in the spring of 1862, down to the James River peninsula, down to attack Richmond, the men were convinced that George McClellan was the greatest military genius of the age.

He might have been a genius, but he was not a genius for achieving victory. What's more, he had serious political disagreements with Lincoln. McClellan was a Democrat; Lincoln was a Republican. McClellan was vehemently opposed to any movement, any twitch of a movement in the direction of emancipating the slaves as part of the war. When that great peninsula campaign failed, [and] when he won a half victory at Antietam in the fall of 1862 but let the Confederate army get away back into Virginia, that was when the rift became critical. Lincoln realized he was going to have to remove McClellan. McClellan was not going to win victories, and, what's more, McClellan was not going to cooperate with him politically. But Lincoln knew that if he made any move to remove McClellan from command, there was that whole Army of the Potomac—one hundred twenty thousand men, when you counted up all the noses—and there was a real chance that that army might have rallied behind McClellan, marched behind him down to Washington, and been part of a *coup d'etat* that would have made McClellan the temporary dictator of the United States for the view of achieving a truce and a negotiated peace.

People warned Lincoln about that. In fact, there was at least one staff officer of McClellan's who was cashiered for talking a little too freely about the plans they had for a *coup d'etat*. Lincoln finally did remove McClellan, and the army cheered McClellan and said, "Lead us to Washington, General. We'll follow you." But two things happened. McClellan, whatever else he was, was not about to overturn his own government. He rode away from the army and made no attempt to lead a *coup d'etat*. The other thing was that the army got a new commander and went back on campaign and had something to occupy itself with.

In those weeks, those two or three weeks after Lincoln removed McClellan, there was nothing that could have kept McClellan from saying to the army and to his officers, most of whom he'd handpicked, "We're going down to Washington, and we're going to sweep that baboon out of office, and we are going to settle this Civil War peacefully." That's why I say that perhaps it was the most critical moment, not only in the war, but maybe in American history. Think what might have happened, first of all, if McClellan had done that and the Civil War had ended as a negotiated peace between two independent countries. Then think, too, what kind of political precedent would have been set for armies and generals to start interfering in the political process. We've seen enough of that in other places in the Western Hemisphere over the last 150 years to know what the United States might have been in for if that had happened.

Two years later, when McClellan was put up as the Democratic candidate for president, he was beaten badly. . . . A lot had happened in two years, from the time when the army was cheering McClellan until 1864 when the army was cheering the man that they came to call, with reverence, Father Abraham.

WHILE I WAS SPENDING a year working at Harvard in 1994–1995 on a project about the history of free will and free choice, I stumbled upon things that Lincoln wrote on the subject. . . . Here was a man who had very broad, free-ranging interests in ideas. He was not just a politician.

His favorite ideas concerned political economy. William Herndon, his law partner, said that there were no books that Lincoln loved to read more than the great nineteenth-century books on political economy: John Ramsey Cullough, John Stuart Mill, Frances Whalen, Henry Kerry. In other words, the great books that were written in the nineteenth century that comprised what we call classical *laissez-faire* liberalism. That's not liberalism as in the way we use the term politically today. It was describing [the theories of] Adam Smith, the classical, market-oriented economics that Lincoln loved to read about.

I CAME INTO MY BOOK with deep respect for Lincoln as a central figure in our history, but there were ways in which Lincoln continued to surprise me. The more I read about his interests, the more I found this man surprising people around him. Let me give you an example: John Hay, who was one of his secretaries in the White House, Brown University grad, young man, sharp as a tack, who would later go on to be a cabinet secretary and had a wonderful career in American politics. Hay came to know Lincoln about as closely as anyone else did during the Civil War. Instead of familiarity breeding contempt, it bred awe on the part of young John Milton Hay. On one occasion Hay wrote in his diary, "Had an interesting talk with the T"—in his diary the T stands for Lincoln because his nickname for him was "Tycoon." "Had an interesting talk with the T about philology, a subject for which the T has a sometimes neglected interest."

Philology? Abraham Lincoln? I think most people would have to scratch their heads for a moment to remember what the world "philology" means. It's the study of language. But Hay would have been surprised if he had known that in the years before the war, Lincoln had actually gone on the Lyceum circuit with a pair of lectures on discoveries and inventions that talked about the origins of human language. Lincoln, in fact, was interested in the origin of language. He was interested in geology and read books on it. He was interested in metaphysics, in philosophy. Herndon recalled how in the law office, he and Lincoln had long discussions about philosophical questions such as free will. Friends of his, like Joshua Speed and his first law partner, John Todd Stuart, spoke of him as having a mind of a metaphysical, philosophical bent with a mathematical exactness about things.

. . . As soon as you put Lincoln's writings and Lincoln's speeches alongside those of Salmon Chase or Charles Sumner or Jefferson Davis, the differences become stark. Davis's speeches are high-flown; the rhetoric is bombastic. It's the literary equivalent of a three-decker novel. Lincoln's prose is spare, direct, eloquent. It's the prose of a lawyer speaking to a jury of twelve plain prairie settlers. He never wasted a moment. Herndon once said that Lincoln was so intent upon getting his ideas made crystal clear that he would ball himself up for hours on end, trying to get just the right words for just the right expression.

WE NEED A BOOK on what Abraham Lincoln thought was the most important document he ever wrote. Not the Gettysburg Address, not the First Inaugural, not the Second Inaugural, but the Emancipation Proclamation. . . . It's the document of Lincoln's that is usually criticized the most severely, yet the funny thing is that the Emancipation Proclamation accomplished more than any other document Lincoln signed. The Gettysburg Address is a great speech, but it didn't do anything. It's not a policy document. The First Inaugural and the Second Inaugural are, likewise, great speeches, but they didn't actually do anything.

The Emancipation Proclamation, at one stroke, was the single greatest social revolutionary document in American history. Yet of all of Lincoln's great documents, it's the one that has been held up to the greatest criticism and sometimes even contempt. [Author and journalist] Lerone Bennett's book about Abraham Lincoln and the Proclamation [is one such example]. In the excerpt from it that appeared in *Ebony* magazine, Bennett asks the question: "Did Lincoln really free the slaves?" Bennett's answer is, "No, he didn't, and the Emancipation Proclamation is tantamount to a fraud." This is why I think we need a book on the Emancipation Proclamation.

Family Relationships

JOHN Y. SIMON

In 1994, C-SPAN worked with the seven original Illinois towns that hosted the 1858 Lincoln-Douglas debates to televise reenactments of them. John Y. Simon joined C-SPAN in Jonesboro, Illinois, on September 17, 1994, to help set the stage for the third debate.

I FOUND [Lincoln's relationship with his father] fascinating. The triggering letter [for my interest] was the one that Lincoln wrote when his father was dying, many miles away, saying that it might be more painful than pleasant to visit him on his deathbed. That letter has always fascinated biographers of Lincoln.

Why is it that Lincoln had such a painful relationship with his own father? Thomas Lincoln really didn't live far from Springfield but was not invited to Lincoln's wedding; never saw his grandchildren, never visited in Springfield at all. Lincoln's estrangement from his father seems to have dated back to his boyhood. It's a puzzle that nobody's solved entirely, but at least I wanted to try my hand at it. I was intrigued by Lincoln's relationship with his father and the triangular relationship with Lincoln's stepbrother, John D. Johnston, who seems to have been Thomas Lincoln's favorite.

On a buggy ride in about 1850 that Lincoln took to the courthouse with William Herndon, he said, "All that I am, or ever hope to be, I owe to my angel mother." That is also a way of passing judgment on his father. She was the mother who died when he was nine. He thought he had inherited his intellect and his character from her and somehow he bypassed his own father. . . .

[OVER THE YEARS, there has been a persistent rumor that his mother, Nancy Hanks, was illegitimate.] There has been a lot of tangled research by genealogists on this, but the evidence is strong that Lincoln himself thought his mother was illegitimate. He had grown up with this crowd of Hanks people, many of them illiterate, and some of them quite likely to give birth without getting married first. He saw this as a kind of stain on himself, and he was troubled by it.

Herndon's Lincoln

DOUGLAS L. WILSON

Doug Wilson, co-director of the Lincoln Studies Center at Knox College, is a two-time winner of the Lincoln Prize. In 1999, he received the prize for Honor's Voice: The Transformation of Abraham Lincoln; *in 2007, he was honored for* Lincoln's Sword: The Presidency and the Power of Words. *Mr. Wilson appeared on C-SPAN's* Booknotes *on March 29, 1998, to discuss* Honor's Voice, *published by Knopf. Knox College in Galesburg, Illinois, was the site of the fifth Lincoln-Douglas debate.*

Far and away the most valuable source about Lincoln is the collection of letters and interviews that were collected by his law partner, William H. Herndon. He was very different from Lincoln. He was outgoing. He was effusive, loquacious. He had strong opinions, he had radical opinions. He was an abolitionist, and Lincoln was not. Herndon had a drinking problem, and Lincoln was a person who rarely drank. But they apparently made a good team because in the firm of Lincoln and Herndon, as we're finding out from the Lincoln Legal Papers Project . . . Herndon really pulled his weight.

[LINCOLN] WAS BORN in 1809 in Kentucky. He lived there seven years before the family moved to southwest Indiana—which was really just woods then—cleared a farm, and built a house. That's where he grew up. He lived there fourteen years. He left [for Illinois] when he was twenty-one.

He was living with his father, and he helped his father build a new cabin near Decatur, Illinois. He'd lived through what they called Winter of the

Deep Snow—1830–1831 was a huge blizzard winter. He took a job working on a flatboat—actually, he first had to build the flatboat because they didn't have one when he got there. [He was] working for a man, taking a cargo of goods down to New Orleans in 1831. When he came back, he went to work in a store that the man who owned the flatboat, Denton Offutt, had set up in the little village of New Salem, which is near Springfield.

[In New Salem], he lived with various people. It's hard to trace exactly. He would sleep one place and take his meals in another place, so when people say, "He boarded with us," usually it meant he took his meals. Sometimes it meant, "He lived with us, but he lived partly in the tavern."

He lived with various people: Mentor Graham, Rowan Herndon. Rowan was a cousin of William Herndon. Mentor Graham was the village schoolteacher. Denton Offutt was an entrepreneur who came into the neighborhood trying to make money. He was something of a con man and a scoundrel. When the store in New Salem didn't pan out, Offutt disappeared and left town, leaving his creditors holding the bag. [Lincoln worked for him] as the storekeeper and the mill operator because Offutt not only bought a store full of goods, he rented the mill at New Salem.

Jack Armstrong was supposed to be the strongest man in the area, the toughest man. He hung out with a group called the "Clary's Grove Boys." When they wanted to test Lincoln, since most newcomers had to be tested—and he looked like a pretty tough customer—they put him up against the best they had, who was Jack Armstrong.

They wanted him to fight, but Lincoln would not fight. Then they said, "Well, let's tussle and scuffle," which is roughhousing. Lincoln said he wouldn't do that, but he would wrestle; wrestling had rules. There were prescribed rules for what could happen. It wasn't a fight; it was basically a test of strength. [Lincoln was] about twenty-two. Jack was a few years older.

John T. Stuart, Lincoln's first law partner, told a reporter who was gathering evidence for a campaign biography that this wrestling match had been the turning point in Lincoln's life. That reporter went and dug up some more stories about it, and it appeared in the first campaign biography in 1860. Because it was such a hit and became a standard part of Lincoln's biography, Herndon went around and interviewed as many people as he could who claimed to know something about it. So we have a lot of testimony in Herndon's letters and interviews about the wrestling match. . . . What Herndon has is all of these interviews and letters, all of this testimony. It's wildly conflicting; it doesn't tell the same story at all.

What are we going to make out of it? . . . The evidence about Lincoln's life that Herndon gathered doesn't all agree. Some of it's clearly wrong;

some of it's irreconcilable. I try to show that it is possible, by sifting through the evidence, to sort some things out. . . . What seems to have happened is that they had agreed to wrestle in a certain way, not in the kind of way that we're familiar with, which is called catch-as-catch-can wrestling, where you try to get hold of your opponent and get the best hold you can and throw him. They agreed to wrestle by taking certain holds. The rules were that you were supposed to throw your opponent down to the ground, but you can't break your hold. If you break your hold, you lose the fall. You [and your opponent] decide how many falls there are going to be, and then you go at it.

Jack Armstrong didn't want to wrestle this way; this was dull. Most people, if you had two well-matched people, would struggle together for a long time. But Armstrong finally agreed. After they had grappled for a long time, he finally reached down and legged [Lincoln]. He grabbed hold of his leg and threw him up and over, which was unfair.

Nobody thought that was so terrible. This is what you expected from Armstrong, and Lincoln went along with it. He took it in good humor. Then when the people who had backed Armstrong—those who had bet their money and their jackknives and their whiskey on Armstrong—tried to claim that they had won, Lincoln said, "No." He would fight anybody who thought that he had been beaten.

That's what people admired—that he took the legging in good humor but drew the line at having his friends lose their money because he hadn't been beaten; he'd simply been fouled.

There is [also] one interesting story that [Lincoln's mother was a wrestler]. The guy who tells it is not particularly known for the truthfulness of his stories as for the colorfulness of his stories. Yet, this would not be out of line with other things we know about his mother, who was known as an independent person, [someone who] had a mind of her own [and engaged in] unconventional behavior, some people said. It's possible that she was a wrestler.

ANN RUTLEDGE WAS THE most beautiful and most eligible young woman in New Salem when Lincoln came there. By the time he knew her, she was already engaged to another man. His name was John McNamar. He left town, saying he was going back East to get his parents and he would come back and marry her, but he was gone two years. She thought that she'd been deserted.

Lincoln, who had a fondness for her all along, apparently, courted her, and she agreed to marry him. She was taken ill in the summer of 1835, a terribly hot, wet summer when there was a huge typhoid epidemic. She died in a few weeks' time. Lincoln was supposed to have taken this, according to the testimony of Herndon's informants, very hard. People were afraid that he was on the verge of insanity, that he was becoming suicidal. He was finally taken in hand by some of his closest friends, who looked after him for a few weeks until be began to come around.

Bowling Green was a sort of father figure for Lincoln. He was the justice of the peace and a great friend of Lincoln's. Mrs. Green says that she and her husband took Lincoln in and looked after him for a good while until he got better. She thought that he was in a very bad way.

There's a great deal of testimony about his so-called crazy spell. He obviously got very despondent, very distressed, after Ann Rutledge's death. Some of the testimony says, no, he wasn't crazy; he was just despondent. No matter how you cut it, everybody agrees that he [had] more than a normal reaction to the death of his fiancée. It was excessive, and the people around him were afraid.

When he came to Springfield in 1837, Lincoln was about twenty-eight years old. We begin to get these reports that Lincoln was a sad man, a gloomy man, that his basic demeanor was [one] of melancholy. Even though he was known as a great storyteller and could convulse an audience at will, his basic demeanor begins to be reported as sad.

By the time that he was a very prominent man, in the 1850s, Herndon said, "Melancholy dripped from him when he walked." Almost everybody talked about this. People who didn't know him and came along later, like Jesse Weik, Herndon's collaborator, couldn't believe that a guy who told such funny stories could be a melancholic person. He went around and interviewed everybody he could find who knew Lincoln, and they all told him the same thing: that Lincoln was a very melancholy, sad person.

Herndon was always wondering about what was the cause of his melancholy. When he discovered the Ann Rutledge story and discovered that Lincoln was temporarily deranged after her death, he thought, "Ah-ha, this must be the cause of his melancholy." I think that eventually he moderated that view and said that he thought it was constitutional.

[James Short] was a friend of Lincoln's in New Salem. When Lincoln had incurred debt in a bad mercantile venture, the noteholders came around and had all of Lincoln's worldly goods put up for auction, including his surveying equipment. He was making his living surveying. So his friend James Short bought his surveying instruments back at the auction and gave them back to Lincoln.

[Short told Herndon: "Once when Mr. Lincoln was surveying, he was put in bed in the same room with two girls, the head of his bed being next to the foot of the girls' bed. In the night, he commenced tickling the feet of one of the girls with his fingers. As she seemed to enjoy it as much as he did, he then tickled a little higher, and as he would tickle higher, the girl would shove down lower, and the higher he tickled, the lower she moved, that is. Mr. Lincoln would tell the story with evident enjoyment. He never told how the thing ended."]

This is James Short telling Herndon this. I'm inclined to believe that he's not trying to put Lincoln down, and he's not trying to embarrass him. He said to Herndon, "This is a story that you won't be able to tell your readers, but I'll tell you because you'll enjoy it." Unless he's making it up, it probably happened. It's interesting to me that the story doesn't have an ending; it's just a beginning. It's left hanging there. Short says that Lincoln would never say how this story ended.

The problem with Herndon's evidence is twofold. One is that it is difficult evidence to work with. We can't be sure that really happened. We know that James Short, who knew Lincoln well and who liked him and regarded himself as his friend, told Herndon this story. It's not a question of yes or no; it's a question of likelihood; it's a question of probability. Not everybody is going to gauge these things the same way.

What happened to Herndon's evidence was that it got a very bad odor in the second quarter of [the twentieth] century. Professional Lincoln historians who prefer documentary evidence—evidence that's contemporary and reasonably objective—said, "Look, this evidence of Herndon's is non-documentary. It's after the fact. It's subject to all the failures of human memory and highly subjective. Therefore, it's not conclusive. And therefore, we shouldn't have anything to do with it."

The Ann Rutledge story [was one] that James G. Randall, the great Lincoln scholar, said had usurped the spotlight; in other words, it occupied too much attention and was too critical in the forming of people's opinion about Lincoln. He said that we ought to concentrate on the presidency and forget about this sort of folklore that Herndon dug up about Lincoln's early life.

Randall, when he laid out the case against the Ann Rutledge story, defined the standards that you need to follow for historical evidence. He defined them almost on a parallel with the evidence needed to convict in a criminal trial. On that basis, we have practically no historical evidence. . . . If we follow his rules, there's almost nothing that we can use.

If we want to talk about Lincoln's early life, then we have no alternative but to try to make something out of Herndon's evidence. We can either say we don't know anything about Lincoln's early life or we can say, "This is what we know, and you have to understand going in, this is the kind of evidence it is. If you sift it out, it looks like this, or possibly this; this is a like-lihood, and so forth."

[LINCOLN WROTE TO HIS FRIEND, Eliza Browning, about another wom-an [named Mary Owens whom he had courted]: "I knew she was oversized, but she now appeared a fair match for Falstaff." She put him in mind of his mother, "from her want of teeth, [her] weather-beaten appearance in gen-eral, and from a kind of notion that ran in my head that nothing could have commenced at the size of infancy and reached her present bulk in less than 35 or 40 years."]

That seems a very cruel way to describe a woman that he proposed mar-riage to. Partly, that letter was written for fun. It was dated April 1 (April Fool's Day) and written to a female confidante of his. She thought when she received it that he was making this story up and that he was just having fun, in fact, about his relationship with Mary Owens. He did court her. We have some letters from that courtship. They are very revealing letters. They show that he was definitely of two minds: He didn't want to be rejected, [but] he sort of encouraged her not to accept his suit, which seems very strange. He said in that letter to Eliza Browning that he eventually had to propose to her, and that when she turned him down, he was shocked. He proposed again. She turned him down again, and then he said he began to feel that maybe he was a little in love with her after all.

He was not the self-confident person that he was on the stump or in the legislature or in court; he was full of self-doubt. He was trying to figure out how to conduct himself. You see it a lot in this period—things that are not part of the legend but are worth knowing.

A lot of people wonder if Lincoln was really describing his mother. Is this a description of his mother, or is this part of the joke [in which] he's just trying to say she was ugly? What kind of a way is that to describe your moth-er? It's a very vexing thing.

[Mary Owens weighed as much as 180 pounds.] We get these different re-ports [about her size]. What we can agree on is something that Mrs. Hardin Bale said, and that was Mary Owens was over standard size for a woman.

Matilda Edwards was a very beautiful young woman. She was about eigh-teen years old in November 1840 when she accompanied her father, who was a state senator, Cyrus Edwards, to Springfield for the legislative session. She stayed with her uncle, who was Mary Todd's brother-in-law; in other words, she stayed in the same house that Mary Todd was living in. She attracted the attention of practically every eligible bachelor in Springfield, and she got a lot of attention and more than a few proposals, if we can trust the testimony about it. One of the people who was attracted to her was Abraham Lincoln.

[Mary Todd] came to live [in Springfield] with her sister, Elizabeth Todd Edwards, in late 1839, just as they were getting geared up for the 1840 campaign. That's how she knew Lincoln. Her brother-in-law and her cousins were all Whig politicians who were associated with Lincoln.

We have testimony that Lincoln was fascinated by her, that she was a creature of excitement, that he would sit and listen to her talk, that they had a lot in common. Most people just go ahead and say they started seeing each other, and they became an item in 1840 and by the end of 1840, they were engaged. It's very hard to find the evidence for that. Her own letters suggest that she may not have been engaged to Lincoln, but they may have had some kind of relationship. She doesn't talk about it in her letters. What seems clear, if we can believe [Joshua] Speed, who was Lincoln's closest friend, is that after Lincoln and Mary were going together, Lincoln changed his mind and decided he wanted to take up with Matilda Edwards. Mary told him that this was dishonorable and that he couldn't do this. He had a violent reaction, according to Speed. He lost it again. They feared for his life; they were afraid he was suicidal.

The Mary Todd "embroilment" is a result of this situation where Lincoln wanted out of their relationship, and Mary resisted. Lincoln emotionally began to sink into despondency. For a week in January of 1841, he was simply out of it. He was dysfunctional. Then she presumably released him, according to some of the testimony. But she wanted him back, and Lincoln felt guilty that he had made her unhappy by breaking up the relationship.

This situation went on for a long time, almost two years, until all of a sudden, unbeknownst to most of their friends, they had been seeing each other and become reconciled. They announced, to the amazement of their friends, that they were going to get married that very day. Lincoln got himself into an entanglement with Mary Todd that he never really could get himself out of. The solution was to marry her.

John J. Hardin, one of Lincoln's political associates from Jacksonville, had a sister, Martinette Hardin. The time of the legislature was a social season. People would come from all over the state to socialize in Springfield. Martinette Hardin left town just as Lincoln was beginning his slide into despondency. As she was leaving, she heard this story that Lincoln was out of commission. She wrote back to her brother with this memorable line: "We hear that Mr. Lincoln has had two cat fits and a duck fit."

We don't know exactly what Lincoln did, but he says in a letter at that time to his law partner, who was in Congress, "I've been making a disgrace of myself, a terrible exhibition of myself, because of my hypochondrism."

We have [Mary Todd's] letters, and we have contemporary letters that make it very clear that Mary was having a gay old time at the same time that Lincoln was in the tank. She was flirting with other men. She gave people the impression that she wanted to marry and was serious about at least one of these people. If she was pining away with love for Lincoln, it's very hard to see that. Her friends couldn't tell it; you can't tell it from her letters.

[HERNDON WROTE: "LINCOLN openly and candidly and sincerely told me that his mother was a bastard."] Herndon wanted to put things like that in his biography, and he got a lot of static for it because people thought it was shameful. As his friends kept saying, even if it's true you shouldn't put that kind of thing into a biography. Herndon thought that was an important part of Lincoln's story. He thought that what Lincoln went through, this sort of family shame, was part of the reason he wanted to distinguish himself. [Nancy Hanks Lincoln's background] is still an area of contention, but most people accept the evidence that she probably was illegitimate. There is a lot about the Hanks family that's very hard to unravel because there are so many Hankses, and they were so obscure, and they all had very similar names. There are many Nancy Hankses that people have been chasing. Sometimes you get the wrong one.

Herndon knew what he heard from Lincoln; he repeated it deliberately. He said where it happened and when it happened and what the circumstances were. Nobody thinks Herndon's a liar. A lot of criticism of Herndon [is] for his opinions and his psychologizing and perhaps his selective use of evidence, but I don't think anybody accuses him of lying.

We do know, with a reasonable amount of assurance, that Lincoln told him this [about his mother]. It's hard to take that too much further.

LINCOLN KNEW WHAT HE was doing when he put his [law] firm together. Herndon tells us that when he was just a young man, just a law student [who] hadn't gotten his license, that Lincoln came to him and said, "Would you like to come in with me?" Herndon thought he was joking. Lincoln said no, he meant it, and Herndon was overwhelmed.

Herndon was a man who owed Lincoln a great deal and who revered him. But the kind of biography he wanted to write [was one in which] he wanted to tell the whole truth. He wanted to get into everything. In his day, biography was supposed to be done sympathetically by your friends, and it was supposed to only talk about the positive and the honorific. He wanted to tell the whole story. He drew a lot of flak for that.

[Herndon wrote that Lincoln's friend Joshua Speed] "told me this story about Lincoln. Speed, about 1839 and '40, was keeping a pretty woman in the city, and Lincoln, desirous to have a little, said to him, 'Speed, do you know where I can get some?' And in reply, Speed said, 'Yes, I do, and if you will wait a moment or so, I'll send you to the place with a note. You can't get it without a note or by my appearance.'"]

There's a hilarious account that Herndon wrote to his collaborator after the biography was pretty well complete. It wasn't to go in the biography. It's hard to know why Herndon wrote this to [Jesse W.] Weik, except that he thought that it was interesting and he also thought it was true. It sounds like a parody of the "Honest Abe" Lincoln story: It's a story about Lincoln [wanting to] go to bed with a prostitute, then determining that he didn't have enough money and deciding that he wasn't going to go through with it because he didn't want to go on credit.

[Herndon wrote that Lincoln told Speed he only had $3 but the woman wanted $5.] Even though it is a preposterous-sounding story and most Lincoln scholars reject it, Herndon thought it was true. Somebody like [Lincoln scholar] David Herbert Donald will say . . . "Well, Herndon's leg was being pulled, and he didn't know it." That is an explanation. It may be that Herndon had the wool pulled over his eyes. This is Herndon recalling a story that he'd heard years ago, presumably, and you can't put any stock in the exact words that he's using. We're not dealing with certainty. We're dealing with likelihood and probability. . . . It all has, it seems to me, some evidentiary value.

We know that Lincoln was very nervous about debt. We have stories about his worrying about his debt. We know that he was very awkward with women. He had a terrible time with women. This was a big problem for him; he didn't have a regular girlfriend. He had gotten himself into a sort of an engagement with Mary Owens, another almost comic affair. What I'm saying is that this story, even though it sounds like a parody and it may be a joke, fits with the other things that we know. That's why I don't think we should just throw it out.

[CARL] SANDBURG WROTE two separate works about Lincoln, which are now combined. The first one was called *The Prairie Years*, about his pre-presidential life, and it started out to be a children's book. Sandburg got very interested in his subject, and so he converted it into a kind of fictionalized biography. He makes up a lot of conversations. He really did a lot of research because he wanted to get it accurate, but he did think that he ought to flesh it out with fictionalizing. He got a lot of criticism for that.

Sandburg wanted to go on and write the story of [Lincoln's] presidency, which he called *The War Years*—a huge work. That's a very different kind of book. He doesn't fictionalize. He tries to write as accurately as he can. But it's maddening for a scholar because he doesn't tell you where he gets any of these anecdotes. If you don't recognize them, you don't know where to find them to test them out.

[Lincoln scholar] James G. Randall said one of the most interesting things about Sandburg's book. Randall said it's more like a pageant. It isn't what a historian would write; it's what a poet would write. But I think *The War Years* is especially well regarded. It has great powers of evocation.

ABRAHAM LINCOLN'S EARLY life is a famous American legend. It's really part of our national identity. We identify with Lincoln and his career. He is the person who rose from poverty and obscurity, gained a profession, gained position in politics, became president and, many think, saved his country. We identify with that rise. There are important things about his rise that we don't know: We don't know how difficult it was. He went through great difficulty and struggle.

He really had great mental problems. He was emotionally very vulnerable and seems to have just lost it. He had to struggle. The actual story doesn't belie the legend—it simply shows that there's a human being behind the hero.

Lincoln and Clay

ROBERT REMINI

Robert Remini talked about his book, Henry Clay: Statesman for the Union, *published by W. W. Norton, in a May 5, 1992, appearance on C-SPAN's* Booknotes.

HENRY CLAY was Abraham Lincoln's ideal of a statesman. Most of the ideas that Lincoln had early on, about economics, about slavery, came right out of Henry Clay. Lincoln was like Henry Clay, to a very large extent, I found. Lincoln quoted Henry Clay in the Lincoln-Douglas debates a total of thirty-seven or thirty-eight times. Clay told whimsical stories the way Abraham Lincoln did. Lincoln moved far beyond Clay in the late 1850s, and was a greater statesman as such, but [Clay] was the man who provided many of the ideas and programs by which the nation was held together, when it seemed to be breaking apart over the Missouri question, over the tariff question, and, of course, over the acquisition of new lands in the Mexican War.

HENRY CLAY REALLY BELIEVED that [slaves] had to be freed and they all had to be sent back to Africa—that the two races could not live together. He feared what would be the consequence. In part politically, he thought that the blacks would assume political power and would do to the whites what the whites had done to them—socially and economically. There would be conflict. So, slavery was something that could not be bridged and the only solution, he felt, was a gradual emancipation in which, as they were emancipated, they would be returned to Africa. These are thoughts that Abraham Lincoln had until the end of the decade of the 1850s. Then I think Lincoln was radicalized, and his views did change. But they had this racist notion about the inferiority of other races, and that was not the black race alone—that included Indians, who were treated as though they were of a lower order.

AND AS SOON AS I BEGAN researching Clay, I realized what an extraordinary figure he was, how important he was, not only for the growth of this country, but its preservation as well. Some historians feel, and I'm one of them, that had the South seceded in 1850, as it threatened—it met in convention in Nashville—that it might have made good on its secession. If there had been a war, they would have won it in 1850, but secession was prevented by Clay with his ideas that constituted the compromise of 1850. This gave the North ten more years to gird its industrial strength, to find Abraham Lincoln, and even then they had a really hard job of beating the Confederates and forcing them back into the Union. So, Clay was a very significant man for the development of this country as well as its preservation.

MANY OF CLAY'S SPEECHES still have an emotional wallop that few others have, and, of course, the fact that a man of Lincoln's stature would regard Clay as his ideal of a statesman, fascinated me even more.

Those Around Him

DAVID HERBERT DONALD

David Herbert Donald appeared on C-SPAN2's Book TV program In Depth *on June 2, 2002. He discussed several of his books, including* Lincoln, *published by Simon & Schuster, which won the Lincoln Prize in 1996. Dr. Donald, who has also twice won the Pulitzer Prize, is a Professor of American History Emeritus at Harvard University. His Lincoln immersion is complete—he lives on Lincoln Road in Lincoln, Massachusetts.*

I would like very much to know the nature of [Lincoln's] friendships and with whom he felt really close, in contrast to people he was simply associated with. I would also like to know much more about his health. We don't know enough about his health. We have some indications, but we historians would like to know how he was feeling, what was wrong with him at particular times in his career. Finally, I would like him to sit down and talk to me about what he was going to do with the Southern states once the war was over.

WILLIAM HERNDON WAS Abraham Lincoln's law partner for sixteen years before the president went to Washington. From about 1844 to 1860, Herndon worked in Lincoln's office and became partner. He studied law under Lincoln, they practiced in the courts together, they lived in the same town. He knew Lincoln very well. After Lincoln's death, Herndon felt that Lincoln was not being well served by his biographers, who were idolizing him and making him a kind of marble figure. So he went around collecting interviews and letters from people who knew Lincoln well, especially in his early days. This is one of the first oral history records, an early attempt at something that historians do now on a large scale.

Those records—which have recently been published by historian Douglas Wilson in a wonderful book called *Herndon's Informants*—are the best records we have of Lincoln's early life. When I wrote about Herndon, my task was to ask what he did as Lincoln's partner, why he undertook a biography, why he wrote this particular kind of biography, and how valid were these observations that he collected. In doing so, I got a chance to be with descendents. Herndon's daughter for example, a dear, sweet lady, was able to tell me about her father. When I was out in Petersburg, which was the successor town of New Salem [Illinois] where Lincoln grew up, people rustled around their barns, and one fine man produced a rather battered image. He said, "It has been damaged by the wet and probably by the mice, but this is a sketch of Herndon's second wife, the beautiful Anna Miles," which is reproduced in my book. So my research gave me a chance to learn something almost firsthand, or at least secondhand, about the Lincoln period and the Lincoln years.

Lincoln's Herndon, published in 1948, was my first book. I was the research assistant of Professor James G. Randall, who was probably the greatest Lincoln scholar we've ever had. He was preparing his four-volume *Lincoln the President*, and I was able to help him on some things by checking materials.

At the same time, I was a graduate student at the University of Illinois and was looking for a dissertation topic. I remember very well Randall coming over to my room one afternoon and saying, "I think I have just the subject for you. You've been learning a lot about Lincoln. We need a book about Lincoln's law partner, Herndon. Herndon's papers have just become available in the Library of Congress. Why don't you write a biography?" And that's how it came out.

HERNDON AND MARY TODD LINCOLN never got along very well. They probably managed, on the whole, to be civil to each other during Lincoln's lifetime. But after his death, when Herndon began collecting stories, some of them were not favorable to Lincoln; some of them talked about Ann Rutledge as the only true love in his life. Once this happened [Mary] turned on [Herndon], and they became bitter enemies. She attacked him as a poor, drunken wretch that was just a hang-around of Lincoln. He attacked her as being eccentric, erratic, and bad. They fought with each other until the end of her life.

Poor Mary was a highly neurasthenic lady. Things frightened her. The other side of it has also to be said, that here was a women with two, sometimes three, small children, left alone much of the time in Springfield, her husband out on the circuit for maybe as much as six weeks at a time. She saw nothing of him. She had to raise the family—and think what it meant to raise a family in those days. She had to cook over a terribly hot stove in a tiny little kitchen. She had to scrub and do the laundry. She had to pump water from the well. She had to clean the house. She had to take care of these three rather raucous young boys. She was constantly under nervous strain, and there was never enough money.

It's rather easy to see how she could become frightened, hysterical. This was part of her background, but it was also a part of the way her marriage was working out. I have great sympathy for Mary Todd Lincoln. Her husband was not an easy man to live with. She was not an easy woman to live with.

WITHOUT HERNDON, WE would know very little about Lincoln's early years. . . . The interviews he collected, the letters that he gathered, these are really the basis for much of the early life of Lincoln. How much one trusts these is another question. They were, after all, collected in every case at least thirty years after the events, sometimes more than that. We all know how easy it is, in retrospect, to exaggerate our relationship to a great man whom we may have known only casually, but becomes a very dearest and best friend in the backward glance of history. I was quite skeptical of Herndon in *Lincoln's Herndon*, though I gave him good marks for good faith in the strong efforts at finding the truth.

Herndon, when he talked about something he personally knew, was nearly always correct. When he was reporting what somebody told him, he was nearly always correct. But sometimes he went off into speculation about what might have been, what Lincoln was thinking about, what could have happened in the Lincoln home, [and these were things] he didn't know about.

WE DON'T KNOW much about Lincoln's mother Nancy Hanks. There was, for a long time, much discussion about whether Lincoln was legitimate. . . . But there is a wedding license of Nancy Hanks and Thomas Lincoln.

Then there is the story of Lincoln's mother's mother. Was she illegitimate? Herndon said, yes, that Lincoln told him so. I think it's doubtful. We have very little evidence to go on, but the basic fact is that Nancy Hanks came from a very large family of many Hankses, a lot of whom were named Nancy or Lucy. It's easy to get them confused, one generation with another.

Lincoln's mother grew up in Kentucky, in a family of modest income and of modest achievement, but a thoroughly respectable kind of family. She married Thomas Lincoln. They had three children—Abraham, Sarah, and a young boy, Thomas, who died in infancy.

Nancy Hanks Lincoln died shortly after they moved to Indiana. For a time there, the Lincoln family was decimated. There was only the father and these two little children with nobody to care for them. It was not clear they were going to survive. Thomas decided he had to marry again, so he packed up, leaving the little children in the wilderness, and moved back to Kentucky to look for another bride. He found a person that he had known earlier, perhaps even wooed earlier, Sarah Bush, who had married a Johnston. She was a widow by this time. She had some debts. She needed a husband, he needed a wife, and they decided to get married. They packed up and took her belongings, which included a chest of drawers, the first piece of furniture Abraham Lincoln ever saw, a Bible, and a few things, and went back to Indiana.

Sarah Bush Lincoln found these two little infants in his cabin, absolutely bedraggled. No clothes, no food, nobody caring for them. She was shocked beyond measure. She took those little children, she scrubbed them up, and made clothes for them. She dressed them up; she treated them as if they were her own children. She had children of her own [who] she brought with her, but there was no discrimination whatsoever. She was the best possible stepmother you could have. She ought to go down in history as the stepmother of all time.

IT IS TRUE [THAT] Lincoln did not attend his father's funeral. He never wrote about it and never said anything about it, so we have to speculate. Lincoln and his father had never been really very close. They were very different in personalities, Thomas Lincoln being a rather lethargic, lazy, good-natured, good-humored man. Abraham Lincoln was striving, ambitious, and eager to get ahead. They didn't get along well. They didn't fight; they just didn't get along well. So he didn't see much of his father.

His father lived nearly a day-and-a-half trip from Springfield. When he became ill, the family around him, including Lincoln's stepbrother, began writing to Abraham Lincoln, saying that Father is sick, he needs this, he needs that. Lincoln kept sending them money. He kept giving them advice about what to do; he kept the property from being foreclosed under Thomas Lincoln, all of those things. It didn't ever satisfy the entourage around Thomas Lincoln.

Lincoln kept feeling that the people around Thomas were playing on his father's illnesses to get Lincoln's support, more money, and even a visit. About this time, Mary Lincoln delivered another baby. She was not ill, but she was not up and about yet. Receiving news that his father was on his deathbed, I think that Lincoln thought, "Oh, not again. They're going to tell me that same old story. I'll take two days off and get out to Charleston and find out he's in pretty good health. I'll give him some money and have to come home and Mary will have missed me." So he just didn't go. . . .

There was not enough emotion there that would cause him to say, "Come hell or high water, I've got to be there at my father's death."

Robert Todd Lincoln, after graduating from Harvard, served briefly in the United States Army. After the Civil War, he went on to become a lawyer and an attorney for the railroads [and later] was the eighth president of the Pullman Corporation. [He was appointed] ambassador to England, and became a very wealthy man who built a magnificent residence in Vermont at Hildene, which is now open to the public.

ROBERT TODD LINCOLN was a stiff man who did not give in easily to bursts of either laughter or affection. He was, as sometimes was said of the Lincolns, more of a Todd than he was Lincoln.

Robert and his father did not get along particularly well. Very few fathers and sons of that age were on friendly, affectionate terms. Robert Todd Lincoln grew up as a lonely boy, and was sent off to college where he did reasonably well. . . . His mother didn't want him to serve in the army. His father said he ought to have the right to if he wished.

After his father's death, Robert Todd Lincoln was very sensitive on the subject of his father and his father's reputation. When Herndon began publishing the stories about Ann Rutledge as the only woman Lincoln ever loved, [Robert thought,] "What about Mary Todd Lincoln, the widow?" When Herndon published stories that Lincoln's mother was illegitimate, and stories of domestic abuse and high outrage in the Lincoln household, Robert simply clammed up. He would not talk about the whole subject to anybody. He kept his father's papers secret. Not until the 1890s did he allow two official biographers, John Hay and John G. Nicolay, the chance to use those papers. After they finished, Robert Todd Lincoln kept the papers locked up until he presented them to the Library of Congress shortly before his death. He did so with the proviso that they shouldn't be opened until 1947, when presumably everybody involved with Herndon would be dead. He wanted to keep his family's reputation sacrosanct; this is something one can understand and respect.

PROFESSOR JAMES G. RANDALL made a massive and definitive exploration of Herndon's sources about Ann Rutledge and came to the conclusion that there was no engagement. She was a lovely young lady and Lincoln was fond of her, as he was fond of many young people in New Salem. She fell ill and died, and he grieved sadly, as he grieved many others and that's the end of it, Randall claimed.

I included that view, which I helped to research, in *Lincoln's Herndon*, my first book. Then over the years, various things began to happen. First of all, Professor John Y. Simon began looking into these sources. What's more,

Douglas Wilson collected the sources and looked at them very carefully and concluded that there really is a lot of evidence that there was more than just a friendship, that there was a real relationship here, and probably an engagement.

I was influenced by that [point of view] when I wrote my Lincoln biography. More recently, in my new book . . . *Lincoln Men*—a study of Lincoln's friendships—I've gone back to my earlier view. First of all, I have reread the evidence, and most of it is indeed secondhand and hearsay. Most important, the one bit of contemporary evidence by a man named Isaac Cogdall, who claimed to have talked to Lincoln himself about it, has been proven to be false. A very careful scholar in New York, Dr. C. A. Tripp, has made a computer analysis of that testimony and advised that this was not Lincoln's language.

I CAME BACK TO the belief that Ann Rutledge was indeed a beautiful young girl, that Lincoln admired her, and that he grieved mightily when she died. That's about all there was to it. The idea that she was the only woman Lincoln ever loved and that his mind walked out, as Herndon said, on the "uncolumned air" after her death or that he never loved his wife, Mary Lincoln, because his heart was buried in Ann Rutledge's grave—I think all of this is nonsense. I hope it will remain that way.

CERTAINLY LINCOLN was depressed at times. There are some specific episodes that one can connect with Lincoln's depression. He was very sad when Ann Rutledge died, and as he said, "The cold rain was beating on her grave." He was certainly deeply depressed when the engagement he had with Mary Todd was broken off. He was depressed when he was defeated for the Senate of the United States. He was depressed after many of the defeats in the Civil War.

It wasn't a depression in the sense that it meant something more than feeling very sad or wishing things were different. It [doesn't mean] clinical depression, a medical condition. . . . This is one reason why I wish I could have had a chance to talk to Abraham Lincoln about his medical condition. We don't have any evidence that there was prolonged medical, clinical depression.

We do know that he was a man of moods, that he was often unhappy. Who would not be if you had six hundred thousand men being killed around you? But it was not something that impaired his work as president.

SALMON CHASE

I FOUND THE GREAT, unpublished diary of Salmon P. Chase, who was Lincoln's secretary of treasury. Finding it, I began going through it. I thought it fascinating, began editing it, and published it as *Inside Lincoln's Cabinet*, which gives a pretty close view of, for instance, how the Emancipation Proclamation was drawn up.

I learned that Mr. Chase was, first of all, handsome, that he was widely admired, that he was arrogant, that he was thoroughly disliked by most of his contemporaries, and that he was insatiably ambitious. He had, as Abraham Lincoln said, a little worm eating away in him, just like a worm in an ear of corn. He had the ambition to become president, and he could never get over it. It spoiled his public career.

[Chase swore in Andrew Johnson as Lincoln's successor, following the assassination.] That was a very moving occasion at a terrible time when it was not clear that the government was going to stand, with the president of the United States assassinated and an attempt on the life of the secretary of state, William Seward. There had been a plan to assassinate Johnson and others as well, so it was a frightening time.

Chase went to Johnson, whom he did not like, to administer the oath of office because Chase was by then chief justice of the United States. He gave him the oath of office, and you can imagine the regret in his mind—but not in his voice—because he thought he, Salmon P. Chase, should be in that chair: "I should be taking that office. If Lincoln is dead, I should be the successor."

IN THE LINCOLN years, a surprising number [of administration officials kept diaries]. The best diary of the Civil War years is that by Gideon Welles, the secretary of navy. Maybe this is because the secretary of navy didn't have that much to do. . . . He wrote a voluminous diary, which has been published in three volumes. It is the best inner history of the Lincoln years.

EDWARD BATES

EDWARD BATES, THE attorney general, also wrote a diary, but it's fairly arid and pedestrian. One of Lincoln's close friends and a senator from Illinois, Orville Browning, kept the most disappointing diary of the period. It's been published in two enormous volumes, and if you go to one of the momentous days of the year when, for example, Lincoln is going to issue the Emancipation Proclamation, you expect to find him telling Browning, his close friend, what was happening. Instead, it says, "Weather heavy today, expected rain this afternoon." It was a most dreary, pedestrian diary, though it's got some gems in it.

The Chase diary is one of the better diaries. It was not all that frequent at the time, nor has it been all that frequent since, for cabinet members to keep diaries. In very recent times, they may be afraid to keep them lest they be subpoenaed.

EDWIN STANTON

EDWIN STANTON WAS Lincoln's great secretary of war. He was appointed in early 1862 to succeed Simon Cameron. Cameron was a rather sleazy Pennsylvania character who had, among other things, embezzled money intended for the Indians, so he's sometimes called the Winnebago Chief. He had made a mess of the War Department. He couldn't administer anything, and finally he was edged out. He was literally sent to Siberia; he was made American Minister to Russia.

In his place, Lincoln needed somebody who was efficient, organized, and had a good deal of political support. Edwin Stanton had been a member of [President James] Buchanan's cabinet briefly. He had a good deal of political experience, he was a superb lawyer, and he was highly efficient.

He was also brusque. He could be rude to absolutely anybody, including the president. [People] would come in to Lincoln and ask, "Can't you give me a pardon for my son? I know he deserted from the army, but he really is a good boy, and if you could just say that you've given him a pardon." Lincoln would say, "I can't give him a pardon. If I did, Secretary Stanton would shoot me." They played good cop, bad cop. It was a very effective relationship.

[Lincoln and Stanton met years earlier when both worked as attorneys on a railroad case.] I'm sure Lincoln remembered it, but he never mentioned it. To my knowledge, Stanton never mentioned it. It was as though it never had happened.

. . . It was a celebrated railroad case. Lincoln was hired as one of the attorneys in order to have somebody from Illinois because an Illinois railroad was involved. The case was heard in Cincinnati. Stanton was the principal attorney. Lincoln arrived a bit late, looking bedraggled with his old green umbrella tied together with a string at the top. His clothes never seemed to fit him no matter how well he tried to dress. He came into the courtroom, wearing an old linen duster, which swept down his back, as Stanton said, looking like a map of Africa. Stanton asked his colleague, "Who is that gorilla?"

He would not let Lincoln have any part of the proceedings. Lincoln watched the case as it was held and went back home much chagrined by the whole affair, but it didn't poison their future relations. Lincoln held no grudges. He was a generous man. Stanton, by the way, was not a generous man.

GEORGE McCLELLAN

[GEN.] GEORGE McCLELLAN certainly deserves some careful psychoanalytical treatment. Lincoln did visit George McClellan very frequently, trying to urge him on, to get going [with the war]. He would say encouraging things to him such as "Oh, the army's in the best shape I ever saw; your plan is wonderful." Always with the subtext of, let's get going on it.

McClellan wouldn't move. He had built-in resistance to moving. Lincoln was impervious to all sorts of personal difficulties. [There is] the incident when Lincoln comes to call on McClellan one evening, one of his usual evening calls, to find out how things are going. Lincoln said to [McClellan's] aide, "I'll wait here in the parlor until he gets home." McClellan came in late, without looking into the parlor, though he obviously saw the president and started upstairs. Lincoln waited and waited, and finally asked the aide, and was told the general's gone to bed. Anybody else, any other president of the United States would have been insulted, would have dismissed the general, would have had a scene. Lincoln said, "I will hold McClellan's horse if that [would] do any good to get him moving. All I care about is action." And he couldn't get it.

STEPHEN A. DOUGLAS

LINCOLN AND STEPHEN A. DOUGLAS had been lifelong political rivals, Douglas being the leader of the Democrats in Illinois, and Lincoln competing as the leader of the Whigs and [eventually] of the Republicans. Lincoln really despised Douglas. He thought he was not truthful, that he stretched things and he made up things. Douglas, on the other hand, had a good deal of respect for Lincoln, though he thought that Lincoln was ill-prepared to be a major leader.

The debates in 1858 surprised Douglas, though he was aware that Lincoln was going to be a formidable opponent. He didn't know how clever Lincoln was going to be. When it was over, and Douglas was re-elected, he realized that Lincoln was on the path to greater power.

Douglas was nominated for president in 1860 by a faction of the Democratic Party, Lincoln by the Republicans. If Lincoln had not run, would Douglas have run? We don't know. Chances are, probably not. Douglas had so many enemies in the Democratic Party, [which was] so badly split that it probably could not have united on another candidate.

Once in office, Lincoln turned to Douglas for support, and Douglas gave it unhesitatingly and wholeheartedly. He came to the White House when Lincoln was drafting his proclamation calling for seventy-five thousand [Union army] volunteers and said, "Of course I support this, but it's not enough. You ought to at least double it. You ought to have more than that. It's going to take more than that."

Douglas then went out into Illinois to make speeches to recruit support for the president's policies. Unfortunately, he fell ill about this time and died, so the chief leader of what could have been the loyal Democratic opposition was removed from Congress.

CHARLES SUMNER

SENATOR CHARLES SUMNER was a senator from Massachusetts in the Civil War years. He was one of the great abolitionist leaders. He was head of the Senate Foreign Relations Committee. He was a constant goad and nag at Abraham Lincoln, urging him to get on with abolition. He was one of the principal architects of radical Reconstruction, meaning rights for African Americans and keeping Southern whites disfranchised. He was very much a Republican.

For the last years of life, indeed for most of his life, Senator Sumner had battled for equal rights for people. He was particularly concerned with equal rights for African Americans. He had many African American friends. He thought deeply about the injuries that had been done to them. He sponsored, repeatedly, a civil rights bill. At the time that he was in his death throes, Congress was just getting ready to pass an abridged and emasculated version of his civil rights bill. He told Frederick Douglass and others at his deathbed, "Don't forget the civil rights bill. Don't let it die." They did, indeed, pass it.

[That was] the sentiment of people like Charles Sumner, but, alas, not of the public as a whole. The Republican Party by this time was moving more and more toward becoming conservative, business-oriented, wanting to get out of the South, call the whole thing off [on civil rights], in effect, leading to the era of segregation. It was against this trend that Sumner was fighting, and that led to the big struggles of the Reconstruction era.

ANDREW JOHNSON

LINCOLN NEGATIVELY SELECTED Andrew Johnson [as his second-term running mate]. He didn't want Hannibal Hamlin, his first vice president, who brought him no strength, because [Hamlin's home state of] Maine was going to be wholly Republican. . . . Andrew Johnson was a Unionist, and he might bring some support in the upper South.

Lincoln, like most presidents, really didn't think much about a vice president. He had no idea that he was going to die, he had no idea he was going to be succeeded by Andrew Johnson any more than Franklin Roosevelt had an idea that he would be succeeded by Harry Truman.

Politicians just don't want to think about these things. They think about some current political advantage. Lincoln also thought there was something to be said for letting the Republican convention in Baltimore have its own head.

Republicans had been, in effect, coerced into nominating him [for reelection] by acclamation, so [he figured he could] let them play around a little bit with a vice presidential nomination [because] it doesn't really matter who's vice president. It was a mistake.

MY GUESS IS THAT, in contrast to Andrew Johnson, Lincoln would have managed to get along with the radical Republicans in his party [who shaped Reconstruction policies]. Some of them were close personal friends of his. Charles Sumner was one of them. If you can believe Mary Lincoln's stories, he and Abraham Lincoln used to get together and tell stories and joke just like two schoolboys. This is from the stately Massachusetts senator [who carried himself with] this stature of morality. I think Lincoln would have managed to get along with these people much better than Johnson.

Second, I think Lincoln had much more sensitivity toward African Americans and their plight. Johnson was a racist. He just by and large didn't like blacks. He didn't think they had any rights that ought to be respected. Lincoln did. He grew to this disposition quite gradually. He had not known any blacks when he grew up.

In the Civil War, Lincoln came to realize the courage and the heroism of black soldiers, and he came to make the friendship of Frederick Douglass, probably the ablest black spokesman of the nineteenth century, and to realize here is a man who could have coped with any problem whatsoever. Lincoln would not have been insensitive to the plight of blacks in the Reconstruction period.

Finally, I think Lincoln would be much more pragmatic. He would not have urged that there be this formula for Reconstruction. Indeed, he'd already worked this out in effect with Sumner.

. . . He was going to play this case by case as he went along. . . . [Lincoln thought] that a statesman had to steer the way one steers on the Mississippi River, from point to point, from this crag, from that bluff, from that buried log. This was the way he was going to run Reconstruction, not by some formula.

The Springfield Junto

ADAM BELLOW

Adam Bellow appeared on C-SPAN's Booknotes *on August 24, 2003, to talk about his book,* In Praise of Nepotism: A Natural History, *published by Doubleday.*

LINCOLN IS the great counter-example; Lincoln is always held up as the model of the self-made man, the person who rose from humble obscurity to become president of the country, based simply on his merit and worth. But this is acknowledged to be a myth. Lincoln was already a very successful railroad lawyer in Springfield, well before he went into politics.

Lincoln came from a family that had a long history of public service. His own father was a failure and had migrated west like many other people looking for greater opportunities. He bought many farms and failed again and again. He kept moving from one state to another, finally ending up in Kentucky, Indiana, Illinois. The relationship between Abe and his father was very strained and harsh. His father wanted Abe to stay on the farm and contribute to the family enterprise, but Abe wanted to go off on his own.

Abe finally did go off on his own and had to become adept at forming friendships and alliances with people who could help him. He had a genius for this kind of thing. He was famous for striking up lifelong friendships on a moment's notice, and he climbed the rungs of these relationships to very prominent positions in the Illinois Republican Party.

One of the most important things he did to help himself was to marry Mary Todd. Mary Todd came from a very well-respected, wealthy Kentucky family. They were a slave-owning family. And she was related by marriage to the circle of Illinois politicians known as the Springfield Junto. It's one of the under-discussed features of American political history. All over America in the nineteenth century, there were juntos. It's a Spanish word—*junto*—

but it really describes a cabal, a group of people who have common political and business interests, and generally intermarry in order to strengthen these bonds. To get ahead in a provincial area like Illinois, you had to have some connection to this group of people.

By marrying Mary Todd, Lincoln acquired a marital connection to the Springfield Junto; it was the making of him. He became the leading lawyer in the state. He was put up for Congress [after serving in] the state assembly, where he performed very significant services, including getting the state capital moved from Vandalia to Springfield, where the members of the junto could exploit the move and the business that would come with it. His reward was being allowed to marry into the junto. Later, these friendships and relationships were instrumental in helping him rise to national office.

Challenging the Incumbent

JOHN SPLAINE

Dr. John Splaine authored A Companion to the Lincoln-Douglas Debates *to accompany C-SPAN's reenactment of the debates in 1994. This text is taken from the introduction of his book, which was published by C-SPAN.*

DEBATES FOR U.S. Senate seats were unusual in 1858. The United States Constitution had placed the election of senators in the hands of the respective state legislatures. Therefore, in 1858 no one directly voted for either Douglas or Lincoln. That happened the next year as the state legislature convened. So, how then did these debates before the people of Illinois come about?

On July 9, 1858, Stephen A. Douglas officially opened his re-election campaign when he spoke at the Tremont House in Chicago. Abraham Lincoln was seated in the audience during Douglas's speech that night and spoke from the same balcony the next evening. Lincoln's peroration there, on July 10, contained words that would continue to resonate, "I leave you, hoping that the lamp of liberty will burn in your bosoms until there shall no longer be a doubt that all men are created free and equal."

A week later, on July 16, Lincoln again watched Douglas speak, this time in Bloomington, Illinois. The next day, they both spoke in Springfield, albeit, at separate times. Politicians, editorial writers, and other citizens were by then beginning to clamor for the two candidates to speak and respond to each other on the same stage at the same time. The two had appeared in the same place and had been on the same platform, but they had not spoken in the presence of the other for the purpose of rebuttal. Lincoln had heard what Douglas had said, and Douglas had read what Lincoln had said, but they had not rejoined each other face to face. What, then, could be done to make it happen?

On July 24, 1858, Lincoln wrote to Douglas proposing an arrangement. Lincoln asked: "Will it be agreeable to you to make an arrangement for you and myself to divide time, and address the same audiences during the present canvass? Mr. Judd, who will hand you this, is authorized to receive your answer; and if, agreeable to you, to enter into the terms of such arrangement."

The next day, Douglas responded:

"Your note of this date, in which you inquire if it would be agreeable to me to make an arrangement to divide the time and address the same audiences during the present canvass, was handed me by Mr. Judd. Recent events have interposed difficulties in the way of such an arrangement."

As the above opening paragraph in Douglas's letter suggested, there were some problems in arranging the joint appearances of the two candidates for the U.S. Senate seat in 1858. Among the problems Douglas cited was that he had already arranged some speaking engagements that left him little time for other speeches. However, Douglas did indicate that he would try to work out an arrangement by which he and Lincoln could jointly appear. He proposed that they do so in the congressional districts where they had not previously spoken. They had both already given speeches in Chicago and Springfield. Douglas concluded his response to Lincoln by saying, "If agreeable to you, I will indicate the following places as those most suitable in the several Congressional Districts at which we should speak to wit: Freeport, Ottawa, Galesburg, Quincy, Alton, Jonesboro and Charleston."

The proposed arrangement was back in Lincoln's corner and he concluded his return correspondence of July 29, 1858, saying, "I agree to an arrangement for us to speak at the seven places you have named, and at your own times, provided you name the times at once, so that I, as well as you, can have to myself the time not covered by the arrangement. As to other details, I wish perfect reciprocity, and no more. I wish as much time as you, and that conclusions shall alternate."

On July 30, 1858, after confirming the times and places for the debates, Douglas ended his response, "I agree to your suggestion that we shall alternately open and close the discussion. I will speak at Ottawa one hour, you can reply, occupying an hour and a half, and I will then follow for half an hour. We will alternate in like manner in each successive place."

Lincoln closed the now historic correspondence between the two men on July 31, 1858, saying, "Yours of yesterday, naming places, times, and terms for joint discussions between us, was received this morning.

Although, by the terms, as you propose, you take *four* openings, and closes to my *three*, I accede, and thus close the arrangement. I direct this to you at Hillsboro, and shall try to have both your letter and this appear in the *Journal* and *Register* of Monday morning."

Thus the debates were scheduled. The verbal flint was at the ready. Lincoln and Douglas were about to set words on fire.

The Debates

HAROLD HOLZER

Lincoln scholar Harold Holzer, author of thirty-two books on Lincoln or the Civil War period, is co-chair of the United States Lincoln Bicentennial Commission. He has appeared on C-SPAN numerous times to discuss the sixteenth president. Among his many recognitions is the 2005 Lincoln Prize for his book Lincoln at Cooper Union: The Speech That Made Abraham Lincoln President, *published by HarperCollins. Mr. Holzer is senior vice president for external affairs for New York's Metropolitan Museum of Art. His book on the Lincoln-Douglas debates inspired C-SPAN's 1994 televised re-creation of the debates.*

There are many misconceptions about the Lincoln-Douglas debates. One is that they were full of high-minded, philosophical, lofty sentiments, which, of course, is not true. Quite the opposite, in fact. The other is that Lincoln cornered Douglas so that he could elevate himself into the presidency and doom Douglas's chances for the presidency two years down the road, which is another misconception. . . .

Stephen A. Douglas was the two-term, New England-born, Illinois-bred senator from Illinois seeking a third term. He was a powerful Democrat in the United States Senate, a leader of the Senate, a leader of efforts to hold off civil war through a series of compromises. He was the father of a doctrine called "popular sovereignty," wherein people in a new territory would have the right, before that territory became a state, to decide for themselves whether to allow slavery in that new territory.

Originally, he was from Vermont, but grew up in Illinois. As a young man, he came to Illinois and dropped the "s" off his name so that he had one "s" instead of two. Otherwise, he would have been perpetually confused with the person whom he didn't like very much, [the noted black abolitionist leader] Frederick Douglass. In fact, he mentioned Douglass during the debates in a derogatory fashion because he saw Frederick Douglass at one of them, riding in a carriage seated next to white women. He used that horrifying spectacle as a warning to the people of Illinois: "This is what Illinois will become if you elect Abraham Lincoln to the Senate." Black people and white people would commingle, which was supposed to send chills of horror down the spines of people from Illinois. So Douglas was a racist in addition to everything else—not unusual in 1858. He was a great public speaker known for ripping his clothes off, one garment at a time, as he spoke in the heat of debate—first his coat, then his vest, then his tie. People would joke that if Douglas had given speeches longer than two hours, he would have wound up on the Senate floor with nothing on but his undergarments.

Aside from being the physical opposite of Stephen A. Douglas—Douglas was called the "Little Giant," and Lincoln, at that point, was known by the nickname "Long Abe"—Lincoln was a one-term congressman. He had served in the 1840s in the Congress as a Whig and he was a co-founder of the new Republican Party, a leader of the Illinois Republicans, and a well-known, successful attorney, but mostly he was known as a party leader, a public speaker on behalf of other candidates. He had tried for the Senate a few years earlier in a campaign that was not really a campaign. It was just decided in the [Illinois] legislature with no campaign, no debates. He had nearly made it, but his party forsook him during the balloting and elected a different fellow.

So [in 1858], he was making his second real effort for the Senate, and this time he said he would only do it if he was nominated for the Senate in advance, which was not the practice in those days. So the Republicans met in convention and nominated Lincoln as their first and only choice for the United States Senate. Lincoln responded with his famous "House Divided" speech—that was his acceptance speech. Thereupon a campaign began, which was unusual because senators were not elected directly by the people in 1858; they were elected by the legislatures, a sort of a parliamentary-style election.

LINCOLN MADE SIXTY speeches during the campaign. The debates were just a fraction of his effort. Douglas made 130 speeches. They really worked those small towns.

THE WHIG PARTY, of which he was a happy and contented member for
the early part of his life—in fact, most of his political career was spent as a
Whig—was just sort of dissolving with the growing immediacy of the slavery
crisis. He and the more advanced of his Whig friends—some of them became Democrats—decided that what was needed was a party that was strictly
against slavery expansion. So he organized in Illinois to convert as many
Whigs as possible into the new party. [They were] old Whigs looking to or-
ganize themselves in a new and appealing way.

[THERE ARE ABOUT FORTY] previous versions of the Lincoln-Douglas debates, and they were all but canonized in *The Collected Works of Abraham Lincoln*, published about forty years ago. All relied on texts that were taken
down at the time by what I call partisan stenographers, hired by the respective political parties. The Republicans hired stenographers to work for the
Republican newspapers; the Democrats hired stenographers to work for the
Democratic newspapers. It was Lincoln who decided, after these debates
were published in the newspapers, to have them published in book form.
He used the approved text of his speeches, [and] the approved text of Douglas's speeches, did some more editing himself, and produced the version
of the debates that we know to this day.

The problem with that is that they differ markedly from the opposition
transcripts. The Democratic transcribers also took down what Lincoln said
and the Republican transcribers also took down what Douglas said. The
purpose was that two or three days after each debate, the full text of the
debate appeared in the newspapers. Of course, there was no recording
equipment at the time and no other way to get the text except to have the
shorthand reporters take down the debates, but what had never been
looked at was the Democratic version of what Lincoln said and the Republican version of what Douglas said.

I suspected that the transcripts would be a lot rougher than the material
that we've come to accept as the authentic texts of the debate, and, in fact,
they were. Lincoln had a great deal of trouble parsing sentences, as I suspected he would. He was nowhere near as eloquent in the soaring moments
of the debate as he was in the transcripts that his fellows, his supporters,
had worked on and he himself had edited. So I thought this [effort to re-
publish the debates] would bring us a little bit closer to that unique political culture that made the debates possible—this rollicking atmosphere of
celebration and spectacle that occurred at each of these debate towns during those months of campaigning.

[WHEN YOU LOOK AT A rundown of where these debates were held, you
can see there were two in August, two in September, and three in Octo-

ber.] Ottawa and Freeport were in the northern part of Illinois. Jonesboro was way in the south; in fact, the part of the state in which that debate took place was called "Egypt." That was the nickname, but no one knew whether that meant it was hot and sultry down there or whether it was because the most famous town there was Cairo. Douglas kept saying during those first two debates, "I want to trot him down to Egypt and bring him to his milk," whatever that means. It was considered a very untoward thing for a senator to say. Charleston is in the middle of the state, and that was where Lincoln's stepmother still lived, not far from there. Galesburg was back a bit north, and it was a college town—Knox College—and the debate took place on the grounds of this rather progressive college, very much for Lincoln. With Quincy and Alton we move back down south and west toward the river. So the towns were all over the state, chosen by Stephen A. Douglas, by the way. He selected the venues because he was in a position to make demands.

KNOX COLLEGE IN Galesburg is still there. They moved the platform that day because it was so windy. They moved it to the side of the college to protect the speakers from the wind, and it created my favorite quote of the debates. Lincoln had to go through the building and out the window to get on the platform, and he said, "At last I've gone through college."

THE PROCESS BEGAN in an interesting way. Douglas was much better financed than Lincoln and much better known, even in Illinois. Lincoln was having trouble getting attention for his nascent campaign. So he devised this idea that he would follow Douglas around to wherever Douglas was campaigning, and after Douglas gave his speech, Lincoln would give a speech in the same place, and, thus, he said, "I'd have the last word on him." In Chicago, Douglas spoke in the afternoon; Lincoln spoke in the evening. In Springfield, their hometown and the state capital, Douglas spoke one day and Lincoln followed him the next day. Well, the Democratic press started to make fun of Lincoln. They said that it was as if he were a circus performer picking up with the menagerie and moving from town to town. The Republican paper, the *Chicago Press and Tribune*, now called the *Chicago Tribune*, proposed this idea of joint debates.

LINCOLN PICKED UP the case immediately and challenged Douglas to debates, and Douglas knew from the beginning that this process could be of no benefit to him. He was coasting at that point. He had a stacked legislature that was almost certainly going to reelect him to the Senate. The last thing he needed was to waste his time debating Lincoln face-to-face—as close to face-to-face as they could get, one fellow being five feet two inches and the other being six feet four inches. But the code of honor of the West dictated that you couldn't very well refuse. Douglas had to accept the debate challenge, but he drew the line when Lincoln said, "Let's meet one hundred times all over the state." Douglas said, "No." Lincoln said, "How about fifty times?" Douglas said, "Forget it." So Douglas said, "We'll meet in the county seats of each county, and we'll leave out Cook County, because you already followed me in Chicago, and we'll leave out Sangamon County, because you followed me in Springfield. So that leaves seven counties, and we'll meet in seven county seats. Take it or leave it." So Lincoln took it.

Each debate was three hours, incredibly enough, and the format was nothing like the debates we have today. The first speaker, the opening speaker, spoke for sixty minutes without stop, and then the rebuttal speaker spoke for one-and-a-half hours—ninety minutes, again uninterruptedly. Finally, the first speaker had thirty minutes to answer the rebuttal—so, three hours altogether, each time. Audiences not only endured this in both the blazing heat of August in Freeport, for example, and Ottawa, but also in the freezing rains that suddenly whipped up in the fall. They loved it. It was spectacle; it was theater; it was religion; it was Fourth of July. These were the biggest events to hit the prairie in these people's lifetimes, and they knew it.

There was no amplification equipment, which makes one wonder about some contemporary descriptions of Lincoln's voice as shrill and unpleasant. Clearly these politicians of the nineteenth century were equipped with incredibly strong voices. It had to have been a prerequisite for a political career because there were twenty thousand people in Freeport, and fifteen thousand or ten thousand at some of the other debate towns. The smallest crowd was the fifteen hundred down south in Jonesboro. These were huge crowds, and they were milling around. There were no seats except for VIPs and for ladies. There was such a crush for the ladies' seats that in one of the debate towns, the entire bench collapsed sending all the ladies down this slanted half-bench to the floor.

At some of the debates, there were no ladies present, but at others, they were there, and they were given the only seats available except for the Conestoga wagons and the covered wagons that some people arrived on. People sat in their wagons. It makes one wonder how many people actually heard the speeches and how many people were out for the celebration. You had ice cream being consumed and picnic barbecues, liquid refreshment—a lot of liquid refreshment—fights breaking out in the back of the crowds, a cannon being fired off. Douglas traveled with his own cannon. That was the only amplification around. His supporters were instructed to fire it every time he got off a good point against Lincoln. So there was lots of noise, lots of crowd yelling and cheering and booing and talking back. They were nothing like the debates today where our candidates make such an intentional and careful effort to take the high ground and to be very calm and not answer [questions]. Negatives and fighting and audience attacks were part of the game.

Immigration was changing the face of Illinois in 1858. Slaveholders were slowly moving out, disappearing into the South, as Illinois was abolishing slavery on its own ground. It was a state really of two halves. The northern half was much like the North in the rest of the United States, committed to stopping the expansion of slavery at a minimum, or abolishing it. Not many people were for abolition. The southern part of the state, bounded by Southern states and the Mississippi River, was very much pro-slavery. One county in Illinois, a county where Lincoln had spent part of his youth, once voted to bar blacks altogether from entering the county—and by a substantial majority. So it was still very much a racist state, believing in the supremacy of the white race but edging toward a liberalization because of population shifts.

[Nationally, the debates] became news after a while. To understand why requires an understanding of the newspapers of the day. They were not nonpartisan like today's newspapers purport to be. They were either Republican newspapers or Democratic newspapers. The Republican papers around the country decided that this fellow Lincoln was making some interesting noise out in the West—it was not the Midwest in those days, but the West—and they began republishing the texts of the debates and also sending correspondents out there to take the measure of the political ferment that they were hearing about. So there were Eastern correspondents on hand. The Democratic papers were publishing Douglas's debates because they saw in Douglas's likely re-election a vindication of "popular sovereignty" and this notion that slavery could expand, in fact, through popular vote.

Lincoln had not done terribly well in the first debate. . . . In Ottawa, this was a new ball game for him. He was a bit outclassed. Douglas posed some rather direct and challenging interrogatories to Lincoln, and Lincoln chose not to answer them in his rebuttal. It was probably a tactical error. He had probably chosen what he wanted to talk about, and he was intent on talking about that. Douglas slaughtered him in the rejoinder, really took him to task for avoiding the issues.

After the Ottawa debate, Lincoln was carried off by his supporters in "triumph." Some of the Democratic press teased that they should have carried him off before the debate started. But even the supporters saw it as sort of a comical thing, because as they carried him off, his pants rose higher and higher until his underwear was exposed. He must have been wearing long underwear even in August. His underwear was exposed to the knees and to see his legs dangling practically to the floor must have been a pretty comical sight. His supporters were not happy when they read the transcript. One of the Chicago Republicans said, "For God's sake, tell him to 'Charge, Chester, charge.'" People wrote to him saying, "You've got to wake up. You've got to fight back."

Along came the Freeport debate, and Lincoln got right back at Douglas and answered all of those interrogatories and posed the famous "Freeport question," which has divided historians ever since about what Lincoln's intention was. He said to Douglas, "Let me ask you something. You talk about popular sovereignty. What if people in the territory, before forming a new state constitution, voted not to have slavery, even down in the South? Would you accept that?" And Douglas said, "I would have to. That's popular sovereignty." Many historians have concluded that that was Lincoln's way of destroying Douglas in the South and ensuring that he could never win a presidential election two years down the road. I have my questions about that, but it was an awfully clever thing to make Douglas admit to.

There were occasions in the debates when Lincoln threatened to stop up Douglas's mouth with a corncob. Douglas used the word "nigger" constantly to taunt Lincoln and Republicans. [Abe Lincoln used the same word] on one or two occasions. Interestingly, he did it in a northern venue; and when he got to Jonesboro, the southern town, he was on very good behavior and actually said, "I know you people don't agree with me, but let me explain my position on race and on slavery," and he was actually quite high-minded at that debate. But, yes, he did use the "n" word.

[DOUGLAS CONSTANTLY REFERRED to "black Republicans" by which] he meant that the party that Lincoln had founded—he meant it in the most pejorative way possible—was cast as an abolition party. They were all pro-black. They were practically black themselves. Nothing worse could be said about a politician by another politician. But when the Democratic papers did the transcripts of Douglas . . . they took out "black" and they just made it "Republican." Whenever Douglas said, "nigger," the Democratic papers changed it to "Negro." That's why I went back to the opposition transcripts, because they didn't have those embellishments and those edits and that softening.

NOT TO CAST A GLOW on bigotry, but it was not unusual to believe in white supremacy if you were white in nineteenth-century America. Lincoln himself had to backtrack during the entire debate proceedings from a speech he made in Chicago before the debate started in which he merely said that the Declaration of Independence, which decreed that all men are created equal, extended not only to whites but to blacks. That, he said, was the intention of the founders of the country. Well, for seven debates, Lincoln hemmed and hawed and explained and revised to get away from the notion that he had actually spoken about racial equality. He had to do that [politically], and he probably believed that he hadn't spoken about racial equality.

THE THING THAT'S probably the most remarkable is that [all seven debates] really were about one thing—slavery. There were lots of diversions. Throughout the debates, you heard Lincoln and Douglas attack each other for the most ridiculous, off-the-subject things. Douglas attacked Lincoln for his record as a congressman during the Mexican War, bringing up a ten-year-old issue, saying he hadn't voted for supplies for the soldiers, and Lincoln had to defend that. Lincoln accused Douglas of conspiring with the chief justice of the United States and the president to nationalize slavery. Lincoln knew that wasn't true. He didn't think that Douglas had had a secret meeting with [Chief Justice] Roger Taney or President James Buchanan and decided that they were going to bring slavery to Maine and Vermont, but part of the debates were about entertainment and weakening your opponent through diversionary tactics, and there was a great deal of that—all these conspiracy theories. Lincoln kept referring to Douglas as "Judge Douglas." It's one of those you-had-to-be-there things, but Douglas had been a judge, and Lincoln had teased Douglas that he had voted as a state legislator to expand the Illinois judiciary specifically so that he could get a judgeship. So every time he called him "judge" instead of "senator," he was digging the knife in a little deeper saying, "You made yourself a judge." But basically the issue was slavery and whether or not it could be expanded morally, legally. The side issue was this issue of equality, which was a new notion for the vast majority of people in Illinois, a new thing for them to deal with. . . .

TO SAVE THE UNION for the future and to permit American democracy to inspire the rest of the world to democracy, [these were ideals in] which Lincoln believed very deeply. The primary goal was to hold the Union together and the moral goal was to stop the spread of slavery. Lincoln believed that if you stopped allowing slavery into new states that were forming all the time in the West, you created a situation in which slavery would disappear in and of itself—no more slave trade, no more foreign slave trade. Slavery would disappear and strangle itself, as he believed the Founding Fathers desired from the beginning. On the notion of political and social equality, I don't think Lincoln was prepared for political and social equality in 1858. The "Great Emancipator" that we think of as the Lincolnian ideal developed four or five years later in his life. He developed quickly, but he wasn't there yet in 1858.

[In these debates], he was saying to all of those who could hear him, "I am a middle-of-the-road Republican. You've heard that I am for equality.

I'm really not for equality. I'm for equality of opportunity. I believe that if you earn bread with your own hands, you should eat it with your own mouth." As he joked later in the debates, "If God meant for one class of citizens to do all the work and another class of citizens to get all the benefits, then he would have made workers with all hands and no mouth and the beneficiaries of their labor with mouths and no hands." It was his way of saying, "People should earn the fruits of their own labors, but don't worry. I'm not going to make jurors of blacks. I'm not going to make voters of blacks. I'm not going to change the nature of politics in the state. I'm not going to empower people who could drive you out of office or compete for wage jobs with your children." This is what he had to do in order to be a viable candidate in Illinois, but he wouldn't have been a candidate in Illinois if he didn't believe that in the first place.

    . . . Obviously Lincoln was not for equality in 1858. Does that make him a racist? It depends on your definition of racism. The debates portray him as less of a racist than Douglas, but one of the things that was eye-opening to me was the beginning of his speech in Charleston. He was coasting. He was the hometown favorite.

He had come to Charleston thirty years before as a young adult. He had come in with his family in an ox cart. They really liked him there. Republicans won that area. Of course, there was no direct election, but Republicans did well in the fall. There were banners all over saying, "Old Abe returns to Charleston," "Pioneer boy comes home." So he was in his element there, and he probably could have said exactly what he wanted to say, but he decided to say, "You have heard some people say that I am for equality of the Negro." An interesting start, but what was even more interesting was the crowd's reaction—laughter. They laughed at the notion that a mainstream politician could have ever said such a thing, which more strongly, more directly, and more irrefutably than at any other moment of the debates, paints a picture of what that electorate was like. The electorate was much more racist than Lincoln, and Lincoln did well to position himself as nimbly as he did and maintain the affections of so many voters.

HOW WOULD LINCOLN do today in politics? It's very hard to transpose the Lincoln who could afford to wear ill-fitting clothes and travel by coach during these debates and generally look like he had slept for twenty-five or thirty hours in his suit when he arrived, didn't shave often enough, and didn't tend to his hair the way our candidates and leaders do today. But obviously he was smart enough to have adapted, and he probably would have been extremely persuasive. Presumably he would change some of his politics to update himself to the twentieth century.

[LINCOLN AND DOUGLAS'S 1858 debates] really give us an idea of what political debating was like before we got as frightened, as we seem to be now, about letting people have the full range of their emotions and their thoughts, and speaking as long as they want, and allowing audiences to do what they wanted. It paints a picture of a political culture that has really vanished from the United States. Maybe it's not a good thing that it has vanished. This idea that people would participate in as many numbers as they did—not paid workers, not political supporters, but ordinary people who came in ox carts and ferries and trains, on horseback or walked, came in such numbers that the towns looked like dust bowls. There was dust rising, enshrouding towns from the numbers of arriving people. It paints a picture of political involvement and excitement about government that we've lost.

Politics and Morality

RICHARD CURRENT

Lincoln scholar Richard Current helped set the scene for C-SPAN's live telecast of the first Lincoln-Douglas debate reenactment in Ottawa, Illinois, on August 20, 1994.

BOTH LINCOLN and Douglas were politicians; they dealt a great deal in irrelevancies, misrepresentations, and alleging conspiracies, each to the other. . . .

An analysis of their debates shows very well that there was a real difference between Lincoln and Douglas's positions, and a difference that I think would be of interest to African Americans today—that is, Lincoln looked ahead to the future. Lincoln did not use race baiting; he did not appeal to prejudice. He recognized it, but he didn't appeal to it. It was Stephen A. Douglas who kept on with the race baiting and using prejudice for politics. When Lincoln did make these defensive statements about not favoring immediate social or political equality, he was driven to it by the constant badgering of Stephen A. Douglas.

LIKE THE OTHER debates between Lincoln and Douglas, the main issue [in the Ottawa debate] was not black rights or even black freedom or the future of slavery. The basic issue was pretty limited to the question of the extension of slavery into the western territories.

Now Lincoln, like many others, believed that if slavery were confined and were not allowed to expand, it would sooner or later—probably sooner—die a natural death. So in that sense, Lincoln was an ultimate abolitionist, not an immediate abolitionist. But it's perfectly true that at the time [of these debates] Lincoln did not stand for political or social equality for African Americans. He specifically said he did not, in response to baiting by Stephen A. Douglas.

On the other hand, it seems to me there's a real difference between the position of Lincoln and the position of Douglas in the debates. There were questions of morality that Lincoln was on the side of and Douglas was against. Lincoln maintained the Declaration of Independence applied to African Americans as well as others. I think Lincoln did look to the ultimate equality of all Americans with regard to natural rights and the rights provided in the Declaration of Independence. But it's very true—the immediate issue in 1858 was not the rights or even the freedom of slaves but the question of confining slavery.

THE DRED SCOTT decision was made in 1857, before the Civil War, and I want to [underscore] that Stephen A. Douglas approved of the decision in the case of Dred Scott. Abraham Lincoln strongly and vigorously opposed it.

[The common view was that] black men had no rights that white men were bound to respect; Lincoln did not believe that. And he did not believe, as the Dred Scott decision held, that slavery was universal, [in other words] even if a slave was taken into free territory, he or she must remain a slave. Lincoln did not agree with that.

LINCOLN ONCE SAID later on, "Whenever I hear someone defending or advocating slavery, I feel like trying it on him personally."

The Jonesboro Debate

JOHN Y. SIMON

On September 17, 1994, John Y. Simon joined C-SPAN for the reenactment of the Lincoln-Douglas debate in Jonesboro, the southernmost town in Illinois.

IN 1858, when the Jonesboro debate was held, Stephen A. Douglas had been a United States senator for [about] twelve years and he was four years younger than Lincoln. There is no doubt that Lincoln must have looked upon him as a successful man. Not only had Douglas achieved a higher office—Lincoln had been a congressman, but only for one term—and the office of senator is normally regarded as a superior one. Douglas seemed to be the more successful man. He was the man of wealth, standing, and celebrity, and Lincoln was the underdog. Lincoln was the one who had to challenge Douglas to debate. Douglas condescended to debate with his less prominent opponent, yet I think there was a kind of personal chemistry between the two as men of nearly equal age and rivals for political eminence.

LINCOLN WOULD tell marvelous stories for which he was always center stage. Douglas would talk much as he did in the debates—he was very much a political man, a political animal. . . . Lincoln was notable for his style of dress. We tend to think that Lincoln dressed like everybody else, but he didn't. He dressed all in black, normally, and wore that hat. Now somebody could have pointed out to him that it was an odd sort of fashion statement—"You're very tall, angular, and the hat makes you look more so." Apparently Lincoln wanted to look like Lincoln. He stood out in a crowd, and he used his appearance as a badge. It was a sign to the voters: Here's somebody different. His wife didn't care for this. She wasn't incapable of saying, "Why don't you dress up and look like you are someone?" But

Lincoln went on looking like Lincoln, usually a little rumpled and certainly not in the fashionable clothes of the era.

LINCOLN'S STATEMENTS on race and on his lack of support for social and political equality for blacks, expressed in the Charleston debate, are now better known than his Gettysburg Address. They've been quoted and re-quoted, and, in many respects, they are a disservice to him since they're uncharacteristic views. I think it's clear that Lincoln was trying to set the record straight on his views on this particular issue. He did himself a service by not saying this in Jonesboro, where they would have been best received, but instead saved them for Charleston, which was essentially a Republican district. It was essential [to a successful campaign] that he not be misidenti- fied as an abolitionist or as somebody who favored social and political equality, and he had to say that loud and clear. His statements on [Negro] inferiority are, in fact, couched in language that gives him the opportunity as a lawyer to change his mind at some later point, as he definitely does.

[WHAT I LIKE LEAST about Douglas is his] lack of antislavery principles. Douglas insisted, time after time, that he did not care whether slavery was voted up or voted down . . . that he cared more for the principles of free government than for all the Negroes in Christendom, which is a non se- quitur, but it's a viciously meant non sequitur. The fact is, he maintained a plantation in Mississippi that was worked by slaves. . . . On the whole, the fact that Douglas tried to stir up racial animosity as a way of winning office puts him at an enormous distance from Lincoln.

Lincoln had to deal with the white population of Illinois—the one that supported the ill-treatment of blacks, the atrocious treatment of blacks, and the Black Exclusion Law that punished free blacks from coming into the state by slapping a heavy fine on them. This was a state in which there was such hostility to blacks that it was very difficult to summon up antislavery sentiment. The amazing thing is, Lincoln did this. He was able to point out that slavery was an amoral, asocial, apolitical evil, and that it should be put on the course of ultimate extinction. That Lincoln could say this in Illinois and gain support . . . is a great tribute to him.

HE WOULD HAVE taken, as he did in these debates, the idea of being an abolitionist as a dreaded charge, one that he certainly wanted to run away from. Abolitionists were people who wanted the immediate end of slavery, without regard to what Lincoln saw as the constitutional protection for the institution of slavery. He was no Owen Lovejoy, who was a very true aboli- tionist and had been one of the founders of the Republican Party. Eventual- ly, of course, Lincoln and Lovejoy came together, but even as president, when he was first inaugurated, Lincoln had no opportunity to act against the institution of slavery. He saw it as protected under the Constitution in the states where it existed—the same point, essentially, that he made in the debates to allay any Southern fears of his election.

Nonetheless, he did say, "If slavery is not wrong, nothing is wrong." He couldn't remember when he did not so think and so believe. It was a remarkable statement of principle from a man who really believed it.

PART 2

WARTIME PRESIDENT

Winning and Governing

DORIS KEARNS GOODWIN

On November 6, 2005, presidential historian Doris Kearns Goodwin joined C-SPAN2's Book TV series In Depth *to discuss her body of work, including* Team of Rivals: The Political Genius of Abraham Lincoln, *published by Simon & Schuster, for which she was awarded the Lincoln Prize in 2006.*

[The Wigwam in Chicago] was constructed for the [1860 Republican] convention. They say it was called the Wigwam because the great chiefs [of the Republican Party] met there. It was part of what allowed Chicago to get the convention—they promised they would build a structure precisely for it.

What's amazing is that when the Republican National Committee met to figure out where they should hold the convention, William Seward wanted it in New York, Salmon Chase wanted it in Ohio, and Edward Bates wanted it in Missouri. Since Lincoln was a dark horse, they all said, "All right, let's have it in Illinois. We don't have to worry about anyone there." Lincoln knew the importance of having it in Chicago. He got the railroads to give discounted fares so people could get to Chicago. Then he was able to pack the hall with his supporters. One of Bates's supporters said if they had [held the convention] in Missouri . . . it's possible that Lincoln wouldn't have been the president.

STEPHEN A. DOUGLAS was not only Lincoln's opponent in 1858 for the Senate race but also an opponent in 1860 for the presidential race. Douglas was very short and rather bullish looking, so he was called the "Little Giant"—he had a huge head. He was also very smart. . . .

Douglas had presumably had difficulties with alcoholism during his life. Drinking a lot, his body was just ravaged by the terrible pressures he put it through. . . . Also during that time, very few candidates actually stumped on their own—it wasn't considered dignified. Yet Douglas had gone all over the country in 1860 trying to win that election, and his body wore down.

The Democratic Party of 1860 was split in three. You had Lincoln as the Republican candidate. Then you had Douglas as the predominant Democratic candidate, but then there were these other two union parties. That's one of the reasons why Lincoln was able to win the election—because of the split in the other party.

At the very end, Lincoln was afraid of [the possibility that] New York, with its great number of electoral votes, would go for Douglas. It was very possible New York might do this because there were a lot of Irish Catholics and a lot of conservative merchants in the cities who wanted to keep trading with the South and didn't want slavery to be such an issue. . . . Even though Lincoln was told at midnight, "You won the election, don't worry," he said "[I'll wait] until I hear New York's totals." If he'd lost New York, the election would have been thrown into the House of Representatives. There would have been no majority.

. . . AFTER LINCOLN BECAME president and the war had started, Douglas was close to dying, but he came to the White House and offered his complete services to Lincoln. He, a Democrat, was saying, "This is not a time for partisanship. I'm with you." That's a moment to remember because it's the last time the two men saw each other. Douglas died a few months later.

[DURING HIS PRESIDENCY, Lincoln] was spending more time with the members of his cabinet than with his wife, Mary. He was almost more married to them. It was such a tense time. They waited for news from the battlefield. They would go to the front. They would relax together at night. When I learned that Lincoln and his cabinet members had been rivals beforehand, I finally realized I had my story.

It turns out that they all kept diaries and because people wrote letters in that period, [their own writing] is an even more intimate source than anything we'll have today. Historians two hundred years from now will never know as much about us as we're able to know about these characters in the nineteenth century. Just in William Seward's family—Lincoln's secretary of state—[there are] five thousand letters. I love reading the letters. You feel like you are right over their shoulders.

For all of the members of that generation, the American experiment in democracy was still new. This generation was coming along [at a time when] politics was the passion of the people, and it's not surprising that all of these men entered political life. When there would be a debate, ten thousand people might come. People would listen to four-hour talks. They say politics back then is what sports are for us today. These men all wanted to become lawyers so that they could become politicians, so they could participate in the public life of our country; that's where the national passion was.

SEWARD IS MY FAVORITE member of Lincoln's cabinet; he reminds me of Winston Churchill. He could drink, he could smoke, he had parties in his house in the 1850s where there'd be so much wine that even Southerners would feel good about the Northerners. Seward was the one who everyone thought would be the [Republican presidential] nominee. He had been the great antislavery orator in the 1850s, the most celebrated name. So many people came to his house [in 1860] waiting for the news that he had been nominated that the champagne had already been uncorked. He was irrevocably disappointed. When Lincoln appointed him secretary of state, Seward thought he would control Lincoln, and Lincoln would be a mere figurehead. He and Lincoln became great friends once he realized who Lincoln was—a very special character.

Salmon Chase was a different kind of character than Seward because he didn't drink, he didn't smoke, [and he was] very religious. He would practice jokes that he could never quite deliver with ease. He kept a diary from the time he was twenty years old, and he was very self-righteous. However, he had been a great abolitionist, so he was an honorable person in the [push] for black equality. He wanted to be president so much that even when Lincoln made him secretary of the treasury, he kept running against Lincoln and tried to maneuver against him to win the second time around. Lincoln bested him.

Edward Bates was an elder statesman from Missouri. People thought maybe he could be president because he was more conservative and came from a border state. When he was a young man, he was very interested in politics like the rest of them. Then he got married to a woman he loved so much he couldn't bear being away from her. When he was on his way to Congress, he said, "Why am I doing this? I miss you; I have this indefinable restless feeling." He clearly wasn't away from her very long because they had seventeen children.

This shows how family life can affect public life. In the nineteenth century, when men wrote about history, they barely mentioned that they had a wife or a family, but you can see [their familial affection] in each one of these cases, even Chase's. He had this beautiful daughter. He had lost three young wives at twenty-two, twenty-five, and thirty. His daughter became his life—his campaign manager and his partner. She married a wealthy older man just to further [Chase's] ambitions, and then she died in poverty.

TODAY, WE HAVE A permanent campaign. The minute a president is elected, he is already thinking of the second term. In Lincoln's day, most previous presidents had just a single term and so they weren't so obsessed about winning re-election. Today, [a president wouldn't put a rival in the cabinet because he] would be worried about giving a platform to his rival, who could then use it against him in the following four years.

The other thing is that these guys were all rivals of one another—not just of Lincoln—and they said terrible things about one another. [They called each other] "unmitigated scoundrels." Half of the time, Stanton and Chase weren't talking to Postmaster Montgomery Blair. They wouldn't go to each other's offices. Can you imagine what would happen if we were to hear on the news tonight that [members] of the cabinet were saying things about each other? It would explode, unless you had a Lincoln to hold it together. He put all the different aspects of the Republican Party—moderates, conservatives, liberals—together in the same tent. [He figured] it was easier to deal with them [that way] than it would have been if they were on the outside.

If you have people who are going to oppose you, who are going to argue and debate you inside your cabinet, then maybe you could hone your skills and be able to deal with the country. If you did well with the country, you wouldn't worry about the next election.

SEWARD, STANTON, CHASE, and Bates . . . all were gossiping about Lincoln and about each other, and they had insight into Lincoln that hadn't always been used in Lincoln biographies. Because I care about their wives and their families, I tried to portray them in my book as full human beings, not just policy makers with Lincoln. It may be that this is partly a woman's perspective [on historical events].

MARY TODD WAS THE belle of Springfield when she was a young girl. . . . She and Lincoln were in the same circle. Even Lincoln and Douglas had been in the same circle when they were young. I love to think of Mary Todd when she was a young girl because there's so much sadness in her later life. We tend to think of her as that older woman who lost three of her four children. One died at three years old. Little Willie died in the middle of the Civil War at [eleven]. Tad, her youngest son, died at eighteen. She was eventually put into an asylum by her oldest son, Robert, because he didn't think she was stable enough to live on her own.

When Lincoln first met her, she was dating Stephen Douglas; she was feisty, a conversationalist, intelligent, and well-educated. She loved poetry and loved politics, which was very unusual for a young woman at that time. When Lincoln first saw her, he came up to her, and seeing her with all her beaus around her, [said], "Mary, I would love to dance with you in the worst way." [After they danced], she laughingly said, "You certainly did." . . . Mary believed in Lincoln early on, which is really quite something. Historians have been unkind to her in a lot of ways, but she was his partner in the 1850s. She had faith in him. I don't think Lincoln needed Mary to give him ambition, as some people suggested. He had all the ambition in the world. Ever since he was young, he wanted to accomplish something so worthy that his story would be told after he died. That would have carried him through, even if he never married.

MARY WAS TRYING to figure out a new social function that would be dramatic for the White House. Most of the White House receptions were open to anybody, so they would be rather crude affairs with backwoodsmen coming in with the diplomats, side-by-side. She decided to have an invitation-only ball, and the invitation became the hottest card in Washington. It was a very exciting event. She planned it for weeks and weeks. Right before the event, her sons Willie and Tad got very sick. She thought she should cancel the ball, but Lincoln decided that since the doctor said they were recovering, it would be all right. They held it, but during the night of the ball, which should have been her triumph, she kept going upstairs to see Willie and Tad. When Willie died not long thereafter, she felt in a certain sense, that it was her pride and desire to do these things in the White House that somehow offended God. That ball was always a terrible memory, even though it was her moment of triumph as a First Lady.

THE SAD THING for Mary was, even when she became First Lady, there was no place for her to find a footing. The Southerners distrusted her because she was married to Abraham Lincoln. The Northerners distrusted her because she had four stepbrothers in the Confederate army. Easterners thought she was crude because she was a Westerner. She tried to redecorate the White House and make it a symbol of the Union as [her] one contribution to his presidency. But at a time when the soldiers didn't have enough money for blankets, it seemed like the wrong thing to be spending money on these "flubdubs," as [Lincoln] put it, in the White House.

Her reputation was really hurt a lot during his presidency. When he died, there wasn't a wellspring of support to help her. It seemed unfair. The government gave Grant a house, they were providing pensions for other people, and they didn't, for a long period, [do anything for Mary]. Supporters finally had to fight to give Mary any kind of a pension. It was in part because she had such bad press during his presidency.

In those last years, she was so worried about money and was unwisely spending it. She may have had some manic depressiveness. There's one point at which she bought three hundred pair of gloves [prompting] her son Robert to fear that he needed to protect her, to put her into an asylum. She was able to get out pretty soon, proving that she was not mentally ill, and went to live in Springfield but had a very sad ending to what should have been a much happier life.

★ ★
★

The Gathering Storm

DAVID HERBERT DONALD

David Herbert Donald appeared on C-SPAN's In Depth *on June 2, 2002, to discuss his many books, including* Lincoln, *published by Simon & Schuster. Dr. Donald's first book,* Lincoln's Herndon, *was published in 1948, and he's since published more than thirty books on the Civil War and the Reconstruction period.*

L incoln was determined that if war came it would not be through his act. He was hoping that war would not come. He believed erroneously that the vast majority of Southern whites were Unionists.

Left to themselves, he thought they would have calmer judgment; they would understand that the Union was so important that they would come back into it. This was a gross mistake, quite clearly, but it was a mistake he operated on, especially during the first year of the war. He didn't want war, he sought to avoid it, he fell into it.

MOST HISTORIANS THESE days would say that slavery was the basic cause of the Civil War, but one has to add to that a lot of other things. Slavery was a part of a Southern culture that became a very different kind of civilization from the rest of the country, from the North. It was a pattern of agrarianism; it was a pattern, in its own way, of paternalism. It was a pattern of racial exploitation that one did not find elsewhere. As the North, especially the New England area, moved off into a modern industrial age, the South was left behind.

At the same time, our constitutional structure gave to the Southern states a very strong political voice. They were able to hold on to control of the Senate right up until the Civil War. That dissonance between economic reality and political fact led to the friction of the 1850s and to the Civil War. But basically, I would have to agree that without slavery there would not have been a Civil War.

In the South, especially, states' rights had been a hallowed tradition. There was a feeling that the citizens of Mississippi or North Carolina ought to decide what [their] particular institutions were, how they were governed and so on, whereas in the Northern states, there was more of a feeling that the government in Washington had to take over to do some things. Building a transcontinental railroad to connect the East and West, tariffs so that we could compete in the world market, encouraging immigration, and so forth. There was a difference in outlook that at base was stolen from the institution of slavery but had around it an encrustation of cultural values that were so very different [from those in the North].

IMMIGRATION PLAYED a great role in increasing the relative power of the Northern and Northwestern states at the expense of the South, which had relatively few immigrants. Most . . . immigrants came from a free tradition— the Irish, many of whom were indifferent on the subject of slavery; and the Germans who came to America were devoted antislavery people. They formed one of the principal constituent elements of the Republican Party.

Immigration played a great role in simply strengthening the Republican Party. . . . As we got to the reallocation of congressional seats according to population, the South was bound to lose more and more representatives as the North gained more and more.

HARPER'S FERRY [NOW part of West Virginia] was an arsenal where weapons were built for the United States Army. It was strategically located at a crucial juncture on the Potomac and Shenandoah rivers. John Brown had the mad idea, with a few people gathered around him after his exploits in Kansas, [that] he was going to . . . seize Harper's Ferry and the weapons there, incite the slaves of the South to rebel, probably march down the Shenandoah into the mountain area, and set up an independent republic that blacks all over the country would join. [From there] they would help overthrow the slave regimes throughout the Southern states.

He did attack Harper's Ferry surreptitiously with a small force. He overcame the guards. He was holed up there, and finally Union troops were sent out under the command of Robert E. Lee [then a U.S. Army colonel] to capture him. He was captured and ultimately executed. This episode sent shivers through the backbones of Southerners throughout the country. It confirmed what they had believed all along: that abolitionists were not content in merely saying let's abolish slavery. They wanted to try to do it by force and to turn the slaves against their masters, to have a slave insurrection to turn the South into another Haiti or Santo Domingo [Dominican Republic].

This was terrifying to Southerners. Think of yourself, for example, in South Carolina where there might be as many as six blacks to every white. If those blacks went into rebellion, if they took arms against you, you feared that there might be widespread massacre. John Brown's raid intensified sectional terror. At the same time, Northerners tried to disclaim responsibility [for the raid] without success; the Southerners blamed it on the Republican Party.

IT IS A MATTER of terrible regret that we were not able to avoid a Civil War. Six hundred thousand young Americans—Northern and Southern— were killed in that conflict, the flower of American youth. There surely ought to have been some way of avoiding that conflict. Would it have been avoided had the South been allowed to secede, set up a separate country, and exist side by side? As Lincoln pointed out, there were so many ties of trade, of commerce, of blood going back and forth that it would be hard to think of such a separation as being at all feasible. There would have been constant episode of border fighting, of disputes. I don't think it would have been like Canada and the United States, I suspect it would have been more like Israel and the Palestinians.

And what about the slaves themselves? Would we really be willing to allow millions of African Americans to remain in bondage for another fifty years, maybe one hundred years? Are we sure that slavery would have been abolished by the South during that time? We don't have any evidence for that. So what is the price of freedom? Are six hundred thousand casualties too much to pay? I don't know. I'm inclined to think that it was a necessary cost, but I say that with sadness and with deep grief and regret.

THE DRED SCOTT DECISION of the United States Supreme Court in 1857 had to do with the status of one slave, Dred Scott, who had been owned in Missouri, taken by his owner into the northwest territory and into Minnesota, and then brought back in to Missouri. The legal question was whether or not he had been freed by living in free territory, taken there by his master.

The case went through the Missouri courts and up to the Supreme Court. The Supreme Court, in a very mixed decision, nine separate opinions, ruled that Dred Scott did not have a right to sue.

The chief justice of the United States, Roger B. Taney of Maryland, declared that blacks were not and could not be citizens of the United States; they were never intended to be and they were inherently unequal. Until that barrier was removed, as it was during the Lincoln years, there could be no equality for blacks in America.

[SOME ARGUE THAT] Lincoln was a racist. So much depends on what you mean by racist. Very few people in the 1860s thought that all people of all races were and should be equal in all respects.

Lincoln grew up not knowing much about blacks. He had prejudices. He outgrew them by the end of the war. He was willing to accept Negroes as people who had the vote, who had fought in the army, and who had, for basic purposes, equal rights. Did Lincoln prolong the war by delaying emancipation? That's almost a ridiculous assertion. There's no evidence whatsoever that the war would have ended had he declared emancipation earlier than he did.

Lincoln never said that all African Americans should be deported to Africa or to any other place. He proposed a voluntary colonization of persons who wished to go either to Africa or to Central America. This was intended as a kind of test round for people who said that blacks simply could not control themselves, that they were a bunch of savages. If there had been such a colony set up in Central America, where exiles from the United States had gone voluntarily to set up a government, making profits and so on, this would disprove that theory. Never in his lifetime did Lincoln say that blacks had to be deported or should be deported. . . . The Emancipation Proclamation could only [be enforced in] that area that was outside the control of the Union army. Because of the nature of the Constitution, Lincoln did not have control over the civilian-controlled parts of the country. So slavery remained legal in Kentucky and in Maryland until much later on. But during that period, Lincoln worked assiduously to bring about the Thirteenth Amendment, which would really abolish slavery everywhere. [To ensure passage], he pigeonholed congressmen; he brought them [into the White House] one after another to cajole and even coerce them into voting for that measure, which was the ultimate measure of freedom.

WE TENDED TO THINK of the Constitution as simply a body of ideas that had been agreed upon, a formula by which government should be operating. For the first sixty years of our country's national life, the Declaration of Independence was too often thought of as a rhetorical exercise. Lincoln brought those two [documents] together specifically in the Gettysburg Address . . . linking together not merely liberty and union, but liberty, freedom, and union. Putting the Constitution and the Declaration together, this was the important political theory from the Lincoln administration.

LINCOLN CAME TO Washington [to be inaugurated]. He had with him only his friend Ward Lamon, a major from the army who was on detached duty, and a couple of friends. They were going to go through Baltimore. They received news that they would be mobbed, and he had to sneak through the city during the night, which gave a very bad tone to the opening of his administration.

There was almost no security [around him at the White House after he was inaugurated]. There was one rather decrepit Irish doorkeeper named [Edward] McManus, who was at the door [of his office], but practically anybody could come in.

. . . Every day, people just came strolling into the White House. If you were visiting in Washington and you had a few hours on your timetable, you probably thought, "Wouldn't it be nice to go and say hello to the president? So you went to the White House. Nobody challenged you. There might be people on the steps waiting to see the president about [appointment to] office, but you would just go on past them up the stairs to his office on the second floor of the White House. This was before the day of executive office buildings and that kind of thing. There he was in his office, and you went in to present yourself. "I'm Josiah Williams from Ohio, and I just wanted to say hello." Lincoln, bless him, would get up, and he would smile and say, "Oh, how nice of you to come by, Mr. Williams." He would shake hands with you and maybe he would tell you a little story and laugh at it. Then he would sort of clap you on the back and escort you to the door. You wouldn't quite know what happened, but you would be escorted out.

There was an effort at security when Lincoln was living out at the Soldiers' Home, about three miles out of Washington, where it was supposed to be cooler in the summertime. They tried to have a cavalry escort [for the three-mile trip], but the Lincolns found them noisy and distracting. So for the most part, there wasn't anybody protecting him. Lincoln would just ride alone in his carriage or on horseback. It is simply remarkable that nobody killed him earlier than they did.

WE DO KNOW THAT on at least one occasion Lincoln was riding out to the Soldiers' Home . . . and somebody shot at him. There was a hole in the cap that he was wearing at that time. Mary was very disturbed about it, but Lincoln pooh-poohed it by saying, "Oh, it's probably just some hunter that was out, and he shot by mistake."

[TOWARD THE END, ON April 4, 1865, he traveled with light security to a conquered Richmond, Virginia.] This was a wonderful day. At last, after all these years, it was clear the war really was just about over. Lee had been forced out of Richmond, the Confederate armies were in retreat, a final victory was within sight. Lincoln decided he would take a break from the White House and go down the river and visit Grant's army. He came up from the Petersburg [Virginia] area. He wanted to visit Richmond, the capital of the Confederacy, to see what it had been like.

It's kind of an amusing story. He was to be escorted up there, first of all, on a proper boat, a tugboat as it turned out, from the Union navy. Fairly far along, [he encountered] obstructions placed in the channel. He couldn't get over them. So the tugboat had to stop, and he had to get out into a smaller vessel. Uncomplainingly, Lincoln and his small entourage, including his little boy Tad, got into the smaller boat. They went along for a while and then got a message that the boat was needed for other military purposes, and they would have to get off into a rowboat. So he uncomplainingly got off into the rowboat with Tad and a few of his entourage and went along.

He said, "You know, this reminds me of a little story." He was always reminded of a little story. "When I first came into office, there was a man who came to me applying for office from Illinois, I believe it was. He said, 'I want to be secretary of state; won't you appoint me?' And I said, 'I'm sorry, I can't do that, I've already appointed Secretary Seward.' 'Oh,' he said, 'well, can't you appoint me consul general to Paris?' 'No,' I said, 'that post is already filled.' 'Well, could you appoint me collector of customs in Austin?' 'No, that post is already filled.' 'Well,' said the man, 'at least, at least could you give me an old pair of pants?'" Said Lincoln, "It pays to be humble, and I'm not upset by coming to Richmond in a rowboat."

He arrived in a rowboat; nobody was expecting him, and then the crowds assembled, nearly all blacks. The blacks in Richmond thronged around him and began falling on their knees and saying, "Praise God, we're delivered! Praise God, bless Abraham!" And Lincoln said, "Don't do that. You cannot do that. Pray to your God; don't pray to me."

He wanted to walk into Richmond. Can you imagine this? Can you imagine right after World War II, the American president strolling through Berlin? You can't imagine it. He strolled through Richmond, he came to the capital of the Confederacy, he sat in Jefferson Davis's desk where all the orders were issued that had been used to fight the Union army all these years. He walked through the town, he got a carriage, he went around and then got back to his boat. It was a moment of triumph and one of the pure unadulterated moments of triumph Lincoln ever had in what was really a short life.

LINCOLN DID HAVE A recurring dream, usually on the eve of what proved to be some major Union victory. He dreamed that he was on a great ship sailing off on an uncharted sea, off into the distance. This dream was a symbol for him that some great news was about to occur.

He told his cabinet of this dream toward the end of his administration because he was sure that this had been [a good sign] before with some of the great battles. Grant rather solemnly reminded him that one of the battles had not been that much of a victory after all. But Lincoln was sure that this dream meant the end of the war and that peace was coming.

. . . How much credence do we put on this? We certainly believe that Lincoln had this dream and that he told people about it at the time. Why did he have it? I don't think any of us know. Does this tell us anything about his spiritual state? I doubt it. It simply tells about the worries, the anxieties, the pressures this man was under after the four years of exhaustive endeavors to finish this war, and now, finally, he believed he was going to be successful.

An Early Plot Against Lincoln

STEPHEN B. OATES

The Approaching Fury: Voices of the Storm, 1820–1861, *published by HarperCollins, was the topic of an interview conducted with Stephen B. Oates as part of C-SPAN's* Booknotes *series on April 27, 1997. Mr. Oates is Professor of History Emeritus at the University of Massachusetts, Amherst.*

I'm not sure anybody [else] really believes that there was an actual assassination plot to kill Lincoln, and Lincoln himself had doubts after it was over with. However, I don't have any doubt in my mind at all that there was an assassination attempt, a plot to kill President-elect Abraham Lincoln in Baltimore as he came through in 1861 to go to Washington to be inaugurated as president.

The source is Allan Pinkerton, the detective from Chicago. His agents had gone to Baltimore and worked their way into this little pro-secessionist group of [people who were] violent and determined to take Maryland out of the Union and who had worked up this plot to shoot him. There were assassination threats even before he left Springfield, and so General Winfield Scott and William H. Seward, secretary of state, both warned Lincoln, "Don't let your family travel with you, because God knows what could happen. There could be an obstruction; the train could go off the track."

So he told Mary, "You can't come with me," and she threw a fit because she did not want to be separated from him. She became insecure and got migraine headaches when they were separated. Besides, she was a proud woman and a tough woman. She had predicted he was going to become president of the United States when he didn't believe it himself. She thought her place was at his side and she didn't want to be left behind.

They had to work out a deal that he went on another train to Indianapolis and then, after that, they traveled on the same train. It sounds to me like she got the better of the compromise.

Things went swimmingly until they got to Philadelphia. This was where Pinkerton came in. He met Lincoln and had the president of the railroad with him, and he said, "You know, Mr. Lincoln, there's no doubt about the fact that there is a pro-secessionist plot to murder you when you come through Baltimore in a couple days. I think we ought to get you on the night train and slip you through Baltimore when nobody's aware of it and get you through that city before anything can happen to you."

Lincoln said, "I can't do that. I promised to speak tomorrow in Philadelphia at Independence Hall and to raise the flag, and I've got to do that. I also promised to meet with the legislature in Harrisburg. If, after that, you still think that there is a plot and you think that my life is in danger, then, all right, I'll surrender myself to you."

His old Illinois friend, Norman Judd, was along and working with Pinkerton. Judd was absolutely certain there was a plot. So after Lincoln met his [Pennsylvania] obligations, they disguised him in a cap and an old suit jacket so that he . . . didn't look like Abraham Lincoln. He had grown a stubble beard because a girl in upstate New York had suggested it to get him more votes; she thought he would be more handsome if he had a beard. We'll leave that to posterity to decide whether he was more handsome with or without the beard. In any case, nobody recognized him. He got in a carriage, and they whisked him away to West Philadelphia. There, they put him onboard a train, the rear berth of the rear car . . . [that] one of the Pinkerton agents had rented for an invalid brother. Here was the president-elect of the United States crawling into this tiny little berth, which hasn't got anything in it but a mattress. He was so long-legged that he was all scrunched up.

He couldn't stand what he was doing. He had had to leave Mary and the children behind, and she had cried because she did not want her husband, if his life was in danger, to go without her. . . . On this night ride to Baltimore, that was all Lincoln could think about. "My God, what have I done?"

They got to Baltimore and they had to switch train stations, so there was a trolley that pulled his car from one depot to the next. Then, when they got to the depot where another train would connect with them to bring them to Washington, they just sat there. This was about two in the morning.

The only thing they could hear was a drunk outside singing "Dixie," carrying on through the night. Lincoln turned to Judd and said, "I reckon there'll be a high old time in Dixie, by and by." Finally, the train that was going into Washington picked them up and pulled them without incident.

Of course, the news leaked out that the president-elect had sneaked through Baltimore. The press made a field day out of it. The *New York Times* and a number of other publications talked about how Lincoln was a coward and a baboon, particularly a coward for coming in like that. *Vanity Fair*, I think it was, had a cartoon of a scarecrow Lincoln in Scottish kilts dancing and sneaking his way into the capital with a cloak on. The press really demeaned him.

Later that afternoon, in comes poor Mary, and she's got an awful migraine headache because she had just endured the worst episode of her life going through Baltimore. People were yelling and screaming, "Hurray for Jefferson Davis!" and "Where's that Republican, Lincoln? Goddamn him! Bring him out! Show his face!" Mary said, "They were looking for you, Father"—the name she called Lincoln. "They were looking for you, and they leered at us and jeered at us. Oh," she said, "it was the most miserable experience I've ever had."

Lincoln told much of this story himself. Norman Judd also wrote an account of it, and Pinkerton wrote an account of it, and reporters dug up some information about it. There was even a reporter who interviewed Mary personally and got her story about what this incident was like for her.

Lincoln and Chase

JOHN NIVEN

John Niven discussed his book Salmon P. Chase: A Biography, *published by the Oxford University Press, on C-SPAN's* Booknotes *program, May 28, 1995.*

[SALMON P. CHASE] and William Seward were the most important individuals in the new Republican coalition. Chase was a Whig, a governor of New York, a U.S. senator from New York—antislavery and a very prominent individual. He almost beat Lincoln; he was the favored nominee in the 1860 convention, but he had been a big shot in politics too long and had too many enemies. Also, he was considered a bit too radical, and so he didn't make it.

Lincoln took all of his [1860 presidential] competitors, both former Democrats and former Whigs, to form his coalition government. He offered the State Department to Seward, and he offered the Treasury Department to Chase. He tried to make a balance between geography and prior political involvement. . . .

[Chase got along with Lincoln] at first, but after a while Chase's insidious ambition and his efforts to undercut Lincoln caused an estrangement. Lincoln put up with him until 1864; then over a patronage dispute, Lincoln finally gave in at the wrong time and accepted Chase's resignation. The New York Customs House was involved, as was the assistant treasurer in New York who was the Treasury Department's primary agent in . . . dealing with the money market and the bankers and that sort of thing.

[About Lincoln, Chase was personally] ambivalent. He surely recognized Lincoln's humane qualities [such as] his generosity. Eventually, he accepted [Lincoln's] political astuteness. On the other hand, Chase was one of these people who was a tidy administrator, and also, of course, he had this tremendous drive to run things. In the beginning, Lincoln did consult with

Chase on military and high policy matters, but as the war developed, Lincoln leaned on Chase less and less. This caused Chase all sorts of irritations and he spread [word of his indignities] among his friends in the Congress.

Lincoln accepted his resignation, which upset Chase—he didn't think it was going to be accepted. Chase yearned for more public duty and more public exposure. He had always thought about the Supreme Court as a possible place anyway, and so he lobbied for himself [to be appointed as a justice]. Lincoln had a lot of what we call radical, or progressive spokesmen— like Charles Sumner, a senator from Massachusetts, [who was] a violently antislavery individual and the conscience of the Senate. Lincoln, who was under great pressure at the time, decided he had to have a progressive, or radical person [on the court]. He had high respect for Chase's abilities, but rather lower respect for his deviousness and his intriguing qualities. Finally, he decided to . . . respond to the pressure, and so he appointed Chase.

[CHASE WAS CHIEF JUSTICE from] December of 1864 . . . until his death in May 1873. [And, when Lincoln's successor Andrew Johnson was impeached, Salmon Chase] was the presiding officer, as the Constitution provides.

★ ★
★

Slavery, the Union, and War

JAMES M. MCPHERSON

This essay is from an interview with Civil War historian James M. McPherson, during which he discussed his book What They Fought For: 1861, *published by the Louisiana State University Press. The interview aired on May 22, 1994, as part of C-SPAN's* Booknotes *series. Among his many honors are a Pulitzer Prize and the 1998 Lincoln Prize.*

The Civil War lasted for four years. It started in April 1861 and ended in April 1865. Six hundred twenty-five thousand soldiers died in the American Civil War—365,000 Union soldiers and 260,000 Confederate soldiers. To give you some idea of what kind of impact the war had on American society with that number of dead, this amounted to 2 percent of the American population of 1861. If 2 percent of the American population were to be killed in a war fought by this country today, five million Americans would be dead.

The Civil War started primarily because, in the generation before 1861, an antislavery movement had grown up in the North that attacked the South's "peculiar institution" as immoral, inhumane, and inconsistent with American ideals of liberty and the Declaration of Independence.

Southerners, slave owners, and the society which they ruled, felt increasingly defensive about this attack on the institution that underlay their economy and society. The Republican Party was founded in the mid–1850s on a platform of restricting the further expansion of slavery—"in order," as one of its leading founders, Abraham Lincoln put it, "to put slavery in the course of ultimate extinction." He was a gradual emancipationist. When that party and that candidate won the presidency in 1860, the Southerners saw the handwriting on the wall. They had lost political control of the national government, and they feared this loss of political control portended an eventual loss of the control of the institution of slavery.

So they seceded to form an independent nation of eleven Confederate states, all of them slave states. The Lincoln administration refused to recognize secession as constitutional or legitimate and argued that if any state or group of states could secede at will then the United States had no national government; in fact, they argued that there was no such entity as the United States if anybody could get out of it at any time, whenever they didn't like how a presidential election came out. So the two sections were polarized over the issues of slavery and secession.

All it needed was a trigger, an incident, to start a war, and that trigger was the Confederate firing on Fort Sumter, the United States installation in the harbor at Charleston, one of the last such United States installations still under national control in the Confederate states. That functioned on Northern public opinion very much like the Japanese bombing of Pearl Harbor did in 1941 on American public opinion. It caused a rise of war fever in the South and a counterpart rise of war fever in the North. As Lincoln said in his Second Inaugural four years later, "The war came and lasted four years, resulted in the destruction of slavery, the destruction of the planter class in the South, and of the social basis for its rule of the South." It also resolved for all time the question of whether a state or any group of states could secede from the United States. No state has tried it since then.

EIGHTY TO NINETY percent of the fighting soldiers in the Civil War were volunteers. Most of them volunteered in the first year of the war. This was a non-coercive, democratic society. The mobilization to fight the Civil War was a kind of do-it-yourself mobilization from the bottom up, from localities, counties, communities, states. During the Civil War, soldiers wrote an enormous number of letters home. Many of them kept diaries. These letters were not subject to censorship during the Civil War; the best place to find out what these men really thought they were fighting for—the purpose of their volunteering to fight and risk their lives—is to go to their personal letters to parents, wives, sweethearts, brothers, and sisters who were eager to hear about their experience as soldiers. Their letters are amazingly frank.

THERE WERE THIRTY-FOUR states in 1860, of which eleven seceded and formed the Confederate States of America. Two other Southern states, Kentucky and Missouri, had a minority of secessionists who formed their own Confederate government, applied for admission into the Confederate congress, and were admitted. So when you see the Confederate flag, it will have thirteen states, and the number of states that remained loyal to the Union was really twenty-three because Kentucky and Missouri were split.

At all times in the war, the Union army had at least twice as many men under arms as the Confederate army. The high point of the war for both sides in terms of the number of men would be 1863 and 1864. By 1864, however, the Confederates had no more manpower on which to call. They had mobilized everybody—every white male between 17 or 18 and 40 or 43, or 45 in some cases, who was not lame or blind. Their numbers began gradually to shrink so that by the end of the war the Union forces outnumbered the Confederate forces about four or five to one.

There were four million slaves and a half a million free blacks, of a population of nearly thirty-two million. A free black was a person living in either the free states where all blacks were free, or a black person in the South who was not a slave, either descended from someone who had been freed a generation or more earlier or who himself had been freed voluntarily by his master. But of the 4.5 million blacks in 1860 at the time of the census—4 million, or 90 percent, were slaves. About 180,000 black soldiers and an estimated 10,000 black sailors fought in the Union army and navy, nearly all of them in late 1862 or later.

At first, the Lincoln administration's war aims were to restore the Union, not to abolish slavery. One of the reasons for this was that Lincoln was trying to keep the border slave states like Kentucky and Missouri and Maryland loyal to the Union. He was also trying to reassure Southerners in the Confederacy that he was not going to precipitately attack slavery.

He was trying to make it a war only for union and not for the abolition of slavery. Since enlisting black soldiers—especially if they'd been former slaves—would be a sign that it was really an antislavery war, the Union army and the Lincoln administration refused to accept black soldiers.

The Lincoln administration completely transformed Northern war aims from that of restoring the old Union to that of destroying the old Union and rebuilding a new union of freedom. "Give the Union a new birth of freedom," as Lincoln said at Gettysburg a year later. Once that commitment had been made, the major transforming commitment in the Civil War, the administration also decided to enlist black soldiers. In late 1862, they authorized the first enlistment on occupied territory in South Carolina where the war had started, on the so-called Sea Islands off the coast, and they recruited two black regiments.

The most famous of the black regiments was the 54th Massachusetts about which the movie *Glory* was made. It consisted mostly of free blacks from the North. Altogether probably 190,000 blacks fought in the Union army. The total number of men who fought for the Union was about 2.1 million, so the black soldiers constituted roughly 9 percent of the total Union armed forces. They fought largely in the last half of the war because they weren't recruited until the war was almost halfway over.

No black soldiers fought in the Confederate army unless they were passing as white. Some light-skinned blacks probably did. Some Confederate soldiers, especially officers, brought their body servants into the army, who in many cases had grown up with them and were very close to them. On occasion some of those body servants were known to pick up a rifle and fight. But there was no official recruitment of black soldiers in the Confederate army until the very end of the war. Out of their desperate shortage of manpower, the Confederate Congress finally passed by a single vote in the Senate in March 1865 the so-called Negro Soldier Bill, which provided for the enlistment of slaves to fight for the Confederacy. Appomattox came only a few weeks later, and none of these men were ever put in uniform to fight.

The Confederate soldiers were fighting for the independence of what they called their country, the Confederate States of America, and they harkened back to the model of the American Revolution. In 1776, Americans declared their independence from the British Empire—they seceded, if you will, from the British Empire in the name of liberty, establishing an independent, free government. The Confederate soldiers said they were doing the same thing in 1861: They were fighting for liberty, for self-government. They were defending their country against invasion from what they now considered to be an alien power that no longer represented their interests. They compared Abraham Lincoln to King George III. They compared the Congress in Washington to the British Parliament of 1776.

As the war went on, and as Northern armies invaded and occupied the South and destroyed its resources, including, ultimately, slavery, many Confederate soldiers became increasingly motivated by notions of revenge, of defending their homeland from these hated "goths and vandals." The Confederates were fighting a defensive war to protect their homeland and the independence of their country.

The Confederacy passed the first conscription law—a draft act—in April 1862, which with a few exempted categories made every white male between eighteen and thirty-five liable. This meant that many plantation owners and overseers were vulnerable to conscription, to the draft. Who was going to stay home and run the plantation? Who was going to manage the slaves? In some cases, only women were left on the plantation—the planter's wife, or maybe the overseer's wife. The idea of leaving one or two or three white women on even a medium-sized plantation with slaves was repugnant to the whole concept of white supremacy and social relations in the South. It also left the plantations inefficient without having somebody to direct them.

The Confederate Congress in the fall of 1862 passed a law exempting one white man for every plantation of twenty or more slaves. It was the so-called Overseer Exemption, or the Twenty Negro Law. This was exceedingly unpopular among non-slaveholders in the South . . . who constituted two-thirds of the Southern families. Their breadwinner, let's say a small farmer who did not own slaves and who was thirty-five years old, was drafted. He left his wife and several children behind to run the farm, and there was no exemption for him. There was a lot of protest and alienation and disaffection within the South against this law.

Only one-third of the Southern whites belonged to slaveholding families. The average number of slaves per slaveholding family was five. An adult male slave in 1860 was worth between $1,000 and $2,000.

To own five slaves was to own quite a lot. To own twenty slaves and, therefore, to be in the planter class and to get an overseer exemption was to be a very wealthy person. Wade Hampton, who was a South Carolina planter and a famous Confederate cavalry commander during the Civil War, owned several hundred slaves . . . on several different plantations in South Carolina and Mississippi and was reputed to be the wealthiest man in the United States in 1860.

THE UNION SOLDIERS said that they were fighting to preserve the nation that was created in 1776, to preserve it from dismemberment and destruction. They, too, appealed to that model of 1776, and it was a powerful motive for Union soldiers. Over and over again, in their letters is the argument that if they lost this war to the Confederacy, it would establish a fatal precedent that would destroy the United States. There would no longer be a united nation. By definition it would be a disunited nation. The next time that a disaffected minority lost a presidential election, they might secede and all of the labor of our ancestors to set up this brave experiment in democracy in 1776 would have been proven a failure.

It's important to remember in understanding the Northern soldiers' perspective that in the mid-nineteenth century the United States was one of the very few republics and by far the largest and most successful republic in the world. Most European countries were monarchies or empires. Other republics, such as those in Latin America, had usually succumbed to dictatorship. When Lincoln said at Gettysburg that "this was the great test whether a nation so conceived and so founded can survive," he struck an important chord among the Northern people. That's what they were fighting for.

[ABOLITIONISTS] WILLIAM Lloyd Garrison, the best known, and Wendell Phillips, were at first very critical of Lincoln because he did not move immediately against slavery. They formed a pressure group on the left, a counterpart of the civil rights activists of the 1960s, and tried to press the president to move more quickly on civil rights, or, in Lincoln's case, on emancipation. . . . Their point of view about Lincoln [was that] he was slow, he was gradual, he was too conservative, deferring too much to the border states, etc. He was under enormous pressure from various sides. From the left, the right, the border states radicals, conservatives, white supremacists, black leaders—he had to strike a balancing act among all of these factions and keep them together on behalf of the war effort and the larger goal, which was to preserve the Union.

THE CIVIL WAR ENDED gradually. The principal Confederate army was the Army of Northern Virginia, commanded by Robert E. Lee. The Army of the Potomac, which had fought Lee for four years, finally brought it to bay at Appomattox, and Lee made the decision to surrender on April 9, 1865, just five days before Lincoln was assassinated. That's often taken as the date that the Civil War ended . . . [but] there were still several other Confederate armies in the field, and they surrendered one by one over the next couple of months.

THIS WAR WAS ABOUT the identity and the future of the United States. If it had come out differently, or if it had never happened, we would be a radically different nation today than we are.

The Fourteenth and Fifteenth Amendments, which defined the legal and constitutional status of the freed slaves, were major accomplishments of the Civil War. They have formed the basis for all civil rights legislation that has happened ever since 1865.

IF I WERE TO TAKE on a controversial [stand] today, it would be on the relationship between slavery and the coming of the Civil War. I would argue that slavery was at the root of what the Civil War was all about. If there had been no slavery, there would have been no war. Ultimately what the Confederacy was fighting for was to preserve a nation based on a social system that incorporated slavery. Had that not been the case, there would have been no war.

The Cost of War

CARL M. CANNON

On December 28, 2003, Carl M. Cannon discussed his book The Pursuit of Happiness in Times of War, *published by Rowan and Littlefield, on C-SPAN's* Booknotes *program.*

 IF THIS COUNTRY has something, a special mission, if American exceptionalism is alive and well, that mission is extending Thomas Jefferson's unalienable rights to people who do not yet have them.

Presidents have wrestled with this, all the presidents before Lincoln, who knew that slavery was wrong—even the slaveholders—and knew that it would take a war to end it. Finally, war was foisted on Lincoln, but he didn't shrink from it. . . . When this country is doing what it should be doing and doing it well, it is [fighting to] extend rights to others.

FREDERICK DOUGLASS AND Lincoln used the words "the pursuit of happiness" [and other references to the Declaration of Independence] constantly at a time when there were two schools within the abolition movement. One [faction] was led by William Lloyd Garrison, who thought that the Declaration and the Constitution were tainted because they had been written by slaveholders and that the Constitution incorporated slavery into the governing structures of the state. Garrison burned the Constitution and the Declaration at a famous speech and said they were pacts with the devil. He was a secessionist from the other side.

But Douglass and Lincoln argued that the words themselves were so powerful and their meaning so obvious that the sins of the people who wrote them were secondary, that we didn't need a new government, we just needed to live up to the creed of the Declaration. Within the abolition movement, that debate was won by Lincoln and Frederick Douglass.

SLAVERY HAD TO BE ended, and Lincoln knew it. It was ended, but the cost was so frightful to people that after the war was over, most Americans questioned whether the cause was just. They questioned war itself. The Civil War started, or helped form, a deep strain of pacifism within America. We were a warlike country in some ways, but now we had this experience that all of the European powers had had. After the Civil War, America really understood how costly war was. It was really the first modern war.

Economic Principles

LEWIS LEHRMAN

Lewis Lehrman appeared on C-SPAN's Sunday evening program, Q&A, on June 26, 2005.

MR. LINCOLN was the best-prepared man [of his time] in economic philosophy, economic theory, and economic institutions. Most people forget that not only was Mr. Lincoln a pro-growth man and a Whig . . . but up until 1854, he had spent his entire life in American politics talking about the principles of economic growth, how we could make America a prosperous country for all people from all walks of life.

Of course, he was [also] antislavery from the very beginning. He didn't have the burden of owning slaves and being against slavery in principle like Henry Clay or Thomas Jefferson.

LINCOLN SET AN example for us. He did not accept slavery in its [existing] form. His campaign, after 1854, was to prohibit the extension of slavery into the territories, while respecting, in every important aspect, the Constitution of the United States. This was a man who probably made the most significant decision of any commander-in-chief in our country's history while at war, [by issuing] the Emancipation Proclamation. And while Lincoln sets an example for us, it doesn't take away from the extraordinary stories of [sacrifice on the part of] the millions of unknown Civil War heroes.

An Economic Nationalist

PATRICK J. BUCHANAN

Patrick J. Buchanan discussed his book The Great Betrayal: How American Sovereignty and Social Justice Are Being Sacrificed to the Gods of the Global Economy *as part of C-SPAN's* Booknotes *series on May 17, 1998.* The Great Betrayal *was published by Little, Brown & Company.*

[**ABRAHAM LINCOLN** had a richer understanding of economics than any politician today.] He was an amazing figure. He was an economic nationalist. His idol was Henry Clay, who's the father of "the American system." In the battle between [Andrew] Jackson and Clay in 1832, Lincoln admitted, "This is my politics. I am an economic nationalist. I don't believe in this free trade, and I believe that tariffs can make us the greatest nation on Earth."

I call Lincoln "The Great Protectionist." He won his nomination by convincing the Pennsylvanians who wanted tariffs on steel and coal that he was one of them. He would write notes to all these [newspaper] editors and say, "Look, I was with Henry Clay, I fought for the tariffs in the 1830s and '40s. And, I'm with you. But don't let the word out to the free traders in the Republican Party." He won that way.

During the Civil War, [the federal government] imposed the Morrill Tariffs, taking them up above 40 percent. This was the economic nationalism that became the philosophy of the Republican Party—all the way through Herbert Hoover.

Lincoln on Taxes

CHARLES ADAMS

On May 9, 1993, Charles Adams, author of For Good &
Evil: The Impact of Taxes on the Course of Civilization,
published by Madison Books, was featured on C-SPAN's
Booknotes.

SLAVERY was never more protected than it was on the eve of the
Civil War. The slavers in the South had won the battle for slavery in
1860. The Supreme Court had handed down the Dred Scott case,
which gave blanket approval to slavery in the country. [I believe that] it was
a tax on the revenue from slavery that caused the Civil War.

In his First Inaugural Address, Lincoln said he had no inclination to interfere with taxes. He said, "I quote from my speeches . . . I have repeated
time and again I'm not going to interfere with slavery. I have no inclination
to do so personally." Congress then passed a resolution, which was to be a
constitutional amendment, protecting slavery in the Southern states. They
had won the battle, and they hadn't fired a shot.

BUT LINCOLN DID say in his inaugural address that the South seceded
from this land. Southerners had walked out—borne their new government
down in Richmond, Virginia. And he said, if they don't want the mails,
that's fine. We won't interfere with their way of life, but we will [continue
to] collect taxes.

When Lincoln was interviewed by a British correspondent from *Frasier's*
magazine, he said there was not going to be any war; he wouldn't use any of
his military forces on the South, except to collect the taxes, and to recover
any forts that had been taken, like Fort Sumter.

Lincoln had given the South an ultimatum of taxes or war. They seceded
. . . because part of Lincoln's platform was to raise the tariff on goods coming into America to 47 percent. This was a very high tax that Southerners

would have to pay if they were to buy foreign goods. If they didn't pay, they would then have to buy Northern goods that were protected, and prices for these were jacked up because there was no competition.

SOUTHERNERS HATED IT. Every time they paid a tax on goods, they knew it was going up North, to the federal government, which was under control of the Republican Party. Or if they bought goods from the North, they knew they were paying through the nose. When they withdrew, the first thing they did in their new Constitution was to lower taxes.

LINCOLN WAS THE most powerful president the United States has ever known because of the way he exercised power over the dissidents in the war. [In the twentieth century] the Russians referred to Abraham Lincoln to justify the deporting of [Soviet-era dissident Alexander] Solzhenitsyn, who was thrown out of the Soviet Union because of their law against slander of the state.

LINCOLN HAD ONE of the leaders of the Democratic Party arrested in Ohio (which was not a war zone), tried before a military court, and convicted of expressing treasonable sentiments because he hated the war. They deported him to the South. The man fled to Canada, where he continued to be strong in the Democratic Party. He had the 1864 [Democratic] convention brand the war a failure. Lincoln had people locked up. He suspended *habeas corpus* [in 1860]. . . . America was very intolerant of anybody who wasn't supporting the war: You were with us or against us. If you expressed disapproval of the war, you were in trouble. Now we permit people freedom of expression, but it's only been in the latter half of the twentieth century. Even during World War I, many people were locked up for expressing treasonable sentiments by simply saying that they thought the war was wrong.

A Predecessor's Opposition

PETER WALLNER

Franklin Pierce: New Hampshire's Favorite Son was written by Peter Wallner and published by Plaidswede. Dr. Wallner participated in C-SPAN's Booknotes *interview series on November 28, 2004.*

[**AFTER HE LEFT** the White House in 1857, Franklin Pierce remained] involved in politics. He was very upset about the move toward the Civil War. He spent two and a half years in Europe after he left the White House. He returned just before John Brown's raid at Harper's Ferry [in 1859]. Pierce was very upset about that and spent a lot of time writing letters to people, sending letters to the papers, and speaking about the need for what he would consider the silent majority to speak out against this fanaticism that he saw happening on both sides, North and South.

When Lincoln was elected and the Southern states began to secede, Pierce proposed that all the living former presidents gather in Washington and issue some kind of a statement. It didn't happen; none of the others would join him. He worked very hard to try to prevent the war from occurring.

WHEN PIERCE DIED, he was very unpopular. . . . His actions during the Civil War made him extremely unpopular. He had spoken out continuously and loudly against the Lincoln administration, particularly against the suspension of the writ of *habeas corpus*, the imposition of martial law, the restrictions on freedom of the press and freedom of speech, which the Lincoln administration imposed on the North. Pierce believed [these restrictions were] unnecessary and unjustified. He spoke out very loudly about this, so much so that he was considered a traitor by many people in the North.

PIERCE REGULARLY declared that slavery was a moral evil he wished didn't exist; he thought slavery was a moral stain on the nation, but he believed it was up to individual states to decide what to do about slavery.

HE ALSO THOUGHT—and he sincerely believed—that if the North hadn't attacked the South so much for this moral sin of slavery, the South eventually, over time, would have ended slavery on its own. He felt the Civil War was unnecessary, and he never [retreated from this position] even at the height of the war itself. He always believed the Civil War was . . . brought upon the nation by fanatics on both sides.

★ ★
★

Lincoln's White House

HAROLD HOLZER

Lincoln scholar Harold Holzer gave C-SPAN an on-camera tour of the Lincoln Bedroom on August 22, 2007. Holzer is the author of many Lincoln books, including Lincoln President-Elect: Abraham Lincoln and the Great Secession Winter 1860–1861, *which was published by Simon & Schuster. This essay is excerpted from that video tour.*

[What's now called the Lincoln Bedroom] was the office and the Cabinet Room [in Lincoln's day]. Lincoln got here around 9 a.m. He was not a very early riser, although he started to rise earlier as the war progressed, and he was required to be on the scene more and more. He worked through the day, here, under the most trying circumstances, under the most demanding routine that can be imagined. It was a routine that was nothing like what our modern chief executives subject themselves to because it involved constant interface with the public—unscreened, no security checks, a constant flow of people, twice a week, five hours a day, later cut down to three hours a day. Lincoln called them "public opinion baths." People would just line up. He would be seated at his desk or at the cabinet table where he opened mail, right in the middle of the room, and he would receive people. He said it was invigorating for him and was what the chief magistrate owed the people who had elected him.

Lincoln worked in the Cabinet Room until late at night unless there was a military action occurring in Virginia, or Pennsylvania, or Maryland, or in the West. In that case, he would walk across the lawn to the War Department and sit at the keyboards of the Military Telegraph Office and wait for war news. He would look over the telegraphers' shoulders and grab the dispatches as they came. Astonishingly enough, the White House was never equipped with a telegraph during Lincoln's time, so he had to travel to get his news. . . . Of course, he would go back to his bedroom or to his family rooms for meals. His private secretaries, who slept in a bedroom right across the hall, would hear him pacing sometimes late at night, back and forth; they would hear the creaking on the floorboards thirty or forty feet from here in the hallway that led to his bedroom. Every once in a while, Lincoln would appear in his night shirt, which was always too short for him, and interrupt his secretaries' sleep to tell them something or read them a story.

Lincoln never slept in the Cabinet Room unless he caught a quick nap on a sofa, but I doubt there was really time for that. He'd just slip down the hall if he wanted to rest or if he wanted to see his boys. Often the boys would come running in to see him here, but this was not a bedroom; it was purely an office—before the Oval Office, this was the president's office.

DURING THE FOUR years he was president, this room was the scene of many historical events. There are many things still in the room directly associated with Lincoln. The painting of Andrew Jackson that remains in the room was over the mantelpiece when Lincoln was president. It was sort of an odd choice. It might have been here when Buchanan was president—Buchanan and Jackson were fellow Democrats while Lincoln made his political bones, as it were, as an anti-Jackson Whig. Around the time Lincoln was elected, a lot of journalists were referring to the fact that Jacksonian firmness was needed to put down the secession crisis. This [sentiment] was repeated over and over again, so I think Lincoln liked the idea that Jackson was watching over his attempt to put down the problems in South Carolina, as Jackson had.

The most famous print in this room is an engraving by Alexander Richie after Francis Bicknell Carpenter's famous painting, now in the Capitol, called *The First Reading of the Emancipation Proclamation.* . . . Carpenter sketched for that painting right in the room. He worked for six months on it. He eventually set up an easel of about seventeen feet by ten feet in the State Dining Room and worked on the painting there. He did portraits of all the cabinet members, and several sketches and one model painting of Lincoln. He worked so meticulously on this painting [of the reading of the Emancipation Proclamation] that some people think by the time he finished it, he had ruined it—he overdid it. The way it looked when it was done is probably reflected in the engraving. Lincoln signed on to be the first buyer of the print but didn't live to get his copy because it wasn't published until 1866.

[The print] shows the day in July 1862 that Lincoln sat in this room with his cabinet members and told them that he had decided to issue a proclamation of emancipation. Some think the picture shows Secretary of State

William Seward objecting, saying, "This is not the right time. We haven't won a major battle, and if you issue the proclamation now, it will be viewed as the last shriek on the retreat." Lincoln [feared the document would be as ineffective as] "the pope's bull against the comet," so they voted not to issue it then, and they waited for battlefield victory. Then, either in this room or in the oval library—no one is quite sure where—Lincoln told his cabinet again in September that he would issue the proclamation. [By then], the Battle of Antietam had been fought, and enough of a victory had been won that it could be issued with some good press behind it.

. . . I don't think [Carpenter, the artist,] ever got to observe a cabinet meeting. He wrote a long memoir of his time here called *Six Months at the White House*, appropriately enough. He later re-titled it *The Inner Life of Abraham Lincoln*, which made Mrs. Lincoln very unhappy. . . . Carpenter did something that had never been done before—he commissioned a photographer from Mathew Brady's studio to come here and take a photograph of Lincoln seated at the cabinet table—in the exact spot in which he wished to paint him in the canvas. So, this room was the first scene of something that has now become quite routine, the White House photograph; but this was the first time it had ever been done. . . .

When the painting was done, it was put on display downstairs in the East Room, and the public was invited to see it. Lincoln looked at it and said, "It's as good as it can be; you've done a great job." Mrs. Lincoln came in and famous for her critical eye, she looked at it and said, "Oh that's a picture of your happy family"—meaning Lincoln with his cabinet.

[WHAT IS NOW] a guest bedroom of the White House was, in Lincoln's day, the office of his Private Secretary John George Nicolay, a twenty-eight-year-old fellow with a German accent, Bavarian born. He was the "Cerberus at the gate," as he was called by people who didn't like him. He kept the official visitors and ordinary people away except during regular office hours. He was also the clerk who brought the state papers to Capitol Hill when they had to be delivered. . . . Across the hall are two rooms that also played in the Lincoln story: One is the bedroom where Nicolay and the Deputy Secretary John Milton Hay slept. This was unusual for the time. Most of the private secretaries who had worked for presidents before Lincoln's time were relatives of the president or the first lady, so they tended to sleep in the family quarters where there were guest bedrooms. But Nicolay and Hay were employees, and Mary Lincoln liked to keep the office and domestic spheres separate, so they slept right across the hall in a rather nice bedroom. To the other side of that bedroom was an office shared by John Hay, the assistant secretary, and a procession of third secretaries, including my favorite, William Osborn Stoddard. His granddaughter is still with us and is the last person who touched the hand that touched the hand of Lincoln. She's quite a priceless piece of evidence of the Lincoln White House years.

Stoddard and Hay dealt with correspondence in that room. Stoddard opened a couple of hundred letters a day. He directed those that were important to Lincoln and sent others to the federal departments. That was the White House office procedure—correspondence, visitors, cabinet meetings, and the general public—"the public opinion baths," streaming through here. In the early days they were looking for favors, looking for jobs; later [people were] looking for pardons, looking for passes into and out of the Confederacy. Lincoln ultimately had to cut down on those public hours because he just didn't have time.

[THE LINCOLN BEDROOM has a copy of the Gettysburg Address on display.] It's the fifth and final handwritten copy. It's not the one Lincoln read from. No one is really 100 percent sure which copy he read from. After coming back and discovering that he had made himself a triumph . . . he was asked to write copies of the Gettysburg Address over and over again for charity fairs. It was a big thing then—the Emancipation Proclamation was also donated to a charity fair. The Gettysburg Address—all 272 words, so it was not that hard to copy—was copied three different times for different people. This last copy was an accident. Lincoln had been asked to donate money for a charity fair, and he wrote his fourth and what he presumed to be his final copy on the front and back of one piece of lined paper. When the recipients opened it up, they thought, this won't do. They wanted to put it in an album of works by illustrious American authors and sell the entire album at the charity fair. So they actually had the gall to go back to Lincoln and say, "You did it incorrectly—try one more time." That's why there is copy number five. It was later owned by a Cuban collector named Oscar Cintas, who ultimately donated it back to the White House. Today it sits in a corner of the room in which we can imagine Lincoln wrote it.

Lincoln had a high pigeonhole desk with little compartments in it where he kept folders of material in his own vicarious filing system. He had one file that he talked about called "Wood and Weed"—that was his "W" file, named for Thurlow Weed, the upstate New York political boss, and Fernando Wood, the mayor of New York City. When asked about it one day Lincoln said, "Thurlow and Fernando, that's quite a pair." He also had a file there with assassination threats marked "A" for assassination.

. . . THE WINDOW [IN the Lincoln Bedroom] is the place, I believe, where Lincoln stood nervously, day after day, in April 1861, wondering what

had become of the Massachusetts regiments that were supposed to be taking railroad cars here to defend Washington against possible invasion by
Confederate troops. They were delayed in Baltimore, attacked on the
streets by a mob. Lincoln's secretary, who worked in the next office, saw
Lincoln standing at that window with his hands behind his back asking,
"When will they come?" over and over again. Not for another couple of
days did they arrive, securing the capital.

. . . THE RECEPTION ROOM and public hallway outside this room were
the only means by which Lincoln could go from the business part of the
White House into his private quarters. If he wanted to go for a meal, or if he
just wanted to go for a rest, he always had to go through these public rooms.
In the reception room there would be a throng of people waiting to see
him—congressmen, the general public, lawyers, diplomats—all herded in
there, waiting for their turn. If he went out into the hallway, there would be
people lined up and down the hallway and down the stairs, all the way to the
front door, all waiting their turn to see the president. . . . Lincoln eventually
found himself absolutely overwhelmed, burdened, annoyed—yes, Abraham
Lincoln did get annoyed—by his inability to move in his own house. He had
a partition built from a door that was between the fireplace and the desk,
through that area into the oval library. This is where he and his wife took
meals and had their sitting room; it was the only sitting room on the floor.
The partition must have been, I would calculate, about seven feet tall because it had to be tall enough for him to pass by without being observed. . . .
Thus, at the end of his first year in office, he finally had a way to sneak out of
here without being pursued by office seekers and favor seekers.

We don't think any of the furniture in the Lincoln Bedroom today is
original to this room. It's hard to imagine, but the desk that was here, the
table that was here, the cabinet chairs that were here, all were scattered. We
do know that the famous Lincoln bed was certainly in the White House
then. It was one of Mary Lincoln's many extravagant purchases, as she began a campaign when she got here to redecorate this entire building. When
she got to the White House with her husband in March of 1861, they had
very different reactions to this place: Lincoln looked around and said, "This
is better than any place we ever lived in." He was right. It had four, five, or
six bedrooms, a beautiful sitting room, and, of course, the office was right
at the house—not bad. Mary thought it looked like a dilapidated country
hotel, and she was very unhappy. She went downstairs and looked at the
public rooms, saw how much damage had been done over the years by sou-
venir seekers, and decided to redecorate—and she did, with a vengeance.
One of the things that she bought was a beautiful bed from a Philadelphia

cabinetmaker. She brought it back here and installed it in the family quarters, and the [ironic] thing about this bed is that it is where, in February 1862, Lincoln's middle son, Willie, died after a bout with typhoid fever. After that, Mary would never go into Willie's room again.

The next time this bed plays in Lincoln's history is when it served as the backdrop for his autopsy, which was performed down the hall in the family quarters. Lincoln's body was not in this bed for the autopsy but on a table stretched out in front of the footboard. Picture this: During the autopsy the doctors searched and searched for the bullet that had ended this great man's life. Suddenly, they hear a clunk as it fell from his body into a basin. Nothing could be heard except the rattling, the spinning of this spent bullet, this tiny thing that had cut off his life. That happened right in front of this bed.

The canopy above the Lincoln bed is just a part of its rich rococo décor. It's very elegant, and it's hard to imagine a child sleeping in this bed, but Mary Lincoln was determined to have nothing but the finest, most elegant, highest style. . . . It was in this room that the superintendent of public buildings was sent by Mary—who didn't have the courage to do an assessment of her spending for her husband—so she sent Mr. French, the superintendent, here to say, "We've overspent the congressional appropriation by a little bit." Lincoln was furious. He pounded the table and said, "It would stink in the nostrils of the American people to know that we've overspent a $25,000 appropriation for 'flubdubs,' for this damned old house, when we can't even have blankets for the soldiers." So he offered to pay for it himself, but Congress made up the difference. He was making about $25,000 a year, which was a lot of money in those days and had so much money that when he died, they found in the drawer some uncashed salary warrants.

. . . IN THE SUMMER, and we know this from his secretary John Nicolay's letters to his fiancée back home in Illinois, the big floor-to-ceiling windows were thrown all the way up to get some air in the Cabinet Room. Nicolay wrote home about bugs—the biggest bugs he had ever seen anywhere in his life—on the papers, on the newspapers, on the books, on the chairs, so we could imagine very unpleasant working conditions here in the summer. In the second summer, Lincoln moved his family to a different location in the warm months. So they did not live here for four or five months in 1862, '63, and '64. They lived in a cottage up North Capitol Street, the Soldiers' Home, and Lincoln was a commuter president who rode to work here in this office, like an everyday commuter would today on a train or bus.

[For a Lincoln historian], being in this room today is sort of like going to heaven without dying. It's the most historic room in the entire life of Abraham Lincoln—there is no place more important to the Lincoln story. That includes, with apologies to all of my friends and curators around the country, the Soldiers' Home, the Springfield home, and all the log cabins between here and Illinois and Indiana. This is the room where one man and his ministers decided to resist secession. In fact, when William Seward saw the painting by Carpenter of the *First Reading of the Emancipation Proclamation*, he said, "That's not the most important moment in the history of this administration. The most important moment is when we sat here and decided to reinforce Fort Sumter." That was the difference between having two countries and one country, and it happened here. This is the room where Abraham Lincoln wrote some of the great state papers and some of the great personal letters in all of American literature—words that were brilliant enough to inspire Harriet Beecher Stowe to say that they should be written for all time in letters of gold.

Most of all, what makes it thrilling is what took place here on January 1, 1863, New Year's Day. One hundred days had passed since the preliminary Emancipation Proclamation had been written, which decreed that if the Southern states didn't give up their rebellion, all of the slaves in the rebellious states would be free from that day and forever. It wasn't an automatic occurrence. There were rumors that Lincoln would extend the deadline, that he would not keep his word, that something would happen that would stop this revolutionary act from going forward. In fact, on that New Year's Day, Lincoln was the host at a huge open house reception downstairs in the East Room for hundreds of people, probably thousands—[there were] hours of handshaking with visitors. He finally made his way up to this room, with no photographer on hand that day, no artist, no witnesses except Seward, the secretary of state, and Seward's son, Frederick. They sat at the table right here, the cabinet table, and unrolled the vellum copy, the official copy of the Emancipation Proclamation, which is now in the National Archives. Lincoln had written it earlier, and it had been transcribed by a calligrapher. Lincoln picked up his pen and put it down. He picked it up again and put it back in the inkwell. Seward and his son wondered, "Is he hesitating? Is he changing his mind?" Then finally, he explained, "I've been shaking hands for hours downstairs, and I can barely feel my own hand. That kind of feeling is not calculated to improve a man's handwriting." He apparently used the word "chorography," which was an archaic word for penmanship. He massaged that massive right hand and waited until the feeling returned. Then he picked up the pen and wrote uncharacteristically

"Abraham Lincoln." He [typically] signed his ordinary letters "A. Lincoln" [instead of] "Abraham Lincoln." He put his pen down and said, "That will do." He said, "If my name ever goes down in history, it will be for this act, and I don't want anyone ever to look at the signature and think it was shaky and conclude that I hesitated."

DESPITE THE PRINT that hangs in this room that shows the Lincoln family gathered in a parlor enjoying time together, the truth is that the Lincolns had very little time together. Mary testified that she was very fortunate if, as she put it, "At eleven o'clock at night, my tired husband comes to my bedroom to discuss the events of the day." He was always working. Robert was not in the White House; he was either at Harvard Law School, or in the army. He later wrote, rather bitterly, that he thought the White House was a gilded prison and that he had scarcely spent five minutes alone with his father during his entire presidency. Willie, who's often shown in these family scenes, died in 1862, less than a year into Lincoln's term. This sent Mary into a mourning from which she never emerged. So the family circle idea was sort of a myth.

Carpenter invented [this Lincoln family myth]. He took Abraham Lincoln down the street to Mathew Brady's gallery, where he posed him for a number of famous photographs—the five-dollar bill photograph, the penny profile photograph, and the famous photograph of Lincoln and Tad reading a book. . . . Showing Abraham Lincoln with his child [was intended] to humanize him. Before his death, Lincoln had a pretty tough image out there. He was the enforcer, he was the man who abridged constitutional rights, he was the man who took slaves away from Southerners, who had already induced five hundred thousand people to their deaths in the Civil War. His image needed amelioration. Carpenter's idea of showing the family was critical to that.

ONE THING YOU have to remember about the White House in Lincoln's time that separates it so dramatically [from today] is that even though war was going on, the doors were generally open, and the grounds were generally open, so this was not a private residence at all. In fact, the Lincolns never used the downstairs unless they were holding a public reception. It was very difficult for them to have privacy downstairs—people just came in and out, came to the public rooms, even uninvited. The Lincolns certainly strolled the grounds; there were marine band concerts here once a week that the president and Mrs. Lincoln and the children often attended until Willie's death. There were flag raisings here, there were moments when troops would come by on the way to battle, or back from service in the military, and Lincoln would go out and make little impromptu speeches, very good speeches. . . . The public marched in and lined up to air grievances, to make requests and demands of the president. He saw them personally. There were no security guards, no metal detectors, there was no frisking, there was no emptying of pockets—it was hard to believe, and it is just frightening to comprehend, to even appreciate that Lincoln survived those four years, considering the violent letters that were aimed at him.

The other thing about this White House is that it was a children's house, in many ways. For four years it had been a bachelor's house under President Buchanan. Lincoln brought in, for his vacations at least, a college-aged young man who was looking for a girlfriend and ultimately found one; a wife who was a senator's daughter; and two youngsters who loved roaming through this house and taking it over. They kept ponies in the stable outside, they rode horses, and they got little uniforms made so they could march with soldiers or sit with soldiers outside—at least Tad did. He became a mascot for the soldiers. The Lincolns also kept pets in the house— cats, dogs, and a goat, which they famously tethered to a wagon and galloped down the main hallway, to the horror of some of the visitors. Lincoln probably thought it would scare them off, so it was a good idea.

There's a long central corridor that leads from this part of the building through the family quarters and separates the family quarters into northern and southern rooms. On the northern side is the oval sitting room and library, which Mary and Abraham filled with books and where the family gathered. As you proceed down the hall on that same side, you have the master suite. Abraham and Mary Lincoln lived in the same suite, but not in the same bedroom, which is exactly the way they lived in Springfield, Illinois. . . . [It was] considered more elegant. Abraham lived in the smaller bedroom and Mary in the larger bedroom. At the very end of the house was a dressing room that they both shared. There was a little hallway that led between them that was private, closed off from the main hallway. Then on the other side of the hallway was Tad's room, then Willie's room, and then a couple of guest bedrooms. In between those rooms was what is called in the Lincoln era scheme, a "washroom." I don't know if it was a full bathroom. There was also a washroom with a toilet in the master suite; and that was just about it for the family quarters.

There is one extraordinary little room . . . which was an open hallway in the Lincoln era. Whenever Lincoln wanted to give a speech here at the White House, which he did on several occasions, he would walk down that corridor, they would hoist open the windows, and he would speak from the second floor window. He gave two very famous speeches there. One was the last speech he ever gave—"We meet today in gladness of heart." It was at that speech that he first broached the idea of extending voting rights to African Americans—even though he limited that opportunity to, as he put it, "the very intelligent," whatever that meant, or to those who had fought in ranks. There was someone in the audience that night, on the lawn, who was listening and turned to his friend and said, "Did you hear that? That means Negro citizenship," and from what we know, he didn't use the word "Negro." He said, "That's the last speech he'll ever make." That man was John Wilkes Booth. Three nights later, Booth shot Lincoln at Ford's Theatre.

When Lincoln was shot, this house turned into a house of mourning. . . . A few months before he died, Lincoln had a nightmare, and for some gruesome reason he decided to tell his wife about it. He woke up and said he heard crying from downstairs and walked downstairs in his nightshirt and saw a catafalque and a coffin in the East Room and said, "Who lies dead here in the White House?" They said, "It's the president. He's been murdered." A premonition? He told enough people that there's not very much question that he actually had this supernatural experience.

Unfortunately, even before the funeral, which took place downstairs, this room had to be turned back into the president's office. Andrew Johnson, after just a few days, moved his office into this very room. Mary, however, really could not leave her bed for weeks and weeks. She stayed inconsolable, weeping, crying, and wailing for about five weeks until she was finally able to summon the courage to walk down the steps for the final time, off to Chicago. She never returned.

Meeting
Harriet Beecher Stowe

PAUL JOHNSON

Paul Johnson discussed his book A History of the American People *(HarperCollins) as part of C-SPAN's* Booknotes *series on April 5, 1998.*

[**IT WAS WIDELY** believed that Harriet Beecher Stowe and her anti-slavery novel *Uncle Tom's Cabin* were at least partly responsible for Lincoln's election and for the chain of events that led to the Southern bombardment of Fort Sumter in 1861.] When she finally got to the White House, Lincoln said to her, "So, you are the little woman who caused this great war?" Stowe left behind some references to her evening at the White House. She had a blow-by-blow account of it in a letter that has, unfortunately, disappeared, so we don't know exactly what happened. But she said the evening was all tremendous fun and that they had a lot of laughter.

Presumably, Lincoln's remark was half in jest and half in earnest because he didn't know exactly what the total impact of *Uncle Tom's Cabin* had been. It was obviously enormous. Whether the war would have happened without it, that's just guesswork. But certainly it was, of all the books published in the nineteenth century, the one that had the biggest impact on politics.

Meeting
Frederick Douglass

MICHAEL BARONE

Michael Barone was featured on C-SPAN2's Book TV program In Depth *on July 1, 2007. Mr. Barone discussed his many books, including* Our First Revolution: The Remarkable British Upheaval That Inspired America's Founding Fathers, *published by Crown.*

FREDERICK DOUGLASS was a great champion of America and someone who helped us make huge progress as a nation. He was an admirer of Abraham Lincoln. They met at the reception after Lincoln delivered his Second Inaugural, the most sublime speech in American history. The usher tried to keep Douglass out [because he] was black, but Lincoln made sure that he was invited in. Lincoln left some people and went over to Douglass and said, "I value your viewpoint as much as anyone's. Would you please tell me what you thought of the speech?" . . . That's a great moment in American history.

★ ★
★

The
Transcontinental
Railroad

DAVID HAWARD BAIN

C-SPAN's Booknotes *program featured David Haward Bain on March 5, 2000. Bain discussed his book* Empire Express: Building the First Transcontinental Railroad, *which was published by Viking. Mr. Bain teaches English and American literature at Middlebury College and has worked with the Bread Loaf Writers' Conference for many years.*

[The Promontory spike was driven into the ground on] May 10, 1869, in Promontory Summit, Utah. They began this whole transcontinental enterprise without having an idea about where [the East and West lines] were going to meet, so it encouraged a kind of a wild, speculative competition. By the time it got to be 1868 and 1869 in Wyoming and Utah, the two competing railroad companies, the Central Pacific from California and the Union Pacific coming out from Omaha, were really just trying to grab as much territory—since they were being paid by the mile—as they could. So when the Union Pacific and the Central Pacific joined in Promontory, it caused a national tumult of celebration. . . .

[The intercontinental railroad would not have been built without taxpayer money]; emphatically not. A good portion of the route was unsettled at that point; it was supposedly federal land that could be given over to the railroads in exchange for their moving westward and eastward. But even with subsidies according to the mile completed, it was something that wouldn't have been done without the taxpayers' purse involved.

Rep. Oakes Ames from Massachusetts was called "The King of Spades." He was heir, along with his brother Oliver, to a very large shovel manufacturing plant in Massachusetts, which really took off during the California Gold Rush, and he became a very wealthy man.

[Ames] went to Congress. He was among the founders of the Republican Party. He was very highly placed. He knew Lincoln very well, and they spent a lot of time together. Lincoln himself anointed Oakes Ames with the purpose of getting involved in the Union Pacific Railroad because the capitalists weren't showing up to invest. It was going nowhere after it was incorporated in 1862, and Lincoln said to Ames, "Ames, take hold of this. It will be the biggest thing in the country." [This happened] right in the middle of the Civil War, a great national project like this with everything going on.

The Union Pacific Railroad started in Omaha on the Missouri River in Nebraska, and the Central Pacific Railroad started in Sacramento, California. The Central Pacific Railroad had to immediately address the Sierra Nevada Mountains, and the two railroad companies just built toward each other.

THE AMERICAN PEOPLE fared positively because of the settlement patterns and the fact that the West was opened up by [the transcontinental railroad]. Of course, there were a lot of very sorry chapters involved with the Plains Indians, with the exploitation of the vast mineral wealth and water wealth out there. But let's face it, we had a large empty space that was still thought of, in most people's minds, as the great American desert, as it had been for fifty years. This became the farmland and the ranchland of the West.

. . . ABRAHAM LINCOLN had two big decisions to make in [the transcontinental railroad]. One was the gauge of the railroad—exactly how wide should the tracks be? It was thought that maybe five feet would be the best route; the other gauge available was four feet eight-and-a-half inches. Today, that seems like a little controversy, but it really depended on how many companies in the United States had already committed to one gauge or the other. It was a hot political issue, and Lincoln finally, in desperation, turned to his cabinet and said, "Well, what do you guys think about all this? What should we do?" He polled them. They all wrote their nomination for what the gauge should be on little pieces of paper, and he put them in his pocket. Then he made the decision that it would be the five-foot gauge. It was basically an arbitrary decision, which was later reversed by congress to the four-foot-eight gauge.

[THE SECOND DECISION] was the Omaha decision: "Where are we going to start this railroad?" There was an interesting little scene in which Lincoln had spread out a map of the Missouri River and was trying to decide, "Well, where exactly are we going to do this?" He looked and saw Council Bluffs, [Iowa], on the east side of the Missouri and Omaha on the other. He'd been hearing testimony for years about what the right way was, and then he finally said, "I may get into trouble about this because I own a few building lots in Council Bluffs, but I'm going to put it there anyway."

Lincoln had guaranteed the loan of a business associate and he had taken the loss as a pledge from a friend so [the property] later passed totally into his control. He was a lawyer and a businessman and he had interests like this. This was not a huge amount of money, but he knew that it had almost the appearance of impropriety. Still, he was convinced that the Platte Valley route was the best way across [Nebraska].

LINCOLN HAD BEEN involved in the railroads before his presidency. He was quite a good lawyer out in Illinois, and he had done a lot of business for different railroads out there. One of his great triumphs was over a controversy involving some river traffic that had hit the abutments of a bridge. He was on the side of the railroad saying that they weren't responsible for accidents like that.

THE LINCOLN [PRESIDENTIAL Railroad] Car was gilt and furnished in silk drapery and had beautiful hardwood appointments. Lincoln took one look at it and said, "I'll never ride in that car." So they retired it to the rail yard. When he was assassinated, it was picked to take him on the long, mournful route back home. It was several weeks worth of a funeral train, which left Washington, DC, and ended up in Springfield, Illinois. You could follow this route and see something about the state of American railroads at that time. You could take a train from Washington to Baltimore, and then from Baltimore up to Philadelphia, and then cross the river and take [a train] from the Camden and Amboy up to New Jersey. Then you could go on a barge to New York and then up along the Hudson River and then transfer, by boat, over to the west side of the Hudson, and so on. It [would take] something like twenty-seven different railroads just to get that distance, and it really demonstrated what a crazy idea it was to have [just] two railroads building seventeen hundred miles across this virtually uninhabited portion of the United States.

LINCOLN WAS SUCH an interesting character, as far as the railroad. He was really the godfather of the Pacific railroad. If he had not thought of [the transcontinental railroad] as being a national priority, it wouldn't have been done during the Civil War. But he insisted, on all sorts of levels, that it be given that kind of support. When he died, the railroad lost an essential spiritual support that it had enjoyed under Lincoln.

★ ★
★

Lincoln and the Telegraph

TOM WHEELER

On November 17, 2007, Tom Wheeler spoke to the Lincoln Forum in Gettysburg, Pennsylvania, about his book Mr. Lincoln's T-Mails: The Untold Story of How Abraham Lincoln Used the Telegraph to Win the Civil War *(Harper-Collins), an event covered for C-SPAN2's Book TV. A telecommunications executive and venture capitalist, Mr. Wheeler also chairs the Foundation for the National Archives.*

One of the things that I found so exciting about Abraham Lincoln was that he was also a technology guy. It is an overlooked thing in Lincoln history that he was a man who had an innate understanding about technology. He was the only president to hold a patent. He was a man who, as a lawyer, made his living representing the new technology of the railroad and the extreme impact that it was having on society. He even tried for a while to lecture—[he had] a speech on discoveries and inventions in which he tried to talk about the importance of technology to mankind. Thank goodness he was comfortable with technology because, here he was, the first president of the United States at the dawn of the telecommunications age who had, in the telegraph, a technology for instantaneous communications that no other leader in history had ever had. He had to figure out how to use it. He had to build a leadership model around it. And, oh yes, he had to do this in the middle of a Civil War. The thing that I found so exciting was the collision of history—Abraham Lincoln's history—and technology and what it tells us about the man.

Some perspectives: Electricity was a vague scientific concept when Lincoln came to Washington. It wasn't until 1879 that Thomas Edison patented the light bulb. The idea of sending messages by sparks of electricity was beyond comprehension for most people. When appropriating legislation for Samuel F. B. Morse's [telegraph test] was on the floor of the House of Representatives in 1843, it was such a wild idea to send messages by sparks that legislative amendments were offered, laughingly, to the same bill to fund mesmerism and other kinds of cult-y ideas.

The legislation authorizing the Morse test barely passed the House of Representatives by three votes. There were almost as many members of Congress who abstained from voting on the bill as voted for it, so concerned were they about associating themselves with this wild idea of sending messages by sparks. That was the kind of environment that Abraham Lincoln came into and had to evolve his use of the telegraph. He first saw a telegraph unit in 1857 when he was [a country lawyer], riding the circuit and staying in the Tazewell House Hotel in Pekin, Illinois. So we're talking about a man who four years later was president of the United States, and during the great American conflict had to figure out in real time just what applications he would make to a technology he had seen only four years previously.

My book is the story of Lincoln's discovery of the application of the new electronic communications technology. It is also the story of a new leadership model that Abraham Lincoln had to build, without text or tutor to guide him—a story that is applicable to us today in our electronic world. It is also the story of how Lincoln used the telegraph to maintain civil supremacy at a crucial time for that concept and how he became commander-in-chief in fact, not just in title, because of his access to the telegraph.

Finally, I think my favorite part of looking at Mr. Lincoln's T-mails is the insight that it provides to Abraham Lincoln. We know of Lincoln in basically three ways: his speeches, his writings, and his telegrams. His speeches and his writings were set pieces. They were designed to convey a message; they were structured. There was thought put into them because they had to stand on their own. His telegrams were off the top of his head, spur of the moment, in response to some kind of stimulus from outside. Since Lincoln kept no diary, the closest thing we will ever see to a transcript of a conversation with Abraham Lincoln are his telegrams.

By 1861, national leaders were flummoxed by the [telegraph's] technology and power, yet they were supposed to use it. The banking industry, railroad industry, financing industry all understood, but the national leaders did not. There was no telegraph line to the White House. There was no telegraph line to the War Department or to the Navy Department. When the United States Army, before the Civil War, wanted to send a telegram, they wrote it out in longhand, gave it to a clerk, and he went and stood in line at the Washington Telegraph Office.

That fact alone makes Abraham Lincoln's adoption and embrace of this technology all the more amazing.

It is possible to watch Lincoln grow through his use of the telegrams. One quick example: In the Battle of First Manassas, Lincoln could hear the cannons thundering over the horizon, twenty-five miles or so away. But the way battles had always been fought was that the national leaders were disconnected. The war was "out there." You couldn't have any real-time conversation [with your commanders]. Lincoln knew something was going on, but messages would have to come by horseback to a telegraph station and then be telegraphed back. They were totally disconnected to the extent that the general in charge had to be awakened by Lincoln during the Battle of First Manassas, because he, General Scott, had taken a nap. That's the way battles were fought. You didn't get involved. You didn't keep pace.

Thirteen months later at the Second Battle of Manassas, Abraham Lincoln was actively involved, telegraphing the field, wanting to know what was going on, and using the technology to reach out. In just that period of time, he had evolved his approach to the technology. There were three phases of Abraham Lincoln's growth in his use of the technology. First, he had to have what I call his "ah-ha" moment, an awakening as to the power of this technology. That took place three months after the Battle of First Manassas at the Battle of Ball's Bluff.

Col. Edward Baker was one of Abraham Lincoln's closest friends. He was leading a Union regiment at Ball's Bluff when he was killed, and the engagement turned into another Union disaster. That day, October 21, 1861, Abraham Lincoln was meeting with his commanding general, George McClellan, in the White House when a messenger came in and handed McClellan a note. McClellan read it and put it in his pocket and did not share it with the president. That note talked about the debacle at Ball's Bluff. But this was information for McClellan, not information, as far as McClellan was concerned, for the president.

Later that afternoon Lincoln walked over to McClellan's headquarters, as he was wont to do, wandering around the various offices of government. He went up to McClellan's clerk, Thomas Eckert, and said, "Anything new from the front?" Eckert said, "There is nothing new in the file, sir." Lincoln walked into McClellan's office because McClellan wasn't there and saw lying on his desk a copy of the telegram talking about Ball's Bluff and Colonel Baker's death and was less than pleased. He came out and confronted Eckert and asked, "Why did you mislead me?" Eckert said, "Sir, I told you the truth. When I saw you coming, I took the telegram and slipped it under the blotter on my desk. You will recall that what I said is: 'There is nothing new in the file, sir.'"

Upon being questioned by Lincoln, it became clear that Eckert was under orders from McClellan not to share this information with the president of the United States and that Secretary of War Simon Cameron was in cahoots with this policy. It was shortly thereafter, for this and several other lapses, that Cameron became the minister to Russia and Edwin Stanton came in as secretary of war. In January of the following year, 1862, Congress passed a law relating to the use of the telegraph and establishing the U.S. Military Telegraph Corps.

Now, the corps may have had in its name "military," the U.S. Military Telegraph Corps, but it was wholly civilian. It was subject to no command by any generals in the field, and it reported to the secretary of the war who, in this case, understood who his boss was. The telegraph wires that McClellan had centralized in his headquarters were taken out, except for the basic needs of running daily operations, and moved to the War Department. It was that great move that put Lincoln in proximity to the telegraph and allowed what we are about to see happen.

For the first fourteen months of his presidency, Lincoln sent fewer than twenty telegraphs, and then on one specific day, he had what I call his electronic breakout. He sent nine telegrams on May 24, 1862, more than he had sent on any day since becoming president of the United States. That week he sent more than he had since taking the oath of office.

Think back to what was happening in May of 1862—it was [Stonewall] Jackson's Valley Campaign. He was threatening Washington. McClellan was stalled outside of Richmond, and he had dissembled with the president in terms of how many troops he had left behind to protect Washington. Lincoln was very concerned about Jackson's threatening of the capital city, so he did something that no other president of the United States, something no other political leader in history had ever done—he assumed direct command of the forces in the field electronically. . . . [In] one of his telegrams to Gen. [John] Fremont, you will see that he told Fremont to move against Jackson at Harrisonburg. . . .

Throughout the history of armed conflict, a general in the field had been the closest thing to a living god. Telegrams changed all of that. Suddenly, the political leadership of the country could communicate in real time with the military forces in the field. There was a reason that Henry V was in Agincourt and Bonaparte went to Russia. Abraham Lincoln changed that history, broke that precedent on May 24, 1862.

We all know Gen. George McClellan, interestingly enough, understood the use of the telegram himself, and he was also the man with whom the president first began developing this new leadership role. It's a realistic expectation to say, "I'm going to use the telegraph to project my voice," and this was how Abraham Lincoln first used the telegraph.

Four days after his electronic breakout [Lincoln sent another noteworthy telegram]. This one was in response to a telegram that Lincoln had received from McClellan, in which McClellan, among other things, had said, quote, "It is the policy and duty of the government to send me by water all the well-drilled troops available." The temerity of this! McClellan telling Lincoln about the policy and the duty of the government.

[This is a telegram that gives us] insight into Lincoln's top-of-the-head thinking. Lincoln started out by responding to some of the activities going on and to some of the things that McClellan had said in his telegram. Then Lincoln got to the point and said, "I am painfully impressed with the importance of the struggle before you. And I shall aid you all I can consistently with my view of due regard to all fronts. But I shall be the judge as to the duty (underlined) of the government in this regard." And then, he scratched that sentence out, which lets you see Lincoln's mind at work. First, he said, "Let me tell you who is running this show, fellow." But then he stopped and said, "Wait a minute. Is this really the best way for me to communicate at this point in time?" And so, he scratched that sentence out. As I said, the Lincoln telegrams allow us an opportunity to look into his real-time thinking, and you can see the struggle that is going on. One of the things that I find so exciting about Lincoln's telegrams is that when you hold this telegram in your hand, you have just one degree of separation from that thinking, from that real-time struggle.

In October of that year, after the battle of Antietam, Lincoln went to see McClellan and urged him to pursue [the Southern commander, Gen. Robert E.] Lee. For five weeks, McClellan had not. Lincoln read a telegram that McClellan had sent to General Henry Halleck, complaining about his sore-tongued and fatigued horses as the reason he couldn't pursue Lee. And again, back to real-time Lincoln: something snapped. He saw that telegram and sat down, took out a piece of paper and wrote: "I have just read your dispatch about sore-tongued and fatigued horses. Will you pardon me for asking what the horses of your army have done since the battle of Antietam that fatigued *anything*?"

This is called changing the relationship between a commander in Washington and his general in the field. It is also an insight into Abraham Lincoln's head, because it was just two weeks later that he dismissed McClellan as the commander of the Army of the Potomac.

THE WAR DEPARTMENT was next door to the White House where the current Old Executive Office Building stands. The second floor, in what used to be the War Department library, was where the Telegraph Office was set up. The benefit to having the telegraph this close to the White House was that Lincoln could be intimately involved and exposed to it. He spent more time in the Telegraph Office than any other place, save the White House itself. If you stop and think about it, the Telegraph Office was the first Situation Room. This was where the president was able to get almost real-time reports from the field, and able to issue commands back.

His habit was that he would walk to the clerk's desk where the "flimsies" were kept—the copies of telegrams that had been received by the War Department for everybody, not just for him. He would reach into the drawer, take out the "flimsies" and go over to a desk by a window overlooking Pennsylvania Avenue and go through them, setting aside those he wanted to come back to for subsequent study.

This is an example of how Abraham Lincoln saw the telegraph as something beyond an extension of his voice. It's obvious to say, "Yes, I will extend my voice using the telegraph." It is less obvious to say, "I'll use it to *listen.*" I think that Lincoln's greatest use of the telegraph was to extend his eyes and ears, not just his voice. This reading of all of the telegraph traffic gave him a picture of what was going on and gave him the ability to insert himself where necessary, to provide his input.

August 1864. We all know it was a dark period in the Union. Confederate General Jubal Early was loose in the Shenandoah Valley. Riots were happening in the cities over the draft. Grant was stalled before Petersburg. There was an election coming up, and Lincoln was sure he was going to lose. In that environment, Lincoln saw a telegram from General Grant to General Halleck in which Grant was expressing concern over what was happening at Petersburg, or rather the lack of what was happening at Petersburg, and the impact that the draft riots might be having on drawing men away from the front. Lincoln saw that and immediately stepped in and inserted his leadership, even though this telegraph wasn't addressed to him. He sent Grant a telegram that read, "I have seen your dispatch expressing your unwillingness to break your hold where you are. Neither am I willing. Hold on with a bulldog grip and chew and choke as much as possible."

It was as good as walking into Grant's headquarters, sizing up the situation and saying, "General, here is how I feel: I am with you." When Grant received this, his telegrapher handed him the note, and Grant picked it up. As he read it, he started chuckling. He said to those around him, "The president has more nerve than any of his advisers." And he did. But the other thing was that Grant was holding in his hand a tool that Lincoln learned to use to communicate that nerve to his general in the field.

I have discussed how there were three phases that Lincoln went through: The first phase was the first fourteen months when he sent fewer than twenty telegrams; the second phase started in May of 1862 and went essentially until Grant came East and took command; the third phase was when Grant was in command. That phase began to evolve the modern model of electronic leadership where you agree on a plan, supervise it electronically, and insert yourself where necessary.

Here is a classic example of how Lincoln exercised this new model of electronic leadership: The back story is that when Jubal Early threatened Washington in the summer of '64, Lincoln had telegraphed Grant, suggesting that Grant might want to come to Washington and assume command because there were so many different generals, all jockeying for their own position and aggrandizement. Grant had missed the nuance in Lincoln's suggestion, and it caused a bit of a rift, but it had been healed over. There was a telegram that followed shortly thereafter in which Lincoln evidenced the fact that he had learned that electronic communications is not the place for nuance; that you have to be very direct.

There are four components to this particular telegram that are significant in this building of the electronic leadership model that Abraham Lincoln developed. He says to Grant, "I have seen your dispatch. . . ." (that's the first point: [The telegraph became his] ears—he is using the telegraph to keep informed) ". . . in which you say, 'I want Sherman put in command of the troops in the field with instructions to put himself up south of the enemy and follow him to the death. Wherever the enemy goes, let our troops go also.' This, I think, is exactly right as to how our force should move." Second leadership point: "I've seen your plan, I understand it, I validate it."

He goes on: "But, please, look at the dispatches you may have received from here since you made that order and discover, if you can, that there is any idea in the head of anyone of, quote 'putting the army south of the enemy or following him to the death in any direction.'" Lincoln's third message: "Watch your people." Then he closes with his fourth and most important message: "I repeat to you, it will neither be done nor attempted unless you watch it every day and hour and force it." His fourth point: "You are in charge, and I've got expectations." Here is, in Lincoln's hand, the embodiment of his growth in the use of the telegraph. I believe it's a message to us today on how to use electronic communications.

LET'S GET OUT OF the battlefield for a second and think about how Lincoln used the telegraph similar to the way that we use e-mail today—to communicate with our families. Mary Lincoln was frequently traveling and absent from Washington and she communicated with Lincoln via telegraph—something that was very rare at the time.

In April of 1864, Mary Lincoln and their eleven-year-old son, Tad, were traveling in New York. She sent a telegram to Lincoln saying, essentially, "We've reached here safely. Hope you are well." That took care of all the formalities; then she got down to business: "Please send me by mail today a check for $50, directed to me, in care of Mr. Warren, Metropolitan Hotel." And then "Tad says, 'Are the goats well?'" Tad had been keeping pet goats at the White House.

The president of United States was in the middle of planning with Grant for the Overland Campaign, but he dropped everything and sent his wife this telegram, which is my favorite out of all one thousand telegrams. He said, "The draft will go to you." In other words, the check is in the mail. "Tell Tad the goats and father are very well, especially the goats."

This is Lincoln coming alive. This is top-of-the-head Lincoln. You can see here both the pressure that he is under as well as how he found refuge in wit.

At a desk overlooking Pennsylvania Avenue, Lincoln conceived and implemented the model for electronic leadership—without text, without tutor, without precedent. Thank God, he was an early adopter.

FIRST AND FOREMOST, my book is a history of a great man at a hinge moment and about a new technology. But I also found my study of Lincoln's telegrams having an impact on the way I use electronic communications. If the role of history is, in fact, to inform us today, Lincoln's telegrams reach out to talk to us about how we communicate today.

Lincoln had a hierarchy of communications, and the bottom rung was electronic communications. First rung was face-to-face. Second was a well-reasoned and well-thought-out letter. When he couldn't do those, when time was of the essence, he sent a telegram.

I find myself using electronic communications as a way to avoid interaction. Why do I send an e-mail instead of getting up and walking down the hall? I found while studying Lincoln's telegrams that I am more sensitive to the fact that this is probably not a good idea.

We saw that his telegrams were short and direct; they weren't an invitation to write an essay. George McClellan would send ten-page telegrams to the president, and he would reply in three or four sentences. Too often we see the blank computer screen as an invitation to an essay and the need to write about everything. For Abraham Lincoln, words mattered.

David Homer Bates, the manager of the Telegraph Office, told the story of how Lincoln would sit at that desk and be writing away and then stop. He would look out the window onto Pennsylvania Avenue and think, trying to find the right word. He would then turn around and start writing again, because words mattered. Too often today, our e-mails are the written equivalent of casual Friday.

We need to think about words like, "Hold on with a bulldog grip and chew and choke as much as possible." That's hard to misinterpret. He was frank and direct, but he understood his limits. We saw his cross-outs in the McClellan telegram. There are many telegrams that he wrote and then said, "No, I don't think I will send that." How many times have I wished I hadn't hit the "send" button on my e-mails? Lincoln showed us that you can vent, but you don't have to send.

Lastly, he showed that the full in-box is an opportunity, not a curse. He took that drawer, and he went through all those telegrams. He picked and chose among them. Those that were responsible, he read. In the equivalent of hitting the "delete" button, he set aside those that he did not need to interact with.

Just when we thought we knew everything about Abraham Lincoln, along come his "T-mails" to connect us with our own electronic experience and to give us new insights into him—to provide us with perhaps the greatest untold story about this great man.

Patriot, Poet

WALTER BERNS

On August 19, 2001, Booknotes featured Walter Berns who discussed Making Patriots, *his book published by the University of Chicago Press.*

IF WE DON'T have wars, we don't need patriotism. On the other hand, we still need patriots who think of the country and think of their fellow citizens and are willing to make sacrifices for their fellow citizens, even if we're not in wartime. We need public spiritedness, and a war, of course, is a great way of inculcating that. Lincoln understood that. In the final paragraph of his First Inaugural, most of which is trying to persuade the Southern states not to secede from the Union, he ends with, "I am loath to close. We are not enemies, but friends. We must not be enemies. Passion may have strained, but must not break our bonds of affection. The mystic chords of memory, stretching from every battlefield and patriot grave, to every living heart and hearthstone, all over this broad land, will yet swell the chorus of the Union, when again touched, as they will be, by the better angels of our nature." I quote that in this context because, of course, Lincoln is relying on memories of battlefields and patriots' graves. That, of course, means wars. What he did [later] at Gettysburg was to use the graves there to swell the chorus of the Union.

It's such a beautiful passage and it's such an unlikely statement to be made by a president of the United States. Only Lincoln could do it, and then only under certain circumstances. The interesting thing about Lincoln is that when he was twenty-eight years old and made a speech to the Young Men's Lyceum of Springfield entitled "The Perpetuation of Our Political Institutions," he knew that these institutions were threatened and might not be perpetuated. He set out to understand the threat and then to figure out how they might be perpetuated. That early speech, the last paragraph of the

First Inaugural, and the Gettysburg Address all fit together. The legend is that he scribbled the Gettysburg Address on the back of an envelope on a train going to Gettysburg. It could be true, but [even so] he had been thinking about this, literally thinking about it, for years. The Gettysburg Address simply didn't come off the tip of his tongue at the last moment.

THE CONSTITUTION DOESN'T use the word "slavery." [It] doesn't appear in the Constitution until the Thirteenth Amendment abolishes it. Frederick Douglass understood this very well and understood the difficulties of overcoming that original sentiment.

Originally—there's really no doubt about this—[the Founders], including the leading Southerners, were antislavery. They understood the incompatibility of slavery and the principles of the Declaration of Independence. Thomas Jefferson, for example, understood this very well indeed. Unfortunately, Jefferson really did nothing to overcome it. Washington freed his slaves. . . . I do think it's necessary for us to go back and read that history and understand the incompatibility of the [founding] principles with what happened and the difficulty of overcoming slavery.

How many of us appreciate the difficulty the Founders had? People sometimes condemn the Founders for not abolishing slavery or for accepting the Constitution without abolishing slavery. Had they done what modern critics say, there would have been two United States—one United States of Southern America, call it the Confederate States of America, and then the United States. And what would have been the consequences of that? Almost all the black people in this country, at that time 90-some-odd percent of them, lived in the South. And almost all of them were slaves there. What was hope for them?

Hope consisted in the Union, and the Founders understood that. Lincoln understood that, so he sometimes is condemned for saying that his first task was to preserve the Union and, second, to emancipate slaves. He understood this, and Frederick Douglass understood this very well. The condition for emancipation was the Union.

If the Confederate States of America, in 1860, had been allowed to go the wrong way as a Confederate States in 1787, slavery would have been a part of [their] original Constitution—and there was really little hope for emancipation under those conditions. First, you [create] the Union in 1787—with the prospect that, in due course, slavery will be abolished. Then in 1860–1865, preserve the Union as a condition of emancipating slaves.

To think of Lincoln is to think of the Declaration of Independence. He made a career of that. He opens the Gettysburg Address saying, "Four score and seven years ago." He's speaking, [in] 1863, of 1776. It's those principles that are antislavery principles. They were violated and forgotten in the beginning, and there was a prospect that they would be violated again, especially in the 1850s when Stephen Douglas of Illinois was largely responsible for the Kansas-Nebraska Act, which opened up these Western territories to slavery under the principle of popular sovereignty. Lincoln insisted, "If you say popular sovereignty, which is to say, you allow the people of the territories to be free or slave [states], that's a violation of the principle of the Declaration," He would not stand for it. He went back into politics because of it, and he became president because of it. He fought the Civil War because of it, and he won the Civil War. The result is the freedom we have.

Lincoln was, by far, the greatest American, probably one of the greatest men in history. Lincoln had his enemies during his lifetime. The manner of his death contributed to his status among us. He was martyred. But Lincoln was a genius—and I use that word sparingly—an astonishing intellect. He understood his own capacities and tried to conceal them, telling bawdy stories and pretending to be just one of the boys.

But much more than that, he was our poet. His words inspire us. One can see that in these monuments, comparing the Jefferson Memorial and the Lincoln Memorial and the reception people have. I go to the Lincoln Memorial with some frequency, largely to see what the response [is from] my fellow citizens. It's different from the Jefferson Memorial. In the Lincoln Memorial, people stand, and they somehow sense the awesomeness of the place. There, carved on the wall are the words of the Second Inaugural and the Gettysburg Address. They read those words and see the seated Lincoln before them, and it moves them. I've seen ordinary American citizens have tears in their eyes when they stand in that place. That's the effect that Lincoln has on Americans.

Lincoln's Writing

WAYNE FIELDS

Booknotes hosted Wayne Fields on April 14, 1996. Fields discussed his book Union of Words: A History of Presidential Eloquence, *which was published by Free Press.*

IT'S VERY difficult to say [if there was ever a president who wrote every word of his inaugural]. We never know for sure, even when we're writing things down, who we're echoing. It seems to me that the president who probably authored more of his material than anybody else is Lincoln, simply because he wrote better than anybody around him. It's difficult to imagine that those words are [from] somebody else, but even Lincoln tried things out on other people, circulated speeches, and changed phrases in response to advisers.

[HIS INAUGURAL SPEECHES embody the] whole crisis of a president who is committed to holding the Union together, the cause of the Union coming apart before he'd ever taken the oath of office, and then, in an era of secession, having to establish the foundation for a rebirth of that Union. Every president before Lincoln had said, as a means of holding the Union together, "If it ever comes apart, it can't be restored." Lincoln had to go against the logic of all those generations of presidents before him. . . .

ONE THING THAT'S STRIKING is who influences presidents, and where they got their notion of the presidency. . . . The first thing [I discovered in my studies of presidential speeches] was that there is this notion of a presidency that seems to be fixed fairly early in a president's life that they often quote from. The other thing I found is that the material that gets quoted [in presidential speeches] changes dramatically. Kennedy was fond of using biblical text, and Lincoln was fond of using biblical text. . . .

[St. Augustine wrote in the fifth century, "There are men who can speak well, but cannot think of anything wise to say. If they take something eloquently and wisely written by others and offer it to the people on the person of the author, they do not do wickedly."] Augustine was speaking primarily about preachers at the time, not about presidents. Yet his point is a valid one for us, too. Part of the test of the presidency is how well the person who holds that office chooses the words that are going to be spoken. The words may be crafted by someone else, but the really important thing is that the message be the right one. . . .

It would have been a mistake for Abraham Lincoln to rely on somebody other than himself for most of his writing, because he was the one who knew those words. He was the one with the wisdom for that particular moment.

War, Weakness, and the Cabinet

RICHARD NORTON SMITH

Presidential historian Richard Norton Smith gave C-SPAN an on-camera tour of the Abraham Lincoln Presidential Museum in Springfield, Illinois, on April 18, 2005, for the museum's inaugural. Smith served as director of the Lincoln Presidential Library and Museum and has directed four other presidential libraries. The following are excerpted observations from his narration along the tour.

It was April of 1861 and Lincoln, above all, did not want to be responsible for firing the first shot. So the first weeks of his presidency were really all about maneuvering the hotheads of South Carolina, in effect, into firing on Fort Sumter. When they did that, two things happened: Lincoln called for troops in the North, and there was an enormous rallying to the flag, real unity that took place in the North. At the same time, not surprisingly, several states of the upper South that had held back decided to secede. One action—that brief siege of the fort in Charleston—really defined the first couple years of the war.

THE FACT OF THE matter is, from Lincoln's standpoint, there were not two nations. If you bought the idea there were two nations and the Confederate States were somehow legitimate, there would be no war. As far as states' rights were concerned in the context of the 1860s, they may have been fine unless you were among the four million black people who were being held in chains.

Over time, Lincoln changed, and his war aims changed. He came to see that a war about interpreting the Constitution—states' rights versus federal rights and the like—had in some ways been superceded by a war about human rights. Halfway through the war, he redefined its meaning. That's what we remember him for today.

The president's office doubled as a cabinet room. In those days, there was no West Wing to the White House, no Oval Office. The cabinet met quite frequently, though some of its members were not happy with the way Lincoln tended to dominate the decision-making process.

It was the summer of 1862, and the president had been hatching this scheme, basically as a military necessity, of emancipating the slaves. He was introducing this to the cabinet, which was divided, reflecting the political divisions: [Secretary of State William] Seward of New York; Salmon Chase, secretary of treasury from Ohio; Edward Bates, attorney general—they all had something in common: They ran against Lincoln for president in 1860.

Lincoln was shrewd. He wanted to keep his enemies close. Someone said to him while he was putting the cabinet together, he really should not appoint these men; there was a possibility that they might eat him up. Lincoln said, "It's just as likely they will eat each other up," and in the end that's very much what happened. . . .

[Edwin] Stanton, a lawyer from Pennsylvania, had clashed swords with Lincoln [when he was] a young, rising lawyer from Illinois. Yet Lincoln was able and willing to overlook the fact that he had been treated pretty shabbily by Stanton and invited him into his cabinet. Stanton was one of the few men around the table who wanted the president to issue the [Emancipation] Proclamation immediately. Remember, Stanton was secretary of war, and he saw this as a source of African American troops fighting for their freedom.

THE EMANCIPATION PROCLAMATION transformed the meaning of the war overnight. Frederick Douglass knew that better than anyone else. He stumped the North, enlisting tens of thousands of African American troops for the Union armies because after January 1, 1863, this was really no longer a war about states' rights. It became increasingly a war about human rights. Anyone who has seen the movie *Glory* knows about the 54th Massachusetts black troops who served historically at Fort Wagner [and] many other places.

THERE WERE MANY PEOPLE who thought they should be [president] instead of Lincoln. There were many people who thought he was slow. Many people thought he was basically a weak man. Nothing that we think of Lincoln today.

Chase schemed and plotted to become president, wanted it badly, toyed with the idea of running in 1864 and was eventually overcome by Lincoln's political guile. He was sidetracked because Roger Taney, chief justice of the

United States, responsible for the Dred Scott decision, a man who arguably did as much as anyone to bring on the Civil War, died very conveniently. Lincoln nominated Salmon Chase to be his replacement.

Seward, secretary of state, went on to be stabbed, almost killed, on the night of April 14. In fact, Seward was intended to be among those killed by the conspirators, as was Vice President Andrew Johnson. Seward was brutally attacked and left for dead. He escaped death only because he had been in a carriage accident and had a neck brace, which in the end saved his life.

[HANNIBAL] HAMLIN WAS a senator from Maine who had been put on the ticket, classically, for political balance, to make sure that New England was part of the Republican coalition in 1860. By all accounts, Lincoln and Hamlin got along well . . . but he was not re-nominated in 1864.

Lincoln could be ruthless where his political interests were concerned. The Republican Party was renamed the Union Party in 1864 and, in an effort to broaden its political appeal, Hamlin was dropped from the ticket, replaced with Johnson, a so-called Democrat from Tennessee. How Hamlin would have been as president is anybody's guess. When Lincoln was asked from time to time [about] the fact that he paid so little attention to his security, he on more than one occasion would say, "No one in the South would want to kill me because I would be replaced by Hamlin," the implication being that Hamlin would be tougher on the South than Lincoln.

LINCOLN WAS ONE of the most—if not *the* most—controversial presidents in American history. . . . [Many newspapers of his day were] harshly critical of the president and in some cases of Mrs. Lincoln as well. It does, among other things, tend to put into perspective modern-day journalistic coverage of the presidency. If you think it's rough today, you ought to look at the nineteenth-century newspapers.

. . . [It was] in the final weeks of a rather close presidential contest between Lincoln and his Democratic rival General George McClellan, who had been, most people would say, a successful general whom Lincoln had sacked earlier in the war and who got his revenge by running against Lincoln in 1864. [The *London Post* wrote this of the president: "Mr. Lincoln will go down to posterity as a man who could not read signs of the times nor understand the circumstances and interest of his own country, could not calculate his own resources nor appreciate those of his enemy, who had no political aptitude, who plunged his country into a great war without a plan, who failed without excuse and fell without a friend."]

There's a lot of difference between journalism and history. People talk about journalism as the first draft of history and there's something to that.

The nice thing about history is that historians' perspectives come with time and the cooling of passions. Also, historians get access to papers and documents that [journalists] didn't have. But the interesting thing about the *London Post* assessment, harsh as it was, people would have agreed with it in October 1864.

IT'S ASTONISHING FOR THE stress, the physical strain he was under, but Lincoln's health actually held up throughout the war. After he came back from Gettysburg in fall of 1863, he went to bed with what we think was a mild form of smallpox. He lost weight. Anyone who looks at pictures of Lincoln . . . will certainly see the aging effect, the physical toll that the war took on him.

THE [GETTYSBURG] STORY sweeps you all the way from July to November. It was November 19, 1863, and the president was delivering the Gettysburg Address, an address by the way, which some of the press at the time judged to be flat and dishwatery. He spoke for two minutes. Edward Everett, the orator, spoke for two hours. . . . [Yet even at the time, Everett understood Lincoln's speech was immortal.] [After Lincoln] delivered the speech, he received a letter from Everett, who said he would have flattered himself if he had come anywhere near the spirit of the occasion in two hours as Lincoln did in two minutes. He asked the president, as a favor, for a copy of the address. And, Lincoln wrote it out [for him] just as he delivered it.

YOU COULD MAKE A CASE that Lincoln was the greatest American president, in part because of the severity of the challenges he faced and, in part, because of the extraordinary capacity for growth he displayed and for the weapons of leadership—of craft, of guile, of eloquence, of strategy—that he was able to summon. He reinvented the United States. It isn't just that he saved the Union. He redefined it.

1863: A Most Difficult Year

JOSEPH E. STEVENS

Joseph Stevens joined C-SPAN's Booknotes *program on June 13, 1999, to discuss his book* 1863: The Rebirth of a Nation, *which was published by Bantam.*

The year 1863 was the pivotal year in American history. It was a year in which the country reinvented itself [not only through] tremendous military conflict, but also [through] a great deal of political change and social change. One of the biggest changes was the federal government becoming much more powerful and intrusive, and state governments enjoying less power.

IN 1863, AT THE START, the Confederacy was extremely close to winning. In December of 1862, Union forces had attacked the Army of Northern Virginia at Fredericksburg, and suffered a disastrous, terrible defeat. The army was demoralized. The people on the home front were demoralized, and politicians from both parties were pretty much ready to give up, saying the Confederacy has won. We can't go on with this. We need to negotiate a boundary.

YOU START OFF THE next year with the Emancipation Proclamation, signed on January 1, 1863. The battle of Gettysburg was fought in early July. The Gettysburg Address was given in late November. You had the battle of Stone's River, which a lot of people know as Murfreesboro. (That's one of those Northern-Southern things: The Southerners call it Stone's River and the Northerners call it Murfreesboro.) It's in middle Tennessee. That battle was right at the beginning of January. The battle of Chancellorsville, [in Virginia] was in May. There was the long-running siege of Vicksburg, which extended from the spring—March or April—through July. The battle of Chickamauga was in Georgia in September and then

Chattanooga on the Tennessee-Georgia border in November. Those are the big battles. Of course, there are all kinds of political battles going on all through that period, which in a lot of ways are as interesting as the military battles. There was this constant drumbeat, especially from the Democratic Party, to negotiate a peace. It's interesting to see Lincoln parrying this and keeping the war going.

LINCOLN HAD SIGNED the preliminary Emancipation Proclamation in September 1862 after the battle of Antietam, and he made it conditional. He said if the South would agree to certain terms that it could be withdrawn, but the deadline was January 1, and the South rejected any sort of negotiations. So he followed through and signed the Emancipation Proclamation.

His objective was twofold: One was to hurt the South militarily. There were four million slaves. They were producing crops. They were being used to dig fortifications and do all sorts of work that freed up the white Southerners to go to the army. So it hurt them militarily. More importantly, Lincoln wanted to change the political dynamic of the war. Davis and the Confederates claimed that they were fighting for liberty, that what they were doing was a second American Revolution. Lincoln felt that he was losing the war of ideas, and by making emancipation a stated war aim, he could then say the Union is fighting not just for the Union but for freedom.

GETTYSBURG WAS IMPORTANT, but I don't think it's as important as some people think. I personally believe that the capture of Vicksburg was the key military event of the year because by capturing it, the Union forces opened the Mississippi River to unimpeded river traffic, and they divided the Confederacy in half. It meant that Arkansas, Louisiana, and Texas were cut off from the rest of the South, and the South was drawing a lot of its foodstuffs and horses for remounts from those areas. So strictly from a military, strategic standpoint, I think Vicksburg was probably the most important battle.

GRANT WAS THE MOST successful general of 1863. [He had been] twiddling his thumbs, mostly, waiting to get his chance. He was in the army. He started out fairly low. He was commissioned as a colonel, worked his way up, gained a big success at Dover, Tennessee. That victory was what really put him into the public eye. That was where he became known as "Unconditional Surrender" Grant because he demanded that the Confederates surrender unconditionally. This was sort of boffo in the press, you know: U.S. Grant, "Unconditional Surrender" Grant. That brought him to the attention of Lincoln and the people at the War Department.

AFTER THE BATTLE AT Gettysburg, the battlefield, as you might imagine, was just a ghastly scene, thousands of bodies of soldiers and horses. It became obvious that something had to be done, or there was going to be a terrible health situation. So it was decided that a national cemetery would be built there. This was done, and a dedication ceremony was arranged. President Lincoln was invited to make a few appropriate remarks. He was not the featured speaker at the dedication. That honor went to a man named Edward Everett, who was the foremost orator of the time. Everett gave a speech that went on for two hours—completely from memory. From all reports, the crowd—there were ten thousand spectators—was entranced with Everett's speech. Afterward, Lincoln got up and read his ten sentences and sat down. Two hundred and seventy-two words. That's it. And yet, those words ring down through the years, and Edward Everett's are long forgotten.

Lincoln explained what all the sacrifice was for; certainly that was something that needed doing—the outpouring of blood was horrifying. There needed to be an exalted reason for this kind of a sacrifice.

Both sides felt that God was on their side. [Southerners were] fighting for liberty, and that's in the American tradition. They felt that the North was seeking to dominate them, and they were fighting for their freedom.

PRESIDENT LINCOLN SELECTED the generals, but as far as controlling their actions on the battlefield, it's rather remarkable how little control he exerted. We think now that the president picks up the phone and says, "Drop a bomb down this chimney in Yugoslavia," and presumably an hour later, it happens. This just was not the case in 1863.

Lincoln was constantly cajoling these generals to be more aggressive, to move faster, to do this and do that. Many of the generals were downright insubordinate. They would ignore his messages. They would not do what he wanted them to do. It was really quite astonishing to me that these West Point–trained generals would treat the commander in chief that way. But this was a different time, and attitudes were different.

IT HAD BEEN OBVIOUS that 1863 was the pivotal year of the Civil War, but the more I got into it, the more I realized that this was really a turning point for the whole country, particularly in the growth and strength of the federal government, industrialization, business practices, and social mores. A year is not that long a period, really, and yet these incredible changes took place in just this 365-day period.

What changed was that the federal government assumed a position that it has increasingly had since then in directing the tone and tenor of national life at the expense of the states.

There was the passage of a national banking law. Interestingly enough, before 1863, states chartered banks, and each bank issued its own currency. You would have hundreds of different kinds of bills and coins and currency floating around from banks of who knows what quality, which really impeded interstate commerce. The national banking law allowed for a national currency, which was a big change in the economy.

Another big thing was conscription. Prior to 1863, the individual states had recruited soldiers and organized them into regiments, picked the commanders, done a lot of the equipping and then sent them off. When the Conscription Act passed, the federal government was saying, "We're going to take charge of this now." The states had a quota: "Recruit so many soldiers, but if you fall below that quota, we're going to send provost marshals in, and we're going to draft people and take them." . . . There was a provision in the conscription law, a very unpopular one, that permitted individuals of means to pay $300 to hire a substitute. . . . There were brokers, people who would find these substitutes—usually they were immigrants right off the boat from Ireland or somewhere. If you were a well-to-do individual, you would go to the broker, pay a certain fee; he would find a person that would go in your place and that was the end of your obligation.

Many people did this. I'm somewhat ashamed to say my own great-grandfather did this. I'm told he regretted it for the rest of his life, but he did. My great-grandfather ran a paper mill in Springfield, Massachusetts, and I assume it was a thriving business and he did not want to leave it. I was a little disappointed perhaps, but also understanding. You ask yourself, if you were in that position and you had the choice, you could pay several thousand dollars and stay home or go to these killing fields, how many of us would choose to go to the killing fields? I'm not sure.

THE REPUBLICANS RAN the Congress then, the so-called radical Republicans, who also tended to be very critical of Lincoln, feeling that he was not prosecuting the war harshly enough. So Lincoln was in the middle and was catching it from both sides.

Lincoln had a number of remarkable talents, and as a politician, he was extremely skillful at tacking a little bit this way toward the radical Republicans and then perhaps tacking back a little bit this way toward the antiwar Democrats.

THERE WERE SOME more terrible battles, but the South was just kind of shrinking in on itself. By 1864, I don't think that there was any question anymore that the Union might lose. That's really one of the extraordinary things about 1863. We look back at history, we feel that whatever happened was inevitable, and that's not true. The Confederacy could have won. I really believe that. If it had won, we would be living in a very different country. That's really one of the amazing things about 1863 and what makes it such an important year.

Word from the Battlefield

JAMES PERRY

Published by John Wiley & Sons, Inc., the book A Bohemian
Brigade: The Civil War Correspondents—Mostly Rough,
Sometimes Ready *was the topic of discussion when author
James Perry appeared on* Booknotes *on May 21, 2000.*

THE CIVIL WAR correspondents called themselves the "Bohemian
Brigade." They thought they were bohemians surrounded by professional soldiers.

MODERN JOURNALISM all began in the Civil War for two basic reasons.
One was the telegraph, of course. This was the first instant-news war in history, and the problem was very much like the Internet today when you
think about it. Journalists could file [stories] immediately, and it caused the
rush to be first. They would take these immense, long rides across broken
countryside on horseback to get to the nearest telegraph station to file. The
other reason was the steam-powered locomotives. You could get on a train
and go back to your own office pretty quickly and file the story that way if
you couldn't get on the telegraph. The army wasn't too keen on making
the telegraph easily available to reporters. They preferred to reserve it for
themselves as much as possible.

MOST OF [THE REPORTERS] were quite young. A lot of them had gone
to college, and they tended to go to small liberal arts colleges, like Trinity
and Beloit and Miami of Ohio and Amherst, places like that. . . . My favorite reporter was a very young man named Henry Wing, who was kissed
by Lincoln—that was what he was most famous for. He was only eighteen
when he went off to cover the war. That was after serving with the Connecticut regiment and [being] wounded at Fredericksburg. So he had had an
amazing career.

GRANT, IN HIS LAST great campaign, had just simply disappeared with his army. They were desperate in Washington—at the White House and at the War Department—to know where he was. Wing, with extraordinary courage and difficulty, rode off from the army through the backcountry. It was filled with all kinds of deserters and Confederate patrols—difficult people of all kinds. He managed to get all the way through, and as he approached Washington, he finally found a Union outpost. He wanted to file a story [about Grant's army] by telegraph, but they wouldn't let him. It was an army telegraph.

Finally, they heard in Washington that there was a reporter at this army station who knew where Grant was. [A Union officer had] ordered him to be arrested. That wasn't what he wanted to hear, so he was going to try to cut a deal that if he was to be allowed to send 150 words or 200 words or whatever it was, to his paper, he [would agree to] come to Washington and report on what he knew.

Lincoln heard about it and said, "None of this arresting him, we'll send a train down." They sent the train down, picked him up, and brought him back to the White House. He came in just covered with dirt and grime, and he noticed Lincoln's whole cabinet was sitting there. He walked in the room. He knew most of these people, but he was in such disreputable appearance that they didn't recognize him. He finally told his story and then when it was all over, he said [to the president], "I have a message from General Grant for you." Before he left, Grant had taken him aside, and said, "If you actually get through and if you see Lincoln, tell him, this time, there's to be no turning back."

The two of them were standing together; Wing was a very short guy, and Lincoln was this extraordinarily tall man. And when he told this story to Lincoln, the president was so overwhelmed that he kissed Wing on the forehead.

Even more dramatic, Wing had had to leave his horse in a little vale, near the woods, and he said, "Mr. President, I worry about Jess"—Jess being the horse. "Tell me about Jess," said President Lincoln. Wing said, "Well, I said I'd come back to get him, and I never lie to horses, Mr. President." Lincoln said, "Henry, we have to do something about that." So the next day, they sent a train down there with some soldiers in the car, and they picked up Jess. The horse was grazing just where he'd been left. They brought Jess back to Washington. Some of the other reporters were so impressed they collected a little fund and bought the horse for Wing.

★ ★
★

The Gettysburg Address

GABOR BORITT

Gabor Boritt is director of the Civil War Institute at Gettysburg
College and the author of sixteen books on Lincoln and the Civil
War. The Hungarian-born author appeared on Book TV's After
Words *program on January 5, 2007, to discuss his book* The
Gettysburg Gospel: The Lincoln Speech That Nobody
Knows, *published by Simon & Schuster. He is co-founder and*
board chairman of the Lincoln Prize, the $50,000 annual
award for the finest work on the Civil War era.

[L incoln gave few prepared speeches during his presidency.] Four, to
be exact. Gettysburg was the first one.
    Lincoln went from Washington to Gettysburg by train. A modern
book might say he was going at the slow pace of twenty-five miles an hour,
that's how it looks to us. If you look at it from his perspective, he was going
at the *amazing* speed of twenty-five miles an hour.

Why did he go to Gettysburg? Certainly to speak to the nation, but there
are many other reasons. Certainly politics were a significant part. He was
running for re-election. It's important [to realize that] if Lincoln had not
been reelected, there would, in my opinion, be no United States. Were that
the case, he would have gone down as the worst disaster, the worst president, and the last president.

The opposition looked on Lincoln as a Republican running for re-election. They looked on Gettysburg as the beginning of the presidential campaign. They weren't entirely wrong. There was a long way to go [in the
fighting], and people were sick and tired of [the war].

One of the many reasons Lincoln went to Gettysburg was to see the battlefield. [Months earlier], he had followed that battle carefully, [although]

he did not look on it, as many others did, as the turning point. . . . He went the day before [the speech] to make sure he would be there on time, and he would have time to look at the entire battlefield. He realized that in spite of how much time he spent looking at maps and looked at the official reports, he did not understand. Gettysburg is a place [where] the land will speak to you. I think it spoke to Lincoln.

[The day he gave the speech, Lincoln was not the star attraction.] Edward Everett, the most famous speaker at the time, spoke for two hours before Lincoln. Today, we make fun of Edward Everett—even academics do. . . . This was a time when there was no Internet, no television, no radio, no organized sports. [Two things drew the public]: one was liturgy and two was politics. Everett did later make fun of his two-hour speech. Nobody speaks for two hours anymore. But that's what was expected [back then]. People traveled a long distance to Pennsylvania. You didn't want just a two-minute speech. You needed a substantial program, and Everett supplied it.

[EVERETT'S] SPEECH WAS beautiful. . . . He looked at history; European history largely, at French, German, and Italian history, and at civil wars, ugly wars. He said Americans will do what others did. When the war is over, they're going to be friends again. He predicted that the country would reunite. At that time, a lot of people made fun of him, but he was right.

There were a lot of people [in Gettysburg that day for Everett's speech]. You have to imagine a town of 2,500 people [with] a minimum of 16,000 visitors, depending on who you believe. The local papers talked about 30,000. The Chicago paper talked about 50,000 visitors. Some newspapers gave higher figures. These people had no place to sleep. Lincoln stayed in the center of town; David Wills was his host. That home normally had five or six people in it. Young Mr. Wills invited thirty-nine people to stay there, which meant nobody had their own bed except the president and Mr. Everett—the two chief guests.

At 11 p.m., the governor of Pennsylvania showed up [at the Wills's home]. Gov. [Andrew] Curtain made Wills the important man of the moment. The governor was grumpy as can be; he was supposed to arrive sooner. He arrived, asked for his room, and Wills looked around and knew there were only two people [not sharing] a bed: Everett and the president. Protocol prevailed. Wills told Mr. Everett, "The governor's going to sleep with you." Mr. Everett didn't like the idea at all. He was almost seventy, and he'd had a stroke earlier in the year. He had a two-hour speech to make the next day from memory. More to the point, he had a bladder problem. He didn't want to sleep with the governor. So finally, the governor left. I still don't know where he slept, if anywhere. So, what do you have there that night?

You have an all-night party. People sang, hollered, and laughed right into the morning. Then there was a change of atmosphere.

[LINCOLN SPOKE BRIEFLY to the revelers outside Wills's home.] That was his first speech. It was a funny speech and, some would say, undignified. He said, "I don't have anything to say, and in my position, I better not say anything foolish." There was this ease with others. Lincoln knew what he was doing.

[Lincoln got to bed] probably before midnight. Everett wrote in his diary, "I did not get to bed until half past 11." Then Everett added, "I couldn't get to sleep until the early hours of the morning, fearing that the executive of Pennsylvania was going to tumble in bed with me." He also couldn't sleep because there was a party going on all night. People were yelling, dancing, and playing. Decades later, people still remembered bands playing until the morning.

PEOPLE CAME FROM long distances. There were veterans, veterans of the battle itself. They stood in a group close to the platform, and they were holding up a sign. When Lincoln finished speaking and the ceremony was over, he went straight to the veterans. He said, "They can speak more eloquently than I can speak." . . . The newspapers said at the time that there had never been such a collection of distinguished individuals in one place.

[IN THE GETTYSBURG Address,] Lincoln's goal was to explain to the people why this war had to go on. It was a bloodbath. Today, people talk about Iraq. Any who die [there] you need to mourn, but at Gettysburg, there were fifty thousand casualties. The [heavy casualties] went on day after day, week after week, year after year [during the Civil War]. His job was to tell the American people why this was going on, why the United States had to be saved, and how slavery had to be ended—and how the two [aims] combined. Lincoln told the American people this is who we are, and it's worth fighting for and worth dying for.

He was always thinking of Southern Americans. He never accepted the idea [that the South] was a separate nation. Surely, in that sense, he spoke to everybody. [Whether] he had hoped that fifty years later people might still remember what he said, we cannot be sure. He hoped that he spoke to the whole nation. At the time, he spoke to the Northerners who needed to carry the burden of the war to its end. That was his main audience.

[SECRETARY OF STATE WILLIAM] Seward gave a speech the night before [Lincoln's]. Seward was actually the backup speaker. People in town did not know for sure if Lincoln was going to come. I found a letter [written] four days before the event addressed to Mr. Seward, asking him to be the speaker if the president could not come. Clearly, Seward had a speech, not unlike Lincoln, that he later published or gave out. In it, he said that we will all be one people. He said, "We're going to mourn our Southern [dead] once the war is over." The two [men] thought very much alike about that.

[THERE ARE CONFEDERATE soldiers buried at Gettysburg.] They are there by mistake. The Confederates were left where they were. There was a movement, even among Northerners to do something about the Confederate dead, but the idea was to let the Confederates pay for it, not us. That was the sharp line. They were not going to be allowed in the national cemetery.

IT'S COMMONLY BELIEVED [that Lincoln wrote the address on the back of an envelope on the train to Gettysburg], but there is no evidence of this. We will never know for certain what happened, but the best evidence is [that he wrote] half of his speech in Washington the night before [traveling] and the second half was finished in Gettysburg. He had a night's sleep—as well as he could sleep with all the noise outside. The next morning he got up, went to the battlefield, came back, and wrote a second version from which I think he spoke.

Lincoln was unique and spoke beautifully, but there's nothing really original about what he was saying. He was summing up for Americans the best thoughts. The words came deep from inside him, words that have been echoed in American conscience for a long time: "Government of the people, by the people, for the people." It's beautiful. There are all kinds of arguments where he got it, and indeed when we begin to call his remarks "The Gettysburg Address," which comes later, people say he plagiarized it. Many others used similar expressions. Indeed, [Daniel] Webster's speech was in Lincoln's mind somewhere deep inside and the expressions in the speech from Weem's *Life of Washington*, again what you read earlier. Here's a man that has no time to write speeches; he was running a war, and he did this quickly—I would say in a day and a half or so. So he reached deep inside himself, and what he found was what had been in his head since he was a young boy, and he put it together beautifully.

THE SPEECH WAS NOT famous immediately, nothing as we looked on it later. A lot of newspapers [at the time] didn't mention it. Thanksgiving came exactly a week after the Gettysburg speech, and Lincoln put out a proclamation. That proclamation received four or five times as much attention as the remarks at Gettysburg. [The proclamation] was put to music, became a hymn, it was everywhere. So there was some reaction by the people—not so much to the speech as to Lincoln himself. The speech itself seemed to largely disappear.

THE GETTYSBURG ADDRESS became a significant element to the reunions of the [Civil War] veterans. [But] the address did not become a central part of our larger culture until the beginning of the twentieth century.

In the first years after Lincoln died, twenty public statues were put up, and in eighteen of them Lincoln is featured holding the Emancipation Proclamation in his hand. We did not have a statue of Lincoln holding the Gettysburg Address until the twentieth century. By the time the reunions took place and the two sides made peace, the Gettysburg Address was important.

DID LINCOLN THINK he failed [in Gettysburg]? There's no evidence of that. Twice, at least, he was asked to make copies [of the speech], to help raise money for soldiers. There's no evidence that the speech ever sold. The Emancipation Proclamation sold for $3,000, which was a lot of money. The only evidence I can find that Lincoln was concerned about how well the speech was received came from a letter that Everett wrote him the day after the event: "In a few words you did much better than I did in two hours." This quote is repeated again and again by scholars to show how Everett understood the importance of the speech at the time. Indeed, Lincoln took [Everett's] letter and showed it to his son and at least a couple other people, which tells you that he wanted Everett to pat him on the back.

What Everett's letter means is open to discussion. If you look at the letter, it doesn't simply say, "Your speech was wonderful." What it said was that your speech was wonderful and then went on to thank the president for taking care of his daughter, Charlotte, who had stayed in the Wills's home as well. She went to Gettysburg with Lincoln and her husband from Washington. In fact, on that funny night when Everett's diary talks about how he couldn't sleep because he was worried about the governor coming to bed, his daughter Charlotte slept [in a bed with] two other women, and the bed broke. Everett's diary says Charlotte took herself to the floor. So, Everett devised a letter praising Lincoln [but] talked about Charlotte. Everett also kept a diary and mentioned the letter, and what he says in his diary is, "I wrote a letter to the president and I thanked him for helping Charlotte." That's it. Was Everett being polite? Did he mean it? It's for you to decide.

[LINCOLN'S ADDRESS] IS secular gospel. It sums up for Americans who we are; it has a sacred quality to it. It is the good news of America. It is America at its best. It's America as it hopes to be—not quite what it is but what it hopes to be—and Lincoln expressed it so beautifully. And the speech, we talk about it as a political speech, but you can read it actually as a religious speech, as some people did, and then you can read it as a secular speech, as some people did. How people understood the speech depended on what was in their heads. The beauty of the speech, in part, is that it was able to encompass so many Americans.

★ ★ ★

Oratory Style

GARRY WILLS

On December 12, 1994, Garry Wills, author of the Pulitzer Prize–winning Lincoln at Gettysburg: The Words That Remade America *(Simon & Schuster), appeared before C-SPAN cameras at the Library of Congress as the library was preparing a rare display one of its two original manuscripts of Abraham Lincoln's Gettysburg Address.*

I t seemed to me that there are three Declarations of Independence: The draft of Jefferson, the congressional document, and then what Lincoln did with the Declaration. The Declaration was so important to Lincoln that I had to spend a lot of time studying how he took the Declaration and made it the hinge for not only [the Gettysburg] Address, but for his whole approach to national union.

LINCOLN HAD DEVELOPED a strategy in dealing with slavery: He posed a dilemma. He did this in the debates with Stephen A. Douglas. "Do you think that the Declaration of Independence matters?"

People would say, "Yes, we celebrate it every year." [Lincoln would say], "Well, then, what do you make of 'All men are created equal?' You might not think that means immediate emancipation or social equality or . . . the vote, or anything, but it must mean something. At a minimum, doesn't it mean one man should not own another man or woman?"

When he came to this stage of his career, this was such an important strategy to him. He had used the Declaration in his First Inaugural speech. [At Gettysburg], he began, "Four score and seven years ago, our fathers brought forth upon this continent a new nation." [He's not referring to] the Constitution. Four score and seven years takes you back to 1776. He says the Declaration is the founding document because it mentions equality.

He took an approach to [the concept of equality that was different from] Jefferson's original approach. Lincoln was very heavily influenced by the Transcendentalists. . . . Their attitude was, when Jefferson said ["All men are created equal"], it wasn't really true for slaves, but it set a benchmark that we should be striving for. We should judge everything in the light of that, including the Constitution. Of course, that was anathema to people who thought that the Constitution was a contract with the states and that you shouldn't try to subordinate it.

If you look at the [Gettysburg] document, you can see that [Lincoln] boiled down his whole approach to that [interpretation of the Declaration]. At the end when he says, "government of the people, for the people shall not perish from the earth"—"the people" was a charged phrase. His attitude was that the people had set up the government with the Declaration of Independence. The states had not contracted, and therefore, they couldn't leave at will because the whole people had made an understanding to be a people.

I SAY THAT LINCOLN remade the nation with these words [at Gettysburg]. People say that's hyperbolic. What I mean is that the whole agony, the struggle, what everybody was doing in fighting the Civil War, crystallized in the American consciousness in this document. It made us rethink things like equality, egalitarianism, what role the Declaration should play in our thinking about ourselves, and how we face up to the Constitution's limitations in dealing with slavery. All of those things are involved here.

A number of people who have criticized Lincoln talked about [the Gettysburg Address] as distorting history, [and they said] that he made us think in a different way, and that maybe we should think in the ways the original drafters of the Constitution or the Declaration of Independence had. That's an argument that goes to original intent and all of those things. It's controversial.

There was a school that said, "Oh, these are just flowery phrases. It's what you would expect to be said at a grave site." [But] it's not at all what you expect. [Lincoln] left out most of the things that you would have expected and that were a part of the normal funeral oratory. There's no mention of anybody's name. North and South are not mentioned. South and the North are treated as part of one people undergoing an experiment to determine whether government of the people, for the people, and by the people will survive. It's very abstract when you contrast it, not only with Edward Everett, but with any of the other nineteenth century funeral orations.

[LINCOLN DELIVERED THE address on] November 19, 1863, which was some time after the battle, which had occurred in the first three days of July. A lot of things had gone on in the interval. Eight thousand bodies were scattered over this village, which only had a population of twenty-five hundred. [The townspeople] didn't know what to do with them. They put the [bodies of] Southerners in mass graves. [Family] members from the states of the Union wanted to come down and get their people and take them back and put them in their family plots, their church plots.

The governor of Pennsylvania decided that we couldn't have people rummaging around looking for their dead—nobody knew they had been just lightly covered over in the summer heat after the battle. He put together a plan in which all eighteen Union states would sponsor a joint cemetery.

It's the first time this had happened, and it created a very complicated series of negotiations. How much did each state have to pay, for instance? If they had gone around and counted each body and done a per-body count that wouldn't have worked. They decided that it would be according to [the size of each state's] congressional representation. The cemetery land was bought. The commission was set up, run by representatives of the eighteen governors involved. People were invited to come and participate in the dedication. Three poets were invited, who turned it down. Lincoln was invited rather late. Edward Everett was invited and asked to give the [keynote] speech.

Everett was the most famous orator left after the great ones of the immediately preceding generation died. He gave these public performances, where he would memorize long texts and deliver them beautifully. He was a classics scholar. He was an ex-senator. He was an ex-secretary of state, an ex-president of Harvard. He was famous for these performances, which were very much admired.

We often hear [that Everett spoke] for two hours, and people think, well, that was a terrible bore. Not at all. People liked long speeches then. It was more like a rock concert format than anything that we would think of as a speech. Lincoln and Douglas talked for three hours when they debated in 1858.

Everett's voice was beautiful. His delivery was beautiful, and he made a big hit in Gettysburg. It was a myth that he spent two hours trying to say something and Lincoln got up and said it in three minutes. That wasn't the case at all. There were two different forms of oratory. Everett was very good.

[GETTYSBURG IS ABOUT eighty miles from Washington.] [Lincoln's] staff set up a train to leave early in the morning—5 or 6 a.m.—to get there in time for the noon ceremony. [But] Lincoln didn't want to take any chances. This was a very important thing to Lincoln . . . so he went the day before and stayed the night at the home of the man who set up the cemetery, stayed there with Everett. They probably looked at each other's speeches the night before to make sure they didn't clash in any way, then got up and took a tour of the battlefield in the morning. They went on horseback out to the cemetery.

It's pretty clear [Lincoln] wrote [his address] in Washington. That was his practice. He prepared his texts very carefully. As president, if he didn't have a text he didn't like to speak, because he weighed his words so well. Modern presidents have ghostwriters write their speeches. Lincoln actually ghostwrote speeches and documents for his cabinet because he wanted to get them just right.

As he was working on the Gettysburg Address in Washington, he called in the landscape architect who set up the [Gettysburg cemetery] and talked to him about the physical setup long before he went.

THE WEATHER WAS FINE [the day of the ceremony]. They were afraid of bad weather. Everett had put it off, because he needed two months [to get ready]. They had wanted to have it in October. They knew they were risking bad weather to have it in November.

Lincoln spoke toward the end. The arrangement was a hymn, a prayer, then the oration, as it's called in the program. Then another hymn, a dirge, and a poem. Then "remarks" by the president. He was there to kind of "cut the ribbon," to say, "This site is dedicated." That's all they expected. So the shortness of [his speech] was not surprising. Nobody really remarked on it at the time.

There are myths that people were taken aback that it was so short, and that a photographer set up and was all ready, and by the time he was ready to take the picture it was all over, and Lincoln had sat down. None of that is true.

Lincoln was interrupted five times for applause. His speech was called a gem [by the press]. Some of the people who didn't like it criticized it very heavily, but the speech took off pretty rapidly. For one thing, it's short enough that it was easy to reprint. It was easy to put on the monument [they erected at the site]. They couldn't put all of Edward Everett's speech on there.

Undoubtedly, accident played some role in the importance of Lincoln's speech. If you had asked Lincoln himself, "Is this your most important speech?" he wouldn't have said Gettysburg. He thought he was going to give many important speeches. [But] the Gettysburg Address was admired; it was sold at charity auctions. That's why we have most of these drafts. He [copied] them to be auctioned off for the war effort, in his own hand.

When he died, he'd only had time to [deliver] the Second Inaugural and a few other things. He was growing as an orator and a thinker, and he expected that this was one speech in what he hoped would be a long series of speeches. He died less than a year and a half after he gave it. . . . So it became kind of his last testament in a way. It became for Lincoln what Washington's farewell address had been.

The Gettysburg Address really boiled down what he thought the whole war was about. He won the war for the interpretation of the agony, of the division of the Union in these words. These became the words that tell us what the Civil War was all about, and in the process tell us what he wanted to make the Declaration of Independence about, and the Constitution. It's not only an important document in itself; it makes us reinterpret these two major documents.

THE NICOLAY DRAFT [of the Gettysburg Address is the one] some think is the original he held in his hand because it was on White House stationery. It was folded. You can see the folds. And he finished writing it with pencil. There are some problems with that theory. Clearly, it is an early draft. There are things in here that are not in the later ones.

There's not a perfect continuation onto the penciled [writing]. A whole clause is dropped, and the little pencilings don't put it together grammatically. It is obviously a composition draft, not in the final form. Maybe one or the other was held by him in his hand as he actually delivered it. It's hard to think that both drafts were because he would have had to improvise the connections between them.

JOHN NICOLAY WAS the young secretary to Lincoln. He was taken on to answer [the president's] mail in 1861, when he was twenty-eight years old. He became so valuable to Lincoln that he undertook diplomatic missions. He was a confidential advisor and a kind of political scout. He hired a friend of his who was only twenty-two at the time, John Hay, as his assistant. The two men lived in the White House up in a corner room and were in twenty-four-hour contact with Lincoln all through the war years. They both kept notes. Hay kept a very complete diary. They wrote the official biography of Lincoln after his death—ten volumes. It took them a quarter of a century to write it.

The Hay draft of the Gettysburg Address [has] been called the most mysterious draft because nobody knew it existed until 1906. It was in the Hay family, and they had never made much of it. When it was produced, people noticed that there were changes in it. [Lincoln] was writing along and putting different things up above, so [historians] thought it must be a composition draft. If you look at the changes, there are things like "We are met" written once, then written again. That's dittography, the kind of thing you do when you're copying out. Or when he says, "be dedicated here to the unfinished work, which they have,"—"work" was omitted. That's hardly what you do when you're composing. You would say "the unfinished task," and then put in "work" if you thought that was better. If you're writing fast, you would come back and put in "work." There was a [belief] in the Hay family that Lincoln had copied the text out for Hay as a favor.

IN LINCOLN'S DAY, THERE were letterpresses. You could make ink copies, but [Lincoln] did everything by hand. The five [copies of the Gettysburg Address] that exist are all in his handwriting. You can see that they're different. Some are written rapidly; some of them he starts very neatly and kind of frays out at the end. He did all of his own texts.

[The surviving copies are] very fragile. Paper chemically deteriorates and changes. Ink fades. The creases will become more damaged if the paper is handled at all. Preservation now—[in] acid-free surroundings and that kind of thing—is a very highly developed art. It has to be, if we want to keep these things. A document like this not only has its intrinsic worth, but forgeries every now and then show up. You can only investigate those by being able to investigate this [authentic original] document. Having it where scholars can get at it, and where occasionally it can be exposed—not too much for the light to bother it—is very important.

IF [THE NICOLAY DRAFT] is a composition draft, there was no reason for Lincoln to [date it]. Even if it was a delivery draft there was no reason. I don't think the Nicolay draft was the final one. I think it's an intermediate one between his early draft, which is probably messier, and the one that he used to deliver. We have not only his five drafts; we have four stenographic reports, of which two are really important. They tell us things that are not in the early drafts.

I'VE SEEN THE BLISS [draft] at the White House, the Everett [draft] at Springfield [Illinois]. The only one I haven't seen is the Bancroft [draft] at Cornell, so I've seen four of the five. . . . There are related things that have disappeared. [Gettysburg innkeeper] David Wills's papers have disappeared. He was the one who ran the whole thing, and he corresponded with Lincoln. Lincoln answered him twice, and those [replies] are gone. David Wills asked for a draft himself. Presumably it was sent to him. That seems to be gone. I have a theory that he sent it up to Edward Everett for printing purposes. [The Bliss copy] is normally in the Lincoln study [at the White House]. Bill Clinton is a big Lincoln fan, and he had moved it onto his desk.

The Nicolay and the Hay drafts are very different. That's a subject for controversy. But these are the most discussed and controversial, and in that sense, probably the most important drafts. The Bliss draft is the final one that he did. He did it very painstakingly and made one correction. Bliss was putting together an auction to raise money. George Bancroft, the historian, was an intermediary who got Lincoln to write something to be [auctioned]. When that copy went, they said, "Oh, it's not the right format. We want a uniform format." So Lincoln had to copy it out all over again. The Bancroft draft was the first one he did for the Bliss auction. That [eventually] went to Cornell. The Bliss version stayed in the Bliss family until they gave it to the White House.

We don't [know precisely which words Lincoln delivered]. You have to put together the newspaper reports, the five documents, and you can approximate. My own guess is that the Everett draft is closest to what Lincoln said, but even there, you would have to make a few additions from the newspaper accounts. The Bliss [version] is the one that's normally printed and used because it is his final draft. He did make a correction in it. He was not trying to give you the delivery document. He was trying to give you what he wanted to go down in history. So we have, in effect, honored that.

Thanksgiving

JAMES LOEWEN

James Loewen discussed his book Lies My Teacher Told Me, *published by The New Press, as part of the* Booknotes *series on March 26, 1995.*

 A LOT OF PEOPLE think that Thanksgiving goes back to 1620, to the Pilgrims. The first point to know about Thanksgiving is that it was actually invented by Abraham Lincoln in the middle of the Civil War. The first official Thanksgiving in our modern history happened in 1863. It was basically giving thanks for the victory of the [Union] troops (particularly during the previous summer in Vicksburg and at Gettysburg) and for the fact that the Union was going to be held together and slavery was going to be ended.

Lincoln and Grant

BROOKS D. SIMPSON

Ulysses S. Grant: Triumph Over Adversity, written by Brooks Simpson and published by Houghton Mifflin Co., was the featured book on Booknotes *on July 16, 2000.*

A POPULAR PERCEPTION is that Ulysses S. Grant and Abraham Lincoln were very tight, that Lincoln had always chosen Grant as his general. That wasn't true. Lincoln often kept Grant at arm's length, [although he] never went to the point of removing him. But Lincoln had doubts about Grant's ability in 1862 and 1863. Lincoln probably never uttered the phrase, "I can't spare this man. He fights," because at the time, he seemed awfully willing to spare Grant.

The Lieutenant General legislation [of 1864] added a third star, reviving a rank that had not been a full rank in the United States Army since the days of George Washington. . . . Congressional Republicans revived this rank and wanted Grant to fill it, in part to take control of the army away from presidents like Lincoln. Lincoln would not support this bill until he found out [for sure] whether General Grant wanted to be President Grant in 1864.

Grant, very shrewdly, wrote letters [to lobby for his promotion] to people who would see Lincoln. One of his former generals, Frank Blair, brother of . . . Montgomery Blair, postmaster general in the Lincoln cabinet . . . had come East to take a turn in congress. Grant wrote Blair a letter that said he didn't have any presidential ambitions at all. He said, "Don't show this letter to anyone unless it be the president himself," which is a clear signal to show the letter to the president and tell him I don't want to become a rival of his in 1864. There were other messages leaked to Lincoln the same way. Lincoln [clearly] checked Grant out before he supported that bill.

[Grant's hometown congressman from Galena, Illinois,] was able to pass the bill in the House. In fact, one of the particular components of the bill that was finally weeded out in [the congressional] committee was taking Grant's name out. At one point, Grant's name was explicitly put in the bill, so it wasn't just legislation reviving the rank, but specifying that the person who would receive the rank would be Ulysses S. Grant.

The Senate argued about this, talking about whether it stripped away the president's right to nominate officers. The bill was still log-jammed in committee when Lincoln leaked word that Grant was an acceptable candidate in part because of his lack of political ambition.

The Soldiers' Home

MATTHEW PINSKER

On December 21, 2003, Booknotes *featured* Lincoln's
Sanctuary: Abraham Lincoln and the Soldiers' Home,
*a book by Matthew Pinsker, published by Oxford University
Press. Mr. Pinsker, the author of numerous articles and essays
on Abraham Lincoln and the Civil War era, is an associate
professor of history at Dickinson College.*

[The Soldiers' Home] was kind of a Camp David for President Lincoln. Robert Anderson of Fort Sumter fame was one of the guiding spirits behind the establishment of the Soldiers' Home, which was an institution for disabled veterans, originally created in the 1850s.

[The Soldiers' Home was located] about three-and-a-half miles [from the White House], on a hilly section of Washington, inside the District but just near the border. A cottage there was built by George W. Riggs, of Riggs Bank fame, in the early 1840s, mostly as a country home for his family. He lived there for several years. After a daughter died, the family decided to move back into the city. In the 1850s, the government bought the grounds and the property, added several buildings and created an institution for disabled soldiers.

The Soldiers' Home was a new experiment. The idea that the government should care for veterans in a home, what they called an asylum, was unprecedented in America. There were precedents in Europe but not in the United States. It took a lot of fighting to get it to happen. Robert Anderson, Winfield Scott, and Jefferson Davis, as a senator, were all moving forces behind the legislation.

When they started to build these Soldiers' Homes—one in Washington, and a couple of others across the country—they were something of a flop.

The soldiers weren't treated properly. The veterans who lived there weren't really well cared for. They didn't understand how to care for them.

They didn't have a recreational facility. They didn't have much medical attention, except for one surgeon on duty. Residents were required to cook and clean for themselves. Some of these men were really struggling to survive. They complained to members of Congress, who considered abolishing the whole thing at the end of the 1850s. The board of commissioners who ran the place made a very smart, very Washington decision.

They said that they needed to cultivate support in the administration, so they started inviting presidents and secretaries of war to spend summers at cottages on the grounds of this institution. It was hilly. It was shaded. It was a beautiful area, about three hundred acres, very pastoral. [President James] Buchanan took them up on the offer and loved it. The only good thing [Buchanan] did for Abraham Lincoln was tell him to use the Soldiers' Home. The week after the inauguration in 1861, both Lincoln and his wife rode out there to take a look.

They were planning to go out to the Soldiers' Home the summer of '61, but the war intruded, so Mary Lincoln took the boys to New Jersey, and President Lincoln stayed in the White House and worked. Then in the summer of 1862, they decided to go to the Soldiers' Home for personal reasons and spent from June until November officially in residence that year.

They went back again the next summer and spent several more months, from late June until late October, and again in the summer of 1864, from early July through early November. Altogether, the Lincolns spent over a quarter of his presidency in residence [at the Soldiers' Home]. During the winter, when they weren't in residence, they would ride back and forth in the afternoon and visit the grounds. It was a standard afternoon ride for them.

AT THE OUTSKIRTS of the District, it was largely rural pasture. Then as Lincoln crossed Boundary Street—I think what's now Florida Avenue—the streets would get increasingly busy. Washington still was not an impressive town. If you read the accounts of foreigners who visited the city, they were amazed at how rundown and rural it was. At the beginning of the war, there were about 61,000 residents. By the end of the war, Washington had more than 200,000 people. It grew to be a big, bustling city.

[THE LINCOLNS] HAD four children. One died as an infant, so during the White House years, they had three children. Robert was the eldest; during the war he was at Harvard. There was a middle son, Willie, who died during the second year of the war. Willie's death was the primary motivation for Lincoln's decision to go to the Soldiers' Home.

Willie's death created grief in both parents, but especially in Mary Lincoln. She had a difficult time grieving for him at the White House. Even though the president had been reluctant to take a vacation at the Soldiers' Home in the summer of 1861, she convinced him that it would be a refuge for the grieving family in the summer of 1862. She had a dispute with some aides over whether or not a band could play outside the White House, and that was finally the trigger that convinced the president to try the Soldiers' Home.

It appears [that their youngest son Tad] had a cleft palate. He may have been learning disabled. He was very cute, rambunctious, but hard to understand. It's not clear that he was reading and writing well. They had a tutor who was very frustrated with his lack of progress. But the soldiers who were guarding the Soldiers' Home and the family loved him. Tad was named third lieutenant in their company. He had a little uniform; he would come to the camp and get his face all grimy. Whenever Tad and Mary Lincoln traveled they would bring back gifts for the soldiers.

Another example of the bond that developed between the family and the guards came at the end of the war. The soldiers made a photo album at their own expense, with a picture of each of them, which they presented to the family, to Tad and his mother. . . .

[IN THE SUMMER of 1862, a New Hampshire officer, Colonel Scott, whose wife was killed in a steamship accident on the Potomac River, decided to go to the Soldiers' Home to directly petition President Lincoln. He wanted permission to enter what was declared a war zone in Virginia to] pick up his wife's body and take her back to New Hampshire for burial.

The idea that a colonel who went through a tragedy like that would approach the president and ask for an exception is an idea that fits with our concept of Abraham Lincoln. But what happened at the Soldiers' Home is interesting. [Colonel Scott] discovered Lincoln in the drawing room or parlor of the cottage with his shoes off. It was late afternoon or early evening on an August day in Washington. It was hot. Lincoln was fanning himself . . . tired at the end of a long day. Scott poured out his heart to him, told him the whole story about his wife and how he wanted to recover her body. All of us would expect Lincoln to respond to that with charity and sympathy, but instead he responded with anger: ["Am I to have no rest? Is there no hour or spot when or where I may escape this constant call? Why do you follow me out here with such business as this? Why do you not go to the War Office, where they have charge of all this matter of papers and transportation?"]

Then he dismissed Scott. He had made a long sort of litany of complaints, but that one complaint sticks in my mind. "Am I to have no rest?"

A weary president in the middle of a tough war, confronted with a personal appeal sent the man away without a favor.

Then the next day . . . Lincoln woke up to what he had done and called for Scott and made the arrangements to allow him to have this. As a historian, I see a story like that and I wonder if it's true.

The details, to an amazing degree, can be corroborated. There was a Baltimore newspaper that reported a list of the survivors, naming Scott, interviewing him, talking about the steamship accident, giving the dates and times of the collision, and even reporting his wife as one of the dead, which, to me, adds lot of credibility to the story.

You see in this one moment . . . this incredible, vivid recollection, supported by some contemporary documents that make me think, the gist of the story probably is true, which is that Lincoln was tired, fed up, and irritable when Scott approached him originally.

There's nothing exactly new about that story, although you can look high and low in Lincoln biographies, and I don't think you'll see it. . . .

WHEN LINCOLN DECIDED to live outside of the White House, it created a security problem. He was commuting every day, living away from the center of town. Also the Soldiers' Home was in a rural area then, relatively easy to attack.

Lincoln would ride back and forth [to the Soldiers' Home] on horseback or in a carriage. The typical route might be down what was then the 7th Street Turnpike into the city, and Rhode Island Avenue to Vermont and then into Lafayette Square. But there were several routes in and out of the city—a variety of options.

[IN THE EARLY DAYS] Lincoln would typically ride alone. . . . In the summer of '62 someone wrote William Seward [secretary of state] to say this was dangerous, that the president shouldn't ride back and forth alone at night to the Soldiers' Home.

Seward was a close associate of the president's. He was in his cabinet, but he was also a friend. Seward responded to this letter and to say that assassination was not an American habit. Don't worry about this, essentially. He said that he himself rode back and forth to the Soldiers' Home all hours of the day. But other people were beginning to worry, not just about assassination but also about the idea of the Confederates launching an invasion into nearby Maryland, which they did after the second battle of Bull Run.

It's shocking to our sensibilities, but you have to remember there was no precedent for assassination or even an assault on the president. There had been a deranged man who attacked Andrew Jackson. There had been some threats against Franklin Pierce, and he'd had a bodyguard briefly. But assassination was something that had not occurred to many people. Of course, some increasingly began to worry about it. And that's why, in the fall of '62, they decided to assign soldiers, an infantry company, to the Soldiers' Home itself and a cavalry escort to follow the president back and forth.

There were about one hundred soldiers in the infantry company, and in that first summer, the company from the cavalry that escorted the president, about eighty-five soldiers. And they rotated them. So in a typical escort, he might have twenty or twenty-five soldiers.

JOHN W. NICHOLS was a private in the company from Pennsylvania. He said that in the summer of '64, one evening, there was a gunshot, and a horse came galloping with President Lincoln on it, hatless. Lincoln claims that the gunshot had scared the horse, somebody had fired a gun off accidentally, and everything was fine. But Nichols and another soldier who was on guard duty with him were suspicious. They walked around the pathways and the grounds of the Soldiers' Home, and they found Lincoln's signature hat with a bullet hole through the crown. He claimed they took the hat to the president the next morning and Lincoln said, "Let's just keep this between us."

That story was published in a newspaper interview after the war. Other people adopted the story and claimed it as their own. I'm not sure I believe that story, either, but it's hard to dispute. It's an eyewitness who is recalling an event. One thing that corroborates that story is important: After the alleged incident took place in the summer of 1864, they increased the security around the president. They began deploying Washington police detectives around the president more frequently in the fall of '64. And there is a letter from a nurse who used to come out to the Soldiers' Home to take care of Tad. She says that "Aunt Mary"—Mary Dimes, the cook—said there had been a lot of threats against the president, and they had been increasing security. So maybe it's believable.

ONE OF THE SOLDIERS in the company, Willard Cutter, was twenty-five at the outset of the war. His father had died just before the war began. His mother was worried. She was recently widowed and now was sending a son off to war. She begged him to write frequently. He said, "You're awfully tenderhearted. Do you think you're the only mother with a son in the army?" But he was a good son, and he wrote her 150 letters, almost one letter a week.

Cutter was with the infantry company originally assigned to the Soldiers' Home in the fall of '62 and spent the rest of the war following the president's family. The president made the decision at the end of the fall to keep the company with him. They went to the White House each winter, and they went out with the family to the Soldiers' Home. So [Cutter was] with the Lincolns for three years, wrote 150 letters [to his mother] that the family kept in a box, which were passed [from] one generation to the next.

Finally, the Cutters donated the letters to a local college, Allegheny College, but the only people who knew about them were Civil War re-enactors from Meadville, Pennsylvania—a group of dedicated amateur historians.

When the Soldiers' Home restoration project, sponsored by the National Trust, became widely publicized around the summer of 2000, the Meadville re-enactors contacted people at the Soldiers' Home and at the National Trust, and they sent a transcript of one of the letters to these folks. When I went down [to Washington] to initialize the restoration project, they passed along a box to me, and in that box was this transcript. I had never heard of Willard Cutter, and I never knew that there were letters from a soldier who guarded the Lincolns. And I had read a lot of Lincoln books.

So I started e-mail contact with these re-enactors and eventually went up to Allegheny College to read these letters. It is a remarkable body of testimony from an admittedly secondary figure, but to me, it was a wake-up call. If so many years can pass and we still haven't examined the testimony of figures like Willard Cutter, then we need to work a little harder at breaking down these boundaries between historians and being better detectives.

THE YEAR 1863 WAS a turning point for the war and for the president's family. In July of 1863, the battle at Gettysburg absorbed the nation; it was the largest conflict of the war. The president was following every detail at the War Department Telegraph Office. On the second day of the battle, his wife was traveling from the Soldiers' Home to Mount Pleasant Hospital, which was not far. There were several hospitals near the Soldiers' Home. There was an accident with her carriage; some of the bolts became loose, and she was thrown. At first, they didn't think her injuries were too severe, but then she got infected, and almost died. She was severely wounded by the infection and struggled for weeks.

This all occurred in the president's life while he was dealing with the aftereffects of the battle of Gettysburg. Gettysburg was a Union triumph, but for the president it was a tremendous disappointment. He wanted General Meade to follow through on the battlefield victory and capture Lee's army before they crossed back over the Potomac River, and he was incredibly agitated that it didn't happen. His agitation over Meade's failure to pursue Lee almost overwhelmed his concern for his wife. This man was struggling between a private crisis and a public catastrophe in his mind, and was stretched to the breaking point.

Robert Lincoln [the oldest son] had very few interactions with his father during the course of the war. They had a strained relationship, but he was back from Harvard that summer. He went to see his father. He'd actually delayed coming back until his father sent him a very sharp note when his mother got sick, saying, "Come home." Robert Lincoln arrived at the White House to accompany his father back to the Soldiers' Home. It was a vivid scene; the president literally put his head on his desk and appeared on the verge of tears. He complained not about his wife but about General Meade in the middle of July 1863: Why couldn't Meade follow through on this victory? Lincoln said, "I could have whipped Bobby Lee myself."

It was a turbulent period, but the Gettysburg victory was the turning point, and the fall of Vicksburg in the West changed the nature of the war. It became clear from that point forward that Lincoln and the Union would prevail. Robert Lincoln said [Mary Todd Lincoln was never the same again] so it was a turning point in her life, too. The head injury might have affected her moods. She had mood swings and health problems. The carriage accident might have made it worse.

[THERE WAS A CEMETERY on the property of the Soldiers' Home] which was a precursor to Arlington National Cemetery. It was a U.S. national cemetery that was created at the beginning of the war and was overrun by gravestones that led to the decision to expand and create a national cemetery on Robert E. Lee's farm in Arlington. President Lincoln reportedly walked along the rows of gravestones at night and during the day when he was collecting his thoughts.

In the summer of 1863 he was living at the Soldiers' Home taking these walks; [the cemetery] was just across the road from the cottage. [Lincoln] returned from the Soldiers' Home to the White House just a few weeks before he went to Gettysburg in late November 1863, to dedicate the national cemetery.

Lincoln collected his ideas for that speech in some measure while he was living [at the Soldiers' Home]. On July 4, 1863, a group of citizens came to serenade the White House and they asked the president to give a speech. They asked the president to talk about the meaning of Independence Day in the middle of this war. Lincoln began his speech by asking, "How long ago was it, eighty odd years?" A few months later his thoughts had coalesced, and he moved from eighty odd years to fourscore and seven years ago. The sanctuary he found at the Soldiers' Home, the ideas he developed walking along those gravestones in Washington before he went to Gettysburg in Pennsylvania is what helped him evolve from eighty odd years to fourscore and develop this idea of the new birth of freedom.

[Lincoln] had evolved to the point where he was comfortable as commander in chief and president, where he was self-assured. He had grown, and that growth was the result of a sense of poise and equilibrium he got in part because he found sanctuary at the Soldiers' Home.

★ ★
★

Photographic Imagery

DAVID WARD

David Ward is a historian at the National Portrait Gallery of the Smithsonian Institution. He was curator of the Portrait Gallery's exhibit "One Life: The Mask of Lincoln" about which he gave this interview to C-SPAN in April 2008 as part of the network's yearlong Lincoln bicentennial coverage.

Lincoln came of political age in a year in which photography was rising as the so-called democratic art. Photography in the nineteenth century allowed a new dynamism to appear in the representation of likenesses. It could be used in many ways; it could be manipulated or posed. What Lincoln realized very early on was that this new democratic art was the art of the people. It was inexpensive, not elite like oil painting. Just as Lincoln represented the democratic impulses of America, photography represented those impulses as well. Lincoln exploited the new technology in innovative ways. Political partisans would display and declare their allegiance by wearing [a political pin or] an image on their person, parading their allegiance and fealty to their champion. This was a dynamic way in which, Lincoln realized, photography could be used for his own advancement, for his party, and for the Union.

AMERICAN POLITICS until then had been oriented toward the Eastern seaboard and the South. The West had been unrepresented largely in the presidency, and Lincoln was not only geographically different, coming from Illinois, but he was socially different. He was a new man who had come out of nowhere. His family background was poor. His aspirations could only be achieved through his own work. The great poet of democracy, Walt Whitman, not even knowing of Lincoln's existence, foretold his appearance as the sixteenth president when he wrote in his political pam-

phlet, "I would be much pleased to see some heroic, shrewd, fully un-
formed, healthy body, middle-aged beard-faced American blacksmith or
boat man, come down from the West, across the Alleghenies, and walk into
the presidency dressed in a clean suit of working attire and with a tan all
over his face, breast, and arms. I would certainly vote for that sort of man."

LINCOLN WAS NOT particularly or conventionally handsome. He was a
striking-looking man, but he admitted that he was no beauty. Nonetheless,
Lincoln's relationship with his photographers was such that he could present himself in a striking and even romantic way. He had tousled hair, a
flamboyant tie; his aquiline features gazed off into the distance.

[THERE'S A LINCOLN] photograph wonderfully mounted in an ornate
case that, when closed, looks almost like a Bible or some form of scripture.
[Inside] is a picture of Abraham Lincoln—the rawboned man from the
West, conventionally unhandsome, and the political champion of the new
emerging Republican party. In this picture, Lincoln is positioning himself
as a national candidate, conveying a sense of authority, a sense of competence that he had to convey in order to convince the rest of the party and
the American people that he could bear the burdens of the office. Lincoln
is beginning to fashion himself in a way that would appeal to Americans,
both as a candidate and ultimately, as he hoped, as president.

Abraham Lincoln went to New York in February 1860, to introduce himself to the Eastern audience—everybody from the common man to the good
and great of the Republican Party, including Horace Greeley, the newspaper
editor. [He went] at the specific invitation of Henry Ward Beecher, the most
popular preacher of his time. Originally, Lincoln was going to speak at
Beecher's church in Brooklyn, but the novelty of his appearance in New
York caused them to move the event to a much larger hall in the Cooper
Union in lower Manhattan. There, Lincoln laid out a very careful legal, historic, and rhetorical brief against slavery, against disunion, and against the
possibility that the South would rebel against the laws of the land.

Lincoln realized, with his command of political symbolism, that words
were not enough. The appeal and charisma of his appearance as a presidential candidate had to be backed up with other signs and instruments. At
the same time that he was laying out this careful constitutional and historical brief, Lincoln had his picture taken by Mathew Brady, the great photographer. Brady created a master image of the picture and also created thousands of what we call *cartes de visites*, images of the presidential candidate on
cards the size of visiting cards. This shows the transformation of high art
into popular art, the use of photography as a way of identifying yourself to

the public not through your writings or through your name, but through your very image.

We remember many of Lincoln's speeches, but, surprisingly enough, he didn't give that many formal orations. Cooper Union is one, as were the First and Second inaugurals, as well as the famous Gettysburg Address. Lincoln realized he could command power by being reticent. As concomitant to that, he knew that he had to keep in fashion for the American people. Here again he relied on photography to present a commanding image, just as he would through his words. [He appeared as] the firm-faced Lincoln, the man setting himself toward the future, the man who had come out of nowhere and become a national presidential candidate.

Lincoln's internal evolution on this issue is very interesting. In 1860, he was asked about his background by a campaign biographer. He said, "My history is what the poet called the short and simple annals of the poor. And neither you nor anyone else will get anything beyond that." Lincoln was not only [referring] to the fact that his life had been hard, as many Americans lives had been hard, but he was also rhetorically sealing himself off from his own past. He was putting aside his youth and upbringing, and setting his ambitions on the presidency.

When traveling from Philadelphia through Maryland to Washington, DC, Lincoln's bodyguard received word that there might be an assassination plot. They advanced the schedule and moved his train in the early morning into Washington, DC. When news of this leaked out, it was greeted with derision from the South and his enemies. A cartoonist created a political image of Lincoln sneaking into town in his nightcap and nightgown to drive home the point of Lincoln's fear. You see a 'fraidy cat arching its back and Lincoln recoiling from the image of the cat, let alone the reality of what faces him. The cartoonist depicts Lincoln with his newly grown beard. There has been speculation about why he chose to grow a beard, having previously been clean-shaven. The common response is an anecdote that a young girl wrote to him and suggested he would look better if he grew a beard. This may be true. We can go beyond this to speculate about the reasons for the beard. It may tie in with the fact that Lincoln knew he was going to war. In times of war and domestic trouble, where violence looks like it will occur, men going back to even the Greek myths have grown beards to assume a more barbaric aspect. He was girding himself for that battle.

IN THE NINETEENTH CENTURY, the Patent Office building [today the site of the National Portrait Gallery] situated at 8th and E streets, was the center of old downtown Washington, equidistant between Capitol Hill and the White House. It was a focal point of Washington life and work. The Patent

Office building was a temple of American invention, which Walt Whitman called the noblest of Washington buildings. Abraham Lincoln's Second Inaugural ball was held on the third floor, and Lincoln himself came to visit the wounded [soldiers] that were brought there. Along its streets were the photography studios of Alexander Gardner, Mathew Brady, and others where Lincoln frequently came to have his picture taken. . . .

The National Portrait Gallery has many images of Lincoln, including two life masks of the president. One was taken in 1860 and the other in 1865. In the nineteenth century, it was in vogue to take plaster casts of people and create an absolute replica of the individual. The 1860 image shows Lincoln un-bearded, fresh-faced, and at the outset of his presidency. The 1865 image was done two months before his assassination. In many ways we can see it as a death mask: His face is careworn; his eye sockets are deep. He now has a beard. The grooves in the plaster show the lines in his face and replicate the tiredness and fatigue. In addition to the life masks, there were also casts created of Lincoln's hands. Lincoln's hands were interesting: large and gnarled. His hands were extraordinarily big and strong. He was self-conscious about them, but they were an emblem of where he came from and where you could go.

[IN APRIL 1863,] the spring campaigning season was about to begin, and the war still had to be won. It was a difficult year for Abraham Lincoln, yet it was capped by a victory at Gettysburg, in which the Union finally defeated the South's invasion of the North for the last time, and the tide began to turn. Lincoln went to Gettysburg in November to commemorate the cemetery there and delivered the Gettysburg Address, probably the most famous oration in American history. The next time that we see Lincoln [in photographs] is after Gettysburg, after that momentous battle had been won and the tide of the war had turned. Lincoln was firmly in charge now. He was in charge of the military and in charge of the civil administration, including his own cabinet, which was fractious at the time. But as the war was being won, its toll was being taken on Lincoln. You can see it in his face. His hair is beginning to recede. We are beginning to see the lines that we see in the [1865] life mask emerging on his face.

In 1909, [an 1864 photographic image of Lincoln] was used to create the new United States penny. It's a profile portrait of Lincoln in which he assumes an almost magisterial pose similar to the classical bust of antiquity. By the [time he posed for this], he was fully attuned to the demands of photography and the image that he wanted to portray. Going from the tousled hair to this monumental bust-like appearance, he had grown fully into the role and fully expressed the charisma and power of the presidency. As

Lincoln achieved in office and mastered the art of government and photography, even his fiercest critics and rivals began to recognize that something extraordinary had happened. The gawky, homely man from Illinois with his trousers ending four inches above his shoes had grown in stature physically and metaphorically. Charles Francis Adams, the haughty aristocrat from Boston, had begun by disparaging Lincoln in both his appearance and intellect. By 1864, even Adams was convinced and described Lincoln as the only man who was capable of doing the job.

The last photograph taken of Lincoln alive was a kind of ambush portrait taken by the paparazzi of the day. A photographer had been taking candid snaps of Lincoln's young son Tad and took advantage of Lincoln's relationship with the boy to get Lincoln to pose for him. Lincoln was not too pleased with this intrusion on his time, but he indulged Tad and stepped out on the balcony of the White House and had his picture taken for immortality.

[Lincoln's last formal sitting with photographer Alexander Gardner came in February 1865.] Lincoln had been to see the defeated Confederate capital [of Richmond], and it was a time for celebration throughout the Union. Yet Lincoln was unable to escape the burdens of his office. He was careworn, shrunken, turned into himself. His eye sockets were even deeper than they had been. The lines on his face were even more funereal. The life mask is beginning to resemble a death mask.

The full formal image that was created in the last session with Alexander Gardner is called the "cracked-plate Lincoln." Gardner, when taking it out of the camera, bent the plate so it cracked in half. We see this line running from the upper left. [It] threw Lincoln's head off to the other side. It is impossible to look at the picture and not see the foreshadowing of the death of Lincoln two months later. In many ways, the crack seems to foreshadow the path of John Wilkes Booth's bullet. And in Lincoln's face we can see even more the cares and the toil and the wearing out of the man during the war.

[The cracked-plate Lincoln] is one of the great works of art in American history. It marks the arrival of photography as a genuine form of art instead of just a mechanical process. In the picture, we see the full range of the photographer's ability to convey not just a likeness, but to suggest an inner man.

★ ★
★

At the End

JAY WINIK

Historian Jay Winik appeared on Booknotes *on July 20, 2000, to discuss his book* April 1865: The Month That Saved America *(HarperCollins), which was the recipient of the first Walt Whitman Civil War Roundtable Award. Mr. Winik is senior scholar of history and public policy at the University of Maryland and a frequent commentator for national news organizations such as the* Wall Street Journal *and the* New York Times.

The question of how wars end is every bit as important as why they start or how they're fought. Put differently, far too many civil wars throughout history ended quite badly. Think of Northern Ireland; it's gone on for some two hundred years. Think of Lebanon, Rwanda, Cambodia. Think of the horrors of the Middle East or the Balkans. Our Civil War could have ended just as badly, with the same terrible, tragic consequences, but didn't. Why?

[CONSIDER] THE MONTH of April 1865. Let's not take it in the South, but let's move it into the North to a meeting that Abraham Lincoln had with his two top generals, U. S. Grant and Bill Sherman. He wanted to talk about the war: when it would end, what would happen, how it would happen. One of the first things he said to Grant was, "Must more blood be shed; must there be a final bloody Armageddon?"

Picture Lincoln for a second. Just imagine it in your mind's eye: he was so exhausted and worn by this tornado and wreckage of war. He was thirty pounds underweight. His hands were routinely cold and clammy. He was so sick of this ongoing war, he had recently held a cabinet meeting from his bed. Grant shook his head sadly and said, "Lee being Lee"—Robert E. Lee, the commanding general of the Confederate army—"more blood will be shed."

Then Lincoln talked about his other great fear: He worried about the Confederates taking off into the hills with their hearty horses and hearty men; in other words, guerrilla warfare. That was an option that lay before the Confederates. That was what Lincoln feared; that was what Grant feared; it was what Sherman feared. When Lee was about to be surrounded—he was surrounded in the south and east and west, every direction but north—it was at that point where he convened a council of war. In this council one of his most trusted aides, E. P. Alexander, said, "We can take to the hills like partridges and rabbits. A little more bloodshed now will make no difference."

He was talking about what Jefferson Davis, the Confederate president, was calling for: guerrilla and partisan warfare—in effect, the Vietnamization of America. This was the decision that lay before Robert E. Lee.

It was in City Point [Virginia] that Lincoln, in that same meeting where he talked about his fears of guerrilla warfare . . . did something quite unique. Abraham Lincoln said, "When this war is over, there must be no hangings; there must be no bloody work." What was looming large in his mind was the specter of the French Revolution because it loomed large in the minds of all Americans. . . . In the French Revolution, the revolutionaries started out with the best of intentions, and before everybody knew it, they were guillotining the opposition and each other, and soon it would engulf the entire continent.

What Lincoln was saying was, "There must be no French Revolution here." It was prescient, it was visionary, and it was one of Lincoln's finest acts. Grant would carry it out brilliantly at Appomattox during the surrender, where rather than treating Lee like a defeated, dishonored foe, he would treat him with great dignity and grace. It would be one of the most poignant scenes in our history.

Throughout history, far too many civil wars end with bloodshed—with hangings or killings or beheadings. Think about the morning that Lee made this fateful decision that he was going to surrender. He straightened himself up and said, "Now I must go meet General Grant, and I would rather die a thousand deaths than do that." History has, more often than not, telescoped and simplified what happened, said that Lee was vain and quixotic in retreat, and then said there was the dignity of Appomattox, the end of the war, end of story.

In truth, it was far richer. How would Lee be treated when he went to meet U. S. Grant? Lee didn't know. What we do know is that Lee, that morning, was actually quite nervous, uncharacteristically so. He was speaking in mumbled half-sentences. He should have been nervous because throughout history, as he knew all too well, defeated generals and revolutionaries and traitors were typically beheaded, or they were hanged, or they were imprisoned or, like General Napoleon, they were exiled.

That very morning, the *Chicago Tribune* editorialized: "Hang Lee." Just days earlier, in the Union capital of Washington, DC, Andrew Johnson, the vice president of the Union, went out with several senators and before a thronging crowd of hundreds, maybe over one thousand, and gave a rousing speech in which he said, "We must hang Davis; we must hang Lee. We must hang them twenty times." So, Lee didn't know what to expect. That Grant would treat him with such tenderness and dignity, it's such a rich scene. He was carrying out Lincoln's vision at City Point of no bloody work, no hangings. But it was really unique in the chain of history.

[Grant and Lee] didn't know each other well at West Point, but what is interesting are the bonds that are forged in war. Let's go to the Wilderness Campaign, the six-week campaign in 1864, before they began the siege in Richmond and Petersburg; it was where Lee and Grant squared off for the first time.

In the first two days of the Wilderness, Grant lost 17,500 men. He went into his tent that night and wept like a baby. The next morning when he came out, everybody expected him to do what every other Union general had done: retreat. Memorably, Grant said, "We will fight it out if it takes all summer." Of course, it would take all year. Just a few weeks later, at Cold Harbor, in the first nine minutes alone, Grant would lose ten thousand men. That was twice as many men as the Confederates would lose in the entirety of the Gettysburg conflict. He did it within ten minutes. In this entire six-week skirmish, Grant would lose as many men as Lee had in his entire army, and he would lose as many men as we would lose in the entirety of the Vietnam War. So out of this ghastly warfare, this bloody battling, the irony was that these two men came to respect each other, to almost fear each other, and to admire each other.

. . . Interestingly enough, when they first walked into Appomattox Court House, Lee was wearing his finest uniform because, as he said, "Now I must become General Grant's prisoner." Grant, who kept him waiting for thirty minutes, came in a mud-spattered private's blouse. Later, Grant would apologize for how he was attired.

Picture this scene for a second: this small home, the Wilmer McLean house, in Appomattox Court House, a little village of about eight structures and rolling hills. Outside in these rolling hills were thousands of men who were standing at rapt attention, watching this amazing piece of historical theater take place. In fact, when the surrender was over, everything would be ripped apart from the Wilmer McLean house: the desk, the pens, the floorboards, and the wallpaper. Even a tree that Lee himself leaned against that morning would be ripped apart so there was nothing left except for a hole. Everybody knew that history was taking place that day, and they wanted a piece of it.

Grant came inside this small home and rather than talking about the surrender, they talked about the old days. Grant said, "I remember you from the Mexican War." Lee looked at him and said, "All these times in this battle, I've tried to recall your face. I could never quite do it." They continued to chat happily. Grant told us that they continued on, and it was eventually Lee who said, "I suppose we must discuss the object at hand, the surrender."

So though they didn't know each other, the bonds that were forged and the closeness they had almost defied the fact that they were the greatest of nemeses one could imagine.

Robert E. Lee surrendered to U. S. Grant, [in] this dignified, honorable surrender, yet he only surrendered his army. There were still three Confederate armies in the field. There were over 175,000 men, their murderous gunbarrels hot to the bitter end. There was Jefferson Davis, the Confederate president, calling for guerrilla warfare. Even Mary Lee, Robert E. Lee's wife, who was directly descended from Martha Washington and great-granddaughter by marriage to George Washington, said, "Robert E. Lee is not the Confederacy. Richmond is not the Confederacy." That was how volatile the situation still was.

Lincoln feared [and wondered] how much longer would the war last. A week? Three weeks? Three months? Six months? Lincoln knew that throughout history, such timespans had been enough to start, fight, and win wars, to unseat great dynasties or to complicate the reconciliation to come. Five days later, Lincoln was dead. He was killed on April 14 at 10:14 at night. William Seward, the Union's secretary of state, was stabbed five times. [Lincoln's] wife was soon screaming, "They've murdered my husband! They murdered my husband!" Only Andrew Johnson escaped unscathed.

The irony of that night was that Andrew Johnson was also invited to Ford's Theatre. He turned it down, saying, "I'm tired. I want to have a quiet, little supper and then turn in." He did this not realizing that on the very floor above him in his hotel was another deadly assassin who was going to plunge a knife into his heart. At the last second, the assassin got cold feet, and so Johnson escaped. Had Johnson been assassinated that night, there would have been a complete decapitation of the Union government.

ONE OTHER THING that really struck me about that night in the Petersen House, [was] when Lincoln lay dying. We heard a lot about Alexander Haig during the attempted assassination of Ronald Reagan saying, "I'm in control here," and how that was seen as a really rogue act. Well, on the night of April 14 and then April 15, when Lincoln died, from this small room in the center of the Petersen House, the secretary of war for the Union, Edwin Stanton, was literally running the country. He had become the president, the vice president, the secretary of war, the secretary of state, and a comforter-in-chief, all wrapped into one. It shows you just how different the world they inhabited was from ours.

[Mary Todd Lincoln's reaction to her husband's assassination] struck a chord of both poignancy and pathos in me because her husband has just been shot. His brains had essentially been blown out before her eyes. That night, she was weeping and wailing by his side. At one point—again, to show the power of Edwin Stanton—Mary had gotten so out of hand that at one juncture, he screamed, "Take that woman out of there." It would never happen with a modern first lady. But in fact, Mary was actually removed to the front room of the Petersen House where she continued to weep and wail. It was only around 7:19 a.m., or thereabouts, that she was allowed to be back with her husband. She was screaming, "Oh, what have you done to take him from me, God?" Or "Bring Taddy to him. Abe loves him so." It had to have been such a poignant night.

I HAD FIGURED THAT the transition mechanism, vice president becoming president, was all very simple and laid out. The president dies, and the vice president becomes president, end of story. In fact, the picture was far murkier and far more complex in April 1865. Because as it turns out, the founders did not intend for the vice president to become president. They only intended for the vice president to temporarily act as president until there was an election. At that point, there would be a new president. So on that fateful evening, Lincoln was shot, and Seward was ailing with five wounds, and Johnson, whom nobody ever expected to be president, had met with Abraham Lincoln only once by happenstance on the day of the assassination for thirty minutes. To this day, we still don't know what they talked about. Johnson was widely written off as a buffoon in Washington circles. In fact, during the Second Inaugural, while Johnson was rambling on and on because he was drunk that night, the attorney general said, "Take that deranged man out of there." That's what low regard [official Washington had for] Andrew Johnson.

That evening, the temptations were for a regency or a cabinet-style government. After the assassination of Lincoln, there would be such turmoil, such chaos and anarchy gripping the Union capital. The *New York Times* would editorialize: "If this were France, all the country would be in bloody revolution by twenty-four hours." They were in such turmoil that the Union cabinet would soon be discussing whether in effect, a Napoleonic coup was under way. Who did they think was behind it? None other than one of their greatest generals, Bill Sherman. That's why I think it's so important to go back and re-create the world, not as we see it with hindsight, but as they saw it, so we can see the turning points that they confronted.

THE UNION WAS IN total chaos. What took place in the Bennett House in North Carolina [April 1865] was the final surrender of the other principal army of the Confederacy, which was commanded by General Joe Johnston.

THERE WERE TEN days worth of negotiations where Sherman first sat down with Johnston and John Breckinridge, who was a former [Confederate] vice president. At one point, the Confederates would be laying down such terms, and Sherman would move his chair back and say, "Well, see here, who's surrendering to whom?" In fact, Sherman would give very generous terms to the Confederates. In doing so, he thought he was carrying out Lincoln's vision, but he would be sharply rebuked by the Union cabinet, particularly after the death of Lincoln. Grant was actually sent down to talk to Sherman. That was a fascinating scene, too, because in the Union capital when this happened, the attorney general, James Speed, said, "What if Sherman decides to arrest Grant?" Speed and Stanton were convinced that Sherman was potentially thinking of some kind of a coup. As they [feared], he was getting ready to march northward with his legions to take over. That's the kind of chaos and anarchy that was gripping the North post-Lincoln assassination while there were still Confederate armies in the field.

If Johnston and Lee had decided to go to the hills, had started sanctioning guerrilla warfare, we would have been in a real mess. But Johnston instead followed Lee's example and he, too, would surrender, in this act of basic insubordination. In doing so, it would pave the way for this country to become not like the Balkans, not like the Middle East, not like Lebanon or Cambodia or these other civil war–torn countries, but to become America today.

Aftermath

TOM SCHWARTZ

*Illinois State Historian Tom Schwartz joined C-SPAN's Wash-
ington Journal on November 17, 2002, to talk about the
dedication of the Lincoln Presidential Library in Springfield,
Illinois.*

[**LINCOLN'S SECOND** vice president, Andrew] Johnson was a Democrat who, during the Civil War, remained staunchly in favor of the
Union. Tennessee was a very crucial state, and unfortunately was divided in a way where the Union forces controlled the western part [of the
state], which had strong Southern philosophies, while the eastern part of
the state, which was very loyal to the Union, was controlled by the Confederacy. That provided a very volatile situation. Lincoln, and indeed many,
felt that having Johnson represent that kind of Unionist force in Tennessee
was a very positive thing, something that should be promoted. By getting
rid of Hannibal Hamlin from Maine, who was a staunch abolitionist, and
replacing him with Andrew Johnson [as the vice presidential candidate in
1864], people often point to the fact that Lincoln and the Republican Party
were looking forward to reconciliation with the South after the war.

THERE'S NO DOUBT that Reconstruction was an awesome task. Clearly,
Andrew Johnson was not up to the task. It's unclear what Lincoln would have
done differently and whether even he would have been able to overcome all
of the obstacles of Reconstruction. Lincoln was more of an astute politician.
He had a fine-tuned ear to criticism and would have been much more able to
work with Congress and his opposition in looking for a good result.

LINCOLN WAS A MAN of his times, and certainly while growing up he was
always antislavery and in many ways he supported women's right to vote.
He supported the expansion of rights to all people. The fact that he

talked in the 1858 debates about blacks not being equal to whites was a political tactic. Clearly, no abolitionist, no one arguing for the equality of the races, could reasonably have been elected to the Senate in Illinois, or to the presidency.

You have to look at what happened in the presidency and how the war changed the whole landscape of understanding about the question of slavery. Lincoln grew in his understanding about the question. He understood he needed blacks in uniform in order to help the Northern war effort; it would have been very difficult if not impossible to win the war without the black military effort. In that, he saw that blacks needed to be rewarded for their efforts. It was more than just ending bondage but, rather, giving them a place at the table.

LINCOLN REMAINS CONTROVERSIAL to this day. The idea that he was the father of big central government is retold in several recent books, such as Thomas DiLorenzo's *The Real Lincoln*. Most scholars, however, would temper that claim, pointing to the contingencies, the necessities of fighting a civil war and keeping the nation united.

This is a country of many voices, and they all need to be heard. We may not think that they are all reasonable or carry the same weight, but we [believe we should] let people sort through the evidence and come to their own conclusions.

★ ★
★

The Assassination

EDWARD STEERS, JR.

Booknotes hosted Edward Steers, Jr., on February 17, 2002, to discuss his book, Blood on the Moon: The Assassination of Abraham Lincoln, *published by the University Press of Kentucky. Dr. Steers currently serves as the Internet editor of the* Lincoln Herald *and is also an associate editor for* North & South *magazine.*

At the time of the assassination, John Wilkes Booth was one month short of his twenty-seventh birthday. He shot Lincoln point-blank with a 41-caliber Derringer, a single-shot pistol, probably within two feet of the back of his head.

JOHN WILKES BOOTH, at the time one of America's greatest tragedians, [was] of the famous Booth family, a Maryland family, from Bel Air, Maryland. By 1864, he had become certainly one of America's greatest actors and a matinee idol—extremely handsome, personable, well-liked, generous, outgoing. Seems he had everything going for him, and everybody liked him. He had no enemies at all.

ON APRIL 9 . . . Lee surrendered the Army of Northern Virginia. The city of Washington was celebrating wildly every day. There were illuminations [lighting displays] throughout the city. It's hard for us to understand today, but they were rather spectacular—everything is illuminated with all forms of light. Lincoln and Mary Lincoln were having a night out of relaxation, enjoyment, and celebrating what would effectively be viewed as the end of the war.

From Booth's perspective, of course, it wasn't the end of the war: There were still 175,000 Confederate troops in the field—about 85,000 in North

Carolina under Joe Johnston, about 55,000 in the trans-Mississippi area under Confederate General Kirby Smith, and then about 35,000 scattered in various places throughout the South. That's a substantial number of Confederate troops. Now, while it was impractical, the idea [of Booth and his fellow conspirators] was that if there was some way to join up those troops, you would have a formidable force that could face Sherman and Grant and perhaps continue the hopes of the Confederacy.

Booth entered the theater, which was crowded, virtually standing room. He had easy, full run of the theater, being a famous actor and a very close friend of the Ford family, of John Ford and his brother, Harry Clay Ford. Booth could come and go in the theater at will. He had reconnoitered the theater earlier in the day, made all of the arrangements, knew what he was going to do, knew when he was going to do it. So he just simply entered the theater, made his way up the staircase to the dress circle or balcony, and then slowly made his way across the back of the theater to the box.

Abraham Lincoln and his wife, Mary, were sitting on one side; on the other were Major Henry Rathbone and his fiancée and stepsister, Clara Harris. It was just the four of them.

[The bullet] entered the lower left base of Lincoln's skull. While there's some controversy as to the path of the bullet, I think most people agree that it traversed diagonally across the brain, lodging behind the right eye. He went comatose. He slumped in his chair. It wasn't a violent reaction on his part. His head just fell forward. Mary Lincoln, who was sitting right next to him, holding his hand, screamed. Pandemonium broke out. Major Rathbone realized what had happened, jumped up, and began to grapple with Booth.

Booth had a large Bowie knife, which he stabbed Rathbone with in the arm and then vaulted over the balustrade onto the floor of the theater stage, turned towards the audience, by most accounts, yelled "*Sic semper tyrannis*"—"Thus always to tyrants," which is Virginia's state motto—and then exited stage right. [He] went out the rear door into the alley behind the theater, known as Baptist Alley—Ford's Theatre had originally been the 10th Street Baptist Church—where his horse was being held by a young boy who worked for the Fords. He struck the boy, mounted the horse, wheeled around, and galloped down the alley, turned left, went up onto F Street, turned right, and headed for the Capitol grounds.

They tried to administer to [Lincoln] in the box. There were several doctors in the theater. The first doctor to get to the box was Charles Leale, who was an army sergeant. At first, he didn't know how the president was injured or to what extent, but he began to examine him, thinking that perhaps he had a chest wound, had been stabbed. At one point, he ran his fingers through Lincoln's hair and noticed blood on his hand. Then, of course, he found the entry wound. A blood clot had already formed, which essentially suppressed Lincoln's breathing. Leale removed the blood clot, and Lincoln began to breathe quite normally, and his pulse [was] restored. At that point, several other doctors came into the box. They consulted and pretty much agreed that they had to move Lincoln.

Laura Keene was starring in the play. It was a benefit performance for her that evening; that is, all of the proceeds from that evening would go to her as a reward and appreciation for her role as the star. *Our American Cousin*, which is a British spoof on American bumpkins, was a play that Lincoln would have enjoyed very much.

She made her way to the box, which is interesting: How was she able to make her way there? But she did, and she asked Leale if she could rest Lincoln's head in her lap. He said yes, and so she did.

They probably moved him over to the Petersen House, directly across the street, between 10:45 and 10:50. When they lifted him and started to carry him out of the theater, they weren't quite sure where to go. Obviously, they knew they would take him to a building or a home somewhere on the street. As they emerged from the front of the theater onto the sidewalk, they were beckoned by a young soldier across the street, who told them to bring Lincoln into this particular house that was the home of a tailor by the name of Petersen—a rather substantial home, three floors, several rooms. They took him into a back bedroom on what was the second floor.

[There is a remarkable picture from the scene at the Petersen House]. It's one of the most haunting pictures obviously taken very shortly after Lincoln's body was removed and taken back to the White House and everyone had left the Petersen House. There were two brother photographers who boarded at the Petersen House—Julius and Henry Ulke—who later became very well-known photographers in Washington. They brought down their wet plate camera, set it up, and shot a photograph. In that photograph, all the bed clothing was still on the bed. That coverlet on the bed showed up later in a few exhibitions but then disappeared. We don't know what happened to it or where it is today. Hopefully, it is in some private Lincoln collection somewhere.

When he was brought to the Petersen House and put in that bed, Lincoln was stripped naked. They removed all of his clothes and examined his body completely. . . . They agreed that the wound was mortal and there was nothing they could do except make him comfortable. And that's what they tried to do. They brought hot water bottles and mustard plasters, tried to warm his body because his extremities were very cold.

During the night—and he was there for nine hours, from 10:45 p.m. to 7:22 a.m., when he died—fifty-eight people visited the house. Of course, not all at once; there was no way they could fit in that room, [although] several etchings and drawings have shown fifty-eight people standing in the room around the bed; hence it's been dubbed the "rubber room." At the moment of his death, there were perhaps twelve people around the bed.

When they removed his body, it occurred to me that they obviously wouldn't remove a man like Abraham Lincoln naked. I found reports that they had sent for a very plain wooden pine box and wrapped his body in an American flag and placed the wrapped body in the box and then took it back to the White House. [Who knows] what happened to the flag? It would become an American icon.

[Lincoln's assassination] is a story that is filled with a great deal of myths and erroneous information. . . . One of the most prominent is that Edwin Stanton, Lincoln's secretary of war, was somehow behind Lincoln's assassination, that he engineered it together with radical Republicans to eliminate Lincoln, now that the war was essentially over, so that the radical Republicans could have their way with the South.

The myth that I like the best is that Mary Surratt and Samuel Mudd were innocent victims. Mary Surratt was the woman who owned Surratt Tavern in Surrattsville, and the boarding house in Washington not many blocks from Ford's Theatre, which became a center for the conspirators to meet, including John Wilkes Booth. Several of the conspirators boarded for a brief period at Mary Surratt's boarding house.

[Mary Surratt] . . . was one of four who were condemned to death by hanging and became in some ways a *cause celebre*, [though] not nearly as much as Dr. Mudd has. . . . Of course, there were many women who had been hanged, but [she was] the first by the federal government.

[The myth about Mudd was] that Dr. Samuel Mudd was nothing more than a simple country doctor who was prosecuted for nothing more than [applying] the Hippocratic Oath to an injured man who was seeking medical attention. Booth and [co-conspirator David] Herold arrived at Dr. Mudd's house four-and-a-half hours after the assassination. Dr. Mudd had also arranged an important meeting between John Wilkes Booth and Thomas Harbin at . . . the Bryantown Tavern in Bryantown, Maryland, very close to where Dr. Mudd lived.

[AFTER SHOOTING LINCOLN, Booth] headed over the Navy Yard Bridge, over the Anacostia or eastern branch of the Potomac River, directly into southern Maryland and went straight to the Surratt Tavern, which is approx-

imately thirteen miles southeast of Washington, where he picked up a car-
bine, a pair of binoculars, and some whiskey, and then headed on directly
to Dr. Mudd's house, where he arrived at 4 a.m.

There were ten conspirators who were eventually charged with Lincoln's
murder, but there were certainly many more people that had knowledge of
and participated in the conspiracy. . . . There were probably twenty-six
people who could have been charged under Stanton's edict of aiding and
abetting Booth both before and after the murder.

[On the night of the assassination, Secretary of State William] Seward
had been attacked by one of the conspirators, Lewis Powell, a key figure,
and one of the four to be hanged. Twenty-one years old at the time and a
very tall, athletic individual who had served with [Confederate Col. John]
Mosby, he was brought into the conspiracy, we believe, by John Surratt, the
son of Mary Surratt, another key figure and an individual introduced to
Booth by Dr. Mudd. That's another reason that I feel that Dr. Mudd is not
just a co-conspirator but a key conspirator—he brought two very important
people into the conspiracy, John Surratt and Thomas Harbin.

It was all very skillful. This belies one of the common beliefs that Lewis
Powell was of somewhat low mental capability, somewhat a stooge of John
Wilkes Booth. He shows a great deal of intelligence in how he handled himself. He went to Seward's house with a bottle of medicine. When he was met
at the door by one of Seward's servants, he said that Seward's doctor, Tulio
Verdi—who was, in fact, Seward's doctor, so Powell knew this—had sent this
medicine over, and he was to deliver it to Secretary Seward personally. He
forced his way into the hallway of the home and started to go up the steps
when Seward's son, Augustus Seward, met him and challenged him. Powell
still maintained that he was under orders to deliver the medicine only to
Seward.

Seward's son would not allow him further up the staircase. Powell
turned, as if he was going to go down the staircase, but then wheeled
around, pulled out his revolver and fired point-blank at Augustus Seward.
The gun misfired, so he bludgeoned him over the head with it, and very seriously fractured his skull. He then made his way to the Seward bedroom,
where he dove on top of Seward literally, with a Bowie knife, and just began
flailing and stabbing away at him. He was interrupted by a male nurse,
George Robinson, who had come into the room, hearing the shouts and
the screaming. They fought, and he stabbed Robinson.

This was going on at the same time, approximately, that Booth was shooting Lincoln, approximately at 10:30. So it was all coordinated, and that is
important . . . [Seward's] wounds were disfiguring. He was stabbed in the

face and it was a very serious cut that ran from ear to jaw, which disfigured him for life. But it wasn't in any way life-threatening to him. He actually fought back, even though he had a broken jaw—that's what he was recuperating from in bed—and struggled with Powell until help came in the way of George Robinson. Powell then turned, ran out of the room, down the stairs, out the front door, supposedly screaming, "I'm mad! I'm mad!"

David Herold was supposed to be tending Powell's horse outside. Herold, who was one of the conspirators in the plot and one of the four to be hanged, had accompanied Powell to Seward's house. [Herold] was a young twenty-one-year-old, and when he heard the sounds coming out of the Seward house and the screaming, he apparently panicked. We don't know that for sure, but that was the suspicion. He turned and rode away, leaving Powell's horse there but abandoning Powell.

Powell mounted his horse and headed out of the city, or tried to. We think that Herold was to accompany Powell because he didn't know his way around Washington. Presumably, Herold would lead Powell out of the city to rendezvous with Booth. But being abandoned, Powell rode off into the city, and all we know is that his horse was found in the vicinity of a congressional cemetery.

That night, four participated—Booth, George Atzerodt, Herold, and Powell. Atzerodt, was the man . . . who was assigned to assassinate Andrew Johnson, the vice president. Andrew Johnson was living at the Kirkwood Hotel, which was at 12th and Pennsylvania, a short distance away from Ford's Theatre. Atzerodt had taken a room early that morning in the Kirkwood Hotel and at approximately 10:30 p.m. was to go to the hotel, knock on the door, and assassinate Andrew Johnson.

He did go to there, to the Kirkwood, and ordered a drink at the bar. He was within feet of Johnson's room, but apparently his courage evaporated and he turned and fled, mounted his horse, and rode about the city. He saw and heard the commotion on 10th Street and realized that Booth had carried out the assassination of Lincoln. Atzerodt returned his horse to a stable, boarded a trolley, and went down to the Navy Yard and tried to stay there with a friend, but the friend refused to have him. So Atzerodt came back into the city on the trolley and checked into either the Pennsylvania House or Kimmel House Hotel and spent the night there.

Mary Surratt was in her boarding house on H Street where interestingly enough, she was visited at 2 o'clock that morning. She was widowed in 1862, when her husband died and left her with considerable debts but also with property—the Surratt Tavern, surrounding land, and the boarding house in Washington. She had three children—John, Isaac, and a younger daughter, Anna. Isaac was away serving in the Confederate army. John had come back home when his father died in order to help his mother. John actually became postmaster in Surrattsville. He was then discharged for disloyalty [and was] suspected of being a Confederate agent.

[Washington] was within the Union lines, but Washington, DC, was thoroughly a Southern city filled with Confederate sympathizers during the war. You have to remember that most of all the able-bodied men were gone into the Union army or fled south and joined the Confederate army.

Access into Washington was over a series of bridges—Long Bridge, the Navy Yard Bridge, the Benning Road Bridge. All of these bridges were guarded by Union troops, and passage in and out of the city was by permit only. However, it was not all that difficult to pass in and out of the city. It seems to me that most of the attention was paid at night and to people coming into the city, not leaving, because the threat posed to the city of Washington was people coming in, not people going out.

Maryland was in the Union, in essence, by force. The Maryland legislature was prevented from holding a convention to vote on secession. It isn't clear that they would have seceded, but they were arrested, held temporarily until the crisis passed, then released. Maryland remained in the Union, obviously, because Washington, DC, sits in Maryland, and you couldn't have the capital of the Union surrounded by Confederate territory.

Maryland was viewed, in many ways, as a Confederate state, certainly sympathizing with the Confederacy. All of southern Maryland, the six counties of southern Maryland, were as Confederate as Richmond. Maryland sent twice as many men into the Union army as it sent into the Confederate army. Those were mostly from northern and western Maryland.

THERE WERE SIX other conspirators tried: Samuel Arnold, Michael O'Laughlen, Mary Surratt, Edman Spangler, Dr. Mudd, and John Surratt. John Surratt was on his way to Canada. He was in Elmira, New York, at the moment that the assassination took place. He did make his way to Canada and was hidden by Jesuit priests there, who eventually helped him make his way to England. From England, he made his way to the Vatican, and he became a papal *zouave*—part of the papal guards in the Vatican. Ironically, an old schoolmate of his was also a papal *zouave*, and he recognized him as John Surratt. He had used the alias John Watson. Knowing that there was a reward for the capture of John Surratt of $25,000, he turned him in.

Surratt was taken into custody by the papal authorities, but managed a Hollywood-type escape, in which he literally jumped over a high precipice, made his way to the coastline, and boarded a freighter for Alexandria,

Egypt. He was arrested in February of 1867 in Alexandria and brought back to the United States and put on trial in June of 1867.

Samuel Arnold was another one of the conspirators. Samuel Arnold and Michael O'Laughlen . . . were two Baltimoreans who were childhood friends of John Wilkes Booth. Samuel Arnold attended Saint Timothy's Hall, which still exists, in Catonsville, Maryland, as a student. Michael O'Laughlen lived across the street from John Wilkes Booth in Baltimore. The Booths owned a home on Exeter Street, in addition to their home in Bel Air, Maryland.

These were the very first men who John Wilkes Booth recruited into his conspiracy. He met with them in August of 1864 in Baltimore at the Barnum Hotel, and he proposed this plot to capture Abraham Lincoln and take him south to Richmond.

For the capture plot, the motive was to presumably exchange Lincoln, use him as a bargaining chip. During the Civil War, they had a process known as "exchange," where prisoners were exchanged, rank for rank. So you could exchange a private for a private, a general for a general.

This was carried out throughout the war. When Grant became general in command of the army in March of 1864, he suspended prisoner exchange because the South was losing its manpower, and the North could keep replenishing its manpower. Grant realized that it was aiding the Confederacy to allow these Confederate prisoners to be exchanged and go back into the army.

So one of the motives Booth had was to capture Lincoln and take him to Richmond. The question is: How many soldiers is a president of the United States worth? A division? No one really knew.

Booth had actually entered into an earlier plot to capture Lincoln on March the 17th of 1865. He had found out after visiting Ford's Theatre earlier in the day that Lincoln was to attend a special performance of players at Campbell Hospital, which was on the northern boundary of Washington in those days. It's where Florida Avenue exists now, in northeast Washington.

Lincoln was to attend a performance, so Booth quickly gathered together his conspirators, and they went out to the vicinity of Campbell Hospital. Booth had the rest of his conspirators stay at a restaurant nearby while he went to Campbell Hospital, where he learned that Lincoln did not come to the performance; he had canceled his appearance and stayed in Washington.

There are some who feel that, early on, Stanton was a target, as was General Grant. It certainly appears as if Stanton's house was cased, in that an individual showed up there two days before. This came out later in the trial.

But we know nothing more than that, and it may or may not have happened that the house had been cased. Grant certainly appears to have been a target, but Grant left earlier in the afternoon, so he wasn't at Ford's Theatre.

THERE IS NO DIRECT evidence, or even a smoking gun, that you can place this [conspiracy] on the desk of Jefferson Davis. But certainly, the Confederate secret service knew about it and was involved in helping Booth assemble his conspiracy and helped him afterward to escape. So there are those who say—and I happen to believe this myself—that those agents would have never acted on their own and involved themselves with John Wilkes Booth. They weren't rogue agents. This information is something they would have reported up to their superiors, and their superiors clearly would have reported this up to Richmond.

The Civil War, characterized by Winston Churchill as "the last war fought by gentlemen," had deteriorated significantly. By 1864, we see the beginnings of "black flag" warfare, where acts began to take place that were outside the articles of war and outside the recognized rules of warfare, basically targeting civilian populations as well as civilian individuals. Clearly, there was a Union attempt, known as the Dahlgren Raid, to sack Richmond—and, according to papers found on the officer's body, to find Jefferson Davis and his cabinet and kill them.

[In] the Yellow Fever Plot, one of the Confederate agents [was] Dr. Luke Blackburn, a very prominent physician from Kentucky. He helped the Confederacy early on as a blockade runner and made his way to Canada in 1864 at the very time that Jefferson Davis had set up a Confederate secret service in Canada. He developed a plot to introduce yellow fever into the North in several areas—Washington being one of the areas, and New Bern, North Carolina, being one of the areas in Union hands. It was a staging base. There were a lot of Union troops around there. A terrible yellow fever epidemic broke out in Bermuda in the spring of 1864.

Blackburn was recognized internationally as an authority on yellow fever. He offered his services to the Bermuda government, and they readily accepted, but his motives were ulterior. He went there with the idea of collecting infected clothing, both bedding and personal clothing, from individuals who died of yellow fever and then having that clothing distributed among certain populations in certain cities, with the idea of inducing or starting a yellow fever epidemic.

We know today that yellow fever is not contagious. It is carried by a virus transmitted through a mosquito, but it is not transmitted between human beings. But they didn't know that. They thought it was contagious. In fact, at the very time that this clothing was distributed in New Bern, a yellow fever epidemic broke out in which two thousand civilians of New Bern died. The [plotters] didn't cause it; they thought they did, but they didn't.

Blackburn was eventually taken into custody in Canada and put on trial there for violation of the Neutrality Act. The New Bern incident was introduced into that trial, along with his [intention of] introducing [tainted] clothing into Washington, DC. He had also attempted to do this with Abraham Lincoln. He had bought several very fine shirts, dress shirts, which he had packed with yellow fever–contaminated clothing—so he thought—and then put the shirts in a very nice, expensive valise and gave it to one of his agents to deliver to the White House to Abraham Lincoln as a gift.

In all of these acts, the thing that you have to realize is, while you may target an individual, they are indiscriminate. So if this was a contagion, if it had been smallpox, for instance, very likely Abraham Lincoln would have contracted smallpox, as would his wife and children and other people in the White House.

EACH DAY [OF THE assassination trial], all of the testimony was taken down in a form of shorthand known as phonography. It was translated that evening, and copies were made by a very interesting process. Those copies that were made were distributed to the defense counsel, to the prosecution counsel and to the newspapers.

The daily transcripts were communicated to Philadelphia by Morse Code and appeared in the *Philadelphia Inquirer* the next day, verbatim, as they were in the *Washington Intelligencer* in Washington, so people could read the previous day's trial proceedings.

[T. B.] Peterson took the *Philadelphia Inquirer* transcripts from the daily papers and published them in a book, unedited, uncorrected, filled with typographical errors because it was being transmitted by Morse Code, and there were a lot of errors in the transmission. That was the earliest edition to come out, in 1865. That was followed by a second publication by Ben Perley Poor, who was a newspaper man who published a three-volume set of the transcripts, edited—that is, corrected for typographical error. The third publication that came out later, in November of 1865, was by Ben Pittman. He was the man who received the government contract to actually record the daily proceedings of the trial.

Andrew Johnson, by executive order, established a military tribunal and placed the defendants under its jurisdiction. There were approximately

5,000 military tribunals [during the war]. Somewhere between 14,000 and 15,000 individuals were tried by military tribunal.

[Mudd's involvement is still a] very big controversy. In many ways, it's a very interesting story because it shows what can happen in history when people attempt to manufacture history and revise it. The Mudd myth was manufactured by the Mudd family, beginning with his daughter, Nettie Mudd Monroe, when she published a book in 1906 called *The Life of Dr. Samuel A. Mudd.* His grandson, Dr. Richard Mudd, has devoted seventy-plus years to exonerating the grandfather. [But] the meetings with John Wilkes Booth were all arranged. There were three of them that we know of. There may have been more, but we can document three of them. More important-ly, when Booth first began to put his conspiracy together, after meeting with Arnold and O'Laughlen, the very next thing he did was go to Canada. He met in Montreal with a Confederate secret service agent who headed the office in Montreal. He stayed for ten days, and when he left, he carried a letter of introduction from that Confederate agent to Dr. Mudd and a man named Dr. William Queen. Both lived in Charles County, Maryland.

If you think about that, it ties both Dr. Queen and Dr. Mudd to the Confederate secret service directly, and it means that Patrick Martin in Montreal knew Dr. Mudd and knew that he was the man John Wilkes Booth needed to see.

Most of the books that have been written on the assassination have missed a great deal, have not really used the primary sources to the degree that they should have and, in my opinion, have missed some very important aspects of the assassination. In particular [the involvement of] Dr. Mudd . . . and the connection with the Confederate secret service in Canada and the military tribunal, which most historians have treated as an illegal court that lacked jurisdiction, as a kangaroo court. I don't agree with that at all. I think it had legal jurisdiction, and it certainly was not a kangaroo court.

Conspiracy

ROGER MUDD

Longtime network newsman Roger Mudd talked about his famous relative during a Booknotes *interview on June 6, 1999. His book* Great Minds of History *was published by Regnery.*

SAMUEL ALEXANDER MUDD was a country doctor down in Charles County, south of Washington, DC. He owned a few slaves, as many did. He was a known Confederate sympathizer. Into this mix comes this Shakespearean actor, strikingly handsome and dashing—John Wilkes Booth—who is consumed by hatred for Lincoln, the North, and oppression by the Union. He hatches a plan and enlists seven or eight [people], including John Surrat, Mary Surrat, and Dr. Mudd. There is some contention about how close the enlistment [of Mudd] was.

The original plan was that Booth wanted to kidnap Lincoln and abduct him either to Canada or to the South and then ransom him for peace. So Booth needed horses, and during this period leading up to April 14 of 1865, he went about collecting horses. He'd been to Dr. Mudd's house in Bryantown, in southern Maryland. My reading indicates that Dr. Mudd had a meal or two with Booth. As the time drew closer, suddenly Booth decided, "No, it's too hard to kidnap; I'm going to kill him." At that point, four of the so-called conspirators dropped out, including Dr. Mudd. Four stayed with him; the four who stayed were hanged. The four who said they didn't want any part of an assassination got life imprisonment. Dr. Mudd was sent down to Shark Island, [in the] Dry Tortugas. A yellow fever epidemic hit the prison, and he was instrumental in conquering the epidemic.

Andrew Johnson gave Dr. Mudd a pardon. His wife, Mrs. Mudd, had persistently circulated petitions signed by many. Finally, he came home and died a relatively young man from the ravages of the yellow fever disease.

Booth [never stood trial. He] had gotten across the Potomac River into Virginia and was killed on the Garrett farm. He was shot in a barn.

THE MUDD HOUSE is near Surratsville [and] Bryantown, in Charles County, Maryland. [Today, it is owned by the] Samuel Mudd Society, and the house is open for tourists. When the Mudd family, the direct descendants of Dr. Mudd, were very active in petitioning the Congress for total exoneration, they kept thinking that I would [help]. I couldn't help because when you're a member of the congressional press galleries, you sign a pledge that you will not lobby or have an interest in pending legislation. So I've never joined in the lobbying and probably wouldn't.

I'M NOT A DIRECT descendant [of Dr. Mudd]. I'm a collateral descendant, so he was an uncle about six or seven times removed. The direct descendants think that Dr. Mudd is totally innocent, but there is some doubt. There's no question that he was not a part of the assassination plot, but you know what life was like for Jack Ruby and Lee Harvey Oswald after the Kennedy assassination. There's a cry of vengeance [that] swells through the country. You could imagine what it must have been like in April 1865 for anybody [who] was within one hundred miles of the assassination or [had] the most remote connection to the assassination—the public wanted them either hanged or jailed for life.

The Journey Home

RICHARD NORTON SMITH

On April 18, 2005, historian Richard Norton Smith gave C-SPAN viewers a tour of the Abraham Lincoln Presidential Museum a day before its official dedication.

NO ONE WANTED the president of the United States to die in a common theater. They took him into the back room [of a boarding house on 10th Street,] into a room fifteen feet by nine feet, and laid him on a bed that was six inches too short for his frame. The deathwatch began, and it lasted for nine hours.

When the deathwatch ended at the Petersen House, there began an extraordinary pageant of grief that lasted twenty days. There was a funeral train, which retraced [Lincoln's] trip from Springfield to Washington in 1861. Thus, in effect, there were ten funerals along the way in ten major cities.

There never has been a funeral like this. It is estimated that seven million Americans—close to a quarter of the population of the country—actually saw the funeral train or saw Lincoln's remains in one of the ten cities where they were put on display. It ended on May 3, 1865. The trip from Washington went up the East Coast to Baltimore, a city that had by no means always been friendly to Lincoln; to Harrisburg, Pennsylvania; to Philadelphia, where there was a major outpouring of people; to New York City, a city where there had been riots during the Civil War, protesting the draft, and yet a million people turned out. It went up the Hudson Valley to Albany, the capital, and then across upstate New York to Syracuse and Rochester; then over into Buffalo and into Pennsylvania. [The train] stopped in Cleveland, and there was a funeral there. Then across Ohio to Columbus and across the great state of Indiana, up through Lafayette to Chicago.

Then on the morning of May 3, before dawn, the train pulled into Springfield, Illinois. By that time, there were already thousands of people milling around the streets. They had no place to go, no place to stay, but they were drawn there. People from all over America who felt they had to be there for this event.

On election night in 1876, there was a plot by some counterfeiters who wanted to spring their boss from jail. Their plan was to steal Lincoln's body out of its tomb, hide it in an Indiana sand dune, and hold it for ransom for their boss. They had broken into the tomb and removed the casket when they were arrested.

As a result of that grave robbery attempt, Lincoln had a very restless afterlife in and out of the tomb. At one point, his body was hidden near the tomb. People didn't know that. In 1901, Robert Todd Lincoln decreed that his father would be buried under ten feet of concrete and steel so never again would there be any possibility of his being disturbed.

On the day that the body was to be interred for the last time, there was a small group of Springfield residents, one of them said to be [a local schoolboy named] Fleetwood Lindley. He got on his bicycle, pedaled out to Oak Ridge Cemetery. He was there when they opened the casket, and his fame was that he was the last person to look upon the face of Abraham Lincoln.

THERE IS ONLY ONE existing photograph of Lincoln as a corpse. It shows Lincoln lying in state in New York City. There's a wonderful story attached to it: Ron Rietveld was a fourteen-year-old Lincoln [buff] back in 1952. He was doing some research [in Springfield] as the guest of the historical director of the [Illinois State Historical Library]. He found the photograph in the papers of Edwin Stanton's son. The photograph was not supposed to be on exhibit; Stanton had ordered it destroyed. For nearly a century, no one had any idea that the photograph survived.

Transporting Lincoln's Body

H. W. BRANDS

H. W. Brands appeared on Booknotes *on February 25, 1996, to discuss his book,* The Reckless Decade: America in the 1890s, *published by St. Martin's Press.*

WHEN LINCOLN'S BODY was being taken back to Illinois, it was thought that it ought to go in style. After all, this was the president. So they found the most luxurious railroad car they could, the Pullman Palace Car, manufactured by the Pullman Palace Car Company. The problem that George Pullman, owner and president of the company, had was that these cars were taller and wider than most cars at the time, and they often ran into trouble when they would pull up to platforms; sometimes they would be too tall to go under bridges. In order to get Abraham Lincoln, the deceased president, back home, the rail lines decided that they would simply have to make the investment to raise the bridges, to pull the platforms back away from the tracks where they had been. So they did. Now, all of a sudden, there was much more track that could handle the Pullman Palace Cars.

In addition, of course, it was terrific advertising. This was the finest railway car in the world. That was the implicit and, as Pullman put it, the explicit message, of the [Lincoln] funeral procession.

Increasingly, other railways found that they had to follow suit because now one railway could say, "We have the Pullman Palace Car." If the others couldn't match it, then the people who wanted to travel in style would simply take their business elsewhere.

PART 3

CHARACTER

★ ★
★

Lincoln and Religion

ALLEN C. GUELZO

Booknotes *hosted Allen Guelzo, author of* Abraham Lincoln: Redeemer President, *on April 16, 2000. Mr. Guelzo is the Henry R. Luce Professor of the Civil War Era, Professor of History at Gettysburg College, and a two-time winner of the Lincoln Prize, which he received for* Redeemer President, *published by Wm. B. Eerdmans Publishing Company, and* Lincoln's Emancipation Proclamation: The End of Slavery in America, *published by Simon & Schuster.*

Abraham Lincoln was a man who took religious ideas very, very seriously. He took them seriously sometimes in opposing them, but he also took them seriously sometimes in adopting them. In the end, they make Lincoln into a president who has more to say about religion and about the combination of religion and policy than almost any other American president. He also does it more eloquently, almost, than any other American theologian.

At the same time, many religious people, many Christian believers who read my book experience a sense of disappointment because they may have read in a number of other places that Abraham Lincoln was a Christian. Well, the truth of the matter is that he was not. He was exposed to Christian influences all through his life. He knew Christian people. He worked with Christian people, worked with Christian ideas. But Lincoln never joined a church, never was actively involved in any kind of Christian organization; in fact, he really had only the most minimal religious profile in his own day.

What has happened, though, is that after Lincoln's death, there was no shortage of people who wanted to claim Lincoln as being one of their own.

They could do this because Lincoln was a very private person. He was often described as being shut-mouthed and reticent, and he really was. He did not like to talk about himself or his inner life.

His law partner, [William] Herndon—who knew him probably as well as anybody could know someone while not being part of the immediate family—said of him that Lincoln kept half of himself secret, away from the general public, and then he kept half of what was left even from his closest friends. People have rushed into that vacuum and tried to suggest that Lincoln was really heading in the direction [of declaring a religious affinity] or that Lincoln made some kind of secret statement about heading in this direction.

There is a very famous story that suggests that Lincoln was about to join the New York Avenue Presbyterian Church [in Washington] on Easter Sunday 1865. And, of course, he was assassinated on Good Friday. The line of reasoning is that had Lincoln not been shot, he would have joined; he would have made a public Christian association of himself with the New York Avenue Presbyterian Church the following Sunday. It's a very famous story—I've bumped into it any number of times, and there is not a single shred of evidence that it's true.

He was something close to a Deist. He believed in a very general sense that there was a God, or at least there was a force that gave order and shape and predictability to the world and to the universe. But he would not move beyond anything more than that, anything more explicit than that. He believed there was some kind of God, but whether this God was a personal God, whether this God gave active direction and intervention to human affairs, that was a subject that, over the years, he tended to shift his position on a good deal.

He was born into a Baptist family—in fact, a Baptist group who were very sectarian. . . . They were radical predestinarians. In other words, they believed that God ordained every event, whatever came to pass. For that reason, this particular Baptist group, sometimes known as the Separate Baptists, would not sponsor missionaries. If the heathens were going to be converted, God would do it; you did not put yourself into a place where you were going to accomplish it. They did not have a professional, paid clergy. They did not have Sunday schools. They even frowned on involvement in reform movements.

Lincoln grew up in that environment, and, in fact, he was so good at understanding that, in his youth, he would get on top of tree stumps and deliver sermons that he had heard from the Sunday previous almost word for word, because his memory was so good. But this was acting; this was not being part of something. He never joined a Baptist church, never committed himself to a religious organization that way.

He did carry with him—and this is the interesting thing—the stamp of that belief in predestination. He secularized it into a belief in necessity or determinism; like those folks that he grew up with, he did not believe that human beings have free will. He did not believe that human choices come from within ourselves. He often described himself, all through his life, as a fatalist and would say to people, "I do not believe that human beings make their own choices."

He knew the Methodists because so many of them were so aggressive on the frontier in building churches, and sometimes not only building churches, but also building a public profile. One of his most famous political opponents in Illinois was a Methodist circuit-riding preacher, Peter Cartwright. It was Cartwright, first of all, who was his opponent for the congressional seat he ran for in the 1840s. Cartwright was running as a Democrat; Lincoln as a Whig. Cartwright also started what Lincoln called a whispering campaign through the Seventh Electoral District, which suggested that people should not vote for this man, Lincoln, because he was an unbeliever and an infidel and, therefore, could not be trusted.

That accusation provoked the single-most important statement Lincoln ever made about his own personal religious beliefs. That came in the form of a handbill, which was printed and circulated throughout the district prior to the election. In it, Lincoln said, "It's true that I do not belong to a Christian church, and it's true that I have never made any profession of Christian belief, but I've never scorned Christians. I've never criticized Christian churches. I've never been an open scoffer at Christianity. What's more, I believe in this doctrine of necessity. But isn't it true that there are some religious denominations that also believe in a doctrine of necessity?" He was, of course, thinking about the Separate Baptists and a number of other denominations, like the old school Presbyterians. He defended himself by saying, "It's true I believe in this doctrine of necessity, but, look, there are other religious people who believe in it, too. Therefore, the accusations that Cartwright is making against me really fall to the ground because you could just as easily make them about religious people."

He came to Springfield in 1837 and for many years did not associate himself with a church. In fact, he wrote back to New Salem at one point saying that he'd been in Springfield now this period of time and hadn't gone to church because he was afraid he wouldn't know how to behave there. There's some truth to his statement about his anxiety about behavior, but lying behind that is the fact that he really did not have anything in the way of religious beliefs. In fact, people who knew him in those early years in Springfield said that he would gather around him a number of his friends and he would take up the Bible and he would read parts of it aloud and criticize it, scoff at it, saying that this couldn't possibly be true, sometimes to the point where a number of his friends thought he was an atheist.

When he married Mary Todd, she was kind of religiously chilly herself, and for a number of years neither of them went to church. But then in 1850, Lincoln's second oldest son, Edward, died. This provoked a crisis in the Lincoln household. It was a crisis that was met by the pastor of the First Presbyterian Church in Springfield, a Scotsman named James Smith. He ministered to Mary Todd and had a very effective ministry to her, counseling her in her bereavement. Lincoln went to Smith with his perplexity, his questions: "Why did God take my son? I'm perplexed about predestination and providence." From that point on, the Lincoln family affiliated with the First Presbyterian Church, and Lincoln rented a pew there, but he didn't join the church. In fact, sometimes he didn't even come, but he did take this step of associating his family, if not himself personally, with the First Presbyterian Church.

He came to like First Presbyterian because, among the Presbyterian churches, First Presbyterian was an old school church, meaning that it was very loyal to the traditional teachings about predestination. It was a very Calvinist church. Not only did Lincoln feel comfortable with that because he was a fatalist, but when he came to Washington as president, the church that he affiliated his family with there, the New York Avenue Presbyterian Church, was also an old school Presbyterian Church. If he was going to feel comfortable with any kind of formal religion, it would be the old school Presbyterians.

Faith and Morality

DOUGLAS L. WILSON

Doug Wilson appeared on C-SPAN's Booknotes *on May 29, 1998. He discussed his book* Honor's Voice: The Transformation of Abraham Lincoln, *published by Knopf.*

[**LINCOLN**] certainly believed in God, and he seemed to always believe in predestination. The testimony of his friends and much of what he said [demonstrates this]. I don't think there's any doubt, either, that as a young man, he was not religious. He was a skeptic where Christianity was concerned.

THERE'S A GREAT deal of testimony about people who knew him well who told [his law partner and biographer William] Herndon that Lincoln used to be a free thinker, that he even went so far as to make fun of some Christian doctrines, and that he was a scoffer as a young man. He clearly stopped scoffing, and he eventually portrayed himself as being unfortunate in his unbelief. Later than that, apparently he indicated to people that he would be pleased if they could bring about his conversion. That he was an unbeliever until the time he went to the presidency, I don't think there's any doubt. I don't mean an unbeliever in God. I mean an unbeliever in Christian doctrine.

LINCOLN WAS A fairly resolute person, but then he had a lot of difficulties [in his life.] He discovered, as he said to his friend [Joshua] Speed in the summer of 1842, "I've lost the gem of my character, which is my ability to keep my resolves once they are made." He said, "Until I get it back, I can't really do anything." I think that was true, and I think he did get it back. He took the means to get it back.

HE WAS REALLY trying to define himself. We know him as a very honorable person, but he did some things that weren't so honorable. He was trying to figure out, as anybody would who's ambitious and wants to get ahead: What is fair? What is honorable? What price are you willing to pay for getting ahead? Can you do underhanded things? Do you pay a price for them? Can you live with them? How candid do you have to be with people? How much can you shave the truth? Are there situations in which it's okay to dissemble? A number of people said that he thought that in political matters—when you're in political fights and you're fighting a political enemy—you didn't have to be candid. You could say what you wanted to. "Fight the devil with fire," he would say.

Spiritual Beliefs

PAUL JOHNSON

This essay was taken from Paul Johnson's Booknotes *interview, which aired April 5, 1998. Johnson's book* A History of the American People *was published by HarperCollins.*

[**LINCOLN** had no religious beliefs in the conventional sense.] That is certainly what his wife said. She said that he never belonged to a church, and that is almost certainly true. The question of Lincoln and religion is a very big one, and I'm not sure that one can give a straightforward answer to it. What one can say is that during the Civil War—which was agonizing to everyone but particularly to a man like Lincoln because he bore the ultimate responsibility for what was happening—he almost inevitably thought deeply about what mankind was doing on Earth. Why these things happened, why evil existed, how it was to be combated, and how the individual spirit stood in relation to all these questions.

That tended to bring him closer to the idea of a deity. One does detect from his writings and from accounts of his behavior—eyewitness accounts—that he was becoming more and more accustomed to reading the Bible. He read it a lot during those terrible years of the Civil War. It may well be that by the end of the Civil War, he was a believer in God. So when he was killed, he met his Maker believing in him.

Genius

SHELBY FOOTE

On September 11, 1994, author and Civil War historian Shelby Foote appeared on C-SPAN's Booknotes *to talk about his book* Stars in Their Courses: The Gettysburg Campaign, *published by Modern Library. Among other projects, Mr. Foote worked for twenty years to write* The Civil War: A Narrative, *which was published in three volumes between 1958 and 1974. He was also known for his contribution to Ken Burns's 1990 documentary series* The Civil War.

The first word that I have for Abraham Lincoln is genius. There's never been a man who functioned the way Lincoln did. He had never occupied anything resembling an executive position before he came [to Washington] to be president. He knew almost nothing about the office. He didn't know how it ran; he didn't know about departments like the Treasury and so forth. He had done a term in Congress, which familiarized him there. He was very active in politics. The Lincoln-Douglas debates show that the man knew a lot about government, but the actual executive part he learned on the job, and he was just a miracle at it. He was a true genius.

[Stephen A.] Douglas was an interesting man because he had a profound influence on history, if he didn't do but one thing—he ran for office. Up until then, no man ran for the presidency of the United States. You couldn't say, "I want to be president of the United States" or "I should be president of the United States." Nobody would say a thing like that. It was too presumptuous. You sat back and other people said you should be president. Douglas said, "I want to be president. I should be president." Others talked about their theories, but Douglas was the first to campaign. . . . It was unthinkable before Douglas for anybody to campaign.

I'll tell you one impact [the Lincoln-Douglas debates] had: They kept Douglas from becoming president of the United States, and they made Abraham Lincoln president of the United States. . . . During the debates, Lincoln posed a question to Douglas where if Douglas answered yes, he would win the [Senate] election; if he answered no, he would lose the presidential election two or so years later. He had Douglas hoisted on his petard there. Douglas gave the answer that won the senatorial election but would lose him the presidential election.

I USUALLY DON'T like "what ifs," but if Douglas had been elected, it simply would have postponed the problem. The problem was there. Seward called it an "irrepressible conflict," and it would have been there while Douglas was president, or certainly after he left office. All these splits were going on: The Whigs had dissolved; there were issues that were so bitter between the abolitionists in New England and the fire-eaters in South Carolina and various other places in the South that I'm almost willing to believe that with all our genius for compromise, there still wasn't any way to settle this thing except by fighting. The most regretful thing is that the war went on for four years with an incredible savagery. That's the great shame. There was bound to be a fight, but for it to be the fight that it was with literally more than a million American casualties—that need not have been. Something should have stopped it before that.

ANY DEEP SOUTH BOY, and probably all Southern boys, have been familiar with the Civil War as a sort of thing in their conscience. I honestly believe that it's in all of our subconsciouses. This country was just into its adolescence at the time of the Civil War. It hadn't really formulated itself as an adult nation, and the Civil War did that. Like all traumatic experiences that you might have had in your adolescence, it stays with you the rest of your life, certainly in your subconscious, most likely in your conscience, too. The Civil War had the nature of that kind of experience for the country. Anybody who's looked into it at all realizes that it truly is the outstanding event in American history insofar as making us what we are. The kind of country we are emerged from the Civil War, not from the Revolution. The Revolution provided us with a Constitution; it broke us loose from England; it made us free. But the Civil War really defined us. It said what we were going to be, and it said what we were not going to be. It drifted us away from the Southern, mostly Virginia, influence up into the New England and Middle western influence, and we became that kind of nation instead of the other kind of nation.

IT MEANT THE LOSS OF the so-called Southern virtues, some of which are very real—a man's word is his bond, the business of not insulting each other with impunity. Some of these things are very small, but they weigh large on the human scale.

THE CIVIL WAR [also meant] emancipation, and it was immediately followed by true emancipation. I mean, the [Thirteenth Amendment to the] Constitution freed the slaves, not just those who were in rebel hands, as Lincoln's Proclamation claimed.

Emancipation meant the setting free of people who were in slavery. Lincoln's Emancipation Proclamation did not free anybody. What it did was it declared that all slaves not then in territory occupied by the Union would be free as of January 1, 1863, meaning if I can reach out and touch you, you're not free. If you're beyond my reach, you're free. Well, they didn't immediately say, "I am free," and march somewhere. They couldn't. But the real emancipation, the Constitutional amendment freeing the slaves, freed all the slaves.

Slavery is a huge stain on us. We all carry it. I carry it deep in my bones, the consequences of slavery. But emancipation comes pretty close to being as heavy a sin. They told, what is it, seven million people, "You are now free. Hit the road," and there was a Freedman's Bureau, which was a sort of joke. There were people down South exploiting former slaves [after the war]. Three-quarters of them couldn't read or write, had no job, no hope of a job, no way to learn a new job, and they drifted back into this peonage system under sharecropping, which was about all they could do.

TO THIS DAY, WE [as a nation] are paying, and [African Americans] are paying for this kind of treatment. I don't mean there should have been a gradual emancipation. I mean there should have been true preparation to get these people ready for living. [Emancipated slaves] . . . should have been free all along, but they were not prepared for living in the world. They had been living under conditions of slavery, which kept them from living in the world.

WHEN I WAS A GRADE school boy in Mississippi, I knew obscene doggerel about Abraham Lincoln, left over from my parents and grandparents. Yankees were despised. When one of them was so unfortunate as to move to Greenville, Mississippi, he was despised. All that has stopped. A great compromise [exists on how to view Lincoln and the Civil War]. I wish my black friends could [accept it]. The Illinois senator [Carol Moseley-Braun] who didn't want the Daughters of the Confederacy at Richmond to have a Confederate symbol—not the battle flag, just a Confederate symbol on their stationery—got her fellow senators to disallow it. I do not understand that. That's a violation of the compromise, and it's an arousal of bitterness. But she, along with a great many others, do not want to be reminded [of the past]. She has every right to want to hide from history if she wants to, but it seems to me she's trying to hide history from us, and that's a mistake.

[IN LOOKING BACK AT] the Civil War, there has been a great compromise. It consists of Southerners admitting freely that it's probably best that the Union wasn't divided, and the North admitting rather freely that the South fought bravely for a cause in which it believed. That is a great compromise, but we live with that, and it works for us. We are now able to look at the war with some coolness, which we couldn't do before now. I very much doubt whether a history book such as mine could have been written much before one hundred years had elapsed. It took all that time for things to cool down.

Reluctant Emancipator

LERONE BENNETT, JR.

Booknotes hosted Lerone Bennett, Jr., *on September 10, 2000, and talked about his book* Forced Into Glory: Abraham Lincoln's White Dream, *which was published by Johnson Publishing. As a writer and social historian, Mr. Bennett has served as the executive editor of* Ebony *for almost forty years. Bennett has written nine books, including* What Manner of Man, Pioneers in Protest, *and* The Shaping of Black America.

L incoln, from my standpoint, was forced into a glory that he resisted every step of the way. One of his great critics in Washington during the Civil War wrote a paragraph in which he said that Lincoln was literally whipped into glory. . . . One of the basic ideas of my book is that there were all these extraordinary men and women, many of them white, in Washington in 1862 and '63, and the American people generally do not know anything about any of them: James Ashley, Lyman Trumbull, Zachariah Chandler, Salmon Chase. They really pushed Lincoln to glory. Lincoln himself said, "I was driven to it, literally driven to it."

Contrary to what most people think, Abraham Lincoln's deepest desire was to deport all black people and create an all-white nation. It sounds like a wild idea now, but from about 1852 until his death, he worked feverishly to try to create deportation plans, colonization plans to send black people either to Africa or to South America or to the islands of the sea.

One of his greatest utterances—people quote it all the time—[was] . . . "We cannot escape history . . . [We are] the last, best hope of the world." He said these words in a State of the Union message on December 1, 1862, in which he asked Congress to pass three constitutional amendments: one, to buy the slaves; second, to declare free all people who'd actually escaped;

the third one, his proposed Fifteenth Amendment, asked Congress to allocate money to deport black people to another place.

This speech and the "we cannot escape history" ending is the portrait [of Lincoln] everybody knows. Nobody talks about the fact that he was asking Congress to deport black people. That was one of his deepest ideas.

Almost everything I say in my book, I take from Lincoln himself or from documents of the time. It was not just that he wanted to push black people out, he had an idea of this giant vacuum sound—of black people leaving and white people from all over the world coming here and creating an all-white nation. As a matter of fact, in his "I have a dream" speech at Alton, Illinois, in 1858, he called for a white haven for free white people everywhere, the world over.

These are Lincoln's words. The interesting thing about that is that he underlined these four words: *free white people everywhere.* He was passionately committed to deporting black people and creating a white nation. I found that offensive and strange. He believed that deportation was the only way to solve the race problem. He said over and over again that he did not believe that black people and white people could live together in equality in the United States of America.

The first sentence in [my] book says, "I was a child in whitest Mississippi . . . when I discovered for the first time that everything I'd been taught about Abraham Lincoln was a lie." I was ten or eleven. Before then, I believed that this was the Great Emancipator. I was one of these strange children who read everything I could put my hands on, any book, any piece of paper, anything I could find. For some strange reason in Mississippi, in the 1930s, I happened to see a copy of Abraham Lincoln's address at Charleston, Illinois, on September the 18, 1858, in the Lincoln-Douglas debates. I read it, and I was just absolutely shocked. From that point on, I started researching Lincoln and trying to find out everything I could about him. I wasn't trying to get a degree. I wasn't trying to pass a course. [I did it] . . . because I found it difficult to understand how people could say this man was the greatest apostle of brotherhood in the United States of America.

Lincoln is one of the keys to the American personality [and he is also] an industry. All over the country, people are engaged in packaging information on Lincoln, putting together exhibits on Lincoln, doing this and that about Lincoln. It's a whole industry that employs hundreds of people, probably thousands of people.

He is also a religion. He is one of the keys to America. Americans see themselves in Lincoln. American politicians tend to measure themselves by Lincoln. He is a secular saint. I'm proposing that we look at Lincoln [in a way that] is painful to whites but necessary for the health of this country and for what we've got to do about completing the task we started in the Civil War but never finished.

THE EMANCIPATION PROCLAMATION did not free black people. It's doubtful if it ever freed anybody anywhere. Abraham Lincoln was not the "Great Emancipator" or the small emancipator or the medium-sized emancipator. [The Proclamation] . . . enslaved or re-enslaved [people]. . . . Lincoln said in the document, which most people will never read, that he was specifically excluding certain slaves in southern Louisiana and eastern Virginia and elsewhere. Why did he exclude these slaves in Louisiana? Because they were the only slaves he could have freed on January the first, 1863. The Union controlled southern Louisiana and New Orleans. The Union controlled eastern Virginia. . . . All he had to do was just not specifically exclude them. Instead of freeing them, Abraham Lincoln, unfortunately, on January 1, [1863], said, "I'm not talking about you. You're the same as you were, as though this document never existed." So we had about 100,000 slaves in southern Louisiana and 80,000 or so in eastern Virginia, and some 275,000 slaves in Tennessee, who were not touched by it. I estimate that approximately 500,000 slaves were re-enslaved or kept in slavery by the Emancipation Proclamation all across the South.

Abraham Lincoln was a racist. I don't have any joy in making that [statement], but I think truth is important. He used the "N-word" habitually, loved darkie jokes and black-based shows, said in Illinois and elsewhere that he was opposed to black people voting, sitting on juries, intermarrying with white people and holding office. . . . Abraham Lincoln was, contrary to what all the historians say, an equivocating, vacillating leader who prolonged the war, delayed emancipation, and increased the number of casualties.

[My critics] say, "Lerone Bennett said that the Emancipation Proclamation didn't free black people, and he's a terrible man for disturbing the peace of the republic." [Then they say], "Of course, the Emancipation Proclamation didn't free black people. The Thirteenth Amendment—everybody knows that freed the black people." They agree with my first point.

They say, "Lerone Bennett says that Abraham Lincoln was a racist, and he's a terrible man for saying that. Of course, he was a racist. . . . All white people in the nineteenth century were racist." I disagree with that and defend white people in nineteenth century. It's absurd to say that everybody in the nineteenth century was a racist.

The third point is, "Lerone Bennett says that Abraham Lincoln wanted to deport black people and create a white nation." They say, "Of course, he wanted to deport black people—not because he disliked them but because he loved them so much and he didn't think they'd ever be treated right in America."

All of the critics I've seen agree with my basic points. I don't know a reputable historian with a library card anywhere who maintains that the Emancipation Proclamation freed black people. I don't believe one exists. Yet people are screaming and hollering at me, asking, "Why did you say this?" [Because] it's the truth.

. . . White authors have written about sixteen thousand books and monographs on Abraham Lincoln. Black authors have written, in the last 135 years, maybe two or three, maybe four. [My book] is, possibly, the first full-scale reassessment and study of Abraham Lincoln [by a black writer]. In the last 135 years, black authors have paid very little attention to Abraham Lincoln. . . . [Black writer Roy] Basler had an essay in 1935. . . . In predominantly black institutions, in black circles, apart from a few pieces of poetry here and there, Abraham Lincoln has never been the thing in black America that he's always been in white America, which suggests to me that black people know Lincoln, have always known him at a depth beneath words. They have not felt it necessary, not felt a need or the interest to address him the way white historians have addressed him.

FOR THE LAST 135 YEARS, every medium of communication outside of the media controlled [by black people] has said Lincoln was the great savior, the great liberator. "He freed you on January the first out of the goodness of his heart." Large numbers of black people worship Lincoln. They believe that he did what people say he did. It's painful to say to them and to my community and other communities, "He didn't do it. He didn't want to do it. He was a completely different man."

On January 1, 1863, a Thursday, here in Washington, slightly after twelve noon, they had the New Year's reception in the morning. Secretary [of State William] Seward and his son took the document, the Emancipation Proclamation, to Lincoln in the Cabinet Room. Lincoln took a steel-tipped pen, and he moved to the line where he's supposed to sign. All of a sudden, when he got to this line—Lincoln tells this story—his hand started shaking so violently that he couldn't sign it. He dropped the pen. So he took the pen again, and he moved it to the place. He started to sign it, and his hand started shaking so violently that he couldn't sign, and he dropped it again. Lincoln was very superstitious. He stopped in awe. Then he said, "A very simple explanation came to me. I had been shaking hands all that morning at the New Year's reception, and my arm was virtually paralyzed." I think this explanation is too simple, but that's what he said. He finally was able to sign the document.

The poetry, the songs, the scholars, the major newspapers, and the major museum people tell us that at that moment, choirs started to sing over the Alleghenies and over Stone Mountain in Georgia and black people started saying, "Free at last, free at last. Thank God Almighty, I'm free at last." It hurts me to say it's not true. Any slave in Georgia who said, "Free at last," [was] surrounded by Confederate troops on January the first, 1863, [and] was immediately sent to heaven. [Same for] any slave in Alabama who said that. . . . I wish it were true, [but] almost everything we've been told about Abraham Lincoln in the last 135 years is wrong and needs correcting.

We need to research Lincoln's life. We need to know everything we can about him. . . . We need more money dedicated to the task of studying the real emancipators, of studying [abolitionists] Charles Sumner and Thaddeus Stevens and Wendell Phillips—all white men. People tell me everybody was a racist then, [yet] these men were one hundred years ahead of Abraham Lincoln in terms of their understanding of democracy and racial equality in this country.

One complaint of mine is that few, if any, white Americans know who Lyman Trumbull was. Lyman Trumbull was a senator from Illinois in Lincoln's time. He had the traditional problems of many of the white men of the time, but he was far more advanced in his understanding of what liberty required of him. He opposed the Fugitive Slave Act in Illinois at a time when Abraham Lincoln was backing the hunting of men, women, and children. He defeated Abraham Lincoln for the Senate. The reason he defeated Lincoln for the Senate is because Lincoln was too conservative on the issue of slavery in Illinois and in America. Bottom line: Lyman Trumbull came to Washington. He was the author of the first Confiscation Act, which began the Emancipation Proclamation in August 1861. He was the author of the second Confiscation Act, which was the most sweeping act of emancipation passed by Congress or enacted during Lincoln's time, more sweeping than the Emancipation Proclamation.

[Trumbull] was one of the principal authors of the Thirteenth Amendment [making slavery unconstitutional]. [He was] one hundred years ahead of Lincoln but nobody in Illinois knows Lyman Trumbull. . . . They've had no major exhibits in Illinois on Lyman Trumbull. We have had one hundred exhibits on Lincoln, who didn't believe in equality, who did little or nothing to advance the abolitionist process. Why isn't the culture teaching people Lyman Trumbull's name? Or Wendell Phillips? Or Charles Sumner?

UNTIL THE CAPTURE of Atlanta and the nomination of General McClellan on the Democratic ticket late in 1864, almost all members of Lincoln's party thought he was a disaster as a president. Most of them were looking for some alternative candidate. Almost all members of the Washington power structure at that time said that he lacked will, he lacked the resolution, he lacked vision, and that he was prolonging the war by his inadequacies. Lyman Trumbull said Lincoln lacked the resolution needed in this great task. His attorney general, [Edward] Bates, said he lacked will. Others said at the time that he was simply a terrible leader. And yet, 135 years later, almost all the scholars say he was the greatest leader we've ever had in our country, perhaps in the world.

THE ABOLITIONISTS HAD driven the South mad, and they were not going to take Stephen Douglas [as president]. But [if he had been elected president in 1860], he would have tried to create a compromise, extending or modifying his earlier compromise. I don't think it would have worked. I don't think there was any solution that the Southerners would have approved of [to remain in the Union].

Wendell Phillips said it first, that fugitive slaves and abolitionists and the threat of insurrections had driven Southerners mad. In essence, they committed suicide. Lincoln, in his inaugural address, said that he would have personally backed a Thirteenth Amendment, which had already been passed, which would have guaranteed slavery forever in the United States of America. The South refused to accept it.

. . . Lincoln was a compromise candidate. . . . He was not elected because he was a flaming antislavery advocate; he was elected because he was less of an antislavery advocate than Seward and Salmon Chase. The question is: What would have happened if Seward or Chase had been elected president? My view is that emancipation would have come sooner and in a better context than it did under Abraham Lincoln. . . . I don't think Chase and Seward would have gone so far in appeasing the South and the border states.

If Lincoln had not spent two years appeasing Kentucky, if he had mobilized four hundred thousand black soldiers and issued an emancipation order giving the soldiers freedom, the Civil War would have been over in two or three years at most. I don't understand the historians who [talk about] his great leadership. If Franklin Delano Roosevelt had conducted World War II as disastrously as Abraham Lincoln conducted the Civil War in the first two years, America would be a German protectorate today.

THERE HAS BEEN, for 135 years, one of the biggest attempts in all history to hide this man and to make the man entirely different from what he was. Lincoln is a mask for certain deep-seated problems we blacks and whites have resisted and refused to deal with, particularly, the problem of slavery, the problem of emancipation, and the problem of black freedom in this country. Lincoln, far from being a leader, was a man on the fence who denounced the extremists on both sides, who talked out of both sides of his mouth. That is an idea that appeals to many people. Although [academic] people won't tell us who Lincoln was, history knows Lincoln [and knows] that he was a waffling, equivocating person. . . . Many scholars are defending that image of leadership.

[There is a] tendency of major Lincoln biographers to take isolated quotes and use them without giving us the context or the setting. For example, [a] historian whom I admire and respect on other grounds said that the 1862 State of the Union message, where [Lincoln] talked about "the last, best hope of Earth" was one of the greatest statements in the history of the world. He does not tell us that Lincoln was asking Congress to deport black people [in the same speech]. In [another] speech, Lincoln said, "I love the Declaration of Independence, one of the great documents of all time." Two paragraphs later, he said, "Now I don't want you to misunderstand me"—he's talking to ten thousand or twelve thousand white people— "I'm not talking about equality, I'm not talking about making black people equal. I'm not talking about freeing black people in the South. But it's a great document in the abstract."

I have detailed the defenses that scholars built into their work. More often than not, an author will say [Benjamin Thomas's book] is the best one-volume biography of Abraham Lincoln. Thomas's one-volume work is readable. It came at a time when people were groping for some new way to deal with Lincoln, sometime around 1952. It was immediately elevated to the best one-volume treatment of Lincoln available. I went down a list of all the things that Thomas did not tell us.

[In his book, Bennett writes: "Thomas doesn't tell us that Lincoln used the N-word. He doesn't tell us that Lincoln loved N-jokes. He doesn't tell us that Lincoln voted for Jim Crow legislation in the Illinois legislature. He doesn't tell us that Lincoln said there was a natural disgust in the minds of nearly all white people about black and white sex. He doesn't tell us that Lincoln supported the Illinois Black Laws. He doesn't tell us that President Lincoln personally ordered Union officers to return runaway slaves to slave masters. He doesn't tell us that President Lincoln tried for 'nearly a year and a half,' in his own words, to save slavery in the United States."]

This is typical of major biographers on Lincoln. The famous Charleston quote [from the Lincoln-Douglas debates] is the stumbling block. . . . The best biographers will summarize the Charleston quote. . . . On Saturday,

September 18, 1858, Lincoln said to about ten thousand or fifteen thousand white people in the Lincoln-Douglas debate that, "I will say then that I'm not now, nor have I ever been in favor of bringing about, in any way, the social and political equality of the white and black race, that I'm not, nor ever have been, in favor of making voters of Negroes or jurors of Negroes, nor qualifying them to hold office, nor to intermarry with white people." He goes on and on, [and] he ends by saying that he's in favor of white supremacy.

[Those remarks] are a litmus test for Lincoln biographers. The best ones will summarize the quote and will make an excuse for him. The major excuse from Thomas and others is to say that Douglas was pushing him and he had to say this to get elected. But most biographers do not give the full quote. They certainly don't give it in context. They certainly do not tell us that Lincoln voted for Jim Crow laws in the Illinois legislature, voted for a white school system in Illinois as a legislator, said on the platform that he supported the Black Laws, and lived in Illinois and never said a word about an Illinois law that made it a crime for black people to live in Illinois. We don't get any of this in the traditional biographies.

I always raise the question of scholarship. You can't divorce a man from a setting like that and write a biography on him. If you don't tell us about the Jim Crow laws he supported and the fact that he supported the hunting of men, women, and children—the Fugitive Slave law—we have to re-evaluate what we're doing in scholarship.

I HAVE BEEN HONORED by some Lincoln associations. . . . [But I do believe] there ought to be a dialogue between academic people—the Lincoln establishment—and other people who have a different vision of Lincoln.

I would walk [into a Lincoln Forum or Abraham Lincoln Association meeting] and give this same thesis with one exception: I don't believe in [rhetorical] lynching parties. If they want to arrange fifteen people on a platform and say, you speak, and then these fifteen people are going to lynch you, I don't believe in that. But if they want me to make a speech, I'll make it. . . . We need this kind of dialogue, but I've been [down] this road before. In February of 1968, I wrote a small essay in *Ebony* called "Was Abe Lincoln A White Supremacist?" [There were] explosions everywhere. People said, "The republic is in danger." Then people said, "Well, you know, he makes some good points. We ought to re-evaluate Lincoln." But the re-evaluation did not come. That essay has been out there for some thirty-two years [and there's been] no real [academic] response to it.

THE TRUTH IS ITS OWN defense and is absolutely necessary. My response to whites and blacks is [why romanticize] this warm, confident symbol who gives out freedom on January the first, 1863? You can't lie your way to freedom. You can't lie your way to a rainbow nation.

[People in the Lincoln establishment] know who Abraham Lincoln is. They know he was not John Brown. They know he was not Wendell Phillips. They know he was not a major advocate of liberation. They know he did it reluctantly; he did it to save the Union. That's the Lincoln that these people worship. What is that saying? That you don't fight for freedom if it causes problems. They know the Lincoln they're worshiping. . . . I'm saying we ought to teach young white children Wendell Phillips's name. [Phillips] said—years before King, years before Mandela—that he wanted to create a rainbow nation composed of the learned and the ignorant, the old and the young, the black and the white, pagan, Christian, Jew—all in one great procession marching toward a rainbow land. That ought to be taught. If we're going to overcome the madness we're going through in this country, we need to know that white people in this country are going back to [study] Abigail Adams, who really was in favor of the liberation of black people. We need to know about black people like Harriet Tubman and Frederick Douglass.

THE MISINTERPRETATION and misunderstanding of Lincoln on this issue has reached the level of a national scandal. . . . It's the duty of all Americans to begin now to deal with the facts.

Lincoln and Race

MARK NEELY, JR.

The Last Best Hope of Earth: Abraham Lincoln and the Promise of America was written by Mark Neely and published by Harvard University Press. Neely discussed the book during a Booknotes *interview on June 12, 1994. Dr. Neely is a McCabe Greer Professor of History at Pennsylvania State University. As a U.S. political and constitutional historian, working mainly on the period 1787–1877, Dr. Neely won a Pulitzer Prize in history for his book* The Fate of Liberty: Abraham Lincoln and Civil Liberties.

WHERE do you draw the line in Lincoln's life between ambition to gain office and wanting to put political principles in place to make the republic better? You can get historians going on that topic just about any day. Nobody says Lincoln wasn't a great politician. Nobody. Even his enemies say he was a great politician.

THE POET EDGAR LEE MASTERS did not like Lincoln and wrote a very hostile book about him. But [generally] Lincoln gets very good press. He was a wartime president and had many bitter critics. He was involved in the race issue, which was even more explosive then than now and also gave him many bitter critics, black and white. But—and this is an irony—in 1865, at the height of his powers just as the Civil War was ending, Abraham Lincoln was murdered. Overnight he became a martyr to freedom. That had the effect of immediately silencing the critics, and to a substantial degree they've not been heard ever since.

FREDERICK DOUGLASS, the great black abolitionist of Lincoln's day, knew Lincoln personally. After Lincoln's death, Douglass gave what I think is the greatest single speech on Lincoln ever given at the dedication of the

Freedmen's Monument [in Washington, DC]. Douglass stood there on this solemn occasion, and he certainly didn't do what people expected.

Here was a monument built to a substantial degree with the pennies raised from freed slaves, and Frederick Douglass gave the dedication speech and said, "We were only Lincoln's stepchildren. The white people in America were his children. We, the black people, were only his stepchildren. What he did as president, he considered the Union first and my race second." Yet what Douglass said about Lincoln was . . . that when he dealt with him personally he had no sense that Lincoln was conscious of his race at all, that he treated him like any other man. He clearly liked and admired him, but he saw the Lincoln administration from the slaves' perspective, and he would like to have seen [Lincoln] move faster.

STEPHEN A. DOUGLAS was one of Lincoln's principal political rivals and, of course, his opponent in the famous 1858 Senate campaign and in the Lincoln-Douglas debates. These debates are remembered every time we have a presidential campaign today. When we have debates as part of the campaign, I think one is always thinking—one is always hoping—that it will somehow rise to the level of the Lincoln-Douglas debates, or to the level of the Lincoln-Douglas debates in myth.

They were part of the rough and tumble of nineteenth-century American politics. Each was trying to gain an advantage over the other in order to win the election, and so the debates are not philosophical discussions of political principles. They are not glosses on the Constitution. They are not systematic statements of policy for the republic. The debates consist of attempts to gain advantage over the adversary, and, therefore, they lead sometimes to distortions. On the other hand, they are full of illuminating explanations of Democratic and Republican policies of the period. Likewise, they include conspiracy charges—they were false—against the other party in the debates.

So like all of these speeches from political forums, they have to be dealt with with skepticism.

LINCOLN WAS NOT A racial equalitarian. That is, he did not believe in the doctrine of racial equality that would measure up to the standards of [our time], and that disappoints us. But I think the key, in part, lies not only in the racial assumptions of his era but in the politics of the era.

To understand [his famous statement on race at the Charleston debate] you need to understand two critical things. One, it was an answer to Stephen Douglas and the Democrats. In other words, Lincoln would rather not have talked about race at all, but, when forced, he would say some things. . . . Second, and even more important, you've got to understand the political effect of the racial assumptions. Illinois is a perfect example. Illinois was free territory. There was no slavery in Illinois, and yet in 1831, which is just after Abraham Lincoln had moved there, the Illinois state legislature passed a law that required a freed black person who wanted to settle in the state to post a $1,000 bond guaranteeing his good behavior while in the state. Lincoln himself made $150 a year at that time, and no black person could post a $1,000 bond. It was, effectively, exclusion from the state. Later, Illinois made it even clearer. In the 1848 state constitution, one article of the constitution forbids black people to enter the state to settle. When they submitted this constitution to the people, they submitted the article on race separate from the body of the constitution. So we have in 1848 an Illinois referendum on race, and it passed by more than a two-to-one majority. In Lincoln's home county, Sangamon County, it passed by more than a three-to-one majority.

That was the common denominator of racial opinion, and Lincoln had to deal with that realistically. Whatever his personal racial views, he could not ignore those white racial views as registered there. He could not move too fast. It explains many of the things that disappoint us today. It explains to some degree what disappointed Frederick Douglass about Lincoln—that he didn't move a little faster toward emancipation.

The whole scheme of colonization was completely impractical. [Sending slaves to] Africa was out of the question. It was too far away and too expensive. So by the 1850s, the people who were interested in colonization [decided it] would be a voluntary movement to Latin American countries. Even so, it was much too expensive. . . . Lincoln's interest in this idea is problematic, there is no doubt about it. Colonization is a profoundly racist idea. The idea behind colonization—and you have to face it squarely—is that America cannot be a biracial country. If black people were going to be free, they could not remain in America. Lincoln was interested in this idea from at least the early 1850s until 1862. After he announces the Emancipation Proclamation, he never mentions colonization in public again, and after 1864 he has dropped the idea.

The key idea is that Abraham Lincoln changed his mind about things. He grew. I like to test politicians not by what they say but by what they do. What did he do that guaranteed a biracial future for America? Well, in 1863 he accepted black people into the Union armies, and everybody knew that you could not ask a man to fight for his country and then say, "Oh, I'm sorry, this isn't your country any longer." That was a step that guaranteed America's biracial future, and Lincoln took it.

★ ★
★

The Declaration's Influence

PAULINE MAIER

C-SPAN's Booknotes *hosted Pauline Maier on August 17, 1997. Maier's book* American Scripture: Making the Declaration of Independence *was published by Knopf. Dr. Maier is the William R. Kenan, Jr. Professor of American History at the Massachusetts Institute of Technology and also authored* From Resistance to Revolution *and* The Old Revolutionaries.

[**M**y book] is about the Declaration of Independence, about how it was originally drafted, about the event, independence . . . and then how the American people ultimately, with the very eloquent help of Abraham Lincoln, redefined it into a document that served a very different purpose.

[IN 1820 THERE WAS A] desire of that younger generation to recover their revolutionary heritage. The Declaration wasn't the only document that was being recovered. A lot of documents were being reprinted at that point so that they wouldn't be lost. What really got the Declaration of Independence on the American agenda was the controversy over slavery. The statement "all men are created equal" obviously contradicted the existence of a system of slavery because slaves held their status by heredity, and they were not subject to their masters by consent. That drove the defenders of slavery to contest the Declaration of Independence.

The statement "all men are created equal" became particularly controversial. People like John C. Calhoun said, "This is evidently false. People are not born equal. They're born dependent. This is a self-evident falsehood." Others said, "It's a self-evident lie." Now if you were an American who had been raised to hold these traditions, and this document, with a certain amount of reverence, this was offensive. Certainly those who found slavery itself offensive sprung to the defense of the Declaration of Independence. It became very central to the debates.

It was, in part, the attacks on the Declaration of Independence that brought Abraham Lincoln back into politics. Here you have a little-known Illinois lawyer who had served one term in Congress before his constituents turned him out because they had rather different views on the Mexican War than he had. You can see him in his office with his feet up on the desk, reading the *Congressional Globe*—the debates over the Kansas-Nebraska Act—which would have extended slavery into what had been free territory. To him, that was wrong.

He saw the attacks on the Declaration that were being made. He was offended by them, and he went back into politics. He contested, in the first instance, Stephen Douglas, who was one Illinois senator who had sponsored and brought into Congress the Kansas-Nebraska Act. [Lincoln] started attacking him in isolated speeches, and by the time Lincoln was the Republican candidate for the Senate, they had these famous debates. Those were almost exclusively one-issue debates over the expansion of slavery. A good bit of the differences [between the two men] turned on the meaning of the Declaration of Independence.

Members of the Republican Party had taken the Declaration of Independence as a statement of their founding principles. So Lincoln was part of a group; he was not isolated. That is very important to know. He built on arguments he had encountered that had been made by others, and he reinterpreted the document: What does it mean that all men are created equal?

He made sense of it by taking the first statement and [combining] it with the second. "All men are created equal in that they are endowed by their creator with certain inalienable rights." He [fused] the two. He said, "The founders did not say that men are created identical in their appearance or their talents or their physical strength. They are equal in rights. This the founders said, and this they meant." Whether that's what the Declaration said is open to contest, but it doesn't matter. [Lincoln's interpretation] made sense of the document, and it made it rather more like a bill of rights and an important message, not just for black Americans, but for all Americans.

$$\star \; \star$$
$$\star$$

Complex and Imperfect

EDNA GREENE MEDFORD

On April 27, 2008, Edna Medford appeared on C-SPAN's Q&A program for an interview on her book The Emancipation Proclamation: Three Views, *co-authored with Harold Holzer and Frank Williams (Louisiana State University Press). Dr. Medford is an associate professor at Howard University and specializes in nineteenth-century African American history.*

I t's not unusual for me to be one of maybe four or five African Americans, and quite often the only African American woman [at meetings of the Lincoln Forum and other gatherings of Lincoln scholars]. My Howard University colleagues, from time to time, have wondered why I bother to attend those kinds of programs. People generally don't see the Lincoln Forum and Lincoln programs as relevant to African Americans. That's unfortunate because Lincoln and the war were very relevant to us.

[LERONE BENNETT, JR., an author, Lincoln critic, and African American, is] a wonderful scholar who has written some very important works and who is a great researcher, as well. He's right that we have elevated Lincoln to god-like status. I think W. E. B. Du Bois said it best in the 1920s, when he said that we have a tendency to make icons of ordinary men and that once they're dead, we have to elevate them to this godlike status. As a consequence, what we get is someone who is cold and dead. We don't really get the person.

The problem with the way Lincoln is treated in the literature, in historical writing, is that he is flawless; he can do no wrong. He emancipated the slaves by himself. When we do that, we do a disservice to a great man.

Lincoln was very complex. He was very much a nineteenth-century man, but very much unlike nineteenth-century men as well. We do better for him and for the nation—and for an understanding of the Civil War—if we view him in all of his complexity. We're not willing as a nation to do that because he does embody what we believe is America. We think that America is flawless. No nation is.

If we look at him . . . what we see is a very remarkable person. We see someone who is much more powerful than we give him credit for when we say he's a saint and that everything was done correctly.

THE FIRST PEOPLE TO revere Lincoln were the former slaves because they did recognize the significance of the Proclamation. They didn't have benefit of all that we know today about other people who were involved in pushing emancipation, as well. But they remained very much committed to Lincoln's memory for a long, long period of time.

By the time of the Depression, however, things started changing. [Change began] even before that, because African Americans, in revering Lincoln, believed that he had promised something more than just freedom. They defined freedom as full citizenship rights. When they didn't receive it, then quite naturally, they have to go back to the person that they saw as the guarantor of that promise. Even though Lincoln had been assassinated, had left the scene earlier than one would have ever expected, he was still held accountable for African Americans not receiving those full citizenship rights.

IN CERTAIN SEGMENTS of the [African American] community, there are still people who think of Lincoln as a great man. I can't imagine many people who don't think of him as a great man.

How can you discount what he did? He saved the Union. He issued the Emancipation Proclamation, which called for the freeing of at least three million enslaved people. Yes, the Union army did have to come and liberate them before they'd actually have their freedom—some ran away—but he did issue the Emancipation Proclamation. That's important. Lincoln had constitutional constraints in issuing the Proclamation. He couldn't touch enslaved people in those areas that were under Union control because the Constitution did not give the president the opportunity to do that. The Constitution, through the War Powers clause, gave the president the authority to do whatever he needed to do in order to quell a rebellion. So he had to go after those enslaved people who were still in areas still controlled by the Confederacy.

. . . About eight hundred thousand people were not freed by the Emancipation Proclamation, but more than three million were, technically. We do know that they had to make their way to the Union line, or the Union troops had to free them.

. . . [Lincoln's] African American contemporaries, understanding that there would be about eight hundred thousand still enslaved, appreciated the fact that the Proclamation called for the freeing of those three million.

They understood, in Frederick Douglass's words, that once you said people were free in the other parts of Virginia, then all of the enslaved people in the border states—in Maryland, in Kentucky and Missouri and Delaware—would eventually get their freedom as well.

That did happen with the Thirteenth Amendment and Lincoln did support that amendment.

It would have been wonderful if all enslaved people had been freed by the [Emancipation Proclamation], but constitutionally it was not possible to do that.

[AUTHOR AND LINCOLN critic Thomas DiLorenzo] is right that a great number of African Americans freed themselves long before the Emancipation Proclamation was issued, by escaping to the Union lines. The Emancipation Proclamation certainly was not the first effort to make black people free. The first Confiscation Act helped with that. The second Confiscation Act helped with that, as well.

What the Emancipation Proclamation did was give African Americans hope. When [slaves] heard about it, they understood that the most powerful man in the nation had now sided with them.

They already thought of this war as one for their liberation. Then you have Lincoln issuing the Proclamation, and they were seeing this as, "The most powerful man in the country is now on our side. If we can make it to the Union lines now, we truly will have our freedom."

Before that, even though they made it to the Union lines, they couldn't be certain how they were going to be treated. Some of them did leave and came back home. There was this interesting backward and forward movement across the Confederate lines, across the lines of war. It was the Thirteenth Amendment that forever ended slavery in this country, but the Emancipation Proclamation is important.

BEFORE HIS ASSASSINATION, on more than one occasion, [Lincoln] had indicated that he wouldn't have a problem with seeing the "more intelligent" blacks get the right to vote, [along with] those who were veterans, and those who had supported the Union during the war.

He was not for universal suffrage, however. He may have gotten to that point [eventually], but we know that Lincoln did everything very cautiously. The fact that he was even willing to suggest that perhaps the soldiers and the more intelligent should have the right to vote was a step in the right direction.

I'm always bothered by the fact that he was not calling into question unintelligent white men, who had been voting all along. He did indicate, however, that he had a debt to pay to African American men. He said at the end of the war there would be some black men who could hold their heads high because they helped to preserve the Union, and there would be some white men who would have to hang their heads because they helped to hinder it.

That statement suggests that he understood that something had to be given to African Americans, [yet] at the end of his life, he wasn't quite there in terms of extending full equality to all African Americans.

Lincoln was a nineteenth-century man with some of the same prejudices of nineteenth-century men. The thing that distinguished him from other men of his era was that he believed very strongly in equality of opportunity and that people had the right to benefit from their labor. So he was antislavery.

There were many white Americans who were not antislavery or simply didn't care at all what was happening to enslaved people. He did care.

Yes, he did tell racially insensitive jokes. He did believe that white men and women were superior to black men and women. He did promote colonization of African Americans outside of the United States because he believed that as long as African Americans remained in the country, they would be the reason why white men fought each other, and that they would never have the opportunity to excel.

He did not call for forcibly deporting African Americans, but he certainly did encourage colonization. He invited five black men to the White House where he talked to them about the fact that they should go and live elsewhere because white men would never treat them properly, even if they were the most refined. There was some truth to that. We certainly saw that after the Civil War.

African Americans didn't go, however, because we had been in this country at least since 1619, before it was a country. People like Frederick Douglass and others said, "We're not leaving, we built this country. We are entitled to be here as much as anybody else." So, Lincoln did eventually drop it.

DiLorenzo is viewed [by other Lincoln historians] probably in the same way that Lerone Bennett is viewed. Their opinions, their interpretations, are viewed as extremist. I understand why their interpretations are what they are. I don't want to try to put words in their mouths, but I think it's a reaction to what they see as an over-the-top attitude about Lincoln, that he is perfect. You even have people saying, "Well, he ended the war knowing that he was going to get rid of slavery, and the war was all about that." I don't see that when I do the research. In the last several years, I have tried to bring a little bit more balance to an understanding of Lincoln. He doesn't have to be perfect. None of us are. But that doesn't mean that he's not important.

It's easier to love Lincoln than it is to be critical of him. That's very true. Those comments [by DiLorenzo, who said peer pressure precludes Lincoln critics from careers in academia] are a little bit extreme, however. I do have a career. I do have a teaching job. Am I accepted? Are my ideas accepted in the mainstream Lincoln community? To some extent, but not totally.

It's very difficult for people to listen to an African American historian talk about some of the problems with Lincoln. White historians have done it for any number of decades, but it's very difficult for African Americans to do it because the assumption is that you should love Lincoln without question, that you should see him as a god, because after all, he freed you. Any little criticism will be pounced on.

I've had some interesting comments from people after I've been on TV programs. I've had rather nasty e-mails. One lady assured me that she was going to contact C-SPAN and tell them not to ever have me on again. I looked back at that program and thought, what did I say that was terrible? All I said was that Lincoln was very cautious in moving toward emancipation. She apparently took offense to that.

I don't know that I would say that Lincoln critics can't get their books published or can't get a job. That's a little extreme. But there's an attitude out there in America that reveres Lincoln to an extent that it is very uncomfortable [with] anything critical.

[At the Lincoln Forum], the people in the room are very much interested in knowing about Lincoln fully, and not just Lincoln the Great, but Lincoln as he dealt with the issues of the time in a very trying situation, in the midst of war. I have found the people there to be very receptive to what I've had to say.

I've taken my graduate students with me when I attend Lincoln Forum events. They have been pleased with what they've heard there in terms of the learning process because many of them may not have been introduced to Lincoln, at least not to the extent that a lot of people in attendance have. They're hearing lectures from scholars who talk about Lincoln from a variety of perspectives.

There's always that possibility [that my inclusion at the Lincoln Forum constitutes affirmative action]. When I feel that, I have to determine, what am I bringing to the table, even if I am affirmative action? If it means that I am there giving an opinion that may not have been heard [elsewhere], and if one person recognizes the validity of that interpretation, I've done my job.

I'M ON THE ADVISORY council that was set up by the Lincoln Bicentennial Commission. There are about 150 or so of us. I've been working with people on the educational committee of the advisory council and with people at Howard University [in Washington]. I'm going to host an international, scholarly conference on race and emancipation in the age of Lincoln. It's not a Lincoln lovefest but an opportunity to look at issues of race and emancipation in the context of Lincoln's time. I hope that we will be able to discuss issues that were not discussed in 1959, for instance. We're very hard at work on that.

Even though some people think that the celebration of Lincoln's birth is over the top and unnecessary, I think this gives us an opportunity to reassess ourselves, our history, and to talk about how we might be able to improve it. At Howard, we're certainly going to attempt to do so.

TODAY, WHAT I WOULD say about the African American belief about Lincoln is that he was a great president, but not because he freed the slaves. Most people see him in a much broader context than that.

He was one of the great presidents because he was president during a war, because he preserved the Union, and yes, because he was the person who issued the Emancipation Proclamation, which brings the country toward the final ending of slavery throughout the nation.

He's important for all of those reasons, but he's not revered by African Americans in the way that he is by some other Americans. I must say, he's not revered by all white Americans, either.

The celebration of the Lincoln Prize was held in Richmond a few years ago, and there were people picketing, because they felt that Lincoln was a murderer, that he was responsible for the 620,000 people who were killed as a consequence of the war.

There are some Southerners who still feel very negatively about Lincoln. I don't think that African Americans feel negatively about him. African Americans just don't have an opinion about him one way or the other except he was a great president. There's no special feeling for Lincoln, perhaps, as there was when the slaves were emancipated.

[TODAY, THERE TYPICALLY are not large numbers of African American tourists and visitors going to Lincoln historical sites and museums.] I don't want to speak for all African Americans, but I think I understand it. It's because African Americans feel that those places are not for us.

We don't go to national parks, [and] we don't go to presidential libraries because we really don't feel that we're welcome at those places. Right or wrongly . . . we don't feel that we are totally included in America, even today, after all these years.

★ ★
★

Lincoln's Ambition

RICHARD SHENKMAN

Richard Shenkman discussed his book Presidential Ambition: How the Presidents Gained Power, Kept Power, and Got Things Done, *published by HarperCollins, in a* Booknotes *interview on March 21, 1999. Mr. Shenkman has studied America's presidents for nearly two decades as a writer, historian, producer, and journalist and college lecturer and has authored five books concerning American history.*

Abraham Lincoln is the one president who was probably the most ambitious. With all the stereotypes about Abraham Lincoln—country lawyer, Honest Abe, stovepipe hat, all of this kind of stuff—you never hear the word "ambitious" come into the picture, but he was ambitious. His law partner, William Herndon, said, "His ambition was an engine that knew no rest."

Just take this little mental picture—when Lincoln was twenty-three years old, he moved into New Salem, Illinois. He knew nobody, had no money, no power, no connections. He was a poor farm boy. He was a poor farmhand who was earning a living by plowing other people's fields. He didn't have his own farm; he didn't have enough money to rent a real home. He rented out the back bedrooms of different people, and he lived two weeks here, a couple of months there. Six months after moving into New Salem—with one year total education in his entire life—he announced in the local paper he was running for a seat in the state legislature. That's ambition. He lost, but he ran again two years later and won. He kept running his whole life, and he could never run fast enough. No matter how quickly he climbed the pole, he always thought it wasn't quick enough. He always

wanted to get ahead. This is why he was one of the youngest presidents we
ever had.

THE FIRST TWENTY U.S. presidents never lied about their health, and
yet, they had bad health all the time. George Washington, a year after taking office, got pneumonia and nearly died from it. Thomas Jefferson, during his first term, had constant diarrhea. He was always sick. It's one of the
reasons why he was always going back to Monticello, because his physician
said, "If you do a lot of horseback riding, that's going to be a solution."
Who knows? That was not much of a cure. Jackson had abscesses constantly
in his arm and in his lungs from bullet wounds. He'd been in a bar brawl
and taken a shot. He was coughing up blood constantly. He could never get
through a whole eight hours of sleep at night. He had terrible health problems. Then, of course, you come to Abe Lincoln, [who had] melancholia.
He really was the first president who probably should have been on Prozac.
He was depressed all the time.

[EXCEPT FOR GEORGE Washington,] all the other presidents tended to
fudge an awful lot [in times of war]. They played politics with war, even
Abraham Lincoln. . . . Lincoln was determined to win the Civil War, but he
was even more determined, in a way, to win re-election in 1864. He knew
that U. S. Grant was the best general in the army; he knew that after the
great victory at Vicksburg in Mississippi. But Lincoln [initially] declined to
bring Grant east to take over as commander in chief of the Army of the Potomac because he was afraid that Grant, from that position, would then run
for president against him. So he first sent emissaries down to talk to Grant,
to sound him out. After he got word back—and several months had
elapsed—then he finally appointed Grant. He played politics with national
security in the middle of the Civil War when tens of thousands of peoples'
lives were lost. That's what presidents do. Even Abe Lincoln.

Fraternity and Sexuality

MATTHEW PINSKER

This essay was taken from Matthew Pinsker's December 21, 2003, Booknotes *interview where he talked about his book* Lincoln's Sanctuary: Abraham Lincoln and the Soldiers' Home, *published by Oxford University Press.*

Joshua Speed and Lincoln were best friends when they were younger men, and they roomed together as young men. In those years, men shared beds together—men who were friends, men who were strangers. If you traveled, like Lincoln did as a lawyer on a circuit, running from town to town, you were thrown into a lodge. You might be thrown into a bed with another man. Now, to modern sensibility, that seems strange. But it wasn't to them.

[Lincoln and Speed] lived above a grocery store for four years or so and shared a bed but not alone. There were other men in the room. It was kind of a bachelors' hangout. They were close friends during that period. Then Speed got married, Lincoln got married, and they drifted apart.

Speed did come back into Lincoln's life occasionally. He visited Lincoln at the Soldiers' Home toward the end of the war, but they were never as close after those early days in Springfield.

David Derickson was about ten years younger than the president, and he was the captain of an infantry company, Company K of the 150th Pennsylvania [stationed at the Soldiers' Home]. He was from Meadville [Pennsylvania], he was a businessman, but he was a Republican politician.

He showed up with the company in early September 1862, and the president, as a courtesy, asked him to ride with him that second morning into Washington.

As they were riding into the city, they struck up a conversation, and Lincoln felt some sort of connection to him. They talked politics. They both came from relatively similar backgrounds.

Over the next several weeks, he and Derickson became friends. It's a remarkable story about their friendship. He took Derickson with him on a tour of the battlefield at Antietam, and then in late October when Mary Lincoln took Tad and went traveling to New England, Lincoln was alone in the Soldiers' Home cottage. According to the soldiers who were there, he invited Derickson to spend a night in the cottage, and according to the soldiers, Derickson slept in the bed with Lincoln at this cottage.

You can, from a modern perspective, raise an eyebrow over that, thinking about sexuality. They raised eyebrows back then, too, but they didn't think sexuality at all. Their gossip was about how a president could dare to be such close friends with a captain. There were many gossipers in the city. There was a woman who wrote in her diary that a captain was becoming close friends with the president, even riding with him and staying with him in the cottage. She wrote in her diary, "What stuff!" But she had no insinuation about sexual relationships. It was about the willingness of the president to break down class and social barriers. . . .

I think this is one of those instances where Lincoln's private life had a connection to his public decisions. It was the fall of 1862. The war was not going well. Lincoln had made a decision to emancipate slaves from rebel masters, and that was a very controversial thing. He was awaiting election results that were destined to be very disappointing to the Republican Party. He was considering firing General George McClellan, who was [commanding officer of the army and] a controversial figure. This was the final decision to terminate McClellan—it was a big move. Lincoln's wife and son had left him alone in this cottage on the grounds of the Soldiers' Home. He was lonely.

It was not just Derickson. Lincoln reached out to John Hay, his twenty-five-year-old aide, to Edwin Stanton, to a handful of other men. What he was trying to do was to recreate that world he had left behind in Springfield, with Speed and the guys in the grocery store or with the lawyers on the circuit, where they were more carefree, where they just told stories and relaxed. For me, the Derickson story is about how a lonely man found a little emotional support, a fraternity that helped him make some tough decisions.

THE PRESIDENT AND his wife had a difficult relationship to assess from the outside. Some historians think they were incredibly unhappy, and they fought, and others think that it was a relatively stable and happy relationship.

My review of the evidence leads me to think that, from the outside, it seems that by Lincoln's presidential years they had found a working relationship.

. . . One of the soldiers in the infantry company who was guarding the president [during their stays at the Soldiers' Home] received a telegram for Lincoln, and it was urgent. It was late at night, and the president was already asleep. The soldier was told to take it up to the president and wake him up. So he entered the cottage, went upstairs, knocked on the door. The president told him to come in. The soldier walked in, and the president was in bed with his wife. [The soldier] was shocked by this, and then later, years after the war, told the story to Ida Tarbell, a famous journalist and Lincoln biographer. She decided not to put it in her biography because it was a little too racy. I put it in my book because we have different sensibilities now. I think it's the first time we have an eyewitness who claimed to see the president and his wife sharing a bed together in that stage of their life.

PEOPLE WHO REALLY FOCUS on human behavior in that way, they see some value in stories like these and talk about them. . . . But none of them really explored the details of [Lincoln's relationship with Derickson.]

Obviously, the [Derickson] story has some political repercussions in the current context, but you try not to worry about that when you research history. . . . I don't think Lincoln was gay, and I don't think he had gay encounters. . . . My book is not an investigation of Lincoln's sexuality. Anybody who tells you that they know one way or the other, they're telling you more about themselves than about Abraham Lincoln. These intimacy issues are matters almost beyond the scope of normal history.

On the emotional questions—did the president need emotional intimacy, where did he find it, and how did he find it—I think that's a real subject worth exploring and debating and discussing. I was happy to do it. I didn't worry about the repercussions.

★ ★
★

Lincoln's Empathy

DORIS KEARNS GOODWIN

C-SPAN2's Book TV program In Depth *featured Doris Kearns Goodwin on November 6, 2005. Goodwin has written many books, including* Team of Rivals: The Political Genius of Abraham Lincoln *(Simon & Schuster) and the Pulitzer Prize–winning* No Ordinary Time: Franklin and Eleanor Roosevelt.

L incoln had this extraordinary empathy; he was able to see both sides of an issue. He gave a great speech when he was a young man . . . in which he argued that you were never going to change the people or the dram sellers who sell by the drink by denouncing them. Anathema breeds anathema; denunciation breeds denunciation. He called for trying to understand. He said the best way into a person's heart was to understand them and not to simply shun them. [Otherwise,] men will retreat within themselves.

[STILL], LINCOLN . . . [recognized] that the only way the war could finally be won was if the Southern capacity to make war was destroyed, which meant destroying the railroads. This was Sherman's March to the Sea. It meant destroying the crops and the cotton that was being sold to make money in order to keep the South in the war. Lincoln figured that unless the Southern capacity to make war was destroyed, it would keep going, and even more people would die.

What Lincoln thought he was preserving was not simply the Union. It wasn't even simply emancipating the slaves. He believed that if the South were allowed to secede, the whole experiment that was democracy would be destroyed. The South would secede, slavery would [continue to exist], and then maybe the West would secede from the East. Everyone in the world would be delighted that this "beacon of hope" that America represented—[this idea] that ordinary people could govern themselves—would be undone. It was something very large that he was fighting for.

ENGLAND AND FRANCE viewed the Civil War as an opportunity to come back and get more land from America, but, more importantly, an opportunity to see the whole democratic experiment fail. They were protecting monarchies; they were protecting a different form of government. If it was proven that ordinary people could not govern themselves, this would be good for [the European powers] and the wealthy classes in England and France. They were the ones supporting the South in the struggle against the North. William Seward, as [Lincoln's] secretary of state, did yeoman's work keeping the English and French out of the war. The masses in England, the working men, were in favor of the Northern cause because they were in favor of emancipation. The ruling powers [in Europe] were trying to maneuver us into a situation where if the North were to lose and if the South split off, then maybe they could pick off [territory in] Mexico.

THERE'S NO QUESTION that in wartime, civil liberties suffer. There's no question that when [Lincoln] undid *habeas corpus*—he had his reasons for doing it. [Union] troops were coming to protect Washington; people in Maryland were preventing them from getting there. He needed to do something to get the troops there or the whole cause would be lost.

LINCOLN THOUGHT A democracy like ours cleared away the artificial weights that prevented people from rising to the level of their own talent. He saw himself as an example of what was so extraordinary about America. He was able to push his way up to the top. He would see in [today's] society problems with education and problems with poverty and that there are whole groups of people who cannot push their way up to the top. [He would] want to help them.

LINCOLN WAS VERY LOYAL politically. It took him a long time to leave the Whigs and become a Republican. . . . He once said that government was there to do for individuals what they could not do well for themselves. He would have a different philosophy than the conservative elements of [today's] Republican Party, but he would probably try to make the Republican Party [move toward] what he believed in, rather than to switch to some other party.

HE DID SAY AT ONE POINT that labor was prior to capital. His whole theory was that labor built a business. . . . [He argued] that capital was subservient [to the interests of workers]. That's in a famous speech. He lived in the age before the Industrial Revolution, before you had robber barons, and before you had full-scale capitalists. It's interesting to wonder what he would think . . . in a later age, [whether he would] look back and retain that desire to see labor prior to capital.

IN THE WHITE HOUSE, the [president's] office and the Cabinet Room were the same. So unlike today, where you've got the Oval Office and then the separate Cabinet Room, there was a big long table where the cabinet met. It was a pretty simple setting. He had a big chair that he liked to sit in, a desk he sat at, and then a table that would be arranged in terms of primacy: secretary of state closest to the president; secretary of treasury next, in terms of which office was most powerful. The incredible thing about the White House and his office in those days [was that] a jobseeker could race in and simply get to Lincoln and talk to him. Those were the days before civil service. He would also have receptions in the White House where anybody could come, backwoodsmen and diplomats alike. The backwoodsmen, it was said, would drag in their mud. They would snip parts of the carpet to take home as souvenirs. People on Lincoln's staff would say, "[Mr.] Lincoln, you can't waste time talking to all these people." He said, "It's my public opinion bath. I need to do it. I need to remember the great popular assemblage from which I've come."

The White House [today] has become so much of a cocoon, and it's so insulated, partly because of security, but partly because of the way it's run. The reason we have these second-term blues with our presidents is because they've lost touch with the people. The first election they've just come from the people. Then the second election, they win it, and all the people who have been with them have also lost touch with ordinary people. Lincoln understood the importance of that.

If public opinion polls were out in his day, he would listen to them. He wouldn't say they don't mean anything. He would educate and shape the public [and] hopefully not be constrained by it. But he used to say, "With universal sentiment, anything is possible. Without it, nothing." In a democracy, the people's opinion matters, so he would try to keep touch. He understood the mood of the people, just like FDR did. It's that intuitive, mystical sense that a leader has.

PERSONALLY, IF I HAD an hour with Lincoln, I would ask him, please tell me some of your great stories. Lincoln was such a storyteller, so gifted. As a young lawyer, he would travel around the [legal] circuit for two months in the spring and two months in the fall. When he went from courthouse to courthouse, if they knew he was in town, people would come from miles around to listen to him stand by a fireplace and tell one story after another. They say that [despite that] sad face of his, once he started telling a story, his eyes would sparkle, and his whole life force would be shown.

HE REVERED THE Constitution and the framers. People who grew up in his generation were not that far from the founding. When he was a young man, he gave a famous speech, the Lyceum speech, in which he said he worried that his generation didn't have the same challenges as the Founding Fathers. He thought, "There's nothing left for our generation except to protect what they've done." He never would have imagined that the anti-slavery movement in the 1850s would lead to his becoming president. It led to a challenge even greater than that faced by the Founding Fathers.

EVERYBODY SAYS [LINCOLN] had a thin, high-pitched voice, which you can't quite imagine from that large a character. But his voice, they said, could range very far. In those days there were outdoor venues, and somehow he could be heard wherever he was. There was one reporter who heard him give one of his first speeches, the Peoria speech in 1854, and wrote about it later. He said when Lincoln first started out, you were aware of the thin, high-pitched voice. You were aware of how awkward [Lincoln] looked. Yet once he started speaking, he spoke with such conviction and with such strength that his voice became louder, and his whole energy was seen in his face. His body would move, and he became a different person. Matching the dazzling words that he was able to write, Lincoln's voice was able to deliver them with feeling.

HE DIDN'T HAVE A depth of education, but he was so deep in the things that he read. As a young child, he had to scour the countryside for books. Everything he could lay his hands on he would read. It was some of the best literature in our history: He read Shakespeare, Aesop's Fables, the King James Bible, poetry. So these cadences got into his soul and heart and allowed him to become that great writer. Literature allowed him to transcend his surroundings. Emily Dickinson once said, "There's no frigate like a book to take us lands away." Through literature, Lincoln was able to go with Shakespeare's kings to England, though he never went there in his life. He was able to go to Spain and Portugal with Lord Byron. That love of books . . . got into his soul in a way. Compare that with education today, [which] is so broad. Our students take so many different courses and fragments of one course and another. Maybe they don't get as deep a feeling for literature as they might, certainly as Lincoln did in the old days. He wrote and edited and wrote. It was part of a muscle in him from the time he was a child [and it] developed more and more. What happens today is that there are so many speechwriters on that White House staff. . . . [Presidents] are not doing [the writing] themselves, so they're not getting better. It isn't part of their importance, but it is important because communicating to the country and being able to give [people] a sense of where you're taking them still remains a central tool for a president.

MOST HISTORIANS WOULD argue that Lincoln's overwhelming strengths were far greater than his flaws. . . . What he might have done after the war—that is the big unknown question of history. Had he lived, would Reconstruction have been different? How would he have treated the South? How would he have ensured that black Americans had rights, even as he brought the South back into the Union? Everybody wonders—if Lincoln hadn't been killed, would things be different?

DYING AT THE HEIGHT of the war, just as it was about to be won, not having to deal with Reconstruction and all the messy problems of peace, probably kept Lincoln's reputation intact. Some say the country would have been better off dealing with Reconstruction [with him] than with Andrew Johnson, even if [Lincoln's] reputation became somewhat diminished. Because Reconstruction was complicated and messy, [it would have been better] to have Lincoln with that great sense of empathy toward the South and at the same time, [the determination to] protect the rights of black Americans. If we had had a better Reconstruction [period] and what followed it had not been as deadly, maybe the whole country would be better off today.

★ ★
★

Commander in Chief

ELIOT A. COHEN

Booknotes *hosted Eliot Cohen on September 22, 2002, for a discussion on his book* Supreme Command: Soldiers, Statement, and Leadership in Wartime, *which was published by Free Press. Cohen is counselor of the Department of State. As a principal officer of the department, he is a special adviser to the secretary and to the bureaus, particularly with regard to matters of war and peace.*

braham Lincoln was probably our greatest war president—even greater than Roosevelt. Lincoln was deceptive. That's a harsh word, but he was a man who worked extraordinarily subtly and indirectly. William Herndon, his law partner, said, "Any man who ever took Lincoln for a simple man usually found himself lying flat on his back in a ditch."

LINCOLN WAS IN MANY ways the most interesting of the group [profiled in my book, which includes wartime leaders Winston Churchill, Georges Clemençeau, and David Ben-Gurion]. Lincoln was a very gentle man. He stayed up late at night trying to figure out ways to commute sentences of sentries who had fallen asleep on guard duty and were sentenced to be shot. He wrote these extraordinary letters of condolence to the daughter of a friend of his who fell in battle [and other] women who were paying a price [during the Civil War].

At the battle of Fredericksburg, Ambrose Burnside, one of his less-able generals, hurled numerous armies at a completely open slope, Marye's Heights. He suffered ten thousand to twelve thousand casualties. [Lincoln] said to somebody in his office, "If we just had a general who was willing to do this every day for a week, . . . the Army of the Potomac would still be a mighty host, the rebel army would be shattered, the insurrection would be over, and the [Union] restored. The war won't be over until we find a general who understands that arithmetic. "

That is a pretty cold-blooded statement. This tremendously humane man was willing to support Grant when they were taking these awful casualties in 1864 and 1865.

Take a different example of ruthlessness with Winston Churchill, who also, had a very tender streak to him. One of the most brutal decisions that he made was in June of 1940 after the French had been practically knocked out of the war by the Germans. In order to prevent the French fleet from falling into German hands, he ordered the Royal Navy to attack it and its harbors in Algeria. [British warplanes] killed something like thirteen hundred French sailors. These were people who had been fighting side by side with [Britain] a few weeks earlier. Churchill's description of that was extremely eloquent. He said, yes, this was the hardest decision he ever made. He said there was a great tragedy, but it was absolutely necessary.

There was also a dark side to Clemençeau. He was actually much more up front about it. He once said, "I had children, they turned against me. I had a wife, she left me. I had friends, they betrayed me. I have only my claws, and I will use them." He was not terribly bashful about saying what a tough fellow he was.

ONE OF THE THINGS that [Lincoln, Churchill, Clemençeau, and Ben-Gurion] had, which it seems to me to be a tremendous requirement of good political leadership, is what [Lincoln's Assistant Secretary of War] Charles Dana said about Abraham Lincoln: "He had no illusions." That's one of the reasons why I think all four of these men were also melancholy. They were men without illusions.

[WHO DID LINCOLN FIRE?] The question is, who didn't Lincoln fire? He went through a long series of generals. He began by firing General Irwin McDowell. George McClellan, he kept a little bit longer. McClellan was in for about a year, fired, brought back, and then fired again after a month. Burnside, [was in for] a couple of months. Joseph Hooker lasted about five months. George Meade was . . . really [only] there for about nine months.

Lincoln could be brutal about it, and in my book I talk about a little-known episode in which he fired not just generals, but a major—[Major John J. Key]—who was reported to have said, "We didn't pursue [all-out victory against Confederate forces] after the battle of Antietam in September of 1862 because we actually wanted them to get away." Lincoln called him into the office and asked, "Did you say this?" Major Key said yes. Lincoln said, "You're out."

There's a poignant part, which brings out Lincoln's ruthlessness. McDowell later appealed [to have Key reinstated], and he had these [other] generals making the case. This petition came to Lincoln just after the poor major, who was desperate to get back into war because he was basically a patriotic man, had just made the ultimate sacrifice: his son, captain of the Ohio infantry, had been killed. What further patriotic testimony can you ask for? Lincoln said, "I'm terribly sorry, I've got to make an example of you."

LINCOLN WAS ULTIMATELY quite a good judge of character. This meant that you don't just accept what the military seniority and promotion system coughs up. You may have to reach down and find some rather unprepossessing soul who looks like Ulysses S. Grant. Very early on in the war, Lincoln kept an eye on Grant about whom he had heard both good and bad things. He tried to figure out, "Is this the kind of person who's right for the job?" So in this sense, Lincoln devoted an enormous amount of effort to try to figure out what somebody's character was and how far he could push them.

Tragic Sensibility

GORDON S. WOOD

The Purpose of the Past: Reflections on the Uses of History, *written by Gordon Wood and published by The Penguin Press, was featured on C-SPAN's Sunday program,* Q&A, *on April 13, 2008. Mr. Wood is Alva O. Way University Professor and Professor of History at Brown University. He has written many books, including* The Radicalism of the American Revolution *(Knopf, 1992), which won the Pulitzer Prize for History.*

When you do polling [on presidential popularity] among historians plus the general public, Lincoln comes out either first or second. Washington still [generally ranks] first because he had to start the whole business [of a new nation], but Lincoln is important for saving the Union. He's really an anomaly. People never expected that from him. He came out of nowhere. He had no education or college degree. Who could have thought that he would be the kind of president he was with such sensitivity, with a kind of tragic sense, which was perfect for the event that he had to lead. He was an extraordinary man.

The British have a statue of Lincoln outside the House of Commons. They saw Lincoln as the true American, the man who came from nowhere.

[During Lincoln's time], some people called him "the gorilla." He was gangly and uneducated, but he had a way with words and he had something that nobody expected. He transcended his time. The mid–nineteenth century was full of second-raters as presidents. The nature of democracy led to that. We were just plain lucky that we got someone of Lincoln's stature.

[LINCOLN'S ASSASSINATION] occurred on Good Friday. Think of the symbolism for a heavily Christian nation: his funeral was on Easter. He seemed to be elevated to the heavens in a way that simply wouldn't have been possible for somebody who would have lived out his life and gotten involved in the nitty-gritty politics of Reconstruction, which would have been messy for any president. The first [post-Lincoln president], Andrew Johnson, got impeached—though not convicted—as a consequence of his involvement in Reconstruction.

THAT GET-UP-AND-GO optimism of Americans is a wonderful thing, but it needs to be tempered by the kind of perspective that Lincoln brought to bear on it, [the idea] that there is a tragic side to life. Lincoln captured that. [Author and cultural critic John Patrick] Diggins felt that very strongly.

He was really opposed to what we call "liberal" America . . . not "liberal" in the modern political sense, more in the individualistic sense of acquiring, buying, consuming; individualistic [in the sense that] you don't think about the community, you think only, "What can I do for myself?" Diggins thought Lincoln was an antidote to this.

The American Revolution represented our optimistic side. [It was a fight about] life, liberty, and the pursuit of happiness—individual rights. Manifestly, that's what I suppose we are about.

That trilogy that comes out of the Declaration of Independence stands for America more than Lincoln's brooding presence. [But] it's nice to have a Lincoln in your past and to think about him and what he stood for: He always felt the world was out of his hands. He had a sense of fate. He was very un-American in that sense. He felt that he was being carried along, as the country was, by forces over which he had very little control. That's not an American attitude. We're much more hands on; we're in charge of our own future. Some of Lincoln's sense of limitation is healthy for us; [it brings] some humility.

[GEORGE] WASHINGTON was much more reticent. He was not a great stylist. He was not stupid, but he was uneducated. He never went to college. His words simply don't have the tragic sense Lincoln's had, and he didn't write anything akin to the Gettysburg Address. Washington was not a man of words. He was impressive, but not the way Lincoln was impressive. . . . He fulfilled his terms in office and was very disillusioned to get caught up in the politics of the time. He became the antagonist, in a sense, to Thomas Jefferson, [who was] not his immediate successor, but [came] shortly thereafter.

No one could have anticipated Lincoln's rise. [People] knew he was a great speaker, but he was a one-term congressman. He hadn't really had a lot of experience. He had never run a government; he was never an executive. We worry whether a senator who's had only two years in the Senate is equipped [for higher office], but this is a man who was only a one-term congressman.

There are a lot of people out there who want to read anything about Lincoln [because of] the Civil War. [It was] a tragedy, [one in which] the country killed so many Americans—six hundred thousand plus, one of the greatest losses in our history. That war has a fascination for Americans that will never die as long as our republic exists, and Lincoln is there, brooding over it. If he had been Martin Van Buren or somebody else, [the effect] wouldn't have been the same. So you have the combination of this terrible war, a bloody war by any standard, together with a man who had this tragic sensibility. The combination is almost irresistible for any author.

Enigma

FRANK J. WILLIAMS

Frank Williams, chief justice of Rhode Island's Supreme Court and a notable Lincoln scholar and enthusiast, joined Booknotes *for an interview on November 11, 2002. Williams talked about his book* Judging Lincoln, *which was published by Southern Illinois University Press.*

Each of us has a dark side and a light side, and Lincoln had a dark side, too. He had a temper. Most people don't know that. Fortunately for us and him, he was able to keep it in check most of the time.

His views on race were ambivalent, at best, and racist at worst. That was the culture in which he lived. We see that in comments he made at the Lincoln-Douglas debates. As other scholars have said, he probably would not have won the race for president if he had taken a position more closely aligned with the abolitionists.

In our current generation, there's more a sense of reality, [a feeling] that Lincoln really was not a godlike figure, that he was a human being. He was praised to the heavens after his death, which is unfortunate. He shouldn't be treated as some kind of a votive candle on the shelf somewhere. He did have human foibles. He was a hypochondriac; he was suspicious. He misjudged his generals during the war until he developed the necessary judgment to retain generals who could win battles. This is all part of the growth of a human being, in the first instance, and a leader in the second.

THE PRESIDENT IS commander in chief, as well as chief magistrate of America. [Lincoln's] role in both capacities was important for me to study.

On the whole, he managed these dual roles well. He struggled mightily, as every president does. . . . Many of the issues that Lincoln confronted we now confront, now that we are at war with terrorism, such as the security of our country versus civil liberties. That's why Lincoln remains such a relevant person.

CLEMENT LAIRD VALLANDIGHAM from Ohio [was] a Copperhead who was active in the Democratic Party. He was the Democratic congressman who vociferously opposed the war and the curtailment of civil liberties by Lincoln, especially the suspension of the writ of *habeas corpus*. That's where an imprisoned person has the right to appear before a magistrate to [ask] why he is imprisoned. There has to be probable cause and some crime alleged. During the war, Lincoln—with the ratification of Congress—suspended the precious writ of *habeas corpus*.

"Copperhead" was a metaphor for the snake of the same name. [It referred to] the loyal Unionist, or "Peace Democrats," who would meet secretly and protest and object to the government. It was very vocal and very vicious. To Lincoln's credit, he would not move against [Vallandigham] because of the First Amendment. [He believed that] you were allowed dissension.

[Union General] Ambrose Burnside . . . had a captain dressed in civilian clothes go to a speech where Vallandigham held forth. Burnside had issued a general order that made it treasonable to make utterances against the government. He had [Vallandigham] arrested. He was tried by a military tribunal. He was to be sentenced for a long term in prison. This embarrassed Lincoln, so he had Vallandigham sent into the Confederate lines. The Confederates weren't that happy to have Vallandigham. He finally left by way of Bermuda, then landed in Canada and ran unsuccessfully for governor of Ohio from Canada.

GENERAL GEORGE MCCLELLAN was Lincoln's troublesome general. He had a case of "the slows," to quote Lincoln. Lincoln reinstated him as general after the second battle of Bull Run, but after Antietam, when McClellan refused to follow up the so-called victory, Lincoln finally had the courage to fire him. Remember, McClellan was very popular with his troops. [Lincoln] sent a messenger with an order relieving him from command and appointing Ambrose Burnside, a Rhode Islander, to take his place as commanding general of the Army of the Potomac. Burnside did not want the command; he knew he didn't have the competence for it. We saw that at the battle of Fredericksburg in December 1862.

Lincoln was . . . fifty-one when he was elected, and McClellan was somewhat younger. The Democrats, the loyal opposition, thought that since

[McClellan] was so popular with the troops and America—he was an icon—they would choose him as the Democratic candidate for president in 1864. But there was a conflict from the beginning. They made this former commanding general of the Army of the Potomac the Democratic candidate, but then the peace lovers acquired a "peace platform" in which there was to be an effort at peace without the end of slavery and without, necessarily, reunion. This doomed the Democrats in the 1864 election.

McClellan had been in the military service . . . then became an executive for a railroad, and then came back into the service at the time of the Civil War, like so many people—including Burnside and General Ulysses S. Grant [who] started as colonel of a regiment in Illinois.

[McClellan] was out [of the military when he ran for president]. He had been relieved of duties, even though he continued to hold the rank. He returned home to New Jersey, and he never received an active command again.

[THE 1864 VOTE TALLY WAS] 2,200,000 for [Lincoln] and 1,800,000 against him. Lincoln is sometimes criticized for curtailing civil liberties, but here was a president and a commander in chief who allowed the elections to go forward in wartime. Initially, in 1864, he thought he was going to lose. That is why he wrote the "blind memorandum" in August and had all of the cabinet members initial the back of it. [The memorandum pledged the loyalty of Lincoln and his government to whomever won the 1864 election. Lincoln did not reveal its contents to those who signed.] He expected to lose, and if he did, he would work with the incoming president to either terminate the war or prevail in the war.

It was the first time in American history that soldiers in the field were allowed to cast a ballot. Lincoln took a big gamble, and yet he believed in the basic tenets of democracy and felt that you should not curtail elections.

[Despite McClellan's popularity with Union troops,] Abraham Lincoln, in the field vote alone—not counting the absentee ballots—got 121,152 votes to McClellan's 34,922, demonstrating the ability of Abraham Lincoln to transcend politics and strike a responsive chord in many Americans, including the soldiers in the field. These were the people who were being sent into battle, receiving the casualties and the deaths, yet they believed in this person they came to call "Father Abraham." They were able to differentiate between him and McClellan, who, under the peace platform, would end a war in which they fought so hard to prevail.

[LINCOLN WON 77 PERCENT of the military vote; 54 percent of the civilian vote; and 55 percent of the combined vote.] The fact that the soldier vote was so overwhelming for Lincoln did not affect the outcome, [although] it probably would have affected the tallies in two states—

Connecticut and New York. But what it symbolizes is just how much Lincoln was appreciated by the soldiers in the field.

[LINCOLN'S VIEW ON RACE] evolved to the point where he finally realized that colonization was not going to work. Colonization, or that [idea] of sending African Americans back to [Africa or to Latin America], started way back with Henry Clay. Clay was the perennial presidential candidate and a hero of Lincoln's. Both were Whigs before the Republican Party was created. [Colonization] was their way of saying, "Look, this is going to avoid the dissension and the arguments [over slavery] between the sections of the country and also between those who are free and those who are enslaved." As Lincoln learned, it was a wake-up call: Blacks did not want to return to some colony or to Africa. America was now their home, and he had to deal with them as part of our culture.

The Thirteenth Amendment outlawed "involuntary servitude," to use the exact language, forever and was added to the Constitution at the end of 1865. Lincoln campaigned for this amendment long before his re-election in 1864, which took a lot of guts and courage. He didn't have to say anything, but he did. It was so important to him that he logrolled, used [political] patronage. We have never found any illegal acts that he might have committed to get votes, but the important thing is he wanted the old Congress—that is, the Congress that would go out of existence after his inauguration in 1865—to be the one to pass the resolution that would go to the states for ratification. He succeeded in [gaining passage by the Congress] in February 1865.

It's a close call on whether his offer of patronage to congressmen to get their vote ran afoul of an anti-bribery statute that was already part of the United States code. Very close. We think no money [changed hands], but clearly the implication was that if you were to vote for this resolution, you might be taken care of with one of your constituents or relatives being given a job in the government.

[At the time Lincoln was pressing for passage of the Thirteenth Amendment, there also was an exchange between Jefferson Davis and the Union over] any interest that Lincoln might have had in bringing the war to closure and . . . whether his primary objective was to reunify the North and South. The issue facing Lincoln and the [Union] peace delegation that came to Hampton Roads [Virginia] with Vice President Alexander Stephens of the Confederacy was whether or not there would be reunion with slavery or without it. Lincoln held to the view that the war aims were now reunion and no slavery.

THE FASCINATING PART about Lincoln is that he was an enigma. As much as we know about him in the historical record, in his utterances, in the collected works of his writings and speeches—almost a million words [in total]—he still kept many things very close to his chest. He was a very private person. The challenge is to try to detect what was really going on his mind and what his motivations were and [to understand] the Machiavellian nature of his personality.

PART 4

IN MEMORY

Whitman's Lincoln

DAVID REYNOLDS

Booknotes featured David Reynolds talking about his book
Walt Whitman's America: A Cultural Biography, *which*
was published by Knopf, in an interview on April 28, 1996.

WALT WHITMAN'S two greatest poems after the Civil War were
about Abraham Lincoln. His most popular poem was "O Captain! My
Captain!" which is somewhat conventional, but his great poem was
"When Lilacs Last in the Dooryard Bloom'd."

[Whitman never met Abraham Lincoln] but saw him very often in the
streets and said that once or twice Lincoln would nod to him. Washington
in those days wasn't like today, where the president is usually, for most
people, just an image on the TV screen. In those days, one could actually
make an appointment with Lincoln and see him in the White House. Whitman himself never did that, but seeing him on the street often, he gained
an incredible admiration for—almost a fixation with—Abraham Lincoln,
who became what Whitman called "the martyred chief of America." Whitman spent much of his later years looking back [on that time].

Whitman was asked many times to give a lecture he had written called
"The Death of Abraham Lincoln" in which he relived the assassination. He
thought that in this moment of assassination, America came together in
grief over the death of its "martyred chief," and this was why Lincoln accomplished the social unification that Whitman had hoped his own earlier
poetry might accomplish. Whitman thought that because Lincoln became
such an important cultural icon, that Whitman himself would be the per-
petuator of Lincoln's memory.

He wrote ["O Captain! My Captain!"] in 1865. It was about imagining
Abraham Lincoln as the captain of the ship of state who was now fallen and
bloody on the deck. It was the one Walt Whitman poem that made it into

the school anthologies. It was the one poem that every schoolboy had to memorize. . . .

[Interestingly,] Whitman himself became a little tired of this poem because he was asked time and time again to recite it. After a while, he said, "Damn 'My Captain!' Damn that poem!" He [ultimately] became sick of it because it was his least representative poem—it was more conventional than much of his work, more rhymed with a regular meter.

Depicting Lincoln

ROBERT HUGHES

American Visions: The Epic History of Art in America, written by Robert Hughes and published by Knopf, was featured as part of the Booknotes *series on July 20, 1997.*

THERE is a lot of Lincoln photography. Lincoln was the first president whose image was really magnified by photography, but that's because there was a popular demand for his [image]. He was the first president in the age of photography who really was regarded as popular in an almost demi-godlike way, at least for Northerners. The official paintings of Lincoln are, for the most part, pretty dull, as any other official portraiture tends to be. It's the photographs that we remember Lincoln by.

THERE WAS A PAINTING done in the 1890s called "Memories of 1865" by John Frederick Peter. He was a magic realist whose paintings were quite popular in America. One of the interesting things about Peter is that he had this exceptionally nostalgic coding. It was called "Memories of 1865" because that was the year Lincoln was assassinated. [Peter's painting depicted] Lincoln's daguerreotype, [an early type of photograph produced on a silver plate,] and there was this old rusty Bowie knife, which was one of his studio props picked up on a Civil War battlefield. It's [depicted] hanging over the image of Lincoln like the sword over Damocles. . . . So the knife is figuratively cutting off the head of the house—and it's an allusion to the assassination of the president.

Persistent Rumors

IRVING BARTLETT

Booknotes featured John C. Calhoun: A Biography, *written by Irving Bartlett and published by Norton, on September 18, 1994.*

[**SOUTH CAROLINA** politician John C. Calhoun served in both houses of Congress and was vice president under presidents John Quincy Adams and Andrew Jackson.] The first question I was asked when I went to a social function in South Carolina [was whether John C. Calhoun was actually Abe Lincoln's father]. I was dumbfounded.

And then [this question] was asked again of me out in the backcountry by a black South Carolinian, a schoolteacher who lived in Abbeville where Calhoun had been born.

No, Calhoun wasn't Lincoln's father. But it is possible that Calhoun had some kind of relationship with a barmaid named Nancy Hanks. There was such a person, and Calhoun would have gone through the community where she lived. It's possible that something like that happened.

What interested me was that this legend stayed alive for so long. I discussed this with one person who knew a lot about South Carolina culture, and she said she thought it was because Carolinians didn't want to give Lincoln too much credit. They want to make sure that there was some Carolina blood in Abraham Lincoln.

I think it's more likely that Calhoun had an unspotted personal reputation, and people are unwilling to let people in public life get off scot-free that way. There's a tendency to be fascinated by any story that spots the reputation of the public person who presumably has been considered spotless.

The rumors of John C. Calhoun being Abe Lincoln's father are a fascinating legend that will never go away.

★ ★
★

Collecting Lincoln

FRANK J. WILLIAMS

Frank Williams talked about his book Judging Lincoln, *published by Southern Illinois University Press, in a November 10, 2002,* Booknotes *interview. Mr. Williams currently serves as president of the Lincoln Forum.*

I remember the sixth grade in the Cranston, Rhode Island, public schools. Mrs. Taylor, my teacher, directed me toward Lincoln and the Civil War. I had already had an interest in American history. I sat under this large portrait of Lincoln, and there was something in his face that attracted me. I don't know whether it was the compassion or leadership. My mother had read stories to me from a child's biography of Lincoln a couple of years earlier, so by the time I was eleven, I was already hooked on him. [At] thirteen I decided to become a lawyer because I realized what a good attorney Lincoln was.

Lincoln's story was like the Horatio Alger story—what Gabor Boritt has coined "the right to rise." If Lincoln could make it, I could make it. He was a politician before he became an attorney, but those two careers were inextricably entwined. We think [he worked] five thousand cases as a lawyer on the circuit, or in Springfield, and [handled] over 333 appeals before the Illinois Supreme Court, which is an amazing number.

Lincoln [made more money] than most people know—$5,000 for one case, the Illinois Central Railroad case, which was a tax case. He saved the railroad millions. Lincoln, to quote his last law partner, Billy Herndon, "did not have the avarice to get, but he had the avarice to keep." [He was] very conservative—he saved most of his money.

I'M FASCINATED BY THE leadership issue and how he operated as a president. I wonder about this in my own position as [chief justice of the Rhode

Island Supreme Court]—how would you face crises? We all have them in leadership positions. It's a great comfort to me to know that here's a man who is the quintessential American from humble beginnings, [someone who had] only one year's education in schools, who could rise to become the president of the United States and lead us through a civil war.

I STARTED IN LINCOLN organizations as a senior in undergraduate school, when I attended meetings of the Lincoln Group of Boston. I was very passionate about Lincoln at the time, and I eventually became president [of the group]. Then I became a member of the board of directors of the Abraham Lincoln Association, located in Springfield, Illinois, serving for nine years as president. Then with the encouragement of many Lincoln people on the East Coast, we began what's called the Lincoln Forum, which meets every November in Gettysburg, on the anniversary of Lincoln's Gettysburg Address.

There was a disagreement with my leadership of the Abraham Lincoln Association, and I was not re-elected in 1995. There were many board members who resigned. There was a feeling by many of us that the association concentrated more on the local area of Springfield, Illinois. Some of us wanted more outreach in the study of Lincoln. We wanted to include other Lincoln groups and create an umbrella [organization] to disseminate [information] and studies about Abraham Lincoln.

[THE LINCOLN FORUM IS] this great group of people from all walks of life with different interests in Lincoln and the Civil War. We have a great time when we get together in Gettysburg. It has students, truck drivers, professionals, academics—anyone who has an interest [in Lincoln and] $25 for a membership. We meet at this conclave in Gettysburg every November and publish two bulletins a year about what is going on in the forum and what we're doing in the way of outreach to study and spread the story of Lincoln.

[The modern Lincoln "industry" encompasses] collecting, studying, writing, lecturing, and the conferences that we put together. Of course, there is this core group, whether it's in Springfield or Gettysburg or the Lincoln Group of the District of Columbia or the Lincoln Fellowship of Wisconsin, that really make up the "industry," . . . [which includes] several thousand people, but for hardcore [Lincoln fans], I would say there are under one thousand.

It's good to see a library and museum [in Springfield] that's devoted to Lincoln and his works. I think it will [add to] the ability of people to study him and have more ready access to him. The whole point is to tell the Lincoln story. Not to embellish it, but to have the resources there for people who really want to discern the truth, rather than the perception.

I'm a member of the U.S. Abraham Lincoln Bicentennial Commission. Harold Holzer, [Illinois] Senator Richard Durbin, and [Illinois] Congressman Ray LaHood are the co-chairs. There are fifteen of us who are commissioners. We've created an advisory board of [more than] one hundred to assist in the planning for the celebration of Lincoln's two hundredth birthday on February 12, 2009. [We hope to] reach across the seas like we did in 1959 on the 150th, reach into schools to assist the teachers and the students with a core curriculum. . . .

[I HAVE ONE OF THE largest collections of Lincoln artifacts, or Lincolniana.] I don't know about the number of objects, but it is a big collection. Some twelve thousand books and pamphlets. Ten thousand other items—prints, photographs, statuary, philately, numismatics—and maybe another twenty thousand clippings, which you can use as a resource in my research library. I own 30 percent of the first five hundred items in the Monaghan bibliography, which came out in 1939. These are the most difficult items to get—sometimes one page or a small pamphlet. Since Lincoln died, there have been more than seventeen thousand books, pamphlets, and articles written about him.

The more valuable material I keep in a vault for obvious reasons—many of the prints, statuary, and many of the Lincoln books. In my home, there's a library called "Civil War and Collateral." [There] is the front hallway with Lincoln prints and cartoons. I'm very much infatuated with editorial cartoonists; they were always using Lincoln as a foil. This is an important legacy. It's not only helped me research, but it's something that my wife Virginia and I can leave some day to a school that has no Lincoln and Civil War collection. . . . We started cataloguing it before there was a software program for computers, so whoever gets the collection will have to do the scanning. I wouldn't have a clue [as to its value]—at least a million dollars.

We have what Virginia collects—the gee-gaws and gimcracks—[items like] a presentation copy of the Lincoln-Douglas debates. . . . You know how proud he was of the Lincoln-Douglas debates, even though he lost the Senate race in '58. . . . I have what Robert Todd Lincoln thought was the best likeness of his father. It's an original. I own a *carte de visite*—one of those small visiting cards that were very common during the Civil War—depicting John Wilkes Booth with the devil looking over his shoulder. I also have a pass to the military commission that tried the [assassination] conspirators, signed by General [David] Hunter. And a campaign flag with a misspelling of Lincoln's first name, "Abram" for Abraham.

[I ALSO OWN] AN original oil painting by James Montgomery Flagg, a great illustrator and painter of the early part of the twentieth century. He's known mostly for creating the "I Want You" Uncle Sam poster. I also have a miniature painting of a beardless Lincoln on ivory by an artist by the name of Patterson, done about 1929, and a "Wide Awake" lantern. During the 1860 election, there were these great "Wide Awake" parades in favor of the Republican ticket, and people would carry the lanterns over their shoulder. [I have a photograph of] Mrs. Lincoln in better times wearing a beautiful dress. This is a photograph from Mathew Brady's studio. There was a tax on these photographs. That's why you see a stamp on it. One of the great things that I keep in the bank vault is Lincoln's telegram to a lawyer friend, Samuel Glover in St. Louis; Lincoln is asking for news of what's going on, intelligence.

[DURING LINCOLN'S LIFE], photography was still in its infancy. There was never a composite photograph of the Lincoln family, so all of the artists would create this composite of the family. Malcolm Forbes, publisher of *Forbes* magazine, now deceased, began collecting Lincoln material assiduously in the 1970s. He had been a collector of many other things like Fabergé eggs and miniature lead soldiers. He acquired a fortune in Lincoln documents, many of which were sold . . . by his heirs at Christie's.

[Forbes's collection included] a letter to George Ramsay by Lincoln, where you see Lincoln's sense of humor and character. . . . He's writing to Major Ramsey and says this woman wants work [for her sons]. "See if you can find [them] jobs. Wanting to work is so rare an event it ought to be encouraged." He may have dictated a few letters to his secretaries John Nicolay and John Hay, but most of this was done in his own hand by him.

[Forbes and another Lincoln collector, Ross Perot] competed. I remember one event where they were competing over a printed copy—printed; not in Lincoln's handwriting—of the Emancipation Proclamation that was signed by Lincoln and his Secretary of State William Seward. I think it sold for $270,000.

If you were to get a "clip" signature—that . . . was my first Lincoln document, and it went for $200 in 1970. To get one like it today would cost $5,000. People in olden days thought that clipping the signature from a document would make [it] more valuable, which is ridiculous because you really want the whole document.

You don't need to have wealth to get Lincoln documents. You can start modestly—campaign documents, prints, the little photographs, sheet music, coins, anything that represents the middle period of American history and has a story about Abraham Lincoln.

I LIKE HAVING LINCOLN around me. It's an inspiration to me during my own days at work, [in the chief justice's chambers]. I've owned a bust of Lincoln, which is a copy of the full bust of his head, since I was thirteen years old. I'm especially enamored with these marquettes—these small [ceramic] copies of Lincoln. I also have John Hay and John Nicolay's biography of Lincoln, a first reading of the Emancipation Proclamation, a working model of Daniel Chester French's Lincoln for the Lincoln Memorial. . . . A full-scale model of Lincoln's patent that's in the U.S. Patent Office— Lincoln patented his idea of lifting a vessel over the shoals with ballasts that are underneath the deck. There's also presentation copy by the Free Colored People of New Orleans to President Lincoln in honor of his issuing the Emancipation Proclamation.

THERE HAS BEEN INTEREST [in my collection] from Brown University, which already has a great Lincoln collection, the McLellan Lincoln collection; and from Louisiana State University in Shreveport, which has a triennial conference on the presidents and an International Lincoln Center headed by Professor Bill Pederson. I still need [these materials] for my own research, [but] I'd like to begin sending out duplicates, different printings, because I'm really out of room.

I hope [to donate the collection] while I'm still alive, but if I'm not, there is a provision in my estate plan with the committee to determine where the collection will go. I've already come to terms with that. It's like any material item. We're only here temporarily, and then we pass, just as I'll pass the baton for being chief justice someday to a successor. This collection ought to go the same way.

Lincolniana

LOUISE TAPER

Lincoln collector Louise Taper joined C-SPAN for a tour of the Abraham Lincoln Presidential Library and Museum in Springfield, Illinois, on April 18, 2005. Ms. Taper shared her collection of Lincoln artifacts with the museum for display. She is also co-author of the book Right or Wrong, God Judge Me: The Writings of John Wilkes Booth, *published by the University of Illinois Press.*

If you do an exhibition on Lincoln, people just show up. They want to know more and more about him. It's magic. He started with nothing, and ended up president of the United States, and that's the dream of a lot of people.

[I STARTED COLLECTING Lincolniana] about thirty years ago. I read a book on Abraham Lincoln and wanted to learn about the family, and it just took off. I started reading [more] books. The first book was $12, and it just grew [from there].

I WOULD BUY WHATEVER I could buy. Then I decided I had to focus on what I wanted to collect. I decided that I would be the first woman collector. Most men collect war and battle items from his presidential time; I wanted to collect from every phase of Lincoln's life. I wanted to start from the beginning. So one of the pieces I have is the first known piece that he wrote [from] when he was fourteen. It's a sum book—"Page 1, Mathematics"—and a little poem he wrote.

I bought [a top hat] from a collector. When he first showed it to me, I knew I had to have it. He said, "I'm not selling it." Then after many years,

I got a phone call. It was him, saying, "Do you want the hat?" I was ecstatic. I bought it, and I share it with everyone so people can see it. It belonged to Lincoln. He gave it to a man, and it was passed down.

It actually shows wear and tear from fingers on the brim. We don't know if it's from Lincoln's [fingers] or not, but either Lincoln or whoever had it after him would [hold it]—you can see underneath is the thumbprint and then he just tipped his hat. . . . [To verify authenticity of an item, the seller] has to have the documentation from the time it left Lincoln's hands—who he gave it to, what they did with it. This particular hat is accompanied by a huge file that's very thick. It tells the whole story up until now. The collector who had it before me was here in Springfield, so the hat was used for different functions with different governors. This particular hat has a very good history.

I NEVER WANTED TO get into collecting [items related to] the assassination, but to have a complete collection you have to do it. . . . One of the pieces I have is a letter written by Mary Suratt, one of the conspirators. It was offered to me. [There is also] a scarf given by John Wilkes Booth to a young woman nine months before he killed Lincoln. I bought a series of love letters he wrote to her. He gave her this scarf and a ring . . . and he wrote her six very interesting letters. No one knew about her until these letters were discovered about eight or ten years ago.

[I LOANED PIECES FROM my collection to the Abraham Lincoln Presidential Library and Museum in Springfield, Illinois.] I love the idea that people can walk through there and walk through Lincoln's life. You can enter the log cabin and see how he grew up and then go into a [replica of part of] the White House and see how he lived there. . . . You see his clothing, Mary Lincoln's clothing, their china, crystal, her jewelry, and a lot of personal things. There is an invitation from Willie inviting someone to his birthday party.

I BOUGHT THE [FORD'S Theatre chair] at an auction where there were some other Booth things up for sale. It had been in a collection in a theater museum.

A LOT OF ITEMS WERE hard to get, very unusual pieces [such as] Lincoln's chamber pot from the presidential china service. A collector was at this particular auction where I bought the chair and he bought [the pot] and I wanted to get it from him. He said, "I'm not going to sell it." Then, one day he called me up and said, "I would like to sell it to you," and I bought it. So you do have to wait for pieces.

[THE MOST EXPENSIVE Lincoln item] would be the Gettysburg Address or something like that—any of the famous speeches. I think artifacts have gotten just out of bounds to buy now.

I'm really cautious because you can buy something that might not be good. . . . You have to check if something has been stolen . . . and that has happened before. Or, if it's a manuscript you've bought, it could be a facsimile and not the real thing. If someone is pushing me, saying, "You have to have it now or I will sell to it someone else." I say, "Sell it to someone else."

The Lincoln Cult

THOMAS DILORENZO

Thomas DiLorenzo joined C-SPAN's Q&A *for an interview on May 25, 2008, to talk about his book* Lincoln Unmasked: What You're Not Supposed to Know About Dishonest Abe, *published by Crown Forum. Mr. DiLorenzo is a professor of economics at the Sellinger School for Business and Management at Loyola College in Maryland.*

After the war, after Lincoln was assassinated, the New England clergy began his deification. I have in my research files an old magazine article that has a picture of Abe Lincoln with angel's wings ascending into the sky [from] an open tomb. This was the sort of thing that went on in the immediate years after the Civil War. That led to the deification of the American presidency. It aided this idea that some people call "American exceptionalism," [the notion] that Americans are exceptional people. There was a "new birth of freedom" during the Civil War, the story goes.

Americans attach their own sense of morality to the whole story of Lincoln. That's one reason why I get attacked a lot for trying to criticize certain things that Lincoln did. I've had quite a few debates with the academics who have had careers deifying Lincoln in their writings. I'm an economist, and [in my profession] I'm used to a lot of back-and-forth debates and criticism. For twenty years before I wrote my [first] Lincoln book, I . . . would go to academic meetings [of economists] and that's what we do. We criticize each other, and it's usually constructive criticism. It's not just showboating or trying to attack somebody.

You can criticize Thomas Jefferson, Bill Clinton, George W. Bush, and Franklin Roosevelt, but you can't criticize Lincoln, apparently, in the history profession. I thought that was very unscholarly and unprofessional and closed-minded on the part of some segments of the history profession—a big part of the history profession. I see no reason why you can't take a look at Lincoln, just as you'd look at any other president, and look at the good and the bad.

There's plenty of bad: Lincoln's suspension of *habeas corpus*, the mass arrest of tens of thousands of Northern civilians, and his shutting down of hundreds of opposition newspapers. These are things that most Americans never heard of. I've given public speeches about this, and people are dumbfounded. They accuse me of being a liar because they were never taught this in school. It's all documented; it's not a secret. Historians know about all of this, but the average American doesn't seem to know it unless he reads my books and the books of a few others.

I GREW UP IN PENNSYLVANIA. I played in baseball in Thaddeus Stevens Middle School, [which is named for a leading Lincoln-era abolitionist], and I remember singing the *Battle Hymn of the Republic* in elementary school almost every day. I was educated like most Americans were: I thought [Lincoln] was the savior of the Union and the man who freed the slaves. But there was always something that sounded kind of fishy about that story to me, even when I was a school child. I started educating myself some more about it, and I changed my mind about Lincoln.

I STARTED READING a lot about the Civil War, then I took courses at the Smithsonian, and I went on field trips. It was a hobby of mine. I'm an economics professor at Loyola College in Baltimore, and started thinking of how I could combine my profession, economics, with Civil War history, and thought that writing about Lincoln was the way. The economic side of the story of Lincoln and the Civil War has been underdeveloped, under-told.

IN SOME OF MY WRITINGS, I talk about the "church of Lincoln." He's been deified a great deal. I think it's a very unhealthy thing for society to deify any politician, whether it's Abraham Lincoln or George Washington. There's nothing wrong with praising them for the good things they've done, but it's dangerous to deify a politician. Even the Communist parties [in the] USA have tried to attach their agenda to the martyred Abraham Lincoln and have used him and his words and his deeds for all sorts of purposes, some good and some not so good.

One of the things that really bothered me was when I found out that all of the other countries of the world that ended slavery in the nineteenth century did so peacefully, [as did] New England and Ohio and Pennsylvania and Indiana, the Northern United States. Why was this not an alternative for America? Why was it only in America where there was a war attached to the ending of slavery? . . . I think it could have been possible for us to do what England and Spain and France and Denmark and other countries did: end slavery peacefully.

The purpose of the invasion of the Southern states was what Lincoln said it was, to destroy the secession movement—as he called it, "saving the Union." But all of the death that was attached to that is the thing that haunts me. Was it really necessary for some 650,000 Americans to die? If you standardize that to today's population, which is ten times higher than it was in 1860, you're talking the equivalent of five or six million people dying. That is what hit me hard, that all of that death was necessary just to save the Union. I argue that the Union wasn't "saved" because the Union of the Founders was voluntary. It was no longer voluntary after 1865.

I CALL [LINCOLN] THE POLITICAL son of Alexander Hamilton. Hamilton, as treasury secretary, essentially advocated bringing the British mercantilist system to America. This mercantilist system—it's a tongue-twister of a word—was a system of policies that benefited politically connected businesses at the expense of consumers and other businesses. There were government-sanctioned monopolies in England, for example. There were barriers to international trade as part of it. There was what we today would call corporate welfare, or subsidies to politically favored businesses. Hamilton favored all of this.

After his death, the mantel for this movement to bring British mercantilism to America fell to the Whig Party and Henry Clay, then to the Republican Party. Abraham Lincoln always said that Henry Clay was his political role model. He called him the *beau ideal* of a statesman in one of his speeches. Lincoln spent twenty-eight years of his off-and-on political involvement before becoming president advocating what Henry Clay and Hamilton called the American system of high protectionist tariffs, a central bank run by politicians in the nation's capital, and government subsidies to corporations. The Whig Party thought this would be the key to perpetual political power: Have a bank that could print money [and] tariffs that would block competition so you would have all of the big corporations, mostly in the North, on your side as the Whig Party.

Lincoln picked up that mantel as the Republican nominee and then president. There had been a political battle over these economic policies for about seventy years. The Whigs and the old Federalists of Hamilton's day had very little success in getting any of this done over this time, but it was all put into place during the Lincoln regime. Tariffs went up 45 to 50 percent and stayed there until Woodrow Wilson became president in 1913.

The central bank and the National Currency Act were resurrections of Hamilton's central banking idea. Railroad subsidies, the big subsidies to the railroad corporations, started during the Civil War. [Free-market theorist Friedrich] Hayek would have been opposed to every bit of that. That's all interventionist, anti–free market, big government economic policy. There are a lot of historians who don't understand much about economics. They look at these things and tend to judge these policies by the intentions of the people who advocate them. They'll say, "I think Abraham Lincoln was a great man. He advocated these things, therefore they must have been good ideas." That's essentially the argument that is made. Well, you can agree that he was a great man, and he had good intentions, but these were bad policies, bad for America.

WHEN YOU CONSIDER that he had less than one year of formal education and he became one of the top lawyers in the United States—self-taught—he certainly had greatness. He was brilliant; he was a genius. A great tragedy for America, however, is that he used [his] genius to manipulate the South Carolinians into firing the first shot at Fort Sumter and plunging the whole nation into a war. Then, [after] invading his own country at Fort Sumter—no one was killed or hurt—his response was a full-scale invasion of the entire Southern states.

Wouldn't it have been great had he used this genius to be more statesmanlike and end slavery peacefully like the British and the Spaniards did, and do other things for America, as opposed to [conducting] a four-year war that killed 650,000 Americans?

He promised he would not send warships to Fort Sumter, yet he did. [There is] a letter from Lincoln to his naval commander—Gustavus Fox—thanking him for his assistance in getting the outcome that they desired. The outcome that they desired was getting the South Carolinians to fire on Fort Sumter because Lincoln guessed correctly that the people of the North would rally behind the flag and support the war that he wanted to get into.

At the same time, the Confederates had sent peace commissioners to Washington to offer to pay the South's portion of the national debt and to pay for federal forts like Fort Sumter. Napoleon III of France offered to broker some sort of compromise. Lincoln refused to speak to any of them; he wouldn't see any of them. He was determined to go to war, which he did. He came up with this idea of the mystical Union. In one of his speeches, he talked about the "mystic chords of memory" of the Union. Up to that time, I would argue most Americans understood that the Union was voluntary and that it would be an atrocity, if any state had left, to march an army into that state and kill some inhabitants just to keep it in the Union.

I ran across a big two-volume set of books called *Northern Editorials on Secession* by a man named Howard Perkins. It [contains] reprinted Northern newspaper editorials from 1859, 1860, and 1861 about this whole issue of secession. He concludes that the majority of the newspapers from New York to Cincinnati to Vermont [and] Wisconsin in the North, were in favor of letting the South go peacefully because they believed in the old Jeffersonian dictum that the Union was voluntary. In the Declaration of Independence [are the words that] governments "derive their just powers" from the "consent of the governed." When the Northerners saw the South saying, "We no longer consent to be governed by Washington, DC," most of them said, "Okay, let them go." . . . [Some Northern newspapers] might have thought [the South] was mistaken or wrong-headed, but [said] "Let them go and maybe we can persuade them to come back into the Union at some future date." That seemed to be the attitude of a lot of these newspaper people.

A LOT OF WHAT MOTIVATES the so-called Lincoln scholars is using the whole Lincoln legend to prop up their version of the state. . . . You have people on both sides of the political spectrum that I call court historians, [who] try to use history, the history of Lincoln in particular, to promote their own particular agenda whatever it is, left and right.

There's not enough time in one man's life to read all of the books that come out about Lincoln. . . . Of all of the Lincoln scholars I've read, David [Herbert] Donald, is my favorite mainstream scholar. You learn a lot more from him than any of the others. You read other books about Lincoln [and] they'll take one seven-hundred-word speech and write an entire book about it. That in itself [is]dubious to me. What's usually done is they take it sentence by sentence and then interpret for you, [telling you] what you should think about this sentence. . . . You never get any of that with someone like David Donald.

There's a whole [Lincoln] group in the academic world. There are Lincoln book awards. If you want a career as a historian, as an academic historian, and you want to write books and get book contracts from big publishers, whether it's a big university publisher or a commercial [publisher], you'll get loads of recommendations to do that from . . . what I call a member of the church of Lincoln.

You cannot have a career as an academic historian if you're a critic of Abraham Lincoln. You won't get a job; no one will hire you. Maybe you can teach high school somewhere, but if you get a Ph.D. in history doing research that is critical of Lincoln [you won't have a career in higher education]. You can write a dissertation that's critical of Thomas Jefferson, of George Washington, of any other president, but not Abraham Lincoln.

When my book first came out, rather than arguing with me, a lot of academics started personally attacking me . . . [They said], "He's lying, he made this up, made that up." I'm not that foolish [to think] I'm publishing a book on Abraham Lincoln [and would] get away with something like that.

A lot of the facts of Lincoln's life and experience, such as suspending *habeas corpus* and having the military mass arrest tens of thousands of Northern citizens, [are facts] I laid out and left there. I didn't make any excuses for it. I didn't say he was forced into it, that the devil made him do it. That really upset a lot of the Lincoln scholars.

The way to become a Lincoln scholar is to take something like this atrocious attack on civil liberties in the Northern states and dream up some excuses for it, think of why he had to do it. If you do that, you're a Lincoln scholar. I didn't play that game. I either said nothing or said the obvious, that this was an atrocious infringement on freedom. The Supreme Court agreed with me on this topic. In 1966, there was a statement that the Supreme Court [issued] about the suspension of *habeas corpus.* They said that it is especially important to enforce the Constitution during wartime because Lincoln and others [argued] that we need to suspend constitutional liberty at wartime, and we can return to normalcy after the war. The courts disagreed with that.

When my book first came out, *The Real Lincoln,* I had an e-mail from a syndicated columnist, Paul Craig Roberts, who wrote a blurb for the back of the book. He said, "You're destroying their human capital, that's why they're attacking you." Human capital is a term we economists use for your body of knowledge, your education, your skills, and so forth. You have a lot of people who have spent careers writing books and articles deifying Abraham Lincoln. Then the skunk at the garden party shows up—me.

There are other Lincoln critics, [such as]. . . . [author and *Ebony* magazine editor] Lerone Bennett, Jr., who's a big critic of Lincoln. You can also find articles in academic journals. There's Professor Clyde Wilson from the University of South Carolina and Donald Livingston at Emory University, who are also academic Lincoln critics.

I got a paper from a young man who published in *The Journal of the Abraham Lincoln Association.* His name is Phillip Magness. He wrote a very critical article about Lincoln and his so-called colonization idea. Lincoln had this fetish about colonizing free black people and sending them to Liberia [or somewhere else in] Africa, anywhere but here. Lincoln's idea about equality—he said it many times—was that he didn't believe that black

North Carolina artist Chas Fagan, in his Charlotte studio, puts the finishing touches on a synthetic clay model of Lincoln for a bronze sculpture commissioned by the Union League Club of New York, which was founded in 1863.

C-SPAN camera technician Bill Heffley videotapes outside Lincoln's Cottage, at the Soldiers' Home in Washington, DC, which opened to the public in February 2008 after an eight-year, $15 million restoration by the National Trust for Historic Preservation. The cottage, three miles from the White House, was a retreat for the Lincoln family during their White House years.

(Photo on right) The library in the Lincoln Cottage, Washington, DC.

Lincoln biographer David Herbert Donald, in his personal library at his home on Lincoln Road in Lincoln, Massachusetts. **(Inset)** Presidential historian Doris Kearns Goodwin, Dr. Donald's Massachusetts neighbor, in a 2007 C-SPAN interview conducted at the Map Room in the White House, where she discussed Lincoln's cabinet.

Journalist and cultural historian Lerone Bennett, Jr., from a September 10, 2000, interview for C-SPAN's *Booknotes* series about his book, *Forced Into Glory*.

Doug Wilson appears at the 2007 National Book Festival in Washington, DC, to discuss his book, *Lincoln's Sword*. Dr. Wilson co-directs the Lincoln Studies Center at Knox College in Galesburg, Illinois, one of the sites of the seven 1858 Lincoln-Douglas debates.

▢ President George W. Bush **(left photo)** and President Bill Clinton **(right photo)** accept bronze sculptures depicting the 1858 Lincoln-Douglas debates from C-SPAN CEO Brian Lamb. The bronze sculptures were created by Illinois artist Lilly Tolpo in 1994 to commemorate the Freeport Debate, the second of seven debates held around the state between incumbent Senator Stephen A. Douglas (D) and challenger Abraham Lincoln (R). C-SPAN worked with the seven communities to televise complete re-enactments of each three-hour debate.

📷 Historian Garry Wills at the Library of Congress in Washington, DC, with one of the five known copies of the Gettysburg Address, in a December 1994 C-SPAN telecast, as the document went on public display for the first time in twenty-three years.

📷 Economist Thomas DiLorenzo appears on C-SPAN's *Q&A* series in April 2008 to discuss his books, *The Real Lincoln* and *Lincoln Unmasked.*

📷 **(Photo on right)** Dr. Edna Greene Medford of Howard University in Washington, DC, stands next to a circa 1888 advertisement detailing the political, social, and educational progress of African Americans, part of the university's collection.

▣ Journalist and author Andrew Ferguson at the Petersen House in Washington, DC, where Lincoln died on April 15, 1865, after being shot while attending a play at Ford's Theatre. The theater, closed for renovation through winter of 2009, will reopen with a new Education and Leadership Center **(photo on right)** examining Lincoln's legacy.

■ Presidential historian Richard Norton Smith, flanked by models of Lincoln cabinet members William Seward and Salmon Chase, previews exhibits at the Abraham Lincoln Presidential Museum in Springfield, Illinois, for C-SPAN viewers on April 18, 2005, one day prior to the museum's official public opening.

C-SPAN video journalist Richard Hall edits video for a Lincoln production, part of C-SPAN's coverage of the 2009 bicentennial of Abraham Lincoln's birth.

(Below) Louise Taper, a member of the Abraham Lincoln Bicentennial Commission, and one of the nation's foremost collectors of Abraham Lincoln artifacts in a C-SPAN interview.

(Bottom photo) Among the items in the Taper collection are the blood-stained gloves worn by President Lincoln at Ford's Theatre on the night of his assassination.

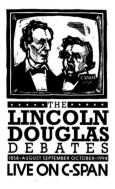 Four of six Abraham Lincoln re-enactors who portrayed the 1858 Illinois Republican Senate candidate in C-SPAN's 1994 televised re-enactments of the seven Lincoln-Douglas debates. From left: B. F. McClerren (Charleston debate); Max Daniels (Ottawa debate); George Buss (Freeport and Jonesboro debates); and Scott Mandrell (Alton debate). Not pictured are re-enactors Michael Krebs (Galesburg debate) and Jack Ingraham (Quincy debate).

people could be equal in America. Back in what he called their native clime, Africa or Haiti or some place like that, Lincoln said, they could be equal. But not here.

Phillip Magness . . . essentially showed that almost up to his dying day Lincoln was working on this. He was working on what to do with the freed slaves after the war. He was wondering, do we have enough ships to send them or to deport them to some other place? During his presidency, he did allocate several million dollars to send some free black people to Liberia in Africa. The man he put in charge of it turned out to be an embezzler, so nothing came of that.

Lincoln held a meeting of some free black men in the White House during his administration, urging them to lead by example and leave the country and go to Liberia. These men wisely said, "No thanks." I'm pleased to see that young scholars like [Magness] are starting to look into the truth. You don't have to be an attacker of Lincoln to write about the truth. American adults can take it.

THERE'S AN OLD BOOK that was published in the 1920s and recently reprinted called *Lincoln and the Railroads*. Lincoln was an attorney for all of the main railroads in the Midwest. He was offered the job of general counsel of the New York Central Railroad, . . . a perfectly legitimate thing. One of the things that I found in this book was that Lincoln bought a bunch of land in Council Bluffs, Iowa, in 1857, around the same time he was offered the job of the general counsel of the New York Central Railroad at a pay of $10,000 a year, which was a very princely sum in those days. He turned [the job] down. Then, a few years later after he got elected president, one of the first things he did was to call a special session of Congress . . . to get the ball rolling on the Pacific Railroad Act. The bill passed about a year or so later and gave the president the right to determine the eastern terminus of the transcontinental railroad. Guess where he chose? He chose Council Bluffs, Iowa. He must have made a killing on that.

There was another instance in this book where Lincoln worked for his client—the Illinois Central [Railroad] in a tax case, which he won—he presented them with a bill for $5,000. That was an enormous bill. The vice president of the Illinois Central said, "My board of directors will not pay a $5,000 bill to a country lawyer from Illinois." So Lincoln sued the Illinois Central. When he went to court, the lawyers for the Illinois Central did not show up, and he won the $5,000 by default. The author of this book, John W. Star, can't prove that there was some sort of corrupt deal between this vice president of Illinois Central and Lincoln, but he strongly suggests there was something. . . . By the way, the [executive] was George B. McClellan. I kept reading it over and over and thought, surely this is not the George McClellan, the [Union] general, but it was. It was the same man . . . who would become [Lincoln's] commander of the Army of the Potomac four years later.

I GAVE A SPEECH IN Springfield, Illinois, last year, and visited Lincoln's home. He lived in a place now in Springfield that's called Old Aristocracy Row. He lived in the biggest house on Old Aristocracy Row, and his law offices are still there. Lincoln and Herndon law offices are about one hundred paces from the Old State Capitol building in Springfield. So he was essentially a lobbyist—[that's] the way we would think of him today—for the railroad companies. That in itself is not corrupt, but I think he did demonstrate some corruption in his career.

[THE 2009 BICENTENNIAL of Lincoln's birth] is going to be quite a big party. There's a commission with all of the big-shot Lincoln scholars, and they've already begun publishing things and putting on television shows. Since I'm a big Lincoln critic, people ask me if I think he should be on Mount Rushmore. I tell them I don't think anyone should be on Mount Rushmore. I think it's unhealthy for society to deify politicians, even the ones I like, like Thomas Jefferson. This whole two hundredth anniversary is sort of like that; it's mostly a celebration of the American state. The people on this commission are so in love with Abraham Lincoln or with the government that is funding it. There's a lot of government money going into it. It's a celebration of itself—the federal government that's putting all of this money behind the [festivities].

There should be a Lincoln Memorial. We're all [okay] with that if the people want to memorialize one of their presidents, but the memorial itself is quite a spectacle. It looks like a Greek temple to me. Washington, DC, is one big city of memorials. My interpretation is they're not necessarily memorializing George Washington or Abraham Lincoln or FDR. It's the government that is memorializing itself with all of these monuments.

I'm a Ron Paul libertarian, politically. . . . I believe in the old Jeffersonian dictum that bigger government means less freedom, in general. This is all promoting bigger government, all of these memorials and monuments to our politicians.

I'VE NEVER BEEN INVITED to speak [at the Abraham Lincoln Association or Lincoln Forum]. I've been around some of these Lincoln scholars before, and I've had some experiences that were appalling. The History

Channel . . . had a series on American presidents. Not all of them—maybe five or six before Lincoln—and they had almost nothing good to say about any of them. The point was to make Lincoln seem even bigger than we think of him now because the others were so bad. They interviewed me, and I must have been totally contrary to that theme. . . . They used about twenty seconds of it, but I think it was just to needle me, to aggravate me, because they twisted my words around to make me say the opposite of what I said about Lincoln during the interview. . . . [So, in the future] I would insist on knowing the ground rules of any kind of debates, rather than being set up.

. . . WE PUT ON AN academic conference in Richmond . . . about different aspects of Lincoln. . . . It was a very low-cost event. It was at the old John Marshall Hotel in downtown Richmond, which was being renovated at the time. We had over three hundred people attend on a beautiful spring day in April on a Saturday.

We had seven academics give talks, and then we had a ninety-minute question-and-answer session at the end. It was all very educational and very stimulating. A lot of people from Washington, DC, drove down to Richmond to see this event and [author and journalist] Andrew Ferguson wrote about it. I was disappointed though. He said almost nothing about the substance of what was said in our conference, but he did mention it in his book.

There was an open question-and-answer session after each presentation, and there were three hundred people in the audience. We left an extra hour-and-a-half at the end just to ask any question of any of the speakers. I've never been to a conference dominated by the Lincoln scholars that did that. They never seemed to let people like myself have an hour-and-a-half to interrogate them about their views. . . . I was the organizer of the conference along with two or three other people. But I didn't have much of a taste for inviting many of these [Lincoln scholars] after they had treated me so shabbily.

I was at another event in Richmond. It was panel discussion with a well-known Lincoln scholar. . . . During the course of this panel discussion this man stands up and says things like, "No private property was ever stolen from a Southern household by Sherman's army." This was in Richmond! I'm astounded at the statement like that. You can go to any Barnes and Noble this afternoon and pick up books on Sherman's March and read the exact opposite about that whole episode. I got to wondering, why would a man like this stand up and say such an obvious falsehood? The impression I got was that he was just trying to make me out to be saying falsehoods because he was the Lincoln scholar, and I was just an economist who picked this up as a hobby. That's what he seemed to be saying, that he was the real expert.

[In] another statement, he denied the killing of civilians by Sherman's army. He said Lincoln never killed any civilians as the commander in chief. Well, of course, [Lincoln] never pulled the trigger and killed anybody, but there have been quite a few books [about civilian casualties during the war]. [Princeton historian] James McPherson, in one of his books, said there were about fifty thousand Southern civilians who just disappeared by the end of the war. Killed, died, one way or another.

You don't have to be a Lincoln critic like me to recognize that there were a lot of civilian deaths in the Southern states during the Civil War. And here's this man [at the conference] denying this. Why would he say such a strange thing? . . . That's how some of the Lincoln people have behaved.

THE THIRTEENTH AMENDMENT freed the slaves, to be sure. Lincoln, late in his term, did support the Thirteenth Amendment. So when the states ratified [it], that's what freed the slaves. During the war, a lot of slaves freed themselves as two huge armies went through and created anarchy and chaos.

The Emancipation Proclamation . . . specifically exempted all of the areas of the United States that were in control of the Union at the time. It was even so specific as to mention each parish in Louisiana where the Union Army was in charge at the time. [The Proclamation couldn't be enforced in] what was called "rebel territory," so it literally didn't have the ability to free anybody. Besides that, the president at this time didn't have the ability to end slavery. There had to be a constitutional amendment, which is what happened eventually. [The idea that the Emancipation Proclamation freed slaves] is one of the great myths of American history.

I went to the new Lincoln presidential museum in Springfield, Illinois, which is really a remarkable technological feat. It's a beautiful museum. They have the face of an ex-slave on a big screen and a voice-over saying what I just said, calling Lincoln's Emancipation Proclamation a sham because it didn't free anybody. I was frankly shocked that they would put this up in the Lincoln museum because I've gotten all kinds of criticism from merely stating the obvious. [In Lincoln's] time, there were newspapers in Europe and America that were saying this. There were abolitionists in the North who were condemning Lincoln because they thought this was a fraud. They thought, "He says he wants to emancipate the slaves, but look at the document; it doesn't emancipate anybody. It only applies to rebel territory, where [the Union] had no ability to emancipate anyone."

I THINK [LINCOLN SCHOLARS] need to get back to pursuing the truth of history in their careers, . . . [and] I might embarrass a few of them into changing their ways. Some of the more thoughtful people might look at what they've been doing in terms of their work and maybe reevaluate. It is a closed society, this whole Lincoln cult. When you're only around other people who think alike and who pressure you to think alike and punish you professionally if you don't think like everyone else, then it's sort of incestuous. That's not good for the expansion of knowledge and for the generation of ideas and learning. There are some thoughtful people in the history profession who would get away from that and start considering alternative ways of looking at Lincoln and the Civil War.

THERE ARE SEVERAL people who like to think of themselves as Lincoln cult leaders. [Author and Claremont Institute fellow] Harry Jaffa . . . has a number of arguments he has come up with over the years and a number of followers who repeat all of these arguments. They tend to personally attack people who disagree with them. The arguments are all basically Lincoln's arguments—that the states were never sovereign, for example. This was Lincoln's argument in his First Inaugural Address [that] the Union created the states, the states didn't create the Union, which I think is just historically untrue. This was the mantra that began with Alexander Hamilton. Jaffa repeats these old Lincoln arguments, and he has a number of followers who do this.

[MOST MAINSTREAM Lincoln scholars] are not really willing to have a conversation about these things. They know the "truth," and anybody who challenges the truth . . . is not to be debated but criticized or attacked or ignored.

★ ★
★

The Lincoln Obsession

ANDREW FERGUSON

This essay was taken from a May 20, 2007, Q&A *interview with author and journalist Andrew Ferguson. Ferguson's book* Land of Lincoln: Adventures in Abe's America *was published by Atlantic Monthly Press. Currently, Mr. Ferguson is a senior editor at* The Weekly Standard *and has written for* The New Yorker, The New Republic, The Washington Post, *and many other national publications.*

I remember going down to see my father who was a member of the Chicago law firm where Robert Todd Lincoln once practiced. Back in those days, people worked on Saturday, and my father would take me down, sometimes, on a Saturday morning. There were pictures of these old guys with walrus moustaches. He showed me one of Robert Todd Lincoln and a little light went off because I was already a Lincoln buff by the time I was six or seven. It was an elevating thing to think that our family had this kind of connection.

I think there is something in the water in Hinsdale, Illinois, which is the town I grew up in. I grew up in an old house on Lincoln Street, and, of course, Illinois is the Land of Lincoln. About a mile away, there was an old house that, according to the legend, Lincoln had stayed at in the 1850s, as a traveling lawyer and politician. So there was this almost mystical presence hovering about of Lincoln consciousness. We also had a family relation to him. One of my ancestors is mentioned in the collected works of Abraham Lincoln as having just died. Lincoln mentions it in a letter. So, Lincoln was never far away.

I TRY AND TELL HOW Lincoln's martyrdom began. You know, it was Good Friday [when he was shot]. By Saturday morning, Holy Saturday, 7 a.m., he was dead. The country knew about it almost instantaneously, thanks to the telegraph. Everyone who had reviled him, at least in the North, suddenly loved him. There were pictures of him being escorted into heaven. There was even talk by preachers, on [Easter] Sunday, the next day—he'd been dead forty-eight hours or less—of his resurrection. Somehow, the country itself would be resurrected through the martyrdom of Father Abraham. The Lincoln cult never quite reached that pitch again, [but] as I found when I traveled around the country, the intensity and the devotion still is very strong among a lot of people.

THE "LAND OF LINCOLN" [campaign] started in the 1950s in Illinois. They needed a state slogan, and a state legislator from central Illinois came up with this idea. He liked the alliteration and everybody took to it. At the time, we had a senator—Everett Dirksen—who fancied himself almost as a reincarnation of Lincoln. He had a big stentorian voice and a florid style, and he traveled the state talking up Lincoln. Then, 1961 comes along. It's the centennial of the Civil War, and that created even more interest in Lincoln. By 1965, you had the one hundredth anniversary of his death, and once again, this sort of fever pitch began of intense Lincoln interest and devotion.

[LINCOLN] IS THIS tepid, uninteresting substance that is ubiquitous. You can't get away from him. He's just there and uninteresting. That was the way I felt until one day—in 2003, I think it was—my wife brought me the newspaper, and it said, "Lincoln statue stirs outrage in Richmond." It seemed like such a non sequitur: Lincoln outrage? I mean how can you get outraged about Lincoln? It's like objecting to the moon. He's too big. He's just there. It turned out that some city fathers in Richmond, Virginia, were trying to put up a statue [of] Abraham Lincoln and his son Tad to commemorate the visit they had made there shortly after the capital of the Confederacy fell in 1865.

Seemed like a wonderful idea to them, but little did they know that a very large portion of their constituents didn't like the idea at all. I read this story and went down to Richmond. I decided to poke around and talk to them, and I saw that there still is a passion about Lincoln. This happens to be a passionate hatred of Lincoln, but he still is capable of arousing all kinds of deep inner stirrings in Americans. So, I wrote a long magazine article about the Richmond statue. When I was done, I thought, "I'm not at the end of this. This is actually a much bigger story." From then, I just took off, got in my car, and went around the country looking for Lincoln.

[Lincoln's modern-day critics] don't like to be called Lincoln haters because it dismisses them. They're often caricatured this way, but they're not a bunch of racist vagabonds. Some of them are quite sophisticated. Thomas DiLorenzo wrote a book called *The Real Lincoln*, which had just come out when the Lincoln statue went up in Richmond, and DiLorenzo was treated as a hero by these Lincoln haters, as I call them, or Abe-a-phobes by another coinage. When I was down in Richmond, the thing that struck me wasn't just the intensity of the hatred for him among these sons of Confederate veterans and Southern nostalgics who thought that the wrong side lost the Civil War. I was also struck by the tepidness of the people who wanted to defend Lincoln.

There was a conference put on at the Virginia Historical Society before the statue was unveiled [involving] a number of Lincoln scholars and other people who were prominent in the field. The Lincoln that they presented—in opposition to this terrible Lincoln that the Lincoln haters had presented—was touchy-feely and almost New Age-y. One of the guys said, "What we love about Lincoln is that he was comfortable with ambiguity, and he was a figure who could always see the other side of an issue." That much is true, but you know there's nothing ambiguous about the way he prosecuted the Civil War. There's nothing ambiguous about the Gettysburg Address. These are ringing declarations of something very important, so I thought, that can't be Lincoln.

I wanted to find out what we know about Lincoln. How did we [come to] know what we know about Lincoln or what we think we know about him? Is he even knowable at all, 140 [plus] years after his death?

From Richmond, I went to [look at] a bunch of books because I also realized from hanging around these Lincoln haters that they knew a lot more than I did. Here I was, a guy who had grown up as a buff, but they were much more conversant in the ins and outs of the Lincoln story than I was. I discovered this character who wrote the first great Lincoln biography, a man named William Herndon, who had been Lincoln's law partner, who was a fascinating character. He called himself an "infidel" and a "freethinker." He was a big boozer, a part-time politician, and a fairly good lawyer, apparently, but he was a very feckless guy who worshipped his law partner and ended up writing the great fountain of Lincoln lore, a book we now call *Herndon's Lincoln*. The story of how he came to write that, how he learned about his law partner and the things he found out that he hadn't expected to find out, is a fascinating story that hasn't been told. I delved into Herndon and saw that you could pull out of Herndon all the strands that led to Lincoln all around the country.

From there, I went to the place where I had first learned to be a buff back in Chicago, Illinois—the Chicago Historical Society, which had once been a shrine to Lincoln. It had wonderful stuff. It had the old carriage that he drove around Washington. It had the bed that he died in. When I was a kid, they also had dioramas that were beautiful little scenes from Lincoln's life. You could stare into them for half an hour at a time, they were so evocative. I wanted to see this, but they were all gone. [Actually,] the bed was still there, and some of the artifacts were still there, but the historical society was no longer a shrine to Lincoln. There was, in fact, very little Lincoln left. I thought that told us something about what's happened to Lincoln.

From there, I decided to go see Lincoln collectors—people who think that they can find Lincoln by buying and holding this stuff that he held himself or that he wrote on. I found that the greatest of all Lincoln collectors is a very wealthy woman who lives, of all places, in Beverly Hills, California, and has a vault that holds a treasure trove of Lincoln. She was kind enough to take me in to show me this. Louise Taper is her name.

We were sitting in her vast living room, and she popped up out of her chair and said, "Do you want to see the really good stuff?" . . . She took me into her vault. She's a woman of superb taste, and she always knew what she wanted in collecting Lincoln. She married a very wealthy philanthropist in Beverly Hills. She'd been a buff for many years herself, and her husband was a very generous man who said, "I'll back you in whatever you want to do." So she really went to town, and for the next ten years she transformed the market in Lincoln collectables by buying one thing after another.

Prices in Lincoln memorabilia went up partly as a result. There are a lot of people in the Lincoln world who resent the inflation of the market [brought about by] Louise, among others. Ross Perot was a big Lincoln collector and drove up a lot of the prices. Malcolm Forbes, too.

The Lincoln world—the scholars—can be very fractious. There is a lot of backbiting and resentment and bitterness and unresolved tension. Louise Taper said, "You know, a lot of [Lincoln] people don't get along, but I get along with everybody." I said, why is that? She said, "Because I've got the stuff." That's true. . . . She's a great collector. This stuff is important to her. This is not a hobby. This isn't stuff she just likes to hang on the wall, so I think when she finally disposes of it, it will be done with great care.

[THE THREE-STATE LINCOLN Heritage Trail] has fallen into disuse. It started in the early 1960s. I got this idea that I wanted to piece it back together again for my own family. Lincoln mysticism is something that's passed from generation to generation. Failing that, I was going to cram it down their throats and see if my own kids were going to take to it. It turned out that I had to cram it down their throats. When you drive around the

Midwest, you'll see the old signs—quite handsome old, silver signs. I couldn't find anybody who knew anything about the old Heritage Trail from the early 1960s, so I got on the phone and called around. Finally, a tourism official in Illinois said, "I know the guy you've got to talk to. He's eighty-seven years old, lives in Champaign, and he was the guy who actually put together the Lincoln Heritage Trail." I called him up, and he was a wonderful man and very talkative. I kind of just gushed at him. I said, "It is such an honor to speak to the man who created the Lincoln Heritage Trail because that's the world I grew up in, when people venerated Lincoln, and they understood how important the past was. They would go to the trouble of making a trail like this."

There was a pause and he said, "Well, thanks, but you know, this was all cooked up by the American Petroleum Institute. They wanted to get people in their cars, buying gasoline. So they came up with this idea of a Lincoln Heritage Trail. There was one back East—a Washington Heritage Trail and a Hiawatha Heritage Trail." You scratch anything in America and pretty soon you find a commercial motive.

I dragged my poor family along the Heritage Trail. The kids were fourteen and twelve and very reluctant. This was a very hot summer. All their friends were going to the beach or Disneyland or up to the mountains; their dad was going to take them driving through the boring Midwest to see Lincoln sites. You can imagine how ecstatic they were. My wife is a history buff, so she was all gung-ho, which I think made it even harder on the kids. If they had had an ally in their mother, it would've been easier on them. I concocted these various strategies to entice their interest. One was that we would go backward through Lincoln's life. Why I thought this was a good idea I'm not sure, but we would start at Springfield, which was the last place he lived in the Midwest, and then we would travel back to the earlier places he'd lived in Illinois and then across the river into Indiana where he'd been a teenager and then end up in the holy of holies, the temple, on a little hill, in Hodgenville, Kentucky. The temple [holds] the cabin in which Lincoln was born.

It is a temple—a Greek temple built by John Russell Pope, who designed the National Gallery of Art. He was a neoclassical architect, a great architect if you like that sort of thing. We were getting down to Lincoln's essence. We were going to finally see the loam that he sprang from, the real elemental Lincoln.

You walk up fifty-seven marble stairs. You open these big brass doors, and there in this sanctum santorum, this holy of holies, is this little tiny cabin. It's extremely moving if you're an American who values our own roots as a rural people. It's [about] people who come from nothing and made this fabulous country. . . . My kids were quite struck by it.

The guard said, "This is what we call a 'symbolic' cabin." I said, "I read a lot about it. There was a whole team of forensic scientists who came in the 1920s and determined that this was the Lincoln cabin." And he said, "No, actually, the History Channel was just here about a year ago filming a show. The park service let them take a core sample and they discovered that the cabin"—in the middle of this holy of holies, in this beautiful sylvan setting—"dated from the 1850s, which is forty years after Lincoln was born. So it's not the cabin."

So, the more you look for [Lincoln, the more] he splits away from you. He's like mercury. You can never pin him down. That's probably because he's been dead for [more than] 140 years. But there was something elusive and mysterious about Lincoln to the people who knew him best; as he comes down to us in history, he's always just out of reach.

Springfield [Illinois] is the town where he lived as a man, practiced law. The only home he ever owned is there. Springfield has tried, from the very beginning, to exploit its Lincoln connections. That is a pejorative term, but exploit is the right word. Lincoln died on a Friday, on Saturday morning word reached Springfield, and that afternoon the city fathers were trying to buy up a parcel of land that they could use as his burial place. The place they chose was right at the intersection of two railroad lines, so that as people went through Springfield, they would see this big tomb that they were going to build for Lincoln and then, maybe, stop and spend the night, spend some money, buy some meals, souvenirs, whatever. They always had this on their mind.

The same impulse is now finally culminated in the Abraham Lincoln Presidential Library and Museum, which cost over $150 million and which opened [in 2005] in Springfield. It's a fabulously expensive and elaborate place. The people in Springfield decided they wanted to have a state-of-the-art museum. They didn't want something old and fuddy-duddy, the kind of thing that would appeal to people like me. They wanted something that would appeal to kids and be loud and noisy, so they sought out what they thought were the best kind of historical museums. [These days,] historical sites, museums, and theme parks are all merging together. One of the guys who's behind that whole movement is Bob Rogers, a former Disney employee. He lives out in Burbank, California, has a huge studio there, with several hundred employees. He has worked for NASA and a number of places in developing these theme park–educational museums. . . . He is a very colorful and brilliant man, full of energy, who brought a Hollywood ethos to Lincoln that had never been there before. A lot of Lincoln scholars were appalled that this vulgarian—that's my term not theirs—would be taking their sainted figure and turning him into a rubber dummy, as they have done.

In various tableaus [at the museum], you see Lincoln in his log cabin, Lincoln in a store in New Salem, Lincoln about to get shot. Life-sized tableaus, they have in the museum. There were certain quarters where there was terrible outrage among Lincoln traditionalists. More often, though, what I saw was, especially in Springfield, "We finally figured out a way to make Lincoln pay. This is actually going to be a moneymaker for us." It has been wildly successful. [But] all of that content had been drained away from Lincoln, and in its place was . . . Disney razzmatazz. What you end up with is a question mark. Why, again, do we love him and revere him? Why have people been obsessed with him for 150 years? It's a question that kept coming up wherever I would go.

WHEN YOU MOVE AROUND really committed Lincoln buffs, scholars, authors, hobbyists, collectors, enthusiasts of all kinds, you start to hear them darkly whisper the word "Springfield." What Springfield represents [to some] is the failure in the preservation of Lincoln. Springfield is extremely possessive of Lincoln. They have wonderful artifacts. Obviously, his home is there. [But] people outside of Springfield think that they're too possessive, that they cling to him, that they don't understand him well enough. I talked to several people who view "Springfield" as a dirty word.

People in Springfield have more or less done as best they can. [But] there's something in the hatred of Springfield among non-Springfield Lincoln buffs that is very much like what Lincoln himself experienced. Easterners thought, "This hick from nowhere, he must be a nobody. He can't have any great talent." Especially in New York, [there are] Lincoln buffs who would say, "How could somebody so great come from nowheres-ville? He should've come from the Upper East Side or at least Yonkers or Nyack." Instead, he came out of this two-horse town in the middle of nowhere, which it still is, actually. To me that is a key to Lincoln's greatness, too.

FRANK WILLIAMS IS THE chief justice of the Supreme Court of the state of Rhode Island, a very impressive man who is, I believe, the owner of the largest privately owned Lincoln collection in America. Louise has the best; Frank has the biggest. Frank is also, by acclamation, partly his own, the leading figure in the Lincoln world. He's ubiquitous. You cannot turn around without bumping into Chief Justice Williams. He's extremely energetic. I think the man must sleep three hours a night because he runs the judicial system of the entire state, even if it is Rhode Island, and does a magnificent job from everything I can tell. He's a man of great integrity.

I want to convey my respect for him, which is formidable. His energies and his ambition are all very laudable. He's done a lot to try and bring Lincoln to life for people. On the other hand, there are moments in talking to him where Lincoln and Frank Williams get kind of mixed up. You're not sure which is one and which is the other. I think the intensity of his personal relationship to Lincoln is such that he draws sustenance from learning about Lincoln's intellectual battles and political battles. There's almost a symbiosis in Chief Justice Williams's mind that is taking place. This is not unusual I should say. He's a perfect example of a phenomenon that's quite widespread among Lincoln lovers.

THE PEOPLE OUTSIDE of Springfield will whisper darkly that it's this blob called Springfield [that] ejected Williams and [Harold] Holzer as [scholarly] reformers because they had come in from outside Springfield. There is an old, sleepy organization called the Abraham Lincoln Association, which was founded in the first centennial; it's been a keeper of the Lincoln flame nationally. To people outside, it is thought of as very provincial and not scholarly and more of a social club for Springfield's first families. According to Williams's account, he came in and he wanted to shake things up. He wanted outreach. He wanted more publicity for the group. He wanted to inspire more scholarly research, and the people in Springfield simply weren't having it. Again, the particulars are up for debate, but after a couple of terms as head of the Abraham Lincoln Association, one group of Springfielders got together and ejected Frank, and many Lincoln people went with him and are no longer members of the association. Or if they are, they have no real other connection to it. Frank went and started the Lincoln Forum, so now you have these two large Lincoln organizations dedicated to advancing the memory and legacy of Abraham Lincoln, and a very large number of the members don't talk to each other.

LINCOLN VERY EARLY ON was used [to make money]. The foremost example was Dale Carnegie, the man who wrote *How to Win Friends and Influence People.* He saw in Lincoln the exemplar of the secret to success. Lincoln, of course, didn't get rich, not really rich. . . . Lincoln was saving the Union and freeing the slaves. [But] Lincoln's personality and his habits and his thought processes and his behavior towards other people, these were things [Carnegie thought] were transferable to the average American if you, as he said, "Ask yourself: What would Lincoln do?" In any given situation, [Carnegie believed] you would be better off and you'd end up making money and you'd become a success and you'd climb the corporate ladder. Carnegie wrote an entire biography of Lincoln and then used Lincoln heavily in *How to Win Friends and Influence People.* This is all back in the 1920s and 1930s, but this tradition is still alive. Lincoln is now used in several places as a management guru and, again, that's a pejorative term that I don't think those people would want to use. But he is considered to be a guy who can give you the secret to capitalistic success and how to climb the corporate ladder and make a buck.

There are people who say Lincoln was gay. Lincoln's been used as a poster boy for manic depression. [Or they say] he was a racist. He was a liberal. He was a conservative. He was a Marxist. The most farfetched has got to be that Lincoln was a great businessman; that Lincoln had a key to business success. Lincoln was a terrible businessman. He was completely disorganized. He was a terrible boss, in the sense that we think of as a boss. He would be a micro-manager one minute and then be totally indifferent to a subordinate in another minute. He kept all of his notes in his hat. He forgot to cash his paychecks.

THERE [STILL] IS A MARKET for Lincoln, as we've seen in [recent years] with the success of James Swanson's book, *Manhunt,* and of course, Doris Kearns Goodwin's magisterial book, [*Team of Rivals*].

We can't shake him. We're never going to get rid of him. And the point of my book is that we can't, and we shouldn't even try.

★ ★
★

Image and Icon

CHAS FAGAN

On May 23, 2008, artist and sculptor Chas Fagan talked with C-SPAN about how he approached his commission for the Union League to create a Lincoln bust. For almost twenty years, Mr. Fagan has worked as a portrait artist, landscape painter, and sculptor, creating nationally recognized works of art.

The hard part of doing a Lincoln likeness is that every one of us has an image in our own mind as to what Lincoln looked like, based on all the photographs and the memorials and the profile on the penny and now on the new version on the five-dollar bill. You have to fight that stereotype in your head and try to get to what he was truly like.

When I see the face of Lincoln, I see the obvious turmoil and trouble, the weight of the world, the weight of the country in his brow, and then I try to pair that with what he is known for, his humor. In every face, if you can get a combination of humor and other expressions built into the same likeness, it makes for a more interactive experience for the viewer.

[I see in him a person who was] very strong. I enjoy the insights that I've had in doing a little research on him. He was so self-aware. There were times where he completely shifted gears in the way he presented himself in public. He was known for being the superb mimic, a guy who could do impressions of anyone. He once . . . jumped up on stage and did this mimicking [of] his [political] opponent. The crowd loved it, and the effect was cathartic, I'm sure. But what he didn't like was how it affected his opponent, so he made a conscious decision to control his natural comedic self. That [speaks] to the seriousness of a man who was able to bring us through one of the very tough periods of our history.

[Before I began this project, I went through] biographies and tried to gather information from my own collection of history books. The harder part was trying to get anecdotes that give a little window into his personality. There are debates as to how many of the jokes and humorous moments attributed to Lincoln are true. There are people who have dedicated great time to [documenting such things], and there are a couple of instances where [history] shows his true humor and ability to think ahead.

There's one example of a diplomat visiting the White House—at that point, I think they stayed at the White House—walking past [Lincoln's] door and seeing him polishing his boots, and having to stop and mention this [by saying], "My goodness, you're polishing your own boots." Lincoln's immediate reaction was, "Why, yes. Whose do you polish?" That type of quick humor was something I tried to capture.

[AS PRESIDENT, LINCOLN allowed sculptors to make "life mask" impressions of his face using clay.] The life mask [I used] was from this one sculptor [Leonard Volk] who was able to get it from him—or off him, literally. [But] the one missing part in all life masks are the eyes. That was the greatest effort for me—to try to have eyes that show a lot of depth and forethought. So, [in my depiction of Lincoln] he's looking a little off to the right. He's in thought—[there is] that heavy vision of the future, [I'm trying to show that] regardless of whatever he had to go through to hold the Union together, whatever political hurdles there were, he was still moving toward his goal.

[MY LINCOLN SCULPTURE] is such a concentrated thing. There are no shoulders. There is no tie. There is no collar. There is just the head, the face, the person. I wanted to make sure that whatever I did was straight from me. [I was] just trying to focus on the personality and the thought within the face, the visage of history, the American conscience—all those things [that are] ascribed to him. I didn't want any kind of distractions. As an artist, I had to forego the wonderful tie that's crooked and the collars [that are] a little off. Lincoln had them in every single photograph, and it would have been wonderful to do, but I think it would have been a little distracting.

[When the life mask I used was created, Lincoln didn't have a beard. To depict his beard in my sculpture] photographs came in very handy. There are wonderful profiles, too, because the shape of the beard is dictated by how full and far it goes. That familiar face and the hair are strictly based on photographs.

I left [his age in this piece] open to interpretation. He looks physically younger [in my sculpture] than he looked later in his presidency, but I wanted to show a resilient man as he was in 1860, when that first mask was taken. A personal touch in terms of sculpting for me is that I like leaving a lot of my work visible. So, [I depicted his hair with] just a series of handfuls of clay—moved and pushed around. A lot has been written about how erratic and windblown his hair always was. I wanted to convey that, too.

I'M NOT AN ART HISTORIAN, but I'm pretty sure that same life mask has to be the basis for a lot of the Lincoln work out there. The original sculpture was done in 1860, and in 1880 or so, someone thought it would be a great idea to raise money for the Lincoln Memorial by selling limited copies of the mask. Even in the 1880s, they sold those copies for $25,000 each. So those copies were out there in the private sector. I think one was used as the basis for the Mount Rushmore likeness, too.

[MY LINCOLN BUST] was done for the Union League Club in New York. I had done a painting for them of President Reagan so I had gotten to know them a little bit. They wanted an emblematic figure of Lincoln because when the Union League was founded, Lincoln played a critical role.

MY BRONZE SCULPTURE and the clay model are life size. There's a little bit of shrinkage that happens with bronze, so it's maybe a couple of percentage points off. . . . [The work was done] in my studio in Charlotte, North Carolina. . . . Inside [the clay model] are aluminum wires. They're rather thick and they're sturdy. That's the core of his skull, and out of that you can make basic shapes with more wire for reinforcement. All the rest [of the sculpture] is me just applying clay and pushing clay around. There's nothing more scientific involved than using your hands. Ninety-five percent [of it] is me moving clay around with my hands, which is the part I love. When sculptures get bigger, it's even more dramatic. But working at this scale—life size—is very comfortable because your fingers are small enough to be able to make some good movement and gesture. It gets a little more complicated around the eyes and the lips, but that's very minor.

THERE IS SOMETHING to fully knowing or getting to know a good hook—a personal characteristic of the subject—and keeping that in the back of your head the whole time when moving clay around. It's that process of just working through it and moving things around to try to pull that likeness out, to pull the personality, to show the person behind the eyes. I can't explain it in any other way, but that's the approach.

It was hard [to declare the sculpture finished]. It's just like in painting. I wanted to keep some of the brushstrokes in because the more movement you see on the clay, the more finger strokes you see, the more energy the piece has. It's not just a finished, smooth surface. There are lots of things that I could still be playing with on this thing. There are some edges on the hair that are distracting. I can see individual little strokes in the beard. But I know that if I were to go in and touch those some more, it would lose a lot of the energy and life. So, there's always a balance. Pulling away and stopping is always a good thing.

I USED A SYNTHETIC CLAY, which does not dry, so the fact that [my original clay model] is actually still here today, is pretty much a miracle because the mold [I used for the bronze casting] was already taken from this form. . . . Normally, when the mold is removed, there's serious damage all over the clay. But in his case, the image came out almost perfectly. The clay itself is a synthetic and oily substance; it's kind of soft. The mold is made of rubber with plaster outside of that.

Normally, [after the mold for casting is created] the clay is just discarded, but I couldn't bring myself to discard Abraham. I don't plan to do anything with it. He just keeps me company in my studio. He'll last as long as the clay lasts, which I'm told is only about twenty-some years before it really starts to deteriorate.

[WHEN I LOOK AT THIS clay model] especially from [the right] angle, what I see is the warmer Lincoln. What I'm always struck by is that different lighting changes the face completely. [Sometimes] the lighting makes him look severe. But from [another] angle, he's got a little warmth to him, a little bit of the famous Abraham Lincoln humor. I notice this every day when it's in my studio. As the sun moves across the sky and the light changes inside, I can look [over at Lincoln] and see a completely different expression from hour to hour.

$$\star \underset{\star}{} \star$$

Lincoln's Relevance

MARIO CUOMO

Booknotes *hosted former New York governor Mario Cuomo on July 25, 2004, for an interview on his Harcourt-published book* Why Lincoln Matters: Today More Than Ever. *Mr. Cuomo has authored books about public policy, social and cultural issues, New York, and his personal and political life.*

[I]n 1955, my older sister, Marie, gave me a copy of Lincoln's collected works.] I had shown an interest in Lincoln already, and she knew it. She was my oldest sister, and education was everything in my household. My parents were immigrants. My mother died at ninety-five, never having been able to read a book in any language, which was something we talked about a lot, the kids in the family. So my sister and older brother were constantly after me [to read] and buying books for me. I wasn't a kid when she did it in '55. I'd been around for a while, but she knew I had an interest in Lincoln, and she thought it would be a good idea. His collected works have become a treasure since then for me.

There are nine volumes, and they have these magic little indexes that were done for a while, additional indexes. I wish they'd kept publishing the collected works because they do find new things from time to time.

To me, the thing that I was totally dazzled by was Lincoln's extreme intelligence, his incredible ability to analyze, his suppleness with the law, and his big ideas for a man who never stepped out of the country except to go to Canada. In New York State, we don't count the Canadian border as foreign policy, but that was the only time he ever left the country. He talked constantly about the rest of the world and the effect of the American experiment [in democracy] on the rest of the world.

For a fellow who went to school for only a year, total, his sense of the big truths in the world, especially on religious issues [was impressive]. He talked a lot about religion. We're confronted now by big religious issues—[such as] abortion and stem cells. His thinking about the fundamental truths, the basic spiritual truths that every religion starts with, was this: "What is your relationship to other human beings? How do you regard other human beings? You're supposed to respect them, love them, if you will, and work with them. What is your mission?" Hebrews say our mission is *Tikkun Olam,* [meaning] "repair the world." Christians say, "Be collaborators in creation." Lincoln wasn't a Christian, he wasn't a Jew, but he said exactly the same thing: "Your whole mission is to try to make this place better, make this living experience better." That's wonderful stuff. We don't have anybody who talks that way now.

[Lincoln] was practicing law when he wasn't being a politician. When he was being a politician, even the people around him [didn't always share his views]. William Herndon, who loved him, was an abolitionist and he wasn't where Lincoln was on the slavery question from the very beginning.

Lincoln did just about everything on his own, unlike most modern politicians. He had to think up the ideas. He didn't sit around with a bunch of Brahmins trying to figure out how to get around the Constitution, which he became extremely adept at. I marvel at the suppleness he showed in dealing with the Constitution and making it sound like he wasn't breaking it in half, when sometimes he was coming very close to doing that.

HE HAD A GREAT reputation as a storyteller. I hate puns, and when I discovered he liked puns that kind of disappointed me. The one that may be the worst [came to him as] he was walking down the street with somebody and saw the sign "T. R. Strong." It was the name of a company. He looked at it and said, "T. R. Strong, but coffee are stronger." [Puns] torture humor. They're too crude a use of humor for a guy like him, whose subtlety I so admire. I'm also glad I never heard any of the bawdier stories he told when he was a young guy.

In my book, I wrote a State of the Union today in Lincoln-esque language. [I talked to] Harold Holzer, who everybody knows is a great Lincoln scholar and an old friend of mine. I said, "Harold, I'm going to write this, I'm going to write it tonight." I said, "Let me try it, just trying to use his language with today's issues—Iraq, terrorism, the huge tax cut, etc." I did it, and Harold called me up and said, "Son of a gun, I think we can make this work." . . . The [result gives you] an idea of [how] Lincoln would speak today.

What Lincoln said, what he believed, the big ideas he offered you, the wisdom he offered [are things] we need desperately now. We're confused;

we're riveted on terrorism and the war, which we need to be. [But] we're still losing men and women, and other innocent people are dying, as well.

[Lincoln] thought about the Civil War. He thought about each battle; but he thought constantly about much more than that. He thought about what was going to happen when he finally did win the war and how he was going to reconcile [the North and South] and how he was going to make us one again and how he was going to preserve us for the benefit of the entire world. That's what we need now.

People came at him and offered all sorts of possible compromises. [They said], "The heck with the South, we'll be better off in the North, we can survive as two countries." He said no to all of that.

All of that would destroy the original idea. The original idea was that we went from the Articles of Confederation to a Constitution to bind us together as one. We had to show we could make it work. [He thought that] if you allow the South to secede, and if you allow them to create their own republic, then eventually, there would be a temptation to have still another fragmentation. The process of fragmentation having been established, [the country] could eventually crumble into particles. I'm sure he was right.

Lincoln said that the whole world was looking at us. There had been attempts at democracies before, but never one like this. Never one with the potential success of this one. This was the big test, to see if we could govern ourselves or whether the first time you have a really passionate disagreement, you're going to break up. He made the right judgment, and that was to pay the price to keep the Union together.

DON'T TRY TO MAKE Lincoln a Republican or a Democrat in today's terms. Don't besmirch him with any of the modern labels. The old ones were bad enough. The modern labels are an absolute joke.

What would you call President Clinton? A conservative? No, no, no. A liberal? No, no, no. He wouldn't like that. Well, then, what do you call him? If the word "conservative" meant anything, why would George Bush have to come from Texas, where he was a conservative, and suddenly become a "compassionate conservative"? If "Democrat" meant anything, why would you have to run as a "new" Democrat? The labels don't mean anything, and they didn't mean much in his time. He was a Whig who became a Republican. He's too supple for that. If you absolutely forced me to give you a label that had only two words to describe him, I'd say, call him progressive and call him pragmatic, and make him a "pragmatic progressive," or a "progressive pragmatist."

What about the role of government? Conservatives would say, as Reagan did and as Clinton did, at one point, the era of big government should be over. Big government is the problem. Little government is what we believe in. Then you go to liberals, and they'd say, "Oh, no, we need more government."

Lincoln didn't fall into that foolish trap. He didn't play that simplistic game. He would say, it's basic: the Constitution brought us together. Government is the coming together of people to do for one another collectively what they could not do as well, or at all privately. If you can use the market system, then use the market system. He'd argue that if you could build all the roads we need in this country, don't ask [President Dwight] Eisenhower to do the [interstate] road program. Just build them and make them toll roads, like Europe. If you could educate everybody in this country through the market system, then Lincoln wouldn't have wasted time saying one of the first things we have to do is [fund] education.

If you had paid attention to Lincoln in the early stages, [he] didn't make these simplistic arguments about government is bad, government is good. [He felt] government was necessary. When it's necessary, you use it. When it's not, you don't.

[Lincoln would have said that with] civil liberties, sometimes you have to play the game with the Constitution. If there's something really at risk, then in this balancing of liberties in the Constitution against protecting the nation and protecting individuals, you lean toward protecting them, even if you have to give up some liberties. He did it with *habeas corpus*.

The opportunity to rise is what [historian Gabor] Boritt talks about in his books on Lincoln, the chance to rise up, the opportunity to work your way to a higher level. [Lincoln] would have said, "Do it through a free-market system. We have to insist that you work as hard as you can the way I did. But then having worked as hard as you can, if you need some help, then the rest of us should chip in to educate you, to give you the skills you need. . ."

[If Lincoln were president today,] he would say, "First of all, don't call it the 'war on terrorism.' You called it that because it allowed you to run up the flag and allowed you to take a vote in Congress. It's not a war like the war in Iraq, where you're taking a specific piece of land against a specific government and it will have a conclusion. This war is not going to have a conclusion, anymore than the war against crime will have a conclusion, or the war against poverty will have a conclusion, or the war against illness will have a conclusion. So get that clear in your mind. It is not the same kind of war.

"Number two, when you find the nation that is truly hosting terrorists and nothing else works but military force, you will have to use it. . . . [But] to think that military force is going to end terrorism is ridiculous. Why? Because the terrorists are willing to give their life to take yours. You can't frighten them with force. You'll need other things. You'll need propaganda to stop the madrassas from teaching young jihadists to kill all infidels."

My favorite thought about Abraham Lincoln is he believed in two things: loving one another and working together to make this world better. I think that's good enough to start a religion with, and that's what he did. He started a civic religion. We need it now.

★ ★
★

Lincoln's Shadow

MERRILL D. PETERSON

Merrill Peterson appeared on C-SPAN's Booknotes *on August 14, 1994. Peterson's book* Lincoln in American Memory *was published by Oxford University Press. A noted Jeffersonian scholar, Mr. Peterson is the editor of the Library of America edition of the writings of Thomas Jefferson. Throughout his career, Peterson has taught at Brandeis University, Princeton, and the University of Virginia and has authored thirty-seven books.*

I live close to Monticello—Thomas Jefferson's home in Charlottesville, Virginia—where I am very active. [Monticello] is a very large organization, and I suppose all those persons there could be said to be involved with the preservation and interpretation of Thomas Jefferson. Then there are the employees of the Jefferson papers in Princeton, New Jersey, and employees of various other adjuncts of Jefferson. There's also quite a bit [done in the preservation of] George Washington. I don't know how they would compare, but I suspect Lincoln is the largest, just as his bibliography is the largest. . . .

There are estimated to be about sixteen thousand items of Lincoln bibliography today. Eventually, there will be some kind of a guide to that vast bibliography, an an updated guide. There hasn't been one for sixty years.

There are significant differences between [Lincoln and Jefferson] and their places in history. Jefferson was a man of great learning, a very bookish man, and a man of the Enlightenment with multifaceted talents. Lincoln, on the other hand, was not a man who read a great deal and was certainly not a well-educated man. He had damn little formal education at all, essentially self-educated and not a multifaceted person. He was a lawyer-politician. His career, as history determined, was essentially encased in the Civil War, a fairly brief period. It did not run over the same period of time as Jefferson and did not involve the tremendous diversity of Jefferson's achievements, which include architecture, education, science. It would be hard to interpret Lincoln in that broad way.

Lincoln was a humanist, an American humanist. But he was not a humanist in the sense that Jefferson was, in terms of being a man of books and learning. Lincoln, later in his life, saw the tremendous excitement of that, but he didn't have the opportunity to do anything about it.

In terms of the roles they have played in American thought and imagination, Jefferson was a man who essentially appealed to the mind, whereas Lincoln appealed to the heart. Lincoln was very much a man who had an affectional relationship to the American people, or the American people developed an affectional relationship with him. That's partly because of the tragedy, the pathos of the assassination, but it's [also] because of the qualities of his personality that were so endearing to many people and so mysterious in many ways. The kind of intellectual appeal that Jefferson has did not really extend to that emotional level.

One thing I found in researching my book, something I hadn't expected at all, was the extent to which everyone who had a memory of Lincoln somehow felt that they had to express it; they had to write it down or tell about it. There's an immense literature of reminiscence, which is not the case with Jefferson. You have some of that, but comparatively little. Most of it talks about Jefferson and the things he did. It doesn't talk about Jefferson as a man of sentiment, as a man of humor, as a man of sorrows. All of that is part of Lincoln.

[Jefferson's importance comes] partly because he was terribly important to the formulation of the fundamental principles of democratic government in America, partly because he was there at a time when the Constitution was being made, when governments were being shaped, and because of the dialogue that was set up between Jefferson and Alexander Hamilton early in our history. They created opposing political forces [that have lasted] throughout our history. [As a result,] Jefferson has been much more used in contemporary politics through the generations.

You can almost write American political history [by focusing on] what Jefferson meant and what he said. There's some of that about Lincoln. But partly because his career was so condensed in the Civil War and involved such things as war powers, and partly because he was a figure for whom there was so much affection, it was very difficult to be partisan about him, particularly after his death. . . .

Clearly, Lincoln was used by the Republican Party for many years. But the Republican Party, by the end of the nineteenth century, realized that it couldn't claim any particular ownership of Lincoln, so it ceased being very tough-minded about that. . . . [By contrast, Jefferson's meaning and legacy] have been in battle, politically, throughout our history.

I WORKED QUITE A LOT at the Illinois State Historical Library in Springfield, which is one of the great libraries of Lincolniana, and also at the Lincoln Library and Museum in Fort Wayne, Indiana, . . .

I visited Hodgenville [Kentucky, Lincoln's birthplace,] and visited a little place that's not very well known anymore—Lincoln Memorial University down at the Cumberland Gap, a small institution started in about 1900 with a very strong commitment to educating the children of Appalachia in the ideals of Abraham Lincoln.

[As I did my research,] my respect for Lincoln grew. More particularly, it just sort of firmed up. I became absolutely convinced that this was a really great figure, a great human being and a great statesman. I suspected this before, but hadn't really made that kind of study of Lincoln. I do not identify myself as a Lincoln scholar, and didn't set out to become a Lincoln scholar. I set out to write this book about the shadow of Lincoln, rather than the historical Lincoln. [To do it,] I had to know the historical Lincoln, and there are things in the book that are revealing about the historical Lincoln that people might not otherwise know. . . .

The discussion of Lincoln's ancestry is something that's sort of been forgotten, but at one time it was terribly important to his life, and perhaps just to bring that back and offer some perspective on that, is useful. One of his first biographers, William H. Herndon, fancied himself as something of a philosopher and psychologist. He was very close to Lincoln for fifteen years. After Lincoln's death, he was devastated, and he set out to write Lincoln's biography, to in effect, become Lincoln's Boswell. But he was incapable at that time of really writing the biography. On his own, he couldn't do it. So he [put together] a huge collection of material on Lincoln. He was mainly responsible for the story of Ann Rutledge, the young woman with whom Lincoln supposedly fell in love at an early age, when he was twenty-three, twenty-four years of age. The story, as Herndon told it, was that she was not only Lincoln's first love, she was his only love, which didn't go down very well with Mary Lincoln, his widow.

Nothing was known about Ann Rutledge until after Lincoln's death. If Lincoln came back and you could ask him a question, one of the first you would ask is, was there an Ann Rutledge and what did she mean to your life? That story is still believed by most people, but it's been discredited by a good many historians, though there's an effort now among serious scholars to revive it and to restore it to the place in Lincoln's life.

The significance of it goes beyond the fact that it was just a love affair between two young people. She died very soon after they had, according to Herndon, fallen in love with each other. Lincoln was devastated by her death, according to Herndon and that was the beginning of Lincoln's melancholia. Other people interpret her death as the thing that made him feel that he had to distinguish himself in some way to justify her, that it made him a man somehow, finally.

There's a lot of psychological significance written into the Ann Rutledge affair. I'm skeptical about it, let's put it that way. James G. Randall, who was the leading twentieth-century scholar, the first serious historical scholar about Lincoln, pretty much undermined that legend and discredited it to the point where it dropped out of scholarly biography. Of course, it's still very much believed by many people. . . . In television docudramas that's always highlighted as the incident around which Lincoln's life was thought to turn. It led to his developing an identity, and it also led to that melancholia that he supposedly had throughout his life.

Lincoln was often given to moods of great sadness and sorrow, depression perhaps, but not clinical depression. There's no evidence at all that Lincoln was clinically depressed in the sense that he could not function effectively at his job or as a human being. He functioned beautifully. Even so, this notion that he was given to depression, that there was a sickness that came out from time to time, is fairly current.

THERE IS ALSO AN anti-Lincoln tradition in America. . . . It is minor most of the time, except in the South, [although there is a] changing Southern image of Lincoln, which has become more and more favorable over time. It was very negative at the beginning but has become more positive, to the point where the South accepts Lincoln as a national hero and can now commemorate him. They couldn't forty or fifty years ago, at least not with great enthusiasm. Still, there is an anti-Lincoln tradition quite beyond that. It's seen in Northern Copperhead-ism, for example. [Antiwar Northerners] hated Lincoln during the Civil War, and they hated the whole tradition of Lincoln. Edgar Lee Masters's book *Lincoln: The Man*, which appeared in the early 1930s, [launched] a devastating attack on Lincoln. It was alleged to be a biography, but basically it was an effort to say that Lincoln had destroyed the country by surrendering it to the money powers during the Civil War. Masters was committed to an old-fashioned populist Jeffersonianism, and he hated Lincoln.

One of the problems that modern conservatives have is that Lincoln had the idea that equality was an important element—[that it was] not only the American creed but, indeed, that equality was an objective to be achieved through the Constitution and the government of the United States. This is something that has bothered them from the beginnings of the neo-conservatism that developed right after the Second World War. If you look at Russell Kirk's *The Conservative Mind,* one of the fundamental books upon which the whole rise of the new conservatism of the 1950s was built, there's almost no discussion of Lincoln. There's no effort to claim Lincoln as a conservative, basically no attention to Lincoln at all.

[AFTER LINCOLN'S DEATH], efforts made in Washington to build a national monument to Lincoln collapsed, so the main effort was the one in Springfield, his hometown, and it was nationally supported. Other states contributed to the building of that monument, and it became the major monument erected to Abraham Lincoln in the period after the Civil War, and for a long time to follow.

There are lots of Lincoln statues. One of the most important is the "Lincoln the Emancipator" statue in Washington, DC—the Freedmen's statue—dedicated in 1876. It was difficult to get that built. It began with the resolution of a recently freed woman in Ohio who argued that the Negro people should build a statue of Abraham Lincoln. She said, "I'll donate $5 of my pay to get the fund started." It was not easy to raise the money, and then developing the concept of the statue took some time, but it is one of the great iconic sculptures in American history.

THE MAJOR THEMES [I explore about Lincoln] . . . all involve myth in one way or another. The myth of Lincoln as a self-made man was clearly there at the time of his apotheosis after his death. This was the idea that he was a man born in absolute poverty with almost no education, who came out of nowhere, had no ancestry, no background, no family that amounted to much, and yet he achieved all this greatness. [This created] a belief that a common, ordinary person in America could excel and rise to the highest office in the land, go from log cabin to the White House. Americans had other examples of that before Lincoln; William Henry Harrison at least professed to be one. But Lincoln was the exemplar in the sense that he was so disadvantaged in his early life.

How much of that [belief that one can rise to greatness] still holds with young people today is an interesting question. I think it's diminished. I don't think young people are as much inspired by this as they were two or three generations ago. Mario Cuomo is one of those who argues that, yes, this theme is still terribly important to the whole idea of opportunity in American culture, fundamental to our existence as a nation. Cuomo makes speeches about this and insists that it was terribly important in his life, that Lincoln was a hero and a model to him and that he thinks [Lincoln is] still a serviceable model in that regard.

THERE HAVE BEEN A lot of popular books written about Lincoln. Ida Tarbell was one of the most interesting popular writers about Lincoln. She was a fine scholar as well. She began in the 1890s as part of *McClure's* magazine, which was a muckraking magazine, so she's better remembered as one of the first muckrakers, [particularly in regard] to John D. Rockefeller and Standard Oil. But she had also this other string in her bow. She was born in the oil region of Pennsylvania, grew up in that area and went to Allegheny College. She became interested in Lincoln and Lincoln remained at her side the rest of her life, even while she turned to lots of other things that were closer to the contemporary political scene. She wrote books that were very personal about Lincoln, books that developed this concept of him as a warm, generous human being, who was also somewhat folksy.

[THE TERM] "APOTHEOSIS" means making someone into a god, making him immortal, in a more civic context rather than an ecclesiastical one—entering a pantheon, in the sense of a civic pantheon. In Lincoln's case, it's the idealization of Lincoln as a hero and saint. One of the interesting questions that one has to ask is: Would Lincoln have been as famous if he had lived longer and died a natural death? The assassination came right at the very end of the Civil War, one day after the American flag was raised again in Charleston, South Carolina, on Good Friday, which evokes the whole symbolism of Christ. To what extent would he have become such a saint and hero if that had not happened?

There is plenty of evidence that Lincoln was being recognized as a very great man both in America and abroad for a year or more before his death, certainly after his re-election as president and his Second Inaugural address, which was actually delivered only about six weeks before his death.

LINCOLN'S REDISCOVERY OF the Declaration of Independence and of its crucial significance in American history, a discovery he made in the 1850s, was one of the most important things that ever happened in American politics. That is now recognized by historians as well as political scientists like Harry Jaffa. He was one of the first scholars in the 1950s and 1960s to return to that dimension of Lincoln—his grasp of the moral imperatives of the Declaration of Independence for defining the meaning and purpose of this country and our politics.

[The Lincoln-Douglas debates] generated so much interest nationally that they helped Lincoln establish himself as a national figure. Then he made his great Cooper Union address in February of 1860, and that introduced him to Eastern audiences. The debates were also important because they helped Lincoln define what was at stake in the coming struggle. What was at stake, as he increasingly defined it, were the fundamental principles upon which this country rested and which had been there at the foundations of the country, July 4, 1776.

At Gettysburg, Lincoln talked about "fourscore and seven years ago"—1776—and that we were "re-founding" the nation on those same principles. That's something that many scholars are now inclined to converge upon. They agree that it is the great significance of Lincoln, and that this contributed greatly to his fame, not only in America, but worldwide.

★ ★
★

Lincoln in Context

JAMES M. MCPHERSON

*James McPherson appeared on C-SPAN2's Book TV program,
In Depth, on March 4, 2001, to discuss his Pulitzer Prize–
winning book* Battle Cry of Freedom: The Civil War Era, *published by the Louisiana State University Press. Mr. McPherson has taught at Princeton University since 1962 and is the George Henry Davis 1986 Professor Emeritus of U.S. History.*

B y the time of the Civil War, and especially by the time Lincoln issued the Emancipation Proclamation, a lot of people were calling themselves abolitionists. It was an idea whose time had come. Back in the 1830s and 1840s when the movement got started, the abolitionists were considered to be fanatics and rabble-rousers, provoking war and violence. It was only because real war and real violence—the Civil War—came along that a majority of the people in the North eventually came to the same conclusion that the abolitionists had been preaching for generations. For the last generation before the war, slavery made a mockery out of American professions of being a land of liberty, and it would destroy the country if slavery wasn't destroyed first.

Abraham Lincoln became the number-one abolitionist, but he had never been an abolitionist in the antebellum sense of the word. The abolitionists were very critical of Lincoln and other political leaders for moving too slowly against slavery. They wanted to make the Civil War [a fight] against slavery immediately. Reading all of their editorials and speeches and letters, I tended to absorb their point of view. But the more I learned about the difficulties that Lincoln faced in holding a coalition together to fight this war—the multitude of pressures from all points on the political compass, the worries that he had to satisfy several different constituencies—the more

I came to appreciate and sympathize with Lincoln's point of view and to wonder if abolitionists might possibly have been a little bit too intolerant.

IF YOU TAKE LINCOLN out of the context of the total spectrum of American opinion and American politics in the 1850s and 1860s and quote some of the things he said from the standpoint of [today], he sounds quite racist. Criticism of Lincoln . . . fails to take account of the context and the pressures and the situation that Lincoln faced at the time. Also, there's a lack of a sense of change in him over time. Lincoln himself moved . . . steadily to the left in the course of the Civil War.

In the first year of the war, Lincoln wanted to reassure Unionists and Northern Democrats that this was a war only for the Union and not a war against slavery. [Later, he made] it a war to emancipate some slaves, and eventually with the Thirteenth Amendment, a war to abolish slavery as the only way to save the Union—as Lincoln said in his Emancipation Proclamation, as "an act of justice itself." At the very end of his life, Lincoln was moving toward incorporation of the freed slaves into the American body politic as equals. If he had lived, he would have continued to move in that direction.

[In] the antebellum period, the question of the status of blacks in the free North was a contested one from the very beginning. Most of the abolitionists were in favor of equal rights for blacks in the North. It started with the Quakers, who were the first abolitionists during the American Revolution, and continued with the more militant phase of abolitionism in the 1830s and 1840s with William Lloyd Garrison, Wendell Phillips, Frederick Douglass, and so on. The abolitionists not only pushed for a moral revolution that would bring about the end of slavery in the South, but they also supported laws that would end discrimination against free blacks in the North. They did succeed in some of the New England states. Rhode Island was one of the few states that actually allowed blacks the right to vote before the Civil War.

The pressures for repressive laws—"black laws"—came from two sources. One was in states like Illinois, Indiana, and Ohio, which had substantial populations of whites who had migrated from the South—from Kentucky, from Tennessee, from Virginia—in the early and middle parts of the nineteenth century and were against equal rights for blacks. [Pressure also came from] the substantial number of immigrants coming into the country in eastern cities like New York, Boston, Philadelphia, and even western cities like Milwaukee and Chicago. They were competing at the lower end in the socio-economic scale with blacks and also [tended] to favor repressive laws.

The Democratic Party was the party of white supremacy in the antebellum period and for a long time after the Civil War, as well. [It helped get] repressive laws passed in response to the interest of these constituents. The abolitionists tried, without much success aside from a few local areas, to move against that. . . . The more mainstream Republicans didn't go as far as the abolitionists in the 1840s and 1850s [and were] more acceptable to a broader range of voters. It might have helped to account for their rising political strength in the 1850s. They were a less objectionable alternative than the full-scale militant abolitionists.

IT IS EASY TO TAKE Lincoln's statements at a particular time out of the context of that time and say he was a racist because this is what he said in 1858, or this is what he said in 1862 to a delegation of blacks who came to the White House, or that he said in his inaugural address in 1861 "I have no purpose and I have no legal authority to interfere with slavery in the states."

It is true that he had no legal authority to interfere with slavery in the states. The Constitution prevented him from doing so. The Constitution protected slavery in the states. Lincoln said over and over again that he intended, or his party intended, to bar the expansion of slavery into the territories. That was enough to provoke the secession of the Southern states and to inaugurate the Civil War. Once the war began, Lincoln did have the power, not as president, but as commander in chief under his war powers, to seize enemy property then used to wage war against the United States. The slaves were that property. So, under that guise, not in 1861, but in 1862 and 1863, he did move against slavery.

It is true that he had called a delegation of blacks—not Frederick Douglass, by the way, they were all blacks from DC—to the White House in August 1862 at a time when he had already made up his mind to issue the Emancipation Proclamation. [He] talked to them about the possibility of colonization, that is, emigration from the country. He had two motives for doing this. One of the main arguments that Democrats were using against emancipation—using it to beat Lincoln over the head throughout the whole Civil War—was that if emancipated, blacks would come North and take away the jobs of white people or rise up and commit violence, rape, and so on in the South. Lincoln realized that white fears and white racism were a powerful obstacle to public support for emancipation. His support for colonization was an effort to convince whites that the race problem in the future might not be quite so bad as their demagogic Democratic leaders were telling them it would be. He hoped to . . . create some degree of white acceptability for emancipation.

LINCOLN WAS IN A long line of leaders going back to Thomas Jefferson who favored, at least in the abstract, liberty and emancipation but were perplexed about how to deal with the racial consequences of emancipation in a society where those few blacks who were free were not granted equal rights. What would be the consequences of large-scale emancipation into this kind of society? In 1862, Lincoln could not yet foresee the possibility of the incorporation of that large black population as equal citizens into American society. But Lincoln's thoughts on this were evolving; they were dynamic, they were changing, and they were constantly moving in a more progressive direction. By the end of his life, just three days before he was assassinated, he was talking about incorporating the freed slaves into American society through a gradual process of granting them equal rights.

To take Lincoln's statements at one particular time and say they represent his position for all time is the wrong way to do it. It was a changing and evolving situation, especially under the pressure cooker of the Civil War, where things changed rapidly, and they changed radically. Lincoln changed with them.

THE PRINCIPAL REFERENCE point in American history for both the Union and Confederacy during the Civil War was the American Revolution. That was the generation of giants that had created the nation and, as Lincoln said in the Gettysburg Address, "We are now being tested whether we're worthy of that heritage." Southerners referred to the American Revolution as a war of independence from a tyrannical power. They said that the American colonies had seceded from the British Empire, and that was exactly what they were doing. They were seceding from the Yankee Empire. They even used that kind of phraseology.

Lincoln and the Northern people said that they were fighting to preserve the nation, created by that revolution of 1776, from dismemberment and destruction. As the war went on, with its dynamic quality of expanding war aims on the victorious Union side to include the abolition of slavery and eventually equal rights for the freed slaves, it moved beyond that reference point to the first revolution. [It] established its own kind of revolutionary quality that the civil rights movement did in the 1960s. Virtually all of the constitutional basis for the advances made by the civil rights movement in the 1960s came out of the Fourteenth and Fifteenth Amendments.

NOBODY CAN SAY WHAT the future history of the United States and of the Confederate States of America after 1861 would have been if the Lincoln administration and Northern people had just let them go. We wouldn't have had a Civil War from 1861 to 1865, but it's at least conceivable that there would have been some kind of a war between these two nations over their access to resources in the West or in the Southwest or somewhere else. On continents with two or more nations rubbing up against each other—[look at] the history of Europe or the history of South America—there have been frequent wars over the centuries.

If the Confederate states had succeeded in creating a separate nation, with or without a war, that would have then constituted a precedent that any disaffected minority might have invoked in the future to secede from the United States. For example, in the 1890s, many Western states felt bitter toward what they [believed as] control of the American economy by the "plutocrats of Wall Street." The populist movement actually won several states in the election of 1892. If there had been a successful precedent of secession when one loses a presidential election, why wouldn't those states then go ahead and secede after they lost the presidential election? . . . It's quite conceivable that if you had just let [the Confederates] go, there would have been three countries or maybe four or five. An alternative scenario is that after a period of years maybe the United States and the Confederate States of America would have negotiated some kind of customs union and maybe an association or alliance of some sort.

THE SEVEN SOUTHERN states that seceded from December 1860 to February 1861 did so in response to the election of Abraham Lincoln on a platform of restricting the future expansion of slavery, which the leading secessionists in these seven states feared meant the ultimate demise of slavery. They regarded the Republican Party as being no better than abolitionists, and they saw the handwriting on the wall in the election of a president who had gotten no Southern votes at all. They had lost control of the national government and therefore had lost control of their destiny within the Union and the destiny of the institution that was the basis of their economy and society.

There can be no doubt that the principal motivation for secession was fear for the future survival of slavery in a nation now dominated by the North and the Republican Party. A series of events brought the question of war or peace down to Fort Sumter. The Confederates fired on Fort Sumter [and] Lincoln called out the troops to suppress an insurrection. Four more Southern states seceded in response. The strongest secessionist areas in those four states—Virginia, North Carolina, Tennessee, and Arkansas— were those areas where slavery was the strongest. So there is a relationship between their secession and slavery as well. In the four border slave states that remained in the Union—Delaware, Maryland, Missouri, and Kentucky—the strongest pro-Confederate regions were also the regions where slavery was the most entrenched.

There is a direct correlation between the degree of commitment to an independent Confederate nation and the degree of the importance of slavery in the society and the economy. That's not to say that the average Confederate soldier had defense of slavery uppermost in his mind as a motive for fighting. Two-thirds of the Confederate soldiers came from non-slaveholding

families. Even many of those Confederate soldiers who came from slaveholding families, in their letters and diaries, talked more about defending their
region, their state, their home, their nation. They talked in terms of an independent nationhood, [and protecting the South] from invasion. They talked
in terms of disdain, contempt, or fear toward the Yankees and toward the
North. There was a feeling that these were two different peoples by 1861.

Most Confederate soldiers took slavery for granted as part of the society
they were fighting to defend. It was not a controversial issue within the
Confederacy. There was not a debate among Confederate soldiers about
whether it was a good idea to be fighting for slavery, as there was among
Union soldiers [who argued] about whether it was a good idea to be risking
their lives to fight for freedom. They had enlisted to fight for the Union,
for the [preservation of the] nation. In the minds of soldiers on both sides
[there was] a kind of American nationalism versus a Confederate nationalism, a loyalty to region and to government that was the principal motive for
fighting. Underlying it in the case of the Confederacy was that there was
this nation—and this society was based on slavery. It was inconceivable for
most Southern whites that their society could exist without slavery.

LINCOLN THOUGHT IN terms of the world impact of the great experiment in
republican government launched [by the United States] in 1776. [America]
was a brave new experiment in a world bestowed by kings, princes, emperors,
and czars. In the middle of the nineteenth century, there were very few stable
functioning republics in the world, and virtually none besides the United
States that were based on broad . . . suffrage, what we call democracy.

THE UNITED STATES WAS on the spot in the nineteenth century. Would
this example succeed? If it succeeded, it might help promote the cause of
democracy, of republicanism, of progress for the middle and lower classes
in other countries as well. That's why Lincoln said the United States was
"the last best hope of earth" for the survival of republican government.
This struggle was significant for more than these United States. It was not
altogether for today, he said; it was for a vast future also.

Lincoln, who never set foot outside the United States, had a vision of just
exactly what was at stake: the forces of democracy and republicanism in
1848, and [the people behind] the uprisings in European countries that
were violently put down in 1848, looked to the United States as the great
example of republicanism in the world. Lincoln was not merely expressing
a kind of American chauvinism when he [said] this. He really was alert to
the existence of the United States as what was called and was almost a
cliché in the nineteenth century: a beacon light of freedom for the op-
pressed of all lands.

PART 5

LINCOLN'S WORDS

HOUSE DIVIDED

June 16, 1858

Delivered in Springfield, Illinois, at the Illinois Republican State Convention

IF WE COULD FIRST KNOW WHERE WE ARE, and whither we are tending, we could better judge what to do, and how to do it.

We are now far into the fifth year, since a policy was initiated, with the avowed object, and confident promise, of putting an end to slavery agitation.

Under the operation of that policy, that agitation has not only, not ceased, but has constantly augmented.

In my opinion, it will not cease, until a crisis shall have been reached, and passed—"A house divided against itself cannot stand."

I believe this government cannot endure, permanently half slave and half free.

I do not expect the Union to be dissolved—I do not expect the house to fall—but I do expect it will cease to be divided.

It will become all one thing, or all the other.

Either the opponents of slavery will arrest the further spread of it and place it where the public mind shall rest in the belief that it is in course of ultimate extinction; or its advocates will push it forward till it shall become alike lawful in all the States, old as well as new-North as well as South.

Have we no tendency to the latter condition?

Let any one who doubts, carefully contemplate that now almost complete legal combination—piece of machinery so to speak—compounded of the Nebraska doctrine, and the Dred Scott decision. Let him consider not only what work the machinery is adapted to do, and how well adapted; but also, let him study the history of its construction, and trace, if he can, or rather fail, if he can, to trace the evidences of design and concert of action, among its chief bosses, from the beginning.

The new year of 1854 found slavery excluded from more than half the States by State Constitutions, and from most of the national territory by congressional prohibition.

Four days later, commenced the struggle, which ended in repealing that congressional prohibition.

This opened all the national territory to slavery; and was the first point gained.

But, so far, Congress only, had acted; and an indorsement by the people, real or apparent, was indispensable, to save the point already gained, and give chance for more.

This necessity had not been overlooked; but had been provided for, as well as might be, in the notable argument of "squatter sovereignty," otherwise called "sacred right of self government," which latter phrase, though expressive of the only rightful basis of any government, was so perverted in this attempted use of it as to amount to just this: That if any one man, choose to enslave another, no third man shall be allowed to object.

That argument was incorporated into the Nebraska bill itself, in the language which follows: "It being the true intent and meaning of this act not to legislate slavery into any Territory or State, nor to exclude it therefrom; but to leave the people thereof perfectly free to form and regulate their domestic institutions in their own way, subject only to the Constitution of the United States."

Then opened the roar of loose declamation in favor of "Squatter Sovereignty," and "Sacred right of self government."

"But," said opposition members, "let us be more specific—let us amend the bill so as to expressly declare that the people of the Territory may exclude slavery." "Not we," said the friends of the measure; and down they voted the amendment.

While the Nebraska bill was passing through congress, a law case, involving the question of a negro's freedom, by reason of his owner having voluntarily taken him first into a free State and then a territory covered by the congressional prohibition, and held him as a slave for a long time in each, was passing through the U.S. Circuit Court for the District of Missouri; and both Nebraska bill and law suit were brought to a decision in the same month of May, 1854. The negro's name was "Dred Scott," which name now designates the decision finally made in the case.

Before the then next Presidential election, the law case came to, and was argued in the Supreme Court of the United States; but the decision of it was deferred until after the election. Still, before the election, Senator Trumbull, on the floor of the Senate, requests the leading advocate of the Nebraska bill to state his opinion whether the people of a territory can constitutionally exclude slavery from their limits; and the latter answers, "That is a question for the Supreme Court."

The election came. Mr. Buchanan was elected, and the indorsement, such as it was, secured. That was the second point gained. The indorsement, however, fell short of a clear popular majority by nearly four hundred thousand votes, and so, perhaps, was not over-whelmingly reliable and satisfactory.

The outgoing President, in his last annual message, as impressively as possible echoed back upon the people the weight and authority of the indorsement.

The Supreme Court met again, did not announce their decision, but ordered a re-argument.

The Presidential inauguration came, and still no decision of the court; but the incoming President, in his inaugural address, fervently exhorted the people to abide by the forthcoming decision, whatever it might be.

Then, in a few days, came the decision.

The reputed author of the Nebraska bill finds an early occasion to make a speech at this capital indorsing the Dred Scott Decision, and vehemently denouncing all opposition to it.

The new President, too, seizes the early occasion of the Silliman letter to indorse and strongly construe that decision, and to express his astonishment that any different view had ever been entertained.

At length a squabble springs up between the President and the author of the Nebraska bill, on the mere question of fact, whether the Lecompton Constitution was or was not, in any just sense, made by the people of Kansas; and in that quarrel the latter declares that all he wants is a fair vote for the people, and that he cares not whether slavery be voted down or voted up. I do not understand his declaration that he cares not whether slavery be voted down or voted up, to be intended by him other than as an apt definition of the policy he would impress upon the public mind—the principle for which he declares he has suffered much, and is ready to suffer to the end.

And well may he cling to that principle. If he has any parental feeling, well may he cling to it. That principle, is the only shred left of his original Nebraska doctrine. Under the Dred Scott decision, "squatter sovereignty" squatted out of existence, tumbled down like temporary scaffolding—like the mold at the foundry served through one blast and fell back into loose sand—helped to carry an election, and then was kicked to the winds. His late joint struggle with the Republicans, against the Lecompton Constitution, involves nothing of the original Nebraska doctrine. That struggle was made on a point, the right of a people to make their own constitution, upon which he and the Republicans have never differed.

The several points of the Dred Scott decision, in connection with Senator Douglas' "care not" policy, constitute the piece of machinery, in its present state of advancement.

The working points of that machinery are:

First, that no negro slave, imported as such from Africa, and no descendant of such slave can ever be a citizen of any State, in the sense of that term as used in the Constitution of the United States.

This point is made in order to deprive the negro, in every possible event, of the benefit of that provision of the United States Constitution, which declares that—"The citizens of each State shall be entitled to all privileges and immunities of citizens in the several States."

Secondly, that "subject to the Constitution of the United States," neither Congress nor a Territorial Legislature can exclude slavery from any United States Territory.

This point is made in order that individual men may fill up the territories with slaves, without danger of losing them as property, and thus enhance the chances of permanency to the institution through all the future.

Thirdly, that whether the holding a negro in actual slavery in a free State, makes him free, as against the holder, the United States courts will not decide, but will leave to be decided by the courts of any slave State the negro may be forced into by the master.

This point is made, not to be pressed immediately; but, if acquiesced in for a while, and apparently indorsed by the people at an election, then to sustain the logical conclusion that what Dred Scott's master might lawfully do with Dred Scott, in the free State of Illinois, every other master may lawfully do with any other one or one thousand slaves, in Illinois, or in any other free State.

Auxiliary to all this, and working hand in hand with it, the Nebraska doctrine, or what is left of it, is to educate and mould public opinion, at least Northern public opinion, to not care whether slavery is voted down or voted up.

This shows exactly where we now are; and partially also, whither we are tending.

It will throw additional light on the latter, to go back, and run the mind over the string of historical facts already stated. Several things will now appear less dark and mysterious than they did when they were transpiring. The people were to be left "perfectly free" "subject only to the Constitution." What the Constitution had to do with it, outsiders could not then see. Plainly enough now, it was an exactly fitted niche for the Dred Scott decision to afterward come in, and declare that perfect freedom of the people, to be just no freedom at all.

Why was the amendment, expressly declaring the right of the people to exclude slavery, voted down? Plainly enough now, the adoption of it, would have spoiled the nitch for the Dred Scott decision.

Why was the court decision held up? Why, even a Senator's individual opinion withheld, till after the Presidential election? Plainly enough now, the speaking out then would have damaged the "perfectly free" argument upon which the election was to be carried.

Why the outgoing President's felicitation on the indorsement? Why the delay of a reargument? Why the incoming President's advance exhortation in favor of the decision?

These things look like the cautious patting and petting of a spirited horse, preparatory to mounting him, when it is dreaded that he may give the rider a fall.

And why the hasty after indorsements of the decision by the President and others?

We cannot absolutely know that all these exact adaptations are the result of preconcert. But when we see a lot of framed timbers, different portions of which we know have been gotten out at different times and places and by different workmen—Stephen, Franklin, Roger and James, for instance—and we see these timbers joined together, and see they exactly make the frame of a house or a mill, all the tenons and mortices exactly fitting, and all the lengths and proportions of the different pieces exactly adapted to their respective places, and not a piece too many or too few—not omitting even scaffolding—or, if a single piece be lacking, we see the place in the frame exactly fitted and prepared to yet bring such piece in—in such a case, we find it impossible not to believe that Stephen and Franklin and Roger and James all understood one another from the beginning, and all worked upon a common plan or draft drawn up before the first lick was struck.

It should not be overlooked that, by the Nebraska bill, the people of a State as well as Territory, were to be left "perfectly free" "subject only to the Constitution."

Why mention a State? They were legislating for territories, and not for or about States. Certainly the people of a State are and ought to be subject to the Constitution of the United States; but why is mention of this lugged into this merely territorial law? Why are the people of a territory and the people of a state therein lumped together, and their relation to the Constitution therein treated as being precisely the same?

While the opinion of the Court, by Chief Justice Taney, in the Dred Scott case, and the separate opinions of all the concurring Judges, expressly declare that the Constitution of the United States neither permits Congress nor a territorial legislature to exclude slavery from any United States territory, they all omit to declare whether or not the same Constitution permits a state, or the people of a State to exclude it.

Possibly, this is a mere omission; but who can be quite sure, if McLean or Curtis had sought to get into the opinion a declaration of unlimited power in the people of a state to exclude slavery from their limits, just as Chase and Mace sought to get such declaration, in behalf of the people of a territory, into the Nebraska bill—I ask, who can be quite sure that it would not have been voted down, in the one case, as it had been in the other?

The nearest approach to the point of declaring the power of a State over slavery, is made by Judge Nelson. He approaches it more than once, using the precise idea, and almost the language too, of the Nebraska act. On one occasion his exact language is, "except in cases where the power is restrained by the Constitution of the United States, the law of the State is supreme over the subject of slavery within its jurisdiction."

In what cases the power of the states is so restrained by the U.S. Constitution is left an open question, precisely as the same question, as to the restraint on the power of the territories was left open in the Nebraska act. Put that and that together, and we have another nice little nitch, which we may, ere long, see filled with another Supreme Court decision, declaring that the Constitution of the United States does not permit a state to exclude slavery from its limits.

And this may be expected if the doctrine of "care not whether slavery be voted down or voted up," shall gain upon the public mind sufficiently to give promise that such a decision can be maintained when made.

Such a decision is all that slavery now lacks of being alike lawful in all the States.

Welcome or unwelcome, such decision is probably coming, and will soon be upon us, unless the power of the present political dynasty shall be met and overthrown. We shall lie down pleasantly dreaming that the people of Missouri are on the verge of making their State free; and we shall awake to the reality, instead, that the Supreme Court has made Illinois a slave State.

To meet and overthrow the power of that dynasty, is the work now before all those who would prevent that consummation.

That is what we have to do.

But how can we best do it?

There are those who denounce us openly to their own friends, and yet whisper us softly, that Senator Douglas is the aptest instrument there is, with which to effect that object. They do not tell us, nor has he told us, that he wishes any such object to be effected. They wish us to infer all, from the fact that he now has a little quarrel with the present head of the dynasty; and that he has regularly voted with us, on a single point, upon which, he and we, have never differed.

They remind us that he is a great man, and that the largest of us are very small ones. Let this be granted. But "a living dog is better than a dead lion." Judge Douglas, if not a dead lion for this work, is at least a caged and toothless one. How can he oppose the advance of slavery? He don't care anything about it. His avowed mission is impressing the "public heart" to care nothing about it.

A leading Douglas Democratic newspaper thinks Douglas's superior talent will be needed to resist the revival of the African slave trade.

Does Douglas believe an effort to revive that trade is approaching? He has not said so. Does he really think so? But if it is, how can he resist it? For years he has labored to prove it a sacred right of white men to take negro slaves into the new territories. Can he possibly show that it is less a sacred right to buy them where they can be brought cheapest? And, unquestionably they can be bought cheaper in Africa than in Virginia.

He has done all in his power to reduce the whole question of slavery to one of a mere right of property; and as such, how can he oppose the foreign slave trade—how can he refuse that trade in that "property" shall be "perfectly free"—unless he does it as a protection to the home production? And as the home producers will probably not ask the protection, he will be wholly without a ground of opposition. Senator Douglas holds, we know, that a man may rightfully be wiser today than he was yesterday—that he may rightfully change when he finds himself wrong.

But, can we for that reason, run ahead, and infer that he will make any particular change, of which he, himself, has given no intimation? Can we safely base our action upon any such vague inference?

Now, as ever, I wish to not misrepresent Judge Douglas's position, question his motives, or do aught that can be personally offensive to him.

Whenever, if ever, he and we can come together on principle so that our great cause may have assistance from his great ability, I hope to have interposed no adventitious obstacle.

But clearly, he is not now with us—he does not pretend to be—he does not promise to ever be.

Our cause, then, must be intrusted to, and conducted by its own un-doubted friends—those whose hands are free, whose hearts are in the work—who do care for the result.

Two years ago the Republicans of the nation mustered over thirteen hun-dred thousand strong.

We did this under the single impulse of resistance to a common danger, with every external circumstance against us.

Of strange, discordant, and even, hostile elements, we gathered from the four winds, and formed and fought the battle through, under the constant hot fire of a disciplined, proud, and pampered enemy.

Did we brave all then to falter now?—now—when that same enemy is wa-vering, dissevered, and belligerent?

This result is not doubtful. We shall not fail—if we stand firm, we shall not fail.

Wise counsels may accelerate or mistakes delay it, but sooner or later the victory is sure to come.

LINCOLN-DOUGLAS DEBATE
IN CHARLESTON, ILLINOIS

September 18, 1858

Mr. Lincoln took the stand at a quarter before three, and was greeted with vociferous and protracted applause; after which, he said:

LADIES AND GENTLEMEN: It will be very difficult for an audience so large as this to hear distinctly what a speaker says, and consequently it is important that as profound silence be preserved as possible.

While I was at the hotel today, an elderly gentleman called upon me to know whether I was really in favor of producing a perfect equality between the Negroes and white people. [Great laughter.] While I had not proposed to myself on this occasion to say much on that subject, yet as the question was asked me I thought I would occupy perhaps five minutes in saying something in regard to it. I will say then that I am not, nor ever have been, in favor of bringing about in any way the social and political equality of the white and black races, [applause]—that I am not nor ever have been in favor of making voters or jurors of Negroes, nor of qualifying them to hold office, nor to intermarry with white people; and I will say in addition to this that there is a physical difference between the white and black races which I believe will forever forbid the two races living together on terms of social and political equality. And inasmuch as they cannot so live, while they do remain together there must be the position of superior and inferior, and I as much as any other man am in favor of having the superior position assigned to the white race. I say upon this occasion I do not perceive that because the white man is to have the superior position the Negro should be denied every thing. I do not understand that because I do not want a Negro woman for a slave I must necessarily want her for a wife. [Cheers and laughter.] My understanding is that I can just let her alone. I am now in my fiftieth year, and I certainly never have had a black woman for either a slave or a wife. So it seems to me quite possible for us to get along without making either slaves or wives of Negroes. I will add to this that I have never seen, to my knowledge, a man, woman or child who was in favor of producing a perfect equality, social and political, between Negroes and white men. I recollect of but one distinguished instance that I ever heard of so frequently as to be entirely satisfied of its correctness—and that is the case of Judge Douglas's old friend Col. Richard M. Johnson. [Laughter.] I will also add to the remarks I have made (for I am not going to enter at large upon this subject,) that I have never had the least apprehension that I or my friends would marry Negroes if there was no law to keep them from it, [laughter] but as Judge Douglas and his friends seem to be in great apprehension that they might, if there were no law to keep them from it, [roars of laughter] I give him the most solemn pledge that I will to the very last stand by the law of this State, which forbids the marrying of white people with Negroes. [Continued laughter and applause.] I will add one further word, which is this: that I do not understand that there is any place where an alteration of the social and political relations of the Negro and the white man can be made except in the State Legislature—not in the Congress of the United States—and as I do not really apprehend the approach of any such thing myself, and as Judge Douglas seems to be in constant horror that some such danger is rapidly approaching, I propose as the best means to prevent it that the Judge be kept at home and placed in the State Legislature to fight the measure. [Uproarious laughter and applause.] I do not propose dwelling longer at this time on this subject. . . .

Note: the full text of this debate and the six others held between Senator Stephen A. Douglas and Abraham Lincoln as they campaigned for the 1858 Illinois Senate election are available at www.c-span.org/Lincoln200years, and the original source www.nps.gov.

COOPER UNION ADDRESS

February 27, 1860

*Delivered at the Cooper Institute in New York, and sponsored
by the Young Men's Republican Union*

MR. PRESIDENT AND FELLOW CITIZENS OF NEW YORK:

The facts with which I shall deal this evening are mainly old and familiar;
nor is there anything new in the general use I shall make of them. If there
shall be any novelty, it will be in the mode of presenting the facts, and the
inferences and observations following that presentation.

In his speech last autumn, at Columbus, Ohio, as reported in "The New-
York Times," Senator Douglas said:

"Our fathers, when they framed the Government under which we live,
understood this question just as well, and even better, than we do now."

I fully indorse this, and I adopt it as a text for this discourse. I so adopt it
because it furnishes a precise and an agreed starting point for a discussion
between Republicans and that wing of the Democracy headed by Senator
Douglas. It simply leaves the inquiry: "What was the understanding those fathers had of the question mentioned?"

What is the frame of government under which we live?

The answer must be: "The Constitution of the United States." That Constitution consists of the original, framed in 1787, (and under which the
present government first went into operation,) and twelve subsequently
framed amendments, the first ten of which were framed in 1789.

Who were our fathers that framed the Constitution? I suppose the "thirty-nine" who signed the original instrument may be fairly called our fathers who framed that part of the present Government. It is almost exactly
true to say they framed it, and it is altogether true to say they fairly represented the opinion and sentiment of the whole nation at that time. Their
names, being familiar to nearly all, and accessible to quite all, need not
now be repeated.

I take these "thirty-nine," for the present, as being "our fathers who
framed the Government under which we live."

What is the question which, according to the text, those fathers understood "just as well, and even better than we do now?"

It is this: Does the proper division of local from federal authority, or anything in the Constitution, forbid our *Federal Government* to control as to slavery in *our Federal Territories?*

Upon this, Senator Douglas holds the affirmative, and Republicans the
negative. This affirmation and denial form an issue; and this issue—this
question—is precisely what the text declares our fathers understood "better
than we."

Let us now inquire whether the "thirty-nine," or any of them, ever acted
upon this question; and if they did, how they acted upon it—how they expressed that better understanding?

In 1784, three years before the Constitution—the United States then
owning the Northwestern Territory, and no other, the Congress of the Confederation had before them the question of prohibiting slavery in that Territory; and four of the "thirty-nine" who afterward framed the Constitution,
were in that Congress, and voted on that question. Of these, Roger Sherman, Thomas Mifflin, and Hugh Williamson voted for the prohibition, thus
showing that, in their understanding, no line dividing local from federal
authority, nor anything else, properly forbade the Federal Government to
control as to slavery in federal territory. The other of the four—James
M'Henry—voted against the prohibition, showing that, for some cause, he
thought it improper to vote for it.

In 1787, still before the Constitution, but while the Convention was in
session framing it, and while the Northwestern Territory still was the only
territory owned by the United States, the same question of prohibiting slavery in the territory again came before the Congress of the Confederation;
and two more of the "thirty-nine" who afterward signed the Constitution,
were in that Congress, and voted on the question. They were William
Blount and William Few; and they both voted for the prohibition—thus
showing that, in their understanding, no line dividing local from federal authority, nor anything else, properly forbids the Federal Government to control as to slavery in Federal territory. This time the prohibition became a
law, being part of what is now well known as the Ordinance of '87.

The question of federal control of slavery in the territories, seems not to
have been directly before the Convention which framed the original Constitution; and hence it is not recorded that the "thirty-nine," or any of them,
while engaged on that instrument, expressed any opinion on that precise
question.

In 1789, by the first Congress which sat under the Constitution, an act
was passed to enforce the Ordinance of '87, including the prohibition of

slavery in the Northwestern Territory. The bill for this act was reported by one of the "thirty-nine," Thomas Fitzsimmons, then a member of the House of Representatives from Pennsylvania. It went through all its stages without a word of opposition, and finally passed both branches without yeas and nays, which is equivalent to a unanimous passage. In this Congress there were sixteen of the thirty-nine fathers who framed the original Constitution. They were John Langdon, Nicholas Gilman, Wm. S. Johnson, Roger Sherman, Robert Morris, Thos. Fitzsimmons, William Few, Abraham Baldwin, Rufus King, William Paterson, George Clymer, Richard Bassett, George Read, Pierce Butler, Daniel Carroll, James Madison.

This shows that, in their understanding, no line dividing local from federal authority, nor anything in the Constitution, properly forbade Congress to prohibit slavery in the federal territory; else both their fidelity to correct principle, and their oath to support the Constitution, would have constrained them to oppose the prohibition.

Again, George Washington, another of the "thirty-nine," was then President of the United States, and, as such approved and signed the bill; thus completing its validity as a law, and thus showing that, in his understanding, no line dividing local from federal authority, nor anything in the Constitution, forbade the Federal Government, to control as to slavery in federal territory.

No great while after the adoption of the original Constitution, North Carolina ceded to the Federal Government the country now constituting the State of Tennessee; and a few years later Georgia ceded that which now constitutes the States of Mississippi and Alabama. In both deeds of cession it was made a condition by the ceding States that the Federal Government should not prohibit slavery in the ceded territory. Besides this, slavery was then actually in the ceded country. Under these circumstances, Congress, on taking charge of these countries, did not absolutely prohibit slavery within them. But they did interfere with it—take control of it—even there, to a certain extent. In 1798, Congress organized the Territory of Mississippi. In the act of organization, they prohibited the bringing of slaves into the Territory, from any place without the United States, by fine, and giving freedom to slaves so bought. This act passed both branches of Congress without yeas and nays. In that Congress were three of the "thirty-nine" who framed the original Constitution. They were John Langdon, George Read and Abraham Baldwin. They all, probably, voted for it. Certainly they would have placed their opposition to it upon record, if, in their understanding, any line dividing local from federal authority, or anything in the Constitution, properly forbade the Federal Government to control as to slavery in federal territory.

In 1803, the Federal Government purchased the Louisiana country. Our former territorial acquisitions came from certain of our own States; but this Louisiana country was acquired from a foreign nation. In 1804, Congress gave a territorial organization to that part of it which now constitutes the State of Louisiana. New Orleans, lying within that part, was an old and comparatively large city. There were other considerable towns and settlements, and slavery was extensively and thoroughly intermingled with the people. Congress did not, in the Territorial Act, prohibit slavery; but they did interfere with it—take control of it—in a more marked and extensive way than they did in the case of Mississippi. The substance of the provision therein made, in relation to slaves, was:

First. That no slave should be imported into the territory from foreign parts.

Second. That no slave should be carried into it who had been imported into the United States since the first day of May, 1798.

Third. That no slave should be carried into it, except by the owner, and for his own use as a settler; the penalty in all the cases being a fine upon the violator of the law, and freedom to the slave.

This act also was passed without yeas and nays. In the Congress which passed it, there were two of the "thirty-nine." They were Abraham Baldwin and Jonathan Dayton. As stated in the case of Mississippi, it is probable they both voted for it. They would not have allowed it to pass without recording their opposition to it, if, in their understanding, it violated either the line properly dividing local from federal authority, or any provision of the Constitution.

In 1819–20, came and passed the Missouri question. Many votes were taken, by yeas and nays, in both branches of Congress, upon the various phases of the general question. Two of the "thirty-nine"—Rufus King and Charles Pinckney—were members of that Congress. Mr. King steadily voted for slavery prohibition and against all compromises, while Mr. Pinckney as steadily voted against slavery prohibition and against all compromises. By this, Mr. King showed that, in his understanding, no line dividing local from federal authority, nor anything in the Constitution, was violated by Congress prohibiting slavery in federal territory; while Mr. Pinckney, by his votes, showed that, in his understanding, there was some sufficient reason for opposing such prohibition in that case.

The cases I have mentioned are the only acts of the "thirty-nine," or of any of them, upon the direct issue, which I have been able to discover.

To enumerate the persons who thus acted, as being four in 1784, two in 1787, seventeen in 1789, three in 1798, two in 1804, and two in 1819–20—

there would be thirty of them. But this would be counting John Langdon, Roger Sherman, William Few, Rufus King, and George Read each twice, and Abraham Baldwin, three times. The true number of those of the "thirty-nine" whom I have shown to have acted upon the question, which, by the text, they understood better than we, is twenty-three, leaving sixteen not shown to have acted upon it in any way.

Here, then, we have twenty-three out of our thirty-nine fathers "who framed the government under which we live," who have, upon their official responsibility and their corporal oaths, acted upon the very question which the text affirms they "understood just as well, and even better than we do now;" and twenty-one of them—a clear majority of the whole "thirty-nine"—so acting upon it as to make them guilty of gross political impropriety and willful perjury, if, in their understanding, any proper division between local and federal authority, or anything in the Constitution they had made themselves, and sworn to support, forbade the Federal Government to control as to slavery in the federal territories. Thus the twenty-one acted; and, as actions speak louder than words, so actions, under such responsibility, speak still louder.

Two of the twenty-three voted against Congressional prohibition of slavery in the federal territories, in the instances in which they acted upon the question. But for what reasons they so voted is not known. They may have done so because they thought a proper division of local from federal authority, or some provision or principle of the Constitution, stood in the way; or they may, without any such question, have voted against the prohibition, on what appeared to them to be sufficient grounds of expediency. No one who has sworn to support the Constitution can conscientiously vote for what he understands to be an unconstitutional measure, however expedient he may think it; but one may and ought to vote against a measure which he deems constitutional, if, at the same time, he deems it inexpedient. It, therefore, would be unsafe to set down even the two who voted against the prohibition, as having done so because, in their understanding, any proper division of local from federal authority, or anything in the Constitution, forbade the Federal Government to control as to slavery in federal territory.

The remaining sixteen of the "thirty-nine," so far as I have discovered, have left no record of their understanding upon the direct question of federal control of slavery in the federal territories. But there is much reason to believe that their understanding upon that question would not have appeared different from that of their twenty-three compeers, had it been manifested at all.

For the purpose of adhering rigidly to the text, I have purposely omitted whatever understanding may have been manifested by any person, however distinguished, other than the thirty-nine fathers who framed the original Constitution; and, for the same reason, I have also omitted whatever understanding may have been manifested by any of the "thirty-nine" even, on any other phase of the general question of slavery. If we should look into their acts and declarations on those other phases, as the foreign slave trade, and the morality and policy of slavery generally, it would appear to us that on the direct question of federal control of slavery in federal territories, the sixteen, if they had acted at all, would probably have acted just as the twenty-three did. Among that sixteen were several of the most noted anti-slavery men of those times—as Dr. Franklin, Alexander Hamilton and Gouverneur Morris—while there was not one now known to have been otherwise, unless it may be John Rutledge, of South Carolina.

The sum of the whole is, that of our thirty-nine fathers who framed the original Constitution, twenty-one—a clear majority of the whole—certainly understood that no proper division of local from federal authority, nor any part of the Constitution, forbade the Federal Government to control slavery in the federal territories; while all the rest probably had the same understanding. Such, unquestionably, was the understanding of our fathers who framed the original Constitution; and the text affirms that they understood the question "better than we."

But, so far, I have been considering the understanding of the question manifested by the framers of the original Constitution. In and by the original instrument, a mode was provided for amending it; and, as I have already stated, the present frame of "the Government under which we live" consists of that original, and twelve amendatory articles framed and adopted since. Those who now insist that federal control of slavery in federal territories violates the Constitution, point us to the provisions which they suppose it thus violates; and, as I understand, that all fix upon provisions in these amendatory articles, and not in the original instrument. The Supreme Court, in the Dred Scott case, plant themselves upon the fifth amendment, which provides that no person shall be deprived of "life, liberty or property without due process of law;" while Senator Douglas and his peculiar adherents plant themselves upon the tenth amendment, providing that "the powers not delegated to the United States by the Constitution" "are reserved to the States respectively, or to the people."

Now, it so happens that these amendments were framed by the first Congress which sat under the Constitution—the identical Congress which passed the act already mentioned, enforcing the prohibition of slavery in the Northwestern Territory. Not only was it the same Congress, but they were the identical, same individual men who, at the same session, and at the same time within the session, had under consideration, and in progress toward maturity, these Constitutional amendments, and this act prohibiting slavery in all the territory the nation then owned. The Constitutional amendments were introduced before, and passed after the act enforcing the Ordinance of '87; so that, during the whole pendency of the act to enforce the Ordinance, the Constitutional amendments were also pending.

The seventy-six members of that Congress, including sixteen of the framers of the original Constitution, as before stated, were pre-eminently our fathers who framed that part of "the Government under which we live," which is now claimed as forbidding the Federal Government to control slavery in the federal territories.

Is it not a little presumptuous in any one at this day to affirm that the two things which that Congress deliberately framed, and carried to maturity at the same time, are absolutely inconsistent with each other? And does not such affirmation become impudently absurd when coupled with the other affirmation from the same mouth, that those who did the two things, alleged to be inconsistent, understood whether they really were inconsistent better than we—better than he who affirms that they are inconsistent?

It is surely safe to assume that the thirty-nine framers of the original Constitution, and the seventy-six members of the Congress which framed the amendments thereto, taken together, do certainly include those who may be fairly called "our fathers who framed the Government under which we live." And so assuming, I defy any man to show that any one of them ever, in his whole life, declared that, in his understanding, any proper division of local from federal authority, or any part of the Constitution, forbade the Federal Government to control as to slavery in the federal territories. I go a step further. I defy any one to show that any living man in the whole world ever did, prior to the beginning of the present century, (and I might almost say prior to the beginning of the last half of the present century,) declare that, in his understanding, any proper division of local from federal authority, or any part of the Constitution, forbade the Federal Government to control as to slavery in the federal territories. To those who now so declare, I give, not only "our fathers who framed the Government under which we live," but with them all other living men within the century in which it was framed, among whom to search, and they shall not be able to find the evidence of a single man agreeing with them.

Now, and here, let me guard a little against being misunderstood. I do not mean to say we are bound to follow implicitly in whatever our fathers did. To do so, would be to discard all the lights of current experience—to reject all progress—all improvement. What I do say is, that if we would supplant the opinions and policy of our fathers in any case, we should do so upon evidence so conclusive, and argument so clear, that even their great authority, fairly considered and weighed, cannot stand; and most surely not in a case whereof we ourselves declare they understood the question better than we.

If any man at this day sincerely believes that a proper division of local from federal authority, or any part of the Constitution, forbids the Federal Government to control as to slavery in the federal territories, he is right to say so, and to enforce his position by all truthful evidence and fair argument which he can. But he has no right to mislead others, who have less access to history, and less leisure to study it, into the false belief that "our fathers who framed the Government under which we live" were of the same opinion—thus substituting falsehood and deception for truthful evidence and fair argument. If any man at this day sincerely believes "our fathers who framed the Government under which we live," used and applied principles, in other cases, which ought to have led them to understand that a proper division of local from federal authority or some part of the Constitution, forbids the Federal Government to control as to slavery in the federal territories, he is right to say so. But he should, at the same time, brave the responsibility of declaring that, in his opinion, he understands their principles better than they did themselves; and especially should he not shirk that responsibility by asserting that they "understood the question just as well, and even better, than we do now."

But enough! *Let all who believe that "our fathers, who framed the Government under which we live, understood this question just as well, and even better, than we do now," speak as they spoke, and act as they acted upon it. This is all Republicans ask—all Republicans desire—in relation to slavery. As those fathers marked it, so let it be again marked, as an evil not to be extended, but to be tolerated and protected only because of and so far as its actual presence among us makes that toleration and protection a necessity. Let all the guarantees those fathers gave it, be, not grudgingly, but fully and fairly, maintained.* For this Republicans contend, and with this, so far as I know or believe, they will be content.

And now, if they would listen—as I suppose they will not—I would address a few words to the Southern people.

I would say to them:—You consider yourselves a reasonable and a just people; and I consider that in the general qualities of reason and justice you are not inferior to any other people. Still, when you speak of us Republicans, you do so only to denounce us a reptiles, or, at the best, as no better than outlaws. You will grant a hearing to pirates or murderers, but nothing like it to "Black Republicans." In all your contentions with one another, each of you deems an unconditional condemnation of "Black Republicanism" as the first thing to be attended to. Indeed, such condemnation of us seems to be an indispensable prerequisite—license, so to speak—among you to be admitted or permitted to speak at all. Now, can you, or not, be prevailed upon to pause and to consider whether this is quite just to us, or even to yourselves? Bring forward your charges and specifications, and then be patient long enough to hear us deny or justify.

You say we are sectional. We deny it. That makes an issue; and the burden of proof is upon you. You produce your proof; and what is it? Why, that our party has no existence in your section—gets no votes in your section. The fact is substantially true; but does it prove the issue? If it does, then in case we should, without change of principle, begin to get votes in your section, we should thereby cease to be sectional. You cannot escape this conclusion; and yet, are you willing to abide by it? If you are, you will probably soon find that we have ceased to be sectional, for we shall get votes in your section this very year. You will then begin to discover, as the truth plainly is, that your proof does not touch the issue. The fact that we get no votes in your section, is a fact of your making, and not of ours. And if there be fault in that fact, that fault is primarily yours, and remains until you show that we repel you by some wrong principle or practice. If we do repel you by any wrong principle or practice, the fault is ours; but this brings you to where you ought to have started—to a discussion of the right or wrong of our principle. If our principle, put in practice, would wrong your section for the benefit of ours, or for any other object, then our principle, and we with it, are sectional, and are justly opposed and denounced as such. Meet us, then, on the question of whether our principle, put in practice, would wrong your section; and so meet it as if it were possible that something may be said on our side. Do you accept the challenge? No! Then you really believe that the principle which "our fathers who framed the Government under which we live" thought so clearly right as to adopt it, and indorse it again and again, upon their official oaths, is in fact so clearly wrong as to demand your condemnation without a moment's consideration.

Some of you delight to flaunt in our faces the warning against sectional parties given by Washington in his Farewell Address. Less than eight years before Washington gave that warning, he had, as President of the United States, approved and signed an act of Congress, enforcing the prohibition of slavery in the Northwestern Territory, which act embodied the policy of the Government upon that subject up to and at the very moment he penned that warning; and about one year after he penned it, he wrote LaFayette that he considered that prohibition a wise measure, expressing in the same connection his hope that we should at some time have a confederacy of free States.

Bearing this in mind, and seeing that sectionalism has since arisen upon this same subject, is that warning a weapon in your hands against us, or in our hands against you? Could Washington himself speak, would he cast the blame of that sectionalism upon us, who sustain his policy, or upon you who repudiate it? We respect that warning of Washington, and we commend it to you, together with his example pointing to the right application of it.

But you say you are conservative—eminently conservative—while we are revolutionary, destructive, or something of the sort. What is conservatism? Is it not adherence to the old and tried, against the new and untried? We stick to, contend for, the identical old policy on the point in controversy which was adopted by "our fathers who framed the Government under which we live;" while you with one accord reject, and scout, and spit upon that old policy, and insist upon substituting something new. True, you disagree among yourselves as to what that substitute shall be. You are divided on new propositions and plans, but you are unanimous in rejecting and denouncing the old policy of the fathers. Some of you are for reviving the foreign slave trade; some for a Congressional Slave-Code for the Territories; some for Congress forbidding the Territories to prohibit Slavery within their limits; some for maintaining Slavery in the Territories through the judiciary; some for the "gur-reat pur-rinciple" that "if one man would enslave another, no third man should object," fantastically called "Popular Sovereignty;" but never a man among you is in favor of federal prohibition of slavery in federal territories, according to the practice of "our fathers who framed the Government under which we live." Not one of all your various plans can show a precedent or an advocate in the century within which our Government originated. Consider, then, whether your claim of conservatism for yourselves, and your charge or destructiveness against us, are based on the most clear and stable foundations.

Again, you say we have made the slavery question more prominent than it formerly was. We deny it. We admit that it is more prominent, but we deny that we made it so. It was not we, but you, who discarded the old policy of the fathers. We resisted, and still resist, your innovation; and thence comes the greater prominence of the question. Would you have that question reduced to its former proportions? Go back to that old policy. What has been will be again, under the same conditions. If you would have the peace of the old times, readopt the precepts and policy of the old times.

You charge that we stir up insurrections among your slaves. We deny it; and what is your proof? Harper's Ferry! John Brown! John Brown was no Republican; and you have failed to implicate a single Republican in his Harper's Ferry enterprise. If any member of our party is guilty in that matter, you know it or you do not know it. If you do know it, you are inexcusable for not designating the man and proving the fact. If you do not know it, you are inexcusable for asserting it, and especially for persisting in the assertion after you have tried and failed to make the proof. You need to be told that persisting in a charge which one does not know to be true, is simply malicious slander.

Some of you admit that no Republican designedly aided or encouraged the Harper's Ferry affair, but still insist that our doctrines and declarations necessarily lead to such results. We do not believe it. We know we hold to no doctrine, and make no declaration, which were not held to and made by "our fathers who framed the Government under which we live." You never dealt fairly by us in relation to this affair. When it occurred, some important State elections were near at hand, and you were in evident glee with the belief that, by charging the blame upon us, you could get an advantage of us in those elections. The elections came, and your expectations were not quite fulfilled. Every Republican man knew that, as to himself at least, your charge was a slander, and he was not much inclined by it to cast his vote in your favor. Republican doctrines and declarations are accompanied with a continual protest against any interference whatever with your slaves, or with you about your slaves. Surely, this does not encourage them to revolt. True, we do, in common with "our fathers, who framed the Government under which we live," declare our belief that slavery is wrong; but the slaves do not hear us declare even this. For anything we say or do, the slaves would scarcely know there is a Republican party. I believe they would not, in fact, generally know it but for your misrepresentations of us, in their hearing. In your political contests among yourselves, each faction charges the other with sympathy with Black Republicanism; and then, to give point to the charge, defines Black Republicanism to simply be insurrection, blood and thunder among the slaves.

Slave insurrections are no more common now than they were before the Republican party was organized. What induced the Southampton insurrection, twenty-eight years ago, in which, at least three times as many lives were lost as at Harper's Ferry? You can scarcely stretch your very elastic fancy to the conclusion that Southampton was "got up by Black Republicanism." In the present state of things in the United States, I do not think a general, or even a very extensive slave insurrection is possible. The indispensable concert of action cannot be attained. The slaves have no means of rapid communication; nor can incendiary freemen, black or white, supply it. The explosive materials are everywhere in parcels; but there neither are, nor can be supplied, the indispensable connecting trains.

Much is said by Southern people about the affection of slaves for their masters and mistresses; and a part of it, at least, is true. A plot for an uprising could scarcely be devised and communicated to twenty individuals before some one of them, to save the life of a favorite master or mistress, would divulge it. This is the rule; and the slave revolution in Hayti was not an exception to it, but a case occurring under peculiar circumstances. The gunpowder plot of British history, though not connected with slaves, was more in point. In that case, only about twenty were admitted to the secret; and yet one of them, in his anxiety to save a friend, betrayed the plot to that friend, and, by consequence, averted the calamity. Occasional poisonings from the kitchen, and open or stealthy assassinations in the field, and local revolts extending to a score or so, will continue to occur as the natural results of slavery; but no general insurrection of slaves, as I think, can happen in this country for a long time. Whoever much fears, or much hopes for such an event, will be alike disappointed.

In the language of Mr. Jefferson, uttered many years ago, "It is still in our power to direct the process of emancipation, and deportation, peaceably, and in such slow degrees, as that the evil will wear off insensibly; and their places be, *pari passu,* filled up by free white laborers. If, on the contrary, it is left to force itself on, human nature must shudder at the prospect held up."

Mr. Jefferson did not mean to say, nor do I, that the power of emancipation is in the Federal Government. He spoke of Virginia; and, as to the power of emancipation, I speak of the slaveholding States only. The Federal Government, however, as we insist, has the power of restraining the extension of the institution—the power to insure that a slave insurrection shall never occur on any American soil which is now free from slavery.

John Brown's effort was peculiar. It was not a slave insurrection. It was an attempt by white men to get up a revolt among slaves, in which the slaves refused to participate. In fact, it was so absurd that the slaves, with all their ignorance, saw plainly enough it could not succeed. That affair, in its philosophy, corresponds with the many attempts, related in history, at the assassination of kings and emperors. An enthusiast broods over the oppression of a people till he fancies himself commissioned by Heaven to liberate them. He ventures the attempt, which ends in little else than his own execution. Orsini's attempt on Louis Napoleon, and John Brown's attempt at Harper's Ferry were, in their philosophy, precisely the same. The eagerness to cast blame on old England in the one case, and on New England in the other, does not disprove the sameness of the two things.

And how much would it avail you, if you could, by the use of John Brown, Helper's Book, and the like, break up the Republican organization? Human action can be modified to some extent, but human nature cannot be changed. There is a judgment and a feeling against slavery in this nation, which cast at least a million and a half of votes. You cannot destroy that judgment and feeling—that sentiment—by breaking up the political organization which rallies around it. You can scarcely scatter and disperse an army which has been formed into order in the face of your heaviest fire; but if you could, how much would you gain by forcing the sentiment which created it out of the peaceful channel of the ballot-box, into some other channel? What would that other channel probably be? Would the number of John Browns be lessened or enlarged by the operation?

But you will break up the Union rather than submit to a denial of your Constitutional rights.

That has a somewhat reckless sound; but it would be palliated, if not fully justified, were we proposing, by the mere force of numbers, to deprive you of some right, plainly written down in the Constitution. But we are proposing no such thing.

When you make these declarations, you have a specific and well-understood allusion to an assumed Constitutional right of yours, to take slaves into the federal territories, and to hold them there as property. But no such right is specifically written in the Constitution. That instrument is literally silent about any such right. We, on the contrary, deny that such a right has any existence in the Constitution, even by implication.

Your purpose, then, plainly stated, is that you will destroy the Government, unless you be allowed to construe and enforce the Constitution as you please, on all points in dispute between you and us. You will rule or ruin in all events.

This, plainly stated, is your language. Perhaps you will say the Supreme Court has decided the disputed Constitutional question in your favor. Not quite so. But waiving the lawyer's distinction between dictum and decision, the Court have decided the question for you in a sort of way. The Court have substantially said, it is your Constitutional right to take slaves into the federal territories, and to hold them there as property. When I say the decision was made in a sort of way, I mean it was made in a divided Court, by a bare majority of the Judges, and they not quite agreeing with one another in the reasons for making it; that it is so made as that its avowed supporters disagree with one another about its meaning, and that it was mainly based upon a mistaken statement of fact—the statement in the opinion that "the right of property in a slave is distinctly and expressly affirmed in the Constitution."

An inspection of the Constitution will show that the right of property in a slave is not "*distinctly* and *expressly* affirmed" in it. Bear in mind, the Judges do not pledge their judicial opinion that such right is *impliedly* affirmed in the Constitution; but they pledge their veracity that it is "*distinctly* and *expressly*" affirmed there—"distinctly," that is, not mingled with anything else—"expressly," that is, in words meaning just that, without the aid of any inference, and susceptible of no other meaning.

If they had only pledged their judicial opinion that such right is affirmed in the instrument by implication, it would be open to others to show that neither the word "slave" nor "slavery" is to be found in the Constitution, nor the word "property" even, in any connection with language alluding to the things slave, or slavery; and that wherever in that instrument the slave is alluded to, he is called a "person"—and wherever his master's legal right in relation to him is alluded to, it is spoken of as "service or labor which may be due"—as a debt payable in service or labor. Also, it would be open to show, by contemporaneous history, that this mode of alluding to slaves and slavery, instead of speaking of them, was employed on purpose to exclude from the Constitution the idea that there could be property in man.

To show all this, is easy and certain.

When this obvious mistake of the Judges shall be brought to their notice, is it not reasonable to expect that they will withdraw the mistaken statement, and reconsider the conclusion based upon it?

And then it is to be remembered that "our fathers, who framed the Government under which we live"—the men who made the Constitution— decided this same Constitutional question in our favor, long ago—decided it without division among themselves, when making the decision; without division among themselves about the meaning of it after it was made, and, so far as any evidence is left, without basing it upon any mistaken statement of facts.

Under all these circumstances, do you really feel yourselves justified to break up this Government unless such a court decision as yours is, shall be at once submitted to as a conclusive and final rule of political action? But you will not abide the election of a Republican president! In that supposed event, you say, you will destroy the Union; and then, you say, the great crime of having destroyed it will be upon us! That is cool. A highwayman holds a pistol to my ear, and mutters through his teeth, "Stand and deliver, or I shall kill you, and then you will be a murderer!"

To be sure, what the robber demanded of me—my money—was my own; and I had a clear right to keep it; but it was no more my own than my vote is my own; and the threat of death to me, to extort my money, and the threat of destruction to the Union, to extort my vote, can scarcely be distinguished in principle.

A few words now to Republicans. *It is exceedingly desirable that all parts of this great Confederacy shall be at peace, and in harmony, one with another. Let us Republicans do our part to have it so. Even though much provoked, let us do nothing through passion and ill temper. Even though the southern people will not so much as listen to us, let us calmly consider their demands, and yield to them if, in our deliberate view of our duty, we possibly can.* Judging by all they say and do, and by the subject and nature of their controversy with us, let us determine, if we can, what will satisfy them.

Will they be satisfied if the Territories be unconditionally surrendered to them? We know they will not. In all their present complaints against us, the Territories are scarcely mentioned. Invasions and insurrections are the rage now. Will it satisfy them, if, in the future, we have nothing to do with invasions and insurrections? We know it will not. We so know, because we know we never had anything to do with invasions and insurrections; and yet this total abstaining does not exempt us from the charge and the denunciation.

The question recurs, what will satisfy them? Simply this: We must not only let them alone, but we must somehow, convince them that we do let them alone. This, we know by experience, is no easy task. We have been so trying to convince them from the very beginning of our organization, but with no success. In all our platforms and speeches we have constantly protested our purpose to let them alone; but this has had no tendency to convince them. Alike unavailing to convince them, is the fact that they have never detected a man of us in any attempt to disturb them.

These natural, and apparently adequate means all failing, what will convince them? This, and this only: cease to call slavery *wrong*, and join them in calling it *right*. And this must be done thoroughly—done in *acts* as well as in *words*. Silence will not be tolerated—we must place ourselves avowedly with them. Senator Douglas's new sedition law must be enacted and enforced, suppressing all declarations that slavery is wrong, whether made in politics, in presses, in pulpits, or in private. We must arrest and return their fugitive slaves with greedy pleasure. We must pull down our Free State constitutions. The whole atmosphere must be disinfected from all taint of opposition to slavery, before they will cease to believe that all their troubles proceed from us.

I am quite aware they do not state their case precisely in this way. Most of them would probably say to us, "Let us alone, do nothing to us, and say what you please about slavery." But we do let them alone—have never disturbed them—so that, after all, it is what we say, which dissatisfies them. They will continue to accuse us of doing, until we cease saying.

I am also aware they have not, as yet, in terms, demanded the overthrow of our Free-State Constitutions. Yet those Constitutions declare the wrong of slavery, with more solemn emphasis, than do all other sayings against it; and when all these other sayings shall have been silenced, the overthrow of these Constitutions will be demanded, and nothing be left to resist the demand. It is nothing to the contrary, that they do not demand the whole of this just now. Demanding what they do, and for the reason they do, they can voluntarily stop nowhere short of this consummation. Holding, as they do, that slavery is morally right, and socially elevating, they cannot cease to demand a full national recognition of it, as a legal right, and a social blessing.

Nor can we justifiably withhold this, on any ground save our conviction that slavery is wrong. If slavery is right, all words, acts, laws, and constitutions against it, are themselves wrong, and should be silenced, and swept away. If it is right, we cannot justly object to its nationality—its universality; if it is wrong, they cannot justly insist upon its extension—its enlargement. All they ask, we could readily grant, if we thought slavery right; all we ask, they could as readily grant, if they thought it wrong. Their thinking it right, and our thinking it wrong, is the precise fact upon which depends the whole controversy. Thinking it right, as they do, they are not to blame for desiring its full recognition, as being right; but, thinking it wrong, as we do, can we yield to them? Can we cast our votes with their view, and against our own? In view of our moral, social, and political responsibilities, can we do this?

Wrong as we think slavery is, we can yet afford to let it alone where it is, because that much is due to the necessity arising from its actual presence in the nation; but can we, while our votes will prevent it, allow it to spread into the National Territories, and to overrun us here in these Free States? If our sense of duty forbids this, then let us stand by our duty, fearlessly and effectively. Let us be diverted by none of those sophistical contrivances wherewith we are so industriously plied and belabored—contrivances such as groping for some middle ground between the right and the wrong, vain as the search for a man who should be neither a living man nor a dead man—such as a policy of "don't care" on a question about which all true men do care—such as Union appeals beseeching true Union men to yield to Disunionists, reversing the divine rule, and calling, not the sinners, but the righteous to repentance—such as invocations to Washington, imploring men to unsay what Washington said, and undo what Washington did.

Neither let us be slandered from our duty by false accusations against us, nor frightened from it by menaces of destruction to the Government nor of dungeons to ourselves. LET US HAVE FAITH THAT RIGHT MAKES MIGHT, AND IN THAT FAITH, LET US, TO THE END, DARE TO DO OUR DUTY AS WE UNDERSTAND IT.

FIRST INAUGURAL ADDRESS

March 4, 1861

Delivered in Washington, DC

FELLOW-CITIZENS OF THE UNITED STATES:

In compliance with a custom as old as the government itself, I appear before you to address you briefly, and to take, in your presence, the oath prescribed by the Constitution of the United States, to be taken by the President "before he enters on the execution of this office."

I do not consider it necessary at present for me to discuss those matters of administration about which there is no special anxiety or excitement.

Apprehension seems to exist among the people of the Southern States, that by the accession of a Republican Administration, their property, and their peace, and personal security, are to be endangered. There has never been any reasonable cause for such apprehension. Indeed, the most ample evidence to the contrary has all the while existed, and been open to their inspection. It is found in nearly all the published speeches of him who now addresses you. I do but quote from one of those speeches when I declare that "I have no purpose, directly or indirectly, to interfere with the institution of slavery in the States where it exists. I believe I have no lawful right to do so, and I have no inclination to do so." Those who nominated and elected me did so with full knowledge that I had made this, and many similar declarations, and had never recanted them. And more than this, they placed in the platform, for my acceptance, and as a law to themselves, and to me, the clear and emphatic resolution which I now read:

"*Resolved*, That the maintenance inviolate of the rights of the States, and especially the right of each State to order and control its own domestic institutions according to its own judgment exclusively, is essential to that balance of power on which the perfection and endurance of our political fabric depend; and we denounce the lawless invasion by armed force of the soil of any State or Territory, no matter what pretext, as among the gravest of crimes."

I now reiterate these sentiments; and in doing so, I only press upon the public attention the most conclusive evidence of which the case is susceptible, that the property, peace and security of no section are to be in any wise endangered by the now incoming Administration. I add too, that all the protection which, consistently with the Constitution and the laws, can be given, will be cheerfully given to all the States when lawfully demanded, for whatever cause—as cheerfully to one section as to another.

There is much controversy about the delivering up of fugitives from service or labor. The clause I now read is as plainly written in the Constitution as any other of its provisions:

"No person held to service or labor in one State, under the laws thereof, escaping into another, shall, in consequence of any law or regulation therein, be discharged from such service or labor, but shall be delivered up on claim of the party to whom such service or labor may be due."

It is scarcely questioned that this provision was intended by those who made it, for the reclaiming of what we call fugitive slaves; and the intention of the law-giver is the law. All members of Congress swear their support to the whole Constitution—to this provision as much as to any other. To the proposition, then, that slaves whose cases come within the terms of this clause, "shall be delivered," their oaths are unanimous. Now, if they would make the effort in good temper, could they not, with nearly equal unanimity, frame and pass a law, by means of which to keep good that unanimous oath?

There is some difference of opinion whether this clause should be enforced by national or by state authority; but surely that difference is not a very material one. If the slave is to be surrendered, it can be of but little consequence to him, or to others, by which authority it is done. And should any one, in any case, be content that his oath shall go unkept, on a merely unsubstantial controversy as to *how* it shall be kept?

Again, in any law upon this subject, ought not all the safeguards of liberty known in civilized and humane jurisprudence to be introduced, so that a free man be not, in any case, surrendered as a slave? And might it not be well, at the same time to provide by law for the enforcement of that clause in the Constitution which guarantees that "the citizens of each State shall be entitled to all privileges and immunities of citizens in the several States"?

I take the official oath to-day, with no mental reservations, and with no purpose to construe the Constitution or laws, by any hypercritical rules. And while I do not choose now to specify particular acts of Congress as proper to be enforced, I do suggest that it will be much safer for all, both in official and private stations, to conform to, and abide by, all those acts which stand unrepealed, than to violate any of them, trusting to find impunity in having them held to be unconstitutional.

It is seventy-two years since the first inauguration of a President under our national Constitution. During that period fifteen different and greatly distinguished citizens, have, in succession, administered the executive branch of the government. They have conducted it through many perils; and, generally, with great success. Yet, with all this scope for precedent, I now enter upon the same task for the brief constitutional term of four years, under great and peculiar difficulty. A disruption of the Federal Union, heretofore only menaced, is now formidably attempted.

I hold, that in contemplation of universal law, and of the Constitution, the Union of these States is perpetual. Perpetuity is implied, if not expressed, in the fundamental law of all national governments. It is safe to assert that no government proper, ever had a provision in its organic law for its own termination. Continue to execute all the express provisions of our national Constitution, and the Union will endure forever — it being impossible to destroy it, except by some action not provided for in the instrument itself.

Again, if the United States be not a government proper, but an association of States in the nature of contract merely, can it, as a contract, be peaceably unmade, by less than all the parties who made it? One party to a contract may violate it—break it, so to speak; but does it not require all to lawfully rescind it?

Descending from these general principles, we find the proposition that, in legal contemplation, the Union is perpetual, confirmed by the history of the Union itself. The Union is much older than the Constitution. It was formed in fact, by the Articles of Association in 1774. It was matured and continued by the Declaration of Independence in 1776. It was further matured and the faith of all the then thirteen States expressly plighted and engaged that it should be perpetual, by the Articles of Confederation in 1778. And finally, in 1787, one of the declared objects for ordaining and establishing the Constitution, was "*to form a more perfect Union.*" But if destruction of the Union, by one, or by a part only, of the States, be lawfully possible, the Union is *less* perfect than before the Constitution, having lost the vital element of perpetuity.

It follows from these views that no State, upon its own mere motion, can lawfully get out of the Union,—that *resolves* and *ordinances* to that effect are legally void, and that acts of violence, within any State or States, against the authority of the United States, are insurrectionary or revolutionary, according to circumstances.

I therefore consider that in view of the Constitution and the laws, the Union is unbroken; and to the extent of my ability I shall take care, as the Constitution itself expressly enjoins upon me, that the laws of the Union be faithfully executed in all the States. Doing this I deem to be only a simple duty on my part; and I shall perform it, so far as practicable, unless my rightful masters, the American people, shall withhold the requisite means, or in some authoritative manner, direct the contrary. I trust this will not be regarded as a menace, but only as the declared purpose of the Union that will constitutionally defend and maintain itself.

In doing this there needs to be no bloodshed or violence; and there shall be none, unless it be forced upon the national authority. The power confided to me will be used to hold, occupy, and possess the property and places belonging to the government, and to collect the duties and imposts; but beyond what may be necessary for these objects, there will be no invasion— no using of force against or among the people anywhere. Where hostility to the United States in any interior locality, shall be so great and so universal, as to prevent competent resident citizens from holding the Federal offices, there will be no attempt to force obnoxious strangers among the people for that object. While the strict legal right may exist in the government to enforce the exercise of these offices, the attempt to do so would be so irritating, and so nearly impracticable with all, that I deem it better to forego, for the time, the uses of such offices.

The mails, unless repelled, will continue to be furnished in all parts of the Union. So far as possible, the people everywhere shall have that sense of perfect security which is most favorable to calm thought and reflection. The course here indicated will be followed, unless current events and experience shall show a modification or change to be proper; and in every case and exigency my best discretion will be exercised according to circumstances actually existing, and with a view and a hope of a peaceful solution of the national troubles, and the restoration of fraternal sympathies and affections.

That there are persons in one section or another who seek to destroy the Union at all events, and are glad of any pretext to do it, I will neither affirm nor deny; but if there be such, I need address no word to them. To those, however, who really love the Union may I not speak?

Before entering upon so grave a matter as the destruction of our national fabric, with all its benefits, its memories, and its hopes, would it not be wise to ascertain precisely why we do it? Will you hazard so desperate a step, while there is any possibility that any portion of the ills you fly from have no real existence? Will you, while the certain ills you fly to, are greater than all the real ones you fly from? Will you risk the commission of so fearful a mistake?

All profess to be content in the Union, if all constitutional rights can be maintained. Is it true, then, that any right, plainly written in the Constitution, has been denied? I think not. Happily the human mind is so constituted, that no party can reach to the audacity of doing this. Think, if you can, of a single instance in which a plainly written provision of the Constitution has ever been denied. If by the mere force of numbers, a majority should deprive a minority of any clearly written constitutional right, it might, in a moral point of view, justify revolution—certainly would, if such right were a vital one. But such is not our case. All the vital rights of minorities, and of individuals, are so plainly assured to them, by affirmations and negations, guaranties and prohibitions, in the Constitution, that controversies never arise concerning them. But no organic law can ever be framed with a provision specifically applicable to every question which may occur in practical administration. No foresight can anticipate, nor any document of reasonable length contain express provisions for all possible questions. Shall fugitives from labor be surrendered by national or by State authority? The Constitution does not expressly say. *May* Congress prohibit slavery in the territories? The Constitution does not expressly say. *Must* Congress protect slavery in the territories? The Constitution does not expressly say.

From questions of this class spring all our constitutional controversies, and we divide upon them into majorities and minorities. If the minority will not acquiesce, the majority must, or the government must cease. There is no other alternative; for continuing the government, is acquiescence on one side or the other. If a minority, in such case, will secede rather than acquiesce, they make a precedent which, in turn, will divide and ruin them; for a minority of their own will secede from them whenever a majority refuses to be controlled by such minority. For instance, why may not any portion of a new confederacy, a year or two hence, arbitrarily secede again, precisely as portions of the present Union now claim to secede from it? All who cherish disunion sentiments, are now being educated to the exact temper of doing this.

Is there such perfect identity of interests among the States to compose a new Union, as to produce harmony only, and prevent renewed secession?

Plainly, the central idea of secession, is the essence of anarchy. A majority, held in restraint by constitutional checks and limitations, and always changing easily with deliberate changes of popular opinions and sentiments, is the only true sovereign of a free people. Whoever rejects it, does, of necessity, fly to anarchy or to despotism. Unanimity is impossible; the rule of a minority, as a permanent arrangement, is wholly inadmissible; so that, rejecting the majority principle, anarchy or despotism in some form is all that is left.

I do not forget the position assumed by some, that constitutional questions are to be decided by the Supreme Court; nor do I deny that such decisions must be binding in any case, upon the parties to a suit; as to the object of that suit, while they are also entitled to very high respect and consideration in all parallel cases by all other departments of the government. And while it is obviously possible that such decision may be erroneous in any given case, still the evil effect following it, being limited to that particular case, with the chance that it may be over-ruled, and never become a precedent for other cases, can better be borne than could the evils of a different practice. At the same time, the candid citizen must confess that if the policy of the government upon vital questions, affecting the whole people, is to be irrevocably fixed by decisions of the Supreme Court, the instant they are made, in ordinary litigation between parties, in personal actions, the people will have ceased to be their own rulers, having to that extent practically resigned their government into the hands of that eminent tribunal. Nor is there in this view any assault upon the court or the judges. It is a duty from which they may not shrink, to decide cases properly brought before them; and it is no fault of theirs if others seek to turn their decisions to political purposes.

One section of our country believes slavery is *right*, and ought to be extended, while the other believes it is *wrong*, and ought not to be extended. This is the only substantial dispute. The fugitive slave clause of the Constitution, and the law for the suppression of the foreign slave trade, are each as well enforced, perhaps, as any law can ever be in a community where the moral sense of the people imperfectly supports the law itself. The great body of the people abide by the dry legal obligation in both cases, and a few break over in each. This, I think, cannot be perfectly cured, and it would be worse in both cases *after* the separation of the sections, than before. The foreign slave trade, now imperfectly suppressed, would be ultimately revived without restriction, in one section; while fugitive slaves, now only partially surrendered, would not be surrendered at all, by the other.

Physically speaking, we cannot separate. We can not remove our respective sections from each other, nor build an impassable wall between them. A husband and wife may be divorced, and go out of the presence, and beyond the reach of each other; but the different parts of our country cannot do this. They cannot but remain face to face; and intercourse, either amicable or hostile, must continue between them. Is it possible, then, to make that intercourse more advantageous or more satisfactory, *after* separation than *before*? Can aliens make treaties easier than friends can make laws? Can treaties be more faithfully enforced between aliens than laws can among friends? Suppose you go to war, you cannot fight always; and when, after much loss on both sides, and no gain on either, you cease fighting, the identical old questions, as to terms of intercourse, are again upon you.

This country, with its institutions, belongs to the people who inhabit it. Whenever they shall grow weary of the existing Government, they can exercise their *constitutional* right of amending it, or their *revolutionary* right to dismember or overthrow it. I cannot be ignorant of the fact that many worthy and patriotic citizens are desirous of having the national Constitution amended. While I make no recommendation of amendments, I fully recognize the rightful authority of the people over the whole subject to be exercised in either of the modes prescribed in the instrument itself; and I should, under existing circumstances, favor rather than oppose a fair opportunity being afforded the people to act upon it.

I will venture to add that to me the Convention mode seems preferable, in that it allows amendments to originate with the people themselves, instead of only permitting them to take or reject propositions, originated by others, not especially chosen for the purpose, and which might not be precisely such as they would wish to either accept or refuse. I understand a proposed amendment to the Constitution, which amendment, however, I have not seen, has passed Congress, to the effect that the federal government shall never interfere with the domestic institutions of the States, including that of persons held to service. To avoid misconstruction of what I have said, I depart from my purpose not to speak of particular amendments, so far as to say that holding such a provision to now be implied constitutional law, I have no objection to its being made express and irrevocable.

The Chief Magistrate derives all his authority from the people, and they have referred none upon him to fix terms for the separation of the States. The people themselves can do this if also they choose; but the executive, as such, has nothing to do with it. His duty is to administer the present government, as it came to his hands, and to transmit it, unimpaired by him, to his successor.

Why should there not be a patient confidence in the ultimate justice of the people? Is there any better or equal hope, in the world? In our present differences, is either party without faith of being in the right? If the Almighty Ruler of nations, with his eternal truth and justice, be on your side of the North, or on yours of the South, that truth, and that justice, will surely prevail, by the judgment of this great tribunal of the American people.

By the frame of the government under which we live, this same people have wisely given their public servants but little power for mischief; and have, with equal wisdom, provided for the return of that little to their own hands at very short intervals.

While the people retain their virtue and vigilance, no administration, by any extreme of wickedness or folly, can very seriously injure the government in the short space of four years.

My countrymen, one and all, think calmly and *well*, upon this whole subject. Nothing valuable can be lost by taking time. If there be an object to *hurry* any of you, in hot haste, to a step which you would never take *deliberately*, that object will be frustrated by taking time; but no good object can be frustrated by it. Such of you as are now dissatisfied still have the old Constitution unimpaired, and, on the sensitive point, the laws of your own framing under it; while the new administration will have no immediate power, if it would, to change either. If it were admitted that you who are dissatisfied, hold the right side in the dispute, there still is no single good reason for precipitate action. Intelligence, patriotism, Christianity, and a firm reliance on Him, who has never yet forsaken this favored land, are still competent to adjust, in the best way, all our present difficulty.

In *your* hands, my dissatisfied fellow countrymen, and not in *mine*, is the momentous issue of civil war. The government will not assail *you*. You can have no conflict without being yourselves the aggressors. *You* have no oath registered in Heaven to destroy the government, while *I* shall have the most solemn one to "preserve, protect, and defend it."

I am loath to close. We are not enemies, but friends. We must not be enemies. Though passion may have strained, it must not break our bonds of affection. The mystic chords of memory, stretching from every battle-field, and patriot grave, to every living heart and hearth-stone, all over this broad land, will yet swell the chorus of the Union, when again touched, as surely they will be, by the better angels of our nature.

THE EMANCIPATION
PROCLAMATION

January 1, 1863

BY THE PRESIDENT OF THE UNITED STATES OF AMERICA:
A PROCLAMATION.

Whereas, on the twenty-second day of September, in the year of our Lord one thousand eight hundred and sixty-two, a proclamation was issued by the President of the United States, containing, among other things, the following, to wit:

"That on the first day of January, in the year of our Lord one thousand eight hundred and sixty-three, all persons held as slaves within any State or designated part of a State, the people whereof shall then be in rebellion against the United States, shall be then, thenceforward, and forever free; and the Executive Government of the United States, including the military and naval authority thereof, will recognize and maintain the freedom of such persons, and will do no act or acts to repress such persons, or any of them, in any efforts they may make for their actual freedom.

"That the Executive will, on the first day of January aforesaid, by proclamation, designate the States and parts of States, if any, in which the people thereof, respectively, shall then be in rebellion against the United States; and the fact that any State, or the people thereof, shall on that day be, in good faith, represented in the Congress of the United States by members chosen thereto at elections wherein a majority of the qualified voters of such State shall have participated, shall, in the absence of strong countervailing testimony, be deemed conclusive evidence that such State, and the people thereof, are not then in rebellion against the United States."

Now, therefore I, Abraham Lincoln, President of the United States, by virtue of the power in me vested as Commander-in-Chief, of the Army and Navy of the United States in time of actual armed rebellion against the authority and government of the United States, and as a fit and necessary war measure for suppressing said rebellion, do, on this first day of January, in the year of our Lord one thousand eight hundred and sixty-three, and in accordance with my purpose so to do publicly proclaimed for the full period of one hundred days, from the day first above mentioned, order and designate as the States and parts of States wherein the people thereof respectively, are this day in rebellion against the United States, the following, to wit:

Arkansas, Texas, Louisiana, (except the Parishes of St. Bernard, Plaquemines, Jefferson, St. John, St. Charles, St. James Ascension, Assumption, Terrebonne, Lafourche, St. Mary, St. Martin, and Orleans, including the City of New Orleans) Mississippi, Alabama, Florida, Georgia, South Carolina, North Carolina, and Virginia, (except the forty-eight counties designated as West Virginia, and also the counties of Berkley, Accomac, Northampton, Elizabeth City, York, Princess Ann, and Norfolk, including the cities of Norfolk and Portsmouth), and which excepted parts, are for the present, left precisely as if this proclamation were not issued.

And by virtue of the power, and for the purpose aforesaid, I do order and declare that all persons held as slaves within said designated States, and parts of States, are, and henceforward shall be free; and that the Executive government of the United States, including the military and naval authorities thereof, will recognize and maintain the freedom of said persons.

And I hereby enjoin upon the people so declared to be free to abstain from all violence, unless in necessary self-defence; and I recommend to them that, in all cases when allowed, they labor faithfully for reasonable wages.

And I further declare and make known, that such persons of suitable condition, will be received into the armed service of the United States to garrison forts, positions, stations, and other places, and to man vessels of all sorts in said service.

And upon this act, sincerely believed to be an act of justice, warranted by the Constitution, upon military necessity, I invoke the considerate judgment of mankind, and the gracious favor of Almighty God.

In witness whereof, I have hereunto set my hand and caused the seal of the United States to be affixed.

Done at the City of Washington, this first day of January, in the year of our Lord one thousand eight hundred and sixty three, and of the Independence of the United States of America the eighty-seventh.

By the President: ABRAHAM LINCOLN
WILLIAM H. SEWARD, Secretary of State.

GETTYSBURG ADDRESS

November 19, 1863

Delivered in Gettysburg, Pennsylvania, at the dedication of the Soldiers' National Cemetery

FOUR SCORE AND SEVEN YEARS AGO our fathers brought forth upon this continent, a new nation, conceived in liberty, and dedicated to the proposition that all men are created equal.

Now we are engaged in a great civil war, testing whether that nation, or any nation so conceived and so dedicated, can long endure. We are met on a great battlefield of that war. We have come to dedicate a portion of that field, as a final resting place for those who here gave their lives that that nation might live. It is altogether fitting and proper that we should do this.

But, in a larger sense, we can not dedicate—we can not consecrate—we can not hallow—this ground. The brave men, living and dead, who struggled here have consecrated it, far above our poor power to add or detract. The world will little note, nor long remember what we say here, but it can never forget what they did here. It is for us the living, rather, to be dedicated here to the unfinished work which they who fought here have thus far so nobly advanced. It is rather for us to be here dedicated to the great task remaining before us—that from these honored dead we take increased devotion to that cause for which they gave the last full measure of devotion—that we here highly resolve that these dead shall not have died in vain—that this nation, under God, shall have a new birth of freedom and that government of the people, by the people, and for the people, shall not perish from the earth.

SECOND INAUGURAL ADDRESS

March 4, 1865

Delivered in Washington, DC

AT THIS SECOND APPEARING TO TAKE THE OATH OF THE PRESIDENTIAL OFFICE, there is less occasion for an extended address than there was at the first. Then a statement, somewhat in detail, of a course to be pursued, seemed fitting and proper. Now, at the expiration of four years, during which public declarations have been constantly called forth on every point and phase of the great contest which still absorbs the attention, and engrosses the energies of the nation, little that is new could be presented. The progress of our arms, upon which all else chiefly depends, is as well known to the public as to myself; and it is, I trust, reasonably satisfactory and encouraging to all. With high hope for the future, no prediction in regard to it is ventured.

On the occasion corresponding to this four years ago, all thoughts were anxiously directed to an impending civil war. All dreaded it—all sought to avert it. While the inaugeral address was being delivered from this place, devoted altogether to *saving* the Union without war, insurgent agents were in the city seeking to *destroy* it without war—seeking to dissolve the Union, and divide effects, by negotiation. Both parties deprecated war; but one of them would *make* war rather than let the nation survive; and the other would *accept* war rather than let it perish. And the war came.

One eighth of the whole population were colored slaves, not distributed generally over the Union, but localized in the Southern part of it. These slaves constituted a peculiar and powerful interest. All knew that this interest was, somehow, the cause of the war. To strengthen, perpetuate, and extend this interest was the object for which the insurgents would rend the Union, even by war; while the government claimed no right to do more than to restrict the territorial enlargement of it. Neither party expected for the war, the magnitude, or the duration, which it has already attained. Neither anticipated that the *cause* of the conflict might cease with, or even before, the conflict itself should cease. Each looked for an easier triumph, and a result less fundamental and astounding. Both read the same Bible, and pray to the same God; and each invokes His aid against the other. It may seem strange that any men should dare to ask a just God's assistance in wringing their bread from the sweat of other men's faces; but let us judge not that we be not judged. The prayers of both could not be answered; that of neither has been answered fully. The Almighty has his own purposes. "Woe unto the world because of offences; for it must needs be that offences come; but woe to that man by whom the offence cometh." If we shall suppose that American Slavery is one of those offences which, in the providence of God, must needs come, but which, having continued through His appointed time, He now wills to remove, and that He gives to both North and South, this terrible war, as the woe due to those by whom the offence came, shall we discern therein any departure from those divine attributes which the believers in a Living God always ascribe to Him? Fondly do we hope—fervently do we pray—that this mighty scourge of war may speedily pass away. Yet, if God wills that it continue, until all the wealth piled by the bondsman's two hundred and fifty years of unrequited toil shall be sunk, and until every drop of blood drawn with the lash, shall be paid by another drawn with the sword, as was said three thousand years ago, so still it must be said "the judgments of the Lord, are true and righteous altogether."

With malice toward none; with charity for all; with firmness in the right, as God gives us to see the right, let us strive on to finish the work we are in; to bind up the nation's wounds; to care for him who shall have borne the battle, and for his widow, and his orphan—to do all which may achieve and cherish a just and lasting peace, among ourselves, and with all nations.

LAST ADDRESS

April 11, 1865

*Delivered at the White House, two days after the surrender of
General Lee's army*

WE MEET THIS EVENING, NOT IN SORROW, BUT IN GLAD-
NESS OF HEART. The evacuation of Petersburg and Richmond, and the
surrender of the principal insurgent army, give hope of a righteous and
speedy peace whose joyous expression can not be restrained. In the midst
of this, however, He from whom all blessings flow, must not be forgotten. A
call for a national thanksgiving is being prepared, and will be duly promul-
gated. Nor must those whose harder part gives us the cause of rejoicing, be
overlooked. Their honors must not be parceled out with others. I myself
was near the front, and had the high pleasure of transmitting much of the
good news to you; but no part of the honor, for plan or execution, is mine.
To Gen. Grant, his skillful officers, and brave men, all belongs. The gallant
Navy stood ready, but was not in reach to take active part.

By these recent successes the re-inauguration of the national authority—
reconstruction—which has had a large share of thought from the first, is
pressed much more closely upon our attention. It is fraught with great difficulty. Unlike a case of a war between independent nations, there is no
authorized organ for us to treat with. No one man has authority to give up
the rebellion for any other man. We simply must begin with, and mould
from, disorganized and discordant elements. Nor is it a small additional
embarrassment that we, the loyal people, differ among ourselves as to the
mode, manner, and means of reconstruction.

As a general rule, I abstain from reading the reports of attacks upon myself, wishing not to be provoked by that to which I can not properly offer an
answer. In spite of this precaution, however, it comes to my knowledge that I
am much censured for some supposed agency in setting up, and seeking to
sustain, the new State government of Louisiana. In this I have done just so
much as, and no more than, the public knows. In the Annual Message of
Dec. 1863 and accompanying Proclamation, I presented *a* plan of re-con-

struction (as the phrase goes) which, I promised, if adopted by any State, should be acceptable to, and sustained by, the Executive government of the nation. I distinctly stated that this was not the only plan which might possibly be acceptable; and I also distinctly protested that the Executive claimed no right to say when, or whether members should be admitted to seats in Congress from such States. This plan was, in advance, submitted to the then Cabinet, and distinctly approved by every member of it. One of them suggested that I should then, and in that connection, apply the Emancipation Proclamation to the theretofore excepted parts of Virginia and Louisiana; that I should drop the suggestion about apprenticeship for freed-people, and that I should omit the protest against my own power, in regard to the admission of members to Congress; but even he approved every part and parcel of the plan which has since been employed or touched by the action of Louisiana. The new constitution of Louisiana, declaring emancipation for the whole State, practically applies the Proclamation to the part previously excepted. It does not adopt apprenticeship for freed-people; and it is silent, as it could not well be otherwise, about the admission of members to Congress. So that, as it applies to Louisiana, every member of the Cabinet fully approved the plan. The message went to Congress, and I received many commendations of the plan, written and verbal; and not a single objection to it, from any professed emancipationist, came to my knowledge, until after the news reached Washington that the people of Louisiana had begun to move in accordance with it. From about July 1862, I had corresponded with different persons, supposed to be interested, seeking a reconstruction of a State government for Louisiana. When the message of 1863, with the plan before mentioned, reached New-Orleans, Gen. Banks wrote me that he was confident the people, with his military co-operation, would reconstruct, substantially on that plan. I wrote him, and some of them to try it; they tried it, and the result is known. Such only has been my agency in getting up the Louisiana government. As to sustaining it, my promise is out, as before stated. But, as bad promises are better broken than kept, I shall treat this as a bad promise, and break it, whenever I shall be convinced that keeping it is adverse to the public interest. But I have not yet been so convinced.

I have been shown a letter on this subject, supposed to be an able one, in which the writer expresses regret that my mind has not seemed to be definitely fixed on the question whether the seceding States, so called, are in the Union or out of it. It would perhaps, add astonishment to his regret, were he to learn that since I have found professed Union men endeavoring to make that question, I have *purposely* forborne any public expression upon it. As appears to me that question has not been, nor yet is, a practically material one, and that any discussion of it, while it thus remains practically immaterial, could have no effect other than the mischievous one of dividing our friends. As yet, whatever it may hereafter become, that question is bad, as the basis of a controversy, and good for nothing at all—a merely pernicious abstraction.

We all agree that the seceded States, so called, are out of their proper relation with the Union; and that the sole object of the government, civil and military, in regard to those States is to again get them into that proper practical relation. I believe it is not only possible, but in fact, easier to do this, without deciding, or even considering, whether these States have ever been out of the Union, than with it. Finding themselves safely at home, it would be utterly immaterial whether they had ever been abroad. Let us all join in doing the acts necessary to restoring the proper practical relations between these States and the Union; and each forever after, innocently indulge his own opinion whether, in doing the acts, he brought the States from without, into the Union, or only gave them proper assistance, they never having been out of it.

The amount of constituency, so to speak, on which the new Louisiana government rests, would be more satisfactory to all, if it contained fifty, thirty, or even twenty thousand, instead of only about twelve thousand, as it does. It is also unsatisfactory to some that the elective franchise is not given to the colored man. I would myself prefer that it were now conferred on the very intelligent, and on those who serve our cause as soldiers. Still the question is not whether the Louisiana government, as it stands, is quite all that is desirable. The question is, "Will it be wiser to take it as it is, and help to improve it; or to reject, and disperse it?" "Can Louisiana be brought into proper practical relation with the Union *sooner* by *sustaining*, or by *discarding* her new State government?"

Some twelve thousand voters in the heretofore slave-state of Louisiana have sworn allegiance to the Union, assumed to be the rightful political power of the State, held elections, organized a State government, adopted a free-state constitution, giving the benefit of public schools equally to black and white, and empowering the Legislature to confer the elective franchise upon the colored man. Their Legislature has already voted to ratify the constitutional amendment recently passed by Congress, abolishing slavery throughout the nation. These twelve thousand persons are thus fully committed to the Union, and to perpetual freedom in the state—committed to the very things, and nearly all the things the nation wants—and they ask the nations recognition and it's assistance to make good their committal. Now, if we reject, and spurn them, we do our utmost to disorganize and disperse them. We in effect say to the white men "You are worthless, or worse—we will neither help you, nor be helped by you." To the blacks we say "This cup of liberty which these, your old masters, hold to your lips, we will dash from you, and leave you to the chances of gathering the spilled and scattered contents in some vague and undefined when, where, and how." If this course, discouraging and paralyzing both white and black, has any tendency to bring Louisiana into proper practical relations with the Union, I have, so far, been unable to perceive it. If, on the contrary, we recognize, and sustain the new government of Louisiana the converse of all this is made true. We encourage the hearts, and nerve the arms of the twelve thousand to adhere to their work, and argue for it, and proselyte for it, and fight for it, and feed it, and grow it, and ripen it to a complete success. The colored man too, in seeing all united for him, is inspired with vigilance, and energy, and daring, to the same end. Grant that he desires the elective franchise, will he not attain it sooner by saving the already advanced steps toward it, than by running backward over them? Concede that the new government of Louisiana is only to what it should be as the egg is to the fowl, we shall sooner have the fowl by hatching the egg than by smashing it? Again, if we reject Louisiana, we also reject one vote in favor of the proposed amendment to the national Constitution. To meet this proposition, it has been argued that no more than three fourths of those States which have not attempted secession are necessary to validly ratify the amendment. I do not commit myself against this, further than to say that such a ratification would be questionable, and sure to be persistently questioned; while a ratification by three-fourths of all the States would be unquestioned and unquestionable.

I repeat the question, "Can Louisiana be brought into proper practical relation with the Union *sooner* by *sustaining* or by *discarding* her new State Government?

What has been said of Louisiana will apply generally to other States. And yet so great peculiarities pertain to each state, and such important and sudden changes occur in the same state; and withal, so new and unprecedented is the whole case, that no exclusive, and inflexible plan can be safely prescribed as to details and colatterals. Such exclusive, and inflexible plan, would surely become a new entanglement. Important principles may, and must, be inflexible.

In the present *"situation"* as the phrase goes, it may be my duty to make some new announcement to the people of the South. I am considering, and shall not fail to act, when satisfied that action will be proper.

AFTERWORD

My mother was a well witcher in New Salem, Illinois. It was mandatory "volunteer" duty for her and other members of Springfield's Junior League in the 1960s. Each spring, motor coaches and school buses crammed with fourth- and fifth-graders swarmed into New Salem from all parts of the state. The kids found Junior Leaguers in period costume spinning wool, collecting rainwater, working in ash pits to make soap or, in the case of my mom, wandering through town with a quivering branch in search of an underground spring.

The dresses worn by the volunteers fastened hook-and-eye style and came one-size-fits-all. The result could be comical. The frock that comfortably encased the plus-size Junior League matron looked as if it had swallowed my mom, who was fighting trim and even then barely at eye-level with some of her fifth-grade charges. I remember the broiling heat, but to the ladies of the Junior League, cold was the enemy. They piled on the long johns and sweaters underneath. But the period look, heightened by bonnets and shawls, was shattered by their sneakers. It was a long day to spend on your feet, and in the spring the most authentic thing about New Salem is the mud.

There were flax hackles and candle molds and cornmeal chests and lots of pewter. There was a blacksmith shop, a mill, and a tavern. I recall being steered into the tiny cabin where Lincoln worked as the town's postmaster and, later, looking at surveyors' equipment said to be similar to the stuff Lincoln once used. Mostly, though, I remember the pull of the woods and the Sangamon River just beyond the mill. My pals and I wanted to skip the history lesson and do what young Abe would have done—swim, fish, or play soldier in the woods.

Lincoln knew little but failure in New Salem. He seemed to have spent all his time there losing jobs, falling into debt, breaking off romances, and begging friends to put him up. The final insult, I guess, is that his story, which is as compelling as any in our history, can't always hold the interest of the average fifth-grade boy.

This project presented the opportunity to make amends. My friend and fellow Illinoisan Bob Hillman told me C-SPAN was looking for an editor to help manage the project, and he put me in touch with Susan Swain. I visited C-SPAN's Capitol Hill headquarters for a quick interview with both Brian

Lamb and Susan. They hired me right then, apparently on the strength of my credentials of having once lived in Illinois and worked for Brian's hometown newspaper in Lafayette, Indiana.

It's been a dream assignment. I've had the privilege of finally getting to know Abraham Lincoln and his story through the eyes of some of America's finest scholars. The original material for this book was strong because of the careful preparation and thought that Brian devoted to each of the author interviews. The book contains a wider variety of views on Lincoln than you are likely to find in most places, including some views that could be considered quite critical and harsh. That's because Brian insisted on looking at Lincoln and his legacy from as many viewpoints as possible.

The essays here took shape quickly under direction from Susan. She is an editor's editor—brilliant, decisive, unflappable, and creative. Amy Spolrich and CaSandra Thomas poured their energies into the project. They edited, checked facts, rooted through archives, and listened to countless hours of Lincoln programming (in addition to countless hours of Lafayette stories from Brian and me). Lea Anne Long and Molly Murchie were roped in from other C-SPAN departments, turning around assignments with amazing speed in spite of their normal workload. Everyone on Team Lincoln benefited from working in a C-SPAN office culture that has to be unique in the television industry and in Washington. The people at C-SPAN are warm, diligent, professional, and devoted to their mission of public service. It's a tribute to Brian, Susan, and financial chief Rob Kennedy, himself a Springfield native. Springfield's tenacious grip on Lincoln is something that author and journalist Andrew Ferguson touches on in these pages. My father used to say that Lincoln would have packed his carpetbag and gone back to Kentucky if he'd seen what Springfield had done to him. A friend from an old-line Springfield family once said that if your great-great-grandmother didn't sleep with Lincoln, you were new to town.

As a boy there, I couldn't have escaped Lincoln if I had wanted to. Large twin busts of him stood on my father's desk at home. Herndon kids populated my nursery school. His image was in every storefront. Yet I was oblivious.

This project was a journey of rediscovery for me, a trip back home to take in all that I missed the first time. I can only hope that readers—along with my wife, Nancy, and children, Nora, Jeff, and Molly—enjoy it as much as I have.

Jim Cox
June 19, 2008
Washington, DC

ACKNOWLEDGMENTS

C-SPAN's six prior books have all been collaborative projects. This one is no exception. Jim Cox, who had just left *USA Today* after two decades of national and international reporting, came on board for a few months to lead our editorial team. Jim, whose family connections to Lincoln lore are described in the Afterword, dove into this project with such great enthusiasm that his kids were saying "No more Lincoln stories, Dad!" Jim's editorial teammates included Amy Spolrich, who worked tirelessly and with good humor on many editorial aspects of this book, CaSandra Thomas, who became an expert Civil War era fact-checker, and Molly Murchie, a veteran of prior C-SPAN books, who edited several chapters in this book.

Lea Anne Long coordinated photographs and brought experience to the task, having done the same work for prior C-SPAN books. She is the person at C-SPAN who really knows where all the good stuff is filed. Two of our graphic artists contributed to the book's visuals: Leslie Rhodes, who worked with the photos, and Ellen Vest who researched, and then drew by hand, the four Lincoln maps featured in this book. Her boss, Marty Dominguez, vice president of marketing, ran interference on design and photo issues, providing chocolates and good cheer when emergencies struck.

Our relationship with PublicAffairs is long-standing. Their Editor-at-Large Peter Osnos, who has published five books for C-SPAN, first suggested this book to us. Peter saw C-SPAN's Lincoln Bicentennial programming ad in the *New York Times* in April 2007 and called immediately, asking, "Isn't there a book in this project?" As a longtime *Washington Post* journalist, Peter should have known better than to suggest a book with deadlines three weeks prior to the national political conventions. The team at PublicAffairs was patient with our many deadline challenges, including publisher Susan Weinberg, editor Morgen VanVorst, and project editor Lori Hobkirk from The Book Factory. All of these people kept our spirits up as the e-mails and overnight delivery packages of manuscript pages were furiously exchanged.

Susan Swain, one of C-SPAN's co-presidents, is listed as the book's co-editor. She is really the "force" who guided this and all other books published by C-SPAN. Susan has an unusual talent for editing our guests' spoken words into a format that is both informative and enjoyable to read.

Rob Kennedy, who shares the network's co-presidency with Susan, kept everything operating smoothly at the company while Susan was knee-deep in details from the 1860s. Bruce Collins, our in-house counsel of more than twenty-five years, did his usual timely and detailed work on contract issues.

Bob Miron, chairman of BrightHouse Networks is also the chairman of C-SPAN's executive committee. A tip of the hat to Bob, representing our board and our cable affiliates, whose nearly thirty years of financial support for C-SPAN programming and carriage of our three television channels allow us to produce the quality history and nonfiction book programming that forms the content for this book.

And finally, a special thanks to Harold Holzer. His Lincoln scholarship first inspired C-SPAN's Lincoln programming. Harold, who co-chairs the national commission on the Lincoln Bicentennial, picked up the phone when he heard about this book and asked, "How can I help?" Harold's encyclopedic knowledge of Lincoln's life is nothing short of impressive. Mr. Holzer is emblematic of a cadre of historians and nonfiction writers who continually offer their scholarship to the C-SPAN audience. We are all much better informed because of them.

Brian Lamb

AUTHOR BIOGRAPHIES

Charles Adams. Mr. Adams earned a law degree from UCLA and has worked as a tax attorney in California. In 1968, before emigrating to Canada, he began his research into the historical role of taxes and taught history at the International College of the Cayman Islands. The author of several books, his seminal work is *For Good & Evil: The Impact of Taxes on the Course of Civilization* (Madison Books 1993). In 2000, Rowman and Littlefield published his book, *When in the Course of Human Events: Arguing the Case for Southern Secession.*

David Haward Bain. *b. 1949.* Mr. Bain is a Vermont-based writer who lectures on English and American literature at Middlebury College. Born in Camden, New Jersey, and a graduate of Boston University, Mr. Bain was working in publishing in New York City before becoming a full-time writer. His several books include *Empire Express: Building the First Transcontinental Railroad* (Viking 1999) and *The Old Iron Road* (Viking 2004). His reviews appear regularly in the *New York Times Book Review, The Washington Post,* and *Newsday.* He has worked with the Bread Loaf Writers' Conference for many years.

Michael Barone. *b. 1944.* Political commentator Michael Barone is a senior writer for *U.S. News and World Report,* a Fox News analyst, and longtime principal co-author of *The Almanac of American Politics.* A graduate of Harvard and Yale Law School, he is the author of several books, including *Our First Revolution: The Remarkable British Upheaval That Inspired America's Founding Fathers* (Crown 2007).

Irving Bartlett. *b. 1923, d. 2006.* A nationally recognized historian, Dr. Bartlett taught at Carnegie Mellon, MIT, and UMass. The author of *John C. Calhoun* (Norton 1992), he was primarily interested in biographies of nineteenth-century Americans such as Wendell Phillips, a Boston abolitionist; William Ellery Channing; and Daniel Webster. Dr. Bartlett received a Ph.D. in American Civilization from Brown University. He was the founding president of Cape Cod Community College.

Adam Bellow. *b. 1957.* Mr. Bellow, son of Nobel laureate Saul Bellow, is vice president and executive editor at Collins Books and publisher of *The New Pamphleteer*—an online site that publishes e-pamphlets. His twenty-plus-year career as a publisher of books for companies such as Free Press and Doubleday includes titles such as *The Bell Curve* and *The Real Anita Hill.* He is also a former literary editor for the *National Review.* He is the author of *In Praise of Nepotism: A Natural History* (Doubleday 2003).

Lerone Bennett, Jr. *b. 1928.* Social historian Lerone Bennett is executive editor emeritus of *Ebony* his home base for more than fifty years. A Mississippi native and graduate of Atlanta's historically black Morehouse College, he began working as a reporter following graduation. A series of articles originally published in *Ebony* resulted in Bennett's first book, *Before the Mayflower: A History of Black America, 1619–1962.* He's written eight subsequent books, including *Forced Into Glory: Abraham Lincoln's White Dream* (Johnson Publishing 2000), which is an expansion of his 1968 magazine essay, "Was Abe Lincoln a White Supremacist?"

Walter Berns. *b. 1919.* Dr. Berns, professor emeritus at Georgetown University, is a resident fellow at the American Enterprise Institute, specializing in political philosophy and constitutional law. Walter Berns served in the Navy during World War II. After receiving his Ph.D. from the University of Chicago, he served on the faculty of many major universities. He is the author of nine books, including *Making Patriots* (University of Chicago Press 2001).

Gabor Boritt. *b. 1940.* Professor Boritt directs the Civil War Institute at Gettysburg College and serves as the Robert Fluhrer Professor of Civil War Studies. The Hungarian-born author, whose personal story of Holocaust survival and participation in the 1956 Hungarian revolution against the Soviets inspired a documentary film, has written sixteen books on Lincoln and the Civil War, including *The Gettysburg Gospel: The Lincoln Speech That Nobody Knows.* Professor Boritt is also co-founder and board chairman of the Lincoln Prize, the $50,000 annual award for the finest work on the Civil War era.

H. W. Brands. *b. 1953.* Henry William Brands is a professor of History and Government at the University of Texas at Austin, which awarded him a Ph.D. in history in 1985 after an earlier stint as a mathematics and history teacher at the high school and community college level. A prolific writer, Bill Brands has co-authored or edited five books and authored twenty-two books, including *The Reckless Decade: America in the 1890s* (St. Martin's Press 1995). His November 2008 book on FDR is titled *Traitor to His Class.*

Patrick J. Buchanan. *b. 1938.* MSNBC senior political commentator Pat Buchanan worked as a senior aide in the Nixon, Ford, and Reagan White Houses. Buchanan sought the GOP presidential nomination in 1992 and 1996 and was the Reform Party nominee in 2000. A Georgetown alumnus who is also a syndicated columnist, Mr. Buchanan is the author of ten books, including *The Great Betrayal: How American Sovereignty and Social Justice Are Being Sacrificed to the Gods of the Global Economy* (Little, Brown 1998). His latest is *Churchill, Hitler, and The Unnecessary War (Crown 2008).*

Carl M. Cannon. *b. 1953.* Carl Cannon is Washington bureau chief for *Reader's Digest* and a contributing editor for *National Journal.* He took up journalism after graduation from the University of Colorado and spent fifteen years covering the White House. His books include *The Pursuit of Happiness in Times of War* (Rowman and Littlefield 2003) and the co-authored *Boy Genius,* a biography of former White House aide Karl Rove. Mr. Cannon teamed with his father, noted Reagan biographer Lou Cannon, to co-author *Reagan's Disciple* (PublicAffairs 2008).

Eliot A. Cohen. *b. 1956.* Eliot Cohen, a counselor at the State Department, serves as a special advisor to Secretary of State Condoleezza Rice. Awarded his Ph.D. in political science from Harvard in 1982, Dr. Cohen is the Robert E. Osgood Professor of American Foreign Policy at Johns Hopkins SAIS. His books include *Supreme Command: Soldiers, Statesmen, and Leadership in Wartime and Citizens* and *Soldiers* (Free Press 2002).

Mario Cuomo. *b. 1932.* Mario Cuomo served three terms as governor of New York, beginning in 1983. A Democrat and native of Queens, New York, with a law degree from St. John's University, Governor Cuomo has spent much of his career in public life, including one term as lieutenant governor of New York. Today, he is a political and social commentator and writer. He co-edited *Lincoln on Democracy* in 1990 and in 2004 authored *Why Lincoln Matters* (Harcourt). Governor Cuomo serves on the advisory council of the Abraham Lincoln Bicentennial Commission.

Richard Current. *b. 1912.* Dr. Current is Distinguished Professor of History Emeritus at the University of North Carolina, Greensboro. He received his Ph.D. in history from the University of Wisconsin in 1940 and taught at several major universities. A prize-winning historian specializing in pre–Civil War and Civil War America, Dr. Current has published more than twenty books. Among his Lincoln titles is *The Lincoln Nobody Knows,* originally published by McGraw-Hill in 1958 and reprinted several times since. A prize for lifetime achievement was named for Professor Current and is given annually by the Lincoln Forum.

Thomas DiLorenzo. *b. 1954.* Thomas DiLorenzo is a professor of economics at Loyola College in Maryland and on the faculty of the Ludwig von Mises Institute. He holds a Ph.D. in Economics from Virginia Tech. Published frequently in national newspapers, Dr. DiLorenzo is the author of ten books, including *The Real Lincoln* (2003) and *Lincoln Unmasked: What You're Not Supposed to Know About Dishonest Abe* (2007), both published by Three Rivers Press.

David Herbert Donald. *b. 1920.* Born in Goodman, Mississippi, two-time Pulitzer Prize–winning author and Civil War historian David Herbert

Donald is the Charles Warren Professor Emeritus of American History at Harvard University. The University of Illinois awarded him his Ph.D. He is the author of more than thirty books, notably, *Lincoln*, the 1996 winner of the Lincoln Prize. Dr. Donald's Pulitzer Prize–winning biographies are *Charles Sumner and The Coming of the Civil War* (Knopf 1960), and *Look Homeward: A Life of Thomas Wolfe* (Little, Brown 1987). His first book was *Herndon's Lincoln*, published in 1948.

Chas Fagan. *b. 1966.* Chas Fagan is a sculptor, portrait artist, and painter of national prominence based in North Carolina. A native of Ligonier, Pennsylvania, Mr. Fagan graduated from Yale University with a degree in Russian Studies. Sculpting is a more recent art form for Mr. Fagan who has been awarded monumental commissions, including three figures for the National Cathedral altar. In February 2008, he received the commission for the statue of Ronald Reagan that will represent California in the U.S. Capitol's Statuary Hall. He has worked with C-SPAN to create art works for several projects, including individual portraits of all forty-two U.S. presidents for an exhibition that has been touring for a decade. In 2007, he was commissioned by the Union League Club of New York to create a Lincoln bust.

Andrew Ferguson. *b. 1956.* Journalist and social observer Andrew Ferguson, senior editor for *The Weekly Standard,* graduated from Occidental College in Los Angeles in 1978 and received a master's degree in journalism from Indiana University. Since then he has reported for several major publications such as *American Spectator, Reader's Digest, Time,* and the Scripps Howard News Service. In 1992, he took a break from journalism to become a White House speechwriter for President George H. W. Bush. Mr. Ferguson is the author of *Land of Lincoln: Adventures in Abe's America* (Atlantic Monthly Press 2008).

Wayne Fields. *b. 1942.* Professor Fields is a nationally recognized expert on American political rhetoric; his opinion is frequently sought for radio, television, and newspaper coverage of presidential speeches and debates. He is the director of American Culture Studies at Washington University in St. Louis where he also teaches American literature, nonfiction prose, rhetoric, and political argument. His 1996 book is *Union of Words: A History of Presidential Eloquence* (Free Press).

Shelby Foote. *b. 1916, d. 2005.* Novelist and Civil War historian Shelby Foote was born in Greenville, Mississippi. His novels include *Shiloh* (Vintage Books 1952). Mr. Foote may be best known for *The Civil War: A Narrative,* published in three volumes between 1958 and 1974, which led to his on-screen participation in Ken Burns's 1990 PBS documentary series, *The Civil War.* Modern Library excerpted from the Civil War narrative, *Stars in Their*

Courses: The Gettysburg Campaign, publishing it as a separate title in 1994. Mr. Foote was elected to the American Academy of Arts and Letters in 1994 and was on the editorial board of The Modern Library for the selection of the one hundred best books of the twentieth century.

Doris Kearns Goodwin. *b. 1943.* Pulitzer Prize–winning presidential historian Doris Kearns Goodwin wrote *Team of Rivals: The Political Genius of Abraham Lincoln,* which won both the Lincoln Prize and the Abraham Lincoln Institute award in 2006. Born in Brooklyn, New York, Doris Kearns was selected as a White House fellow in 1967. When President Johnson left office, he asked Kearns to help with his memoirs. Her own first book, a bestseller, *Lyndon Johnson & The American Dream* (Harper 1976), came from that experience. Kearns Goodwin was awarded her Ph.D. by Harvard, where she taught for ten years. The author of five books, Kearns Goodwin is also an NBC analyst. She lives in Concord, Massachusetts.

Allen C. Guelzo. *b. 1953.* Allen C. Guelzo is Henry R. Luce Professor of the Civil War Era and Professor of History at Gettysburg College. Born in Yokohama, Japan, to an army family, Allen Guelzo earned a M.A. and a Ph.D. in history from the University of Pennsylvania, and a M.Div. from Philadelphia Theological Seminary. He is the only writer in the history of the two Lincoln prizes (The Lincoln Prize and the Abraham Lincoln Institute Prize) to win both simultaneously, and for two of his books: *Abraham Lincoln: Redeemer President* (Eerdmans 1999) and *Lincoln's Emancipation Proclamation: The End of Slavery in America* (Simon and Schuster 2004).

Harold Holzer. *b. 1949.* Lincoln scholar Harold Holzer, co-chair of the United States Lincoln Bicentennial Commission, has authored or edited thirty-two books on Lincoln or the Civil War period. His 2004 book, *Lincoln at Cooper Union: The Speech That Made Abraham Lincoln President* (Harper-Collins), won a 2005 Lincoln Prize. Educated at the City University of New York, Mr. Holzer had an early career in journalism and politics. Today, Mr. Holzer is senior vice president for external affairs for New York's Metropolitan Museum of Art. He is founding vice-chairman of the Lincoln Forum, has authored hundreds of articles about Lincoln and the Civil War and is a regular organizer or participant in conferences and television productions about the period. His 1993 book, *The Lincoln-Douglas Debates,* inspired C-SPAN's 1994 televised re-creation of the debates. His latest book is *Lincoln: President-Elect* (Simon and Schuster 2008).

Robert Hughes. *b. 1938.* Internationally known art critic and cultural historian Robert Hughes was born in Sydney, Australia. Hughes studied art and architecture at Sydney University. Beginning in 1970, he spent three decades as *Time*'s art critic. A writer and television documentary-maker, he is the author of sixteen books, including *American Visions: The Epic History of Art in America* (1997). He was elected to membership in the American Academy of Arts and Sciences in 1996 and is the only art critic to be a two-time winner (1982 and 1985) of the Frank Mather Award, the nation's highest honor for art criticism.

Paul Johnson. *b. 1928.* Historian, journalist, and author Paul Johnson was born in Manchester, England, and educated at Magdalen College, Oxford. After an early writing career with progressive British publications, his politics evolved, and he served as speechwriter and counselor to British Prime Minister Margaret Thatcher. He is the author of nearly forty books on history, art, religion, travel, and social commentary, including *A History of the American People* (HarperCollins 1997) and *Heroes* (HarperCollins 2007). He was awarded the Presidential Medal of Freedom in 2006 by President Bush.

Lewis Lehrman. *b. 1938.* Investor, business executive, and civic activist Lewis E. Lehrman is senior partner of L. E. Lehrman & Company. Born in Harrisburg, Pennsylvania, Mr. Lehrman received an M.A. in history from Harvard. He was president of Rite Aid, managing director of Morgan Stanley, and the 1982 GOP candidate for governor of New York. Long interested in Lincoln, Mr. Lehrman co-founded with George Gilder the Lincoln and Soldiers Institute at Gettysburg College, which annually awards the Lincoln Prize and the Gilder Lehrman Center for the Study of Slavery, Resistance, and Abolition at Yale, which awards the Frederick Douglass Prize. A member of the Lincoln Bicentennial Commission, Mr. Lehrman received the 2005 National Humanities Medal. His latest book is *Lincoln at Peoria: The Turning Point* (Stackpole 2008).

James Loewen. *b. 1942.* Sociologist James Loewen holds a Ph.D. from Harvard. He taught at the predominantly black Tougaloo College in Mississippi, later moving to the University of Vermont, where he taught race relations for twenty years. He coauthored the prize-winning *Mississippi: Conflict and Change*, which that state rejected for classroom use, leading to the first amendment case, *Loewen v. Turnipseed*. He is the author of the best-selling *Lies My Teacher Told Me* (1995) and *Lies Across America* (1999), published by New Press, critiques of how Americans are taught history.

Pauline Maier. *b. 1938.* Historian Pauline Maier, a native of St. Paul, Minnesota, is the William R. Kenan Jr. Professor of American History at the Massachusetts Institute of Technology and a scholar of the American Revolutionary era. Dr. Maier, who received her Ph.D. from Harvard in 1968, is the author of the award-winning *American Scripture: Making the Declaration of Independence* (Knopf 1997), *From Resistance to Revolution* (1972), and *The Old Revolutionaries* (1980) and numerous other books. She wrote a junior high school textbook, *The American People: A History* (1987) and is an advisor to History News Network.

James M. McPherson. *b. 1936.* James McPherson is the author of the Pulitzer Prize–winning *Battle Cry of Freedom,* which has sold more than six hundred thousand copies and is credited with helping to launch a resurgence of interest in the Civil War. A North Dakota native, James McPherson was awarded a Ph.D. from Johns Hopkins, and he has taught at Princeton since 1962, where he is the George Henry Davis '86 Professor Emeritus of U.S. History. The 2000 Jefferson Lecturer in Humanities and past president of the American Historical Association, and winner of the Lincoln Prize, he has been at the forefront of the battlefields preservation movement. His latest book is *Tried by War: Abraham Lincoln as Commander in Chief.*

Edna Greene Medford. *b. 1951.* An associate professor of history at Howard University, Dr. Medford specializes in nineteenth-century African American history. She teaches courses in Civil War and Reconstruction, Colonial America, the Jacksonian Era, and African American history. Dr. Medford collaborated with Harold Holzer and Frank J. Williams to write *The Emancipation Proclamation: Three Views* (Louisiana State Univ. Press 2006). She is a member of the advisory board of the Abraham Lincoln Presidential Library and Museum and a member of the advisory committee of the Lincoln Bicentennial Commission.

Roger Mudd. *b. 1928.* Veteran network newsman Roger Mudd is a Washington, DC, native who spent much of his career at CBS news covering national issues and politics. In 1980, he joined NBC News, where he co-anchored the evening news for several years and hosted *Meet the Press.* Later, he joined The History Channel as a documentary host. Mr. Mudd received his master's degree from UNC Chapel Hill. His journalism work earned him a Peabody Award and five Emmy Awards. He is an indirect distant relative of Dr. Samuel Mudd, of Lincoln assassination fame. Mr. Mudd is the author of *The Place to Be: Washington, CBS, and the Glory Days of Television News* (PublicAffairs 2008), and of *Great Minds of History* (Wiley 1999).

Mark Neely, Jr. *b. 1944.* Pulitzer Prize–winning historian Mark Neely is the McCabe Greer Professor of Civil War History at Pennsylvania State University. He received his Ph.D. in history from Yale in 1973. For twenty years, he directed the Lincoln Museum in Fort Wayne, Indiana. He is the author of a dozen books on Lincoln and the Civil War, including *The Last Best Hope of Earth: Abraham Lincoln and the Promise of America* (Harvard University Press 1993) and *The Fate of Liberty: Abraham Lincoln and Civil Liberties* (Oxford University Press 1991), which won a 1991 Pulitzer Prize in history.

John Niven. *b. 1921, d. 1997.* John Niven was a nationally known scholar of Jacksonian and Civil War history and the editor of *The Salmon P. Chase Papers.* He published four volumes between 1993 and 1997 and was working on the final volume at the time of his death. A Brooklyn native, he received his Ph.D. from Columbia University in 1955. He was Professor Emeritus of American History at Claremont Graduate School and had chaired the department of history. He produced a number of biographies of prominent figures in American history including *Salmon P. Chase: A Biography* (Oxford University Press 1995).

Stephen B. Oates. *b. 1936.* Civil War historian Stephen Oates is the author of sixteen books on that period, including *The Approaching Fury,* the first in a Civil War trilogy and *With Malice Toward None: A Life of Abraham Lincoln* (American Political Biography Press 2002). Professor of History Emeritus at the University of Massachusetts, Amherst, Dr. Oates was a consultant for Ken Burns's *Civil War* series on PBS. He was the recipient of the Nevins-Freeman Award of the Chicago Civil War Round Table for lifetime achievement in the field of Civil War studies.

James Perry. James Perry is Senior Political Writer Emeritus for the *Wall Street Journal.* He has written several books about two of his main interests—the media and politics—including *Us and Them: How the Press Covered the 1972 Election* and military history, particularly of the Civil War period. These include *Arrogant Armies* (Wiley 1992): *A Bohemian Brigade: The Civil War Correspondents;* and *Touched With Fire: Five Presidents and the Civil War Battles That Made Them* (PublicAffairs 2003).

Merrill D. Peterson. *b. 1921.* Merrill Peterson is Professor of History Emeritus at the University of Virginia, which honored him with a Literary Lifetime Achievement Award in 2005. A native of Manhattan, Kansas, and World War II veteran, Dr. Peterson received his Ph.D. from Harvard in 1950. His first book on Thomas Jefferson won the 1960 Bancroft Prize. A noted Jeffersonian scholar and the editor of the Library of America edition of the writings of Thomas Jefferson, he has written or edited thirty-seven books, including *Lincoln in American Memory* (Oxford University Press 1995), a finalist for the 1995 Pulitzer Prize in history. He was a Peace Corps volunteer in Armenia at the age of seventy-five.

Matthew Pinsker. *b. 1968.* Matthew Pinsker is an associate professor of history at Dickinson College in Carlisle, Pennsylvania, where he holds the Brian Pohanka Chair of American Civil War History. He received his Ph.D. from Oxford in 1995. He has been a fellow at the U.S. Constitution Center. Dr. Pinsker is the author of *Abraham Lincoln* (Congressional Quarterly 2002) and *Lincoln's Sanctuary: Abraham Lincoln and the Soldiers' Home* (Oxford 2003).

Robert Remini. *b. 1921.* Dr. Remini is the official historian of the United States House of Representatives, since 2005. The noted Andrew Jackson biographer is Professor of History Emeritus at the University of Illinois at Chicago. A World War II veteran, he read history onboard ship and returned to his native New York City to pursue his Ph.D. from Columbia. He is the author of more than twenty books, including numerous works about the Jacksonian era. The third volume of his Jackson biography, *Andrew Jackson and the Course of American Democracy: 1833–1845*, won the 1985 National Book Award. He is also the author of *Henry Clay: Statesman for the Union* (Norton 1991).

David Reynolds. *b. 1948.* Dr. Reynolds is Distinguished Professor of English and American Studies at the Graduate Center and Baruch College of the City University of New York. A native of Barrington, Rhode Island, he received his Ph.D. in English from UC Berkeley in 1979. He is the author of many books including *Walt Whitman's America: A Cultural Biography* (Knopf 1995), which won the Bancroft Prize and *John Brown: Abolitionist* (Knopf 2005). David Reynolds's next book is *Waking Giant: America in the Age of Jackson* (HarperCollins 2008).

Tom Schwartz. *b. 1955.* Tom Schwartz was appointed Illinois State Historian in 1993, and has worked for the state since 1985. He directs historical content for the Abraham Lincoln Presidential Museum in Springfield and established the Research Division in the Abraham Lincoln Presidential Library. An Illinois native, he received his Ph.D. from the University of Illinois at Urbana/Champaign. Dr. Schwartz has published more than sixty articles in professional publications and is the senior editor of the *Journal of the Abraham Lincoln Association* and is the historical advisor for the *Journal of Illinois History*.

Richard Shenkman. *b. 1954.* Rick Shenkman, associate professor of history at George Mason University, is the founder and editor of History News Network, a Web site that features historians' perspectives on current events, and was a co-founder of TomPaine.com. A former television journalist, he did graduate studies at Harvard. He continues to be a frequent commentator on network television. Mr. Shenkman is the author of six books, including *Legends, Lies & Cherished Myths of American History* (Morrow 1988) and *Presidential Ambition: How the Presidents Gained Power, Kept Power and Got Things Done* (HarperCollins 1999). His latest book is *Just How Stupid Are We? Facing the Truth About the American Voter* (Basic Books, June 2008).

John Y. Simon. *b. 1933, d. 2008.* John Y. Simon was a professor of history at Southern Illinois University at Carbondale for forty-four years. He was executive director of the Ulysses S. Grant Association and spent much of his academic career as the editor of the *Papers of Ulysses S. Grant* (Southern Illinois University Press). John Simon was also a founder of the Association for Documentary Editing. A scholar of Lincoln and the Civil War who wrote more than one hundred scholarly articles and essays on the period,

Dr. Simon received a lifetime achievement award from The Lincoln Forum in 2004 and a Lincoln Prize in 2005.

Brooks D. Simpson. *b. 1957.* Dr. Simpson is professor of history at Arizona State University. A native of Freeport, New York, he received his Ph.D. from the University of Wisconsin Madison in 1989. In Tennessee, he was assistant editor of the papers of Andrew Johnson. Specializing in Civil War–era history, Dr. Simpson has authored five books and edited or co-authored six others. His book, *Ulysses S. Grant: Triumph Over Adversity,* was published by Houghton Mifflin in 2000.

Richard Norton Smith. *b. 1953.* Presidential historian, author, lecturer, and speechwriter Richard Norton Smith was born in Leominster, Massachusetts, and graduated from Harvard. Mr. Smith has been the executive director of five presidential libraries (Hoover, Eisenhower, Reagan, Ford, and Lincoln) and of the Robert Dole Library in Lawrence, Kansas. He is currently a scholar-in-residence at George Mason University. Mr. Smith has authored biographies of Thomas Dewey, Herbert Hoover, and George Washington. His 2003 biography of Robert McCormick, *The Colonel* (Northwestern University Press) won the JFK's School's Goldsmith Award. His current biographical project is Nelson Rockefeller. A regular television presence on PBS and ABC, Mr. Smith has been a regular consultant to C-SPAN for several presidential history series and frequently provides on-camera commentary for current events.

John Splaine. *b. 1940.* Dr. John Splaine spent thirty-four years at the University of Maryland's College of Education and continues to teach part-time as associate professor emeritus. Boston University awarded him a Ph.D. in education. A New Hampshire native, he began teaching history at the high school level in both New Hampshire and Maryland. From 2001–2003, he held the Amos B. Hostetter Chair at the University of Denver and taught courses in political communication. An education consultant for C-SPAN since 1987, Dr. Splaine was involved in several of the network's special history projects, notably the Lincoln-Douglas Debates series, for which he authored *A Companion to the Lincoln-Douglas Debates* (1994). Among his other books is *The Road to the White House Since Television.*

Edward Steers, Jr. *b. 1937.* Ed Steers had a thirty-year career as a biomedical research scientist at the National Institutes of Health in Bethesda, Maryland, retiring in 1994 to begin a second career as a nonfiction writer. He has written three books about the Lincoln assassination, including *His Name Is Still Mudd* and *Blood on the Moon: The Assassination of Abraham Lincoln.* Dr. Steers, who holds a Ph.D. in molecular genetics from the University of Pennsylvania, is the Internet editor of the *Lincoln Herald* and is also an associate editor of *North & South* magazine.

Joseph E. Stevens. Joseph E. Stevens's first book, *Hoover Dam: An American Adventure* (Univ. of Oklahoma Press 1988), received the John H. Dunning Prize of the American Historical Association. In addition to *1863: The Rebirth of a Nation* (Bantam Dell 1999), he is also the author of *America's National Battlefield Parks* (Univ. of Oklahoma Press 1990) A Princeton graduate, Mr. Stevens lives in Santa Fe, New Mexico.

Louise Taper. Louise Taper of Los Angeles is a thirty-five-year collector of important Abraham Lincoln artifacts and the co-author of *Right or Wrong, God Judge Me: The Writings of John Wilkes Booth* (Univ. of Illinois Press). She serves on the boards of the Abraham Lincoln Association, the Abraham Lincoln Presidential Library and Museum Foundation, the Lincoln Forum, the Lincoln Legal Papers, is a member of the Lincoln Bicentennial Commission, and previously the Lincoln Prize at Gettysburg College. She is also a trustee of Lincoln College. In 2007, the Taper collection was purchased for the Abraham Lincoln Library and Museum by the museum's foundation.

Peter Wallner. *b. 1946. Franklin Pierce: New Hampshire's Favorite Son* (Plaidswede 2007) was written by Peter Wallner, library director for the New Hampshire Historical Society. He was a history teacher and school administrator for thirty years before beginning his research on Franklin Pierce. Dr. Wallner received his Ph.D. in history from the Pennsylvania State University. He continues to teach as an adjunct instructor at the New Hampshire Community Technical College at Nashua, and at Franklin Pierce College, in Concord, New Hampshire.

David Ward. *b. 1952.* David Ward, a historian and deputy editor of the Peale Family Papers at the National Portrait Gallery of the Smithsonian Institution, curated the Portrait Gallery's 2008 exhibit "One Life: The Mask of Lincoln." He holds graduate degrees from Warwick University and Yale and is the author of *Charles Willson Peale: Art and Selfhood in the Early Republic* (UC Press 2004).

Tom Wheeler. *b. 1946.* Tom Wheeler, a Washington, DC-based venture capitalist, has been involved with telecommunications for nearly three decades—as both an entrepreneur and head of two trade associations. An Ohio State alumnus, he is the author of two Civil War era books: *Take Command: Leadership Lessons from the Civil War* (Doubleday 2000) and *Mr. Lincoln's T-Mails: The Untold Story of How Abraham Lincoln Used the Telegraph to Win the Civil War* (HarperCollins 2006). Mr. Wheeler is also chairman and president of the Foundation for the National Archives, which supports the Archives' efforts to teach American history through its documents.

Frank J. Williams. *b. 1940.* Frank Williams, chief justice of the Rhode Island Supreme Court, is a Lincoln scholar and collector of Lincoln artifacts. He has chaired the Lincoln Forum since its inception and previously spent nine years as president of the Abraham Lincoln Association. He is a member of the Lincoln Bicentennial Commission and chairs the Ulysses S. Grant Association. Judge Williams received his law degree from Boston University Law School. He is the author and co-author of about a dozen Lincoln books, including *Judging Lincoln* (Southern Illinois University Press 2002).

Garry Wills. *b. 1934.* Cultural historian Garry Wills, Professor of History Emeritus at Northwestern University, won the Medal for the Humanities in 1998 and the 1993 Pulitzer Prize for general nonfiction for his book *Lincoln at Gettysburg: The Words That Remade America* (Simon & Schuster). The Atlanta native received a Ph.D. in classics from Yale in 1961. He has authored more than thirty-five books.

Douglas L. Wilson. *b. 1935.* Doug Wilson, a two-time recipient of the Lincoln Prize, is co-director of the Lincoln Studies Center at Knox College in Galesburg, Illinois, one of the seven Lincoln-Douglas debate sites. His book, *Honor's Voice: The Transformation of Abraham Lincoln,* won the Lincoln Prize in 1999 as well as the Abraham Lincoln Institute Award, and *Lincoln's Sword: The Presidency and the Power of Words* won the Lincoln Prize in 2007. Dr. Wilson received a Ph.D. in English from the University of Pennsylvania in 1964. He is the author of several other books and numerous academic publications. Dr. Wilson is a member of the advisory committee for the Lincoln Bicentennial Commission.

Jay Winik. *b. 1957.* Jay Winik is the author of the best-selling *April 1865: The Month That Saved America,* which won the first Walt Whitman Civil War Roundtable Award. He is a regular reviewer for the *Wall Street Journal* and contributes to the *New York Times Book Review.* Dr. Winik serves on the Civil War Preservation Trust and is a member of the Lincoln Forum. He holds a Ph.D. from Yale and a master's degree from the London School of Economics. Dr. Winik's earlier career was in foreign policy. He serves on the governing council of the National Endowment for the Humanities and is on the advisory committee for the Lincoln Bicentennial Commission. Dr. Winik lives in Chevy Chase, Maryland.

Gordon S. Wood. *b. 1933.* Gordon Wood is Professor Emeritus of History at Brown University. Dr. Wood received his Ph.D. from Harvard. He was on the faculty there and at the University of Michigan before joining the faculty of Brown in 1969. His 1969 book, *Creation of the American Republic 1776–1787* (Chapel Hill) won both the Bancroft and Dunning prizes. *The Radicalism of the American Revolution* (Knopf 1992) won the Pulitzer Prize for History. Dr. Wood is a trustee of Colonial Williamsburg and was a consultant to the National Constitution Center and the U.S. Capitol renovation.

INDEX

history/biography

ABRAHAM LINCOLN chronicles the life and legacy of America's sixteenth president through the eyes of fifty-six of the country's leading Lincoln historians, journalists, and writers. Richly detailed essays are drawn from C-SPAN interviews with Edna Greene Medford, James McPherson, John Y. Simon, Stephen Oates, Robert Remini, and Paul Johnson, among many others, to create a vivid portrait of Lincoln in a single volume.

In these pages, Doris Kearns Goodwin describes how Lincoln brilliantly organized the 1860 Republican convention, negotiating discount railroad fares to Chicago and packing the house with his supporters. Tom Wheeler shows how Lincoln adopted the new technology of the telegraph to become the first president to get real-time information on the progress of a war and communicate his directives to his commanders in the field. And David Herbert Donald describes Lincoln's April 1865 tour of the vanquished southern capital of Richmond. This unique collection also includes critics of Lincoln, including Thomas DiLorenzo and Lerone Bennett, Jr., who discuss the misinterpretation and mythologization of the president.

Brimming with fascinating, little-known anecdotes, *Abraham Lincoln* deserves a place on the shelf any reader seeking to better understand one of the most important figures in American history.

Brian Lamb, founding CEO of C-SPAN, conducted many of the original interviews that form the essays within this book. **Susan Swain,** C-SPAN's president & co-chief operating officer, oversaw the editing for this book with the help of **Jim Cox.**

Visit **www.c-span.org/lincolnbook**

C-SPAN is directing any royalties from the sale of this book to the nonprofit C-SPAN Education Foundation, which creates teaching materials for middle and high school teachers.

cover design by pete garceau

AVAILABLE AS AN E-BOOK AND AUDIO DOWNLOAD

Visit www.publicaffairsbooks.com
Sign up for our newsletter

publicaffairs
≡IN PAPER≡

$16.95/$21.50 can

ISBN 978-1-58648-774-4

51695

9 781586 487744